Cartography by Department of Geography, University of Toronto
Original research by S. Hryniuk

Peasants with Promise:
Ukrainians in Southeastern Galicia 1880-1900

Peasants with Promise:
Ukrainians in Southeastern Galicia 1880-1900

Stella Hryniuk

Canadian Institute of Ukrainian Studies Press
University of Alberta
Edmonton 1991

This book has been published with the help of a grant from the Canadian Federation for the Humanities, using funds provided by the Social Sciences and Humanities Research Council of Canada.

Canadian Cataloguing in Publication Data

Hryniuk, Stella M., 1939-
Peasants with promise

Includes bibliographical references and index.

ISBN 0-920862-74-8

1. Galicia, Eastern (Ukraine)—History. 2. Galicia, Eastern (Ukraine)—
Social conditions. 3. Peasantry—Ukraine—Galicia, Eastern—History.
I. Title.

DK508.9.G35H79 1991 947'.718 C91-091239-4

Printed in Canada

Table of Contents

Preface

When I began the work that led to this book, my purpose was to examine the cause of the massive emigration of Ukrainian peasants from Eastern Galicia to Canada at the end of the nineteenth and the beginning of the twentieth centuries. Both popular and scholarly explanations of this phenomenon stated that those peasants were representative of their society and were subject to harsh social, political, and economic oppression. Emigration, for them, was an escape from a hopeless situation. That oppression was usually explained as a result of historical circumstances which had placed the Ukrainians of Eastern Galicia under the rule of the Poles in the Austro-Hungarian Empire. Polish policies both hindered the attainment of Ukrainian national and political aspirations and failed to respond to the socio-economic needs of the Eastern Galician Ukrainians. All of that led to the poverty which generated migration.

Although Eastern Galicia and Southern Podillia, the subject of this book, were poor and underdeveloped compared to many parts of Western Europe, the commonly held explanation was not in accord with other evidence. For example, interviews with residents of Manitoba who either had emigrated from Eastern Galicia or were the children of emigrants revealed that if these emigrants had suffered stark poverty, it had occurred during the early Canadian portion of their experience. They left a society which was quite different from the one presented in standard historical interpretations. There were similar discrepancies between these interpretations and the memoirs of former inhabitants. The level of material comfort in their former society seemed to be somewhat higher, and there appeared to be a higher literacy rate in the homeland than was usually acknowledged. One interviewee explained that "they were pretty well-to-do" in the old country but that "there were better prospects in Canada." The general emigration literature also suggested that rising expectations rather than poverty stimulated emigration. "Fleeing poverty" explanations were offered only occasionally.

Thus, before I could state why they emigrated, I needed to know much more about the society from which they came. The "why" of emigration is therefore the subject of another study. Here I have examined aspects of Eastern Galician peasant society as they evolved in the last twenty years of the nineteenth century through a study of the five counties of Eastern Galicia from which came most of the pre-1900 Galician-Ukrainian emigrants to Manitoba. I do not claim that conditions here were representative of Eastern Galicia as a whole.

Although denied access to Soviet archives, I was able to make use of some Austrian ministerial archives transferred to Poland after World War I.

Furthermore, I made extensive use of contemporary Ukrainian newspapers, official Austrian statistical data, and memoirs. Contemporary German-Austrian, Polish, and Ukrainian studies of the economy, agriculture, and other relevant features of Eastern-Galician society, as well as later studies, were useful. Another source was interviews with survivors of the emigration or their offspring resident in Manitoba about pre-emigration conditions in the villages of Eastern Galicia.

I have excluded questions that other historians have investigated in detail, such as the rise of Ukrainian national consciousness and the competition for popular support between Old Ruthenians, Populists, and, a little later, Radicals. My focus has been on developments in a rural area in which debates among intellectuals and politicians were not as significant as they were to the participants in Lviv and elsewhere, or to the historians who have quite properly concerned themselves with such questions. My sources have been in some respects voluminous and in others frustratingly fragmentary. My approach to the topic has benefitted particularly from Eugen Weber's *Peasants into Frenchmen: The Modernization of Rural France, 1870-1914* and Pamela Horn's *The Rural World 1780-1850: Social Change in the English Countryside*. I trust that through this analysis of developments in Southern Podillia in the period 1880-1900 I have generated a new and better understanding of Eastern Galician Ukrainian society.

I would like to express my sincere gratitude to the many people who have helped me during the course of the research and writing of what was initially a doctoral dissertation—Dr. Oleh W. Gerus, my advisor; the staff of the Interlibrary Loans and Slavic Collections of the Dafoe Library, University of Manitoba, without whom this study could not have been completed; the staff at the Catholic University of Lublin, the Library of the University of Illinois, Urbana, and the Oesterreichische Nationalbibliothek in Vienna; the scholars in Manitoba and elsewhere who have shared their ideas and resources with me, especially John-Paul Himka; my father and my uncle Emil; the people of Manitoba whose memories and stories inspired and sustained my faith in this study; the people who typed my work, especially David Webb; Pat Devenney; cartographer Geoffrey Matthews, University of Toronto; and my children, Michael and Angela, who never ceased to believe in me. Special thanks go to Fred for his encouragement from initiation to completion of this work. I acknowledge with gratitude doctoral fellowships from the Social Sciences and Humanities Research Council of Canada and the Canadian Institute of Ukrainian Studies, which facilitated my work immeasurably, and assistance from the Aid to Scholarly Publications Program of the Canadian Federation for the Humanities.

Winnipeg, 1988 *Stella Hryniuk*

List of Tables

List of Maps

List of Illustrations

Acknowledgments

The publisher gratefully acknowledges perrmission to reprint photographs from the following sources: *Istorychno-memuarnyi zbirnyk Chortkivskoi okruhy, Povity: Chortkiv, Kopychyntsi, Borshchiv, Zalishchyky*, ed. Olha Sonevytska, Bohdan Stefanovych, and Roman Drazhnyovsky (New York, Paris, Sydney, and

Toronto: Shevchenko Scientific Society, 1974) (photographs 2, 10, 20, 25); *Terebovelska zemlia: istorychno-memuarnyi zbirnyk*, ed. Iwan Wynnytsky, Wasyl Palidwor, Roman Kryshtalsky and Julian Fryz (New York, Paris, Sydney and Toronto: Shevchenko Scientific Society, 1968) (photographs 3, 4); the V. Stefanyk Library of the Academy of Sciences of the Ukrainian SSR (photographs 5, 6, 7, 8, 16, 17, 27), and the Central State Historical Archive in Lviv (photograph 28).

List of Appendices

Prefatory Note

The units of currency in this study are the kreuzer and the gulden (abbreviated as "kr" and "g"; 100 kr = 1 g). New units of currency, the heller and the crown (Krone) (100 heller = 1 crown) were introduced in 1892, concurrent with Austria's adoption of the gold standard. However, the old currency was only gradually withdrawn, and most prices in Galicia continued to be expressed in kreuzer and gulden (1 gulden = 2 crowns) until the end of the century. To make comparisons easier, prices have, where necessary, been converted from heller and crowns to kreuzer and gulden.

The adoption of the metric system was a slow process in many rural parts of Austria, and traditional measures of weight, volume, area, and length continued to be used. Of the traditional units of measurement, the one most frequently cited was the morg, a measurement of area equivalent to approximately 0.575 hectares. Where appropriate (and possible), metric measures have been used in this study (ha: hectare, hl: hectolitre, kg: kilogram, l: litre, mc: metric centner).

I have used a modified Library of Congress transliteration system. Names of places have been rendered in their Ukrainian version, except where a standard English version exists, e.g., Vienna and Warsaw. Nevertheless, I have retained the Ukrainian "Podillia," even though it is often rendered in English as "Podilia" or "Podolia" (German: Podolien; Polish: Podole).

However, I have used the term Eastern Galicia for the territory known as "Skhidnia Halychyna" in Ukrainian, "Ost-Galizien" in German, and "Galicja Wschodnia" in Polish. The territory of Eastern Galicia was approximately that part of Galicia east of the San River. The Ukrainian inhabitants of Eastern Galicia referred to themselves as "Rusyny" ("Rusini" in Polish) until late in the nineteenth century, when the term Ukrainians ("Ukraintsi" in Ukrainian, "Ukrainer" in German, "Ukraińcy" in Polish) gained popularity. "Rusyny" was translated into German as "Ruthenen" and into English as "Ruthenians." The modern term "Ukrainian" will be used in this study, except in direct quotation and where Ruthenian is part of the title of an association, book, etc.

The following English translations of Ukrainian, Polish, and German terms have been used:

English	German	Polish	Ukrainian
Governor	*Statthalter*	*namiestnik*	*namisnyk*
County	*Bezirk*	*powiat*	*povit*
County Officer	*Bezirkshauptmann*	*starosta*	*starosta*
Reeve	*Vogt*	*wójt*	*viit*
Commune	*Gemeinde*	*gmina*	*hromada*

The following abbreviation has been used in notes throughout this study:

IMZCh *Istorychno-memuarnyi zbirnyk Chortkivskoi okruhy*

All newspaper and periodical citations have been given according to the New Style calendar, e.g. 2 June (Old Style) is 14 June (New Style).

Chapter I

Southern Podillia

Introduction

This is a study of the agricultural and socio-cultural development of the Ukrainian peasant population of five counties of Eastern Galicia in the last two decades of the nineteenth century. The five counties—Borshchiv, Chortkiv, Husiatyn, Terebovlia, and Zalishchyky—are here collectively called "Southern Podillia."[1] They formed a contiguous area in the southwestern corner of what has been traditionally known as the Podillian Plateau. A county was an administrative subdivision of the Austrian portion of the Habsburg monarchy. Each county was comprised of a number of communes. The five counties of Southern Podillia were themselves part of the Austrian Crownland (hereinafter termed Land) of Galicia. They lay at the eastern extremity of the Land; Borshchiv and Husiatyn bordered on the Russian Empire.

Galicia was the largest component Land of Austria.[2] In 1880 it had a population of just under six million. Under the Austrian Fundamental Law of 1867, Galicia and the other Crownlands were granted considerable autonomy, exercised under the authority of unicameral legislatures—in Galicia the Sejm. However, there were definite parameters set on this autonomy; all Land laws required the approval of the Austrian emperor in Vienna (Franz Josef, 1848-1916), and on certain matters the authority of the Austrian bicameral parliament, the Reichsrat, was supreme.[3]

Before they had come under Austrian rule in 1772, the territories which comprised the Land of Galicia had been part of the Kingdom of Poland,[4] whose rule had extended in earlier centuries over large portions of the former Kievan Rus' state.[5] By the late eighteenth century, all the territories of this Kievan state, the homeland of the Ukrainians, had been partitioned between the Russian and Austrian Empires, the Russians obtaining the major portion. However, the centuries of incorporation in the Polish Commonwealth left a lasting legacy. In the eastern part of Galicia the princes, nobles, and gentry—owners of land and for centuries wielders of power—were either of Polish extraction or, if Ukrainian, had for the most part become thoroughly Polonized. That is, they had accepted the language, culture, religion, and way of life of their Polish peers.[6]

Although the Polish aristocracy and gentry lost some of their powers under

Austrian rule, they maintained political hegemony in Galicia, and opportunities to exert their influence were even enhanced by the measures of autonomy granted to Galicia in 1867 and by the exigencies of Austrian politics. Nevertheless, some Austro-Polish politicians and a large portion of the Polish intelligentsia chafed under the mild restrictions of Austrian rule, and dreamed of the resurrection of the Polish state. The basis for such a state could best be laid in Galicia, for while in Austria the Poles were a privileged nationality, in Germany and Russia (the other heirs of the kingdom of Poland) Poles were regarded as inferior and untrustworthy, and their institutions were treated with a heavy hand.[7] Despite the fact that in the 1870s only 45 per cent of the population of Galicia was ethnically Polish, and there was a very definite preponderance of Ukrainians in Eastern Galicia,[8] the Poles were determined to treat Galicia as one unit and to promote the Polish cause therein. In this quest, they encountered resistance from an increasingly influential and articulate national consciousness among the Ukrainians of Eastern Galicia.[9]

Geography and Climate

The five counties of Southern Podillia lay between latitude 48° 30' and 49° 25' North and longitude 25° 25' and 26° 25' East. The Podillian Plateau, a portion of a greater land mass variously called the European Plain and the Russian Plain, is bounded on the west by the Vereshytsia River, on the south and southeast by the Dnister River valley, and on the north and northeast by the valley of the Bug River. In both the north and south the plateau rises to heights of 200-300 metres above sea level, the highest point being 470 metres above the Bug plain. Then it declines sharply on the south into the Dnister valley and, more gradually, toward the Black Sea or Pontian plain.[10]

Geologically, the entire Podillian Plateau is composed of an ancient, stable block of the earth's crust, Precambrian crystalline rock. Over the centuries, as a result of glacier movements and other eroding forces, the surface of the plateau was ground to a relatively smooth but undulating surface, with only occasional outcroppings. To the south lies typical steppe-plain, particularly as the Podillian Plateau merges with the Pontian plain.[11] Besides the plateau formation itself, the most important feature of the general landscape is a dyke-like ridge, called the Medobory or Tovtry, which rises suddenly out of the plain, just south of Ternopil, and stretches in a more or less continuous line from the source of the Seret River to Kamianets-Podilske in the southeast, and east of the counties studied here. It was the result of a barrier reef formed during the Miocene period when a sea covered the northern half of the Podillian Plateau. Its limestone and coral protrusions eroded into fantastic forms, making the Tovtry a rich source for local adventure stories, ballads, and sayings. To some extent it formed a barrier to the outside plain.[12]

Characteristic of this portion of the Podillian Plateau was the web of rivers and streams which cut through it "as tho' with a giant saw."[13] The Dnister River and its northern tributaries gave great variety and beauty to the area. From ponds and bogs, streams turned into wide, deep rivers, then cut into the plateau as they turned south, causing the valleys to become narrower and deeper. They wound their way through steeper and higher valley slopes, which at their entry into the Dnister became true canyons.[14] The Dnister River is said to have had the most beautiful of all those canyons, with walls more than 200 metres high:

> It cuts through the high plateau in adventurous windings, every curve revealing new, beautiful prospects over the high, concave, steep edge, torn by ravines, and the gently rising convex banks. In deep gorges the yari of the tributaries open into the yar of the main stream. Between the defiles stretches the flat, hardly undulating plain. In the summer only endless waving grain-steppes present themselves to the view of the traveller, only here and there a little wood appears in the horizon, or a lone farm. Suddenly the wood seems to end, the traveller is confronted by a deep, steppe-walled (sic) valley, down the sides of which climbs the road. And below, on the silvery river, amid the green of the orchards, lies village after village.[15]

Another visitor to the area noted that the villages were located in the river valleys, "like pearls on a string."[16] Contemporary fears about the erosive force of the rivers were exaggerated, as such erosion had occurred over thousands of centuries, exposing magnificent horizontal rock layers in which red sandstone added brilliant colour to the Podillian canyons.[17] Some ecological damage to the plain and loss of arable land did occur after the felling of forests throughout the eighteenth and nineteenth centuries.

The soil of the Podillian Plateau is one of the richest in the world. Receding glaciers left a deep cover of loess, which gave the soil important minerals and enhanced its natural fertility. The soil of the five counties is of the fertile Black Soil or Chernozem type. Some counties had diverse geological and soil conditions: Terebovlia had many outcroppings of sandstone which provided a great number of stone quarries for local use,[18] while Zalishchyky was located on the northern bank of the Dnister on Precambrian rock. Because of its southern exposure, Zalishchyky was warmer and had a longer frost-free period—all of which allowed for cultivation of special, high-revenue crops such as early ripening tomatoes, apricots, and grapes.[19] The most fertile strip of land in the region was between the Seret and Strypa Rivers, northern tributaries of the Dnister.

The climate of Southern Podillia is continental, warm and moderate for the most part, with temperatures ranging from an average low of -4C in January to an average high of +20C in July.[20] The annual rainfall is 550-700 mm with steady rain in the spring and fall, and occasional downpours and thunderstorms in the summer. The prevailing winds are westerly, although there can be sharp northwesterly winds as well. These winds help to preserve, rather than remove, moisture in the air. The frost-free period is approximately 165 days, but the first frosts may occur as early as 23-5 September and the last as late as 19 May. There are four clearly marked seasons of approximately equal length—spring, beginning in the middle of March; summer in the last third of May; fall, between mid-September and October; and winter by the last third of November. The fall is warm and sunny, which enhances the maturing of late crops of grain and fruit. When the temperatures drop in mid-October, the days tend to be cloudy and sometimes foggy. The temperature drops below 0° in late November, but usually snow does not fall for another month. Snowcover—usually lasting fifty to sixty days—helps retain moisture in the soil and allows for the sowing of winter crops, while the long frost-free period permits a second sowing in the summer.[21]

Despite rapid spring runoff, the water level in the rivers was sufficiently high all year for local needs and the area was rich in underground water. The water table was from one to five metres in the river valleys and ten to sixteen metres in the plateau. Many springs in the river valleys emerged from the various exposed rock strata, including mineral water springs with curative qualities.[22] They provided the local inhabitants with good drinking water and nourished the ponds and rivers.

The Way of Life

Southern Podillia in 1880 was overwhelmingly agricultural. The majority of the people lived in hamlets, villages, and small towns which differed very little from each other. Of the more than 250 settlements about 80 per cent had populations of fewer than 2,000 in 1880.[23] The towns, including the market towns, the county capitals, and the county court seats, though trade and administrative centres, were still mainly animated by the primarily rural nature of the region.[24] Their daily pace was largely set by the plant-growing cycle: slower activity in the late fall and winter, and high activity in the spring and summer. The concepts of work and leisure differed from those of urban-based commentators. Toward the end of the nineteenth century, increased urbanization began to change the social structure as more industry entered the region. Particularly noteworthy at this time was the transformation of the Chortkiv area into a railway and garrison town, with the beginning of some light industry.[25]

Southern Podillia had been bypassed by main trading routes. In the late nineteenth century the region was far removed from major population centres and, until the mid-1880s, was not served by a railway. Major towns did not emerge here because large-scale trade networks were lacking and there was no indigenous social class to generate them. The Polish nobles had their estates serviced by their own artisans and servants. With the exception of one tobacco factory, neither the state nor the nobility invested in industry. Ukrainian villagers always had lived within the framework of a society in which they "knew their place." In addition, their religious and ethical norms indicated that towns and townspeople were somehow unscrupulous, immoral, materialistic, and grasping. People from the village dressed differently from townspeople, even after the turn of the century.[26]

Such mores led these villagers to take a negative attitude toward existing towns. The sources contain hostile comments about urban dwellers, especially the Jews who formed such a large proportion of the town population.[27] A visit to town was often equated by Ukrainian writers with being cheated in business transactions by urban merchants. In 1884 the editor of a Ukrainian newspaper commended the idea of Ukrainian-owned village shops because they made unnecessary a trip during which one would be swindled by Jews.[28] One village had acquired a weigh-scale so that "our villagers who took their grain to town to sell could weigh it at home in advance and thus get around being cheated by Jews."[29] The town was seen as an unwelcome intruder into village life because of visits from the county election commissioners, the county supervisors of health measures, and tax collectors.[30] The town was also perceived as dangerous and expensive, according to one correspondent who maintained that on the way to town one had to pay tolls; livestock being led to market could get lost; there were highway robbers on the road, and thieves in town; one could be fined in town for leaving animals unattended; fire could destroy one's home in one's absence; and one might meet with violence or even death in town.[31] By the end of the century, some of these attitudes were dissipating as mobility increased, but there were still concerns that towns were trade centres monopolized by a dishonest clique.[32] Moreover, the attachment of Southern Podillian peasants to the village remained strong, as can be inferred from the great dislocation experienced by emigrants to Canada, who tried to recreate the same village patterns in their new homeland.[33]

The settlements varied in size and location, if not in their basic modus operandi. They were most often situated in the valleys of the region's many rivers, but could also sprawl up the side of a valley or lie entirely on the plain. For example, Kozachchyna in Borshchiv county was entirely in the valley, while Kryvche in the same county was divided into an upper (horishne) and a lower (dolishne) section corresponding to its topography.[34] Kryvche was further divided into a Christian and a Jewish section, and other villages sometimes had Ukrainian and Polish sectors. Villages could be huddles of houses for 200-300 inhabitants or could contain houses for 3,000 or more people. The proximity of abundant water and particular historic circumstances contributed to this pattern.[35] The large valleys of the Zbruch and Dnister and the northern tributaries of the latter, such as the Seret, Nichlava, and Dzhuryn, were major locations for habitation, but every village seemed to have some river or stream running through it or close by.

The natural beauty of these valleys was further enhanced by numerous orchards in the area, which were a spectacular sight when in bloom. Writing about his native town, Borshchiv, one former inhabitant claimed that the Nichlava River valley "was paradise."[36] Two other villages in Borshchiv county, Shyshkivtsi and Shuparka, were also exceptionally attractive, as was Kolodribka in Zalishchyky county. The woodlands of the valley seemed to hug the "clean peasant homes with their lush orchards," and Shuparka seemed literally to be "drowned in orchards."[37] Bridges and ferries facilitated the movement of people and goods over the streams and rivers. Iron bridges spanned the Zbruch from Husiatyn to the Russian Empire[38] and the Dnister from Zalishchyky to Bukovyna.[39] A smaller bridge crossed the Zbruch at Shydlivtsi. State-owned ferries plied the Dnister at Okopy and a private one ran from Ustechko to the county of Horodenka. The Okopy ferry was leased to an entrepreneur who not only ran the ferry but also operated a tavern on both sides of the river.[40]

Since the topography of the region determined the layout of the settlements, the arrangement of the streets in the various villages formed an irregular, clustered village plan, or occasionally, a ribbon or chain pattern if the ravine was very narrow.[41] Sometimes several villages or hamlets merged, for example, Kolodribka and Synkiv in Zalishchyky county; they belonged to the same parish and the dialect spoken in them was similar.[42] Together, they had 4,383 inhabitants in 1900. Villages in Borshchiv county which were connected in the same manner were Mykhalkiv, Ustia Iepyskopske, and Pylypche (5,185 people). One road, along which a ribbon of settlement stretched, linked them all.[43] Kosiv, Bilyi Potik, and Hramushivka—three villages on the plain in Chortkiv county—were within two kilometres of each other and formed one parish with 4,960 people.[44] People in some villages along the Zbruch River owned parcels of ploughland which were located in the Russian Empire. For example, some in Zaluche, Zelena, and Shydlivtsi paid tax on ploughland to the Russian authorities.[45]

These varied circumstances had manifold social and cultural implications for village inhabitants. Southern Podillian villagers were not as isolated from outside influences as the physical geography might suggest. There are many instances of several villages gathering for some "happening," working together, or sending their village choirs to help celebrate an event in a neighbouring village. For example, people from Pylypche, Ustia Iepyskopske, Horoshova, Ivanie Puste, and Zalissia attended the opening of the reading club in Volkivtsi, Borshchiv county.[46] No doubt it was topography which caused specific names to be given to different parts of villages. Individual roads, fields, hillocks, and forests would be given names such as "past the river," "at the foot of the hill," or "near the Imperial road" as identifiers. Geographical, historical or even personal circumstances influenced this naming process. For example, a forest in Tovstenke, Husiatyn county, was called "Dubyna" because of its many oak (*dub* in Ukrainian) trees.[47] A hillock in Oleksyntsi, Borshchiv county, was called "Panska Stinka," which means "the lord's wall." A story alleged that the hillock had been a secret hiding place for the local gentry landowner during seventeenth-century Turkish incursions. In the late nineteenth century it still had an iron door with a padlock at its entrance.[48]

The terrain also had some impact on weather conditions in the villages. In general, the climate in Southern Podillia was perceived as "raw" and the winters cold, although the mean temperatures do not really bear this out.[49] Rather, in continental European terms, the weather was moderate. In the valley villages it was milder and the winds could be lighter because of the shelter afforded by the valley walls.

While they enjoyed comparatively pleasant weather, the valleys were plagued by steep roads. Throughout the last two decades of the century, commune and county roads, with few exceptions, were poorly built and maintained, and sometimes had very steep gradients. Especially during wet periods, this could affect transportation and communications. Vasyl Havrysh relates how his father, driving a horse-drawn wagon heavily laden with wood, hit a stone, losing the wagon's braking power; it went out of control and killed him when he fell under it. A similar incident, blamed on the steepness of the road, involved his brother on the same road in Kalynivshchyna, but with less drastic consequences.[50] Ivan, in Stefanyk's story "The Stone Cross," also complained of the hard time he and his horse had climbing his hilltop field.[51] There were also several improved imperial and Land roads in the region. Four of the five counties were served by an imperial road, which was a good quality, hard surface road. This "Podillian Highway" traversed the countryside, going north from Zalishchyky to Terebovlia, and then on to Ternopil and Lviv. Zalishchyky county was connected with the large market town of Kolomyia and with Chernivtsi in Bukovyna to the south by the main road as well. The towns of Ternopil, Kolomyia, and Chernivtsi were on railway lines by 1871. There was also a good road connecting Chortkiv with Buchach and Stanyslaviv.[52]

Towns of over 5,000 inhabitants were rare in the region in 1880. Only Terebovlia (6,423), Kopychyntsi (6,221), Skala (6,154), Khorostkiv (5,623), Zalishchyky (5,588), Husiatyn (5,214), and Budzaniv (5,124) fell into this category. These places, as well as sixteen others, possessed the status of "market."[53] Local roads, often in poor condition, connected villages with one another and with a nearby market.

The natural landscape and historic social conditions combined to influence the pattern of land ownership and use in these villages. Usually there was one large estate, consisting of one or more farmsteads (*filvarok*), in the vicinity of each village, which normally was owned by Polish nobles or other wealthy people. By the last quarter of the nineteenth century, they sometimes leased these farmsteads to new entrepreneurs.[54] The estate owners owned most of the woodlands and meadows and had the best fields near the manor itself, while the peasant lands were farther away from their dwellings. Peasant lands also tended to be strips and pieces scattered in many different locations, while manor lands were more consolidated. The time peasants spent getting to their plots reduced their working hours on the land. The fact that their land was scattered and fragmented had both advantages and disadvantages. Scattered fields might have lowered the efficiency of agricultural production, but provided natural crop insurance against weather hazards when no other kind existed.[55]

The internal arrangement of the villages faithfully reflected the socio-cultural life therein. Dominating the centre of most of the villages were the church, parish buildings, belltower, and cemetery. Close by were the school, the commune council building, village shops and tavern.[56] By the end of the century, in most villages and towns, there were buildings erected by Ukrainian or Polish voluntary organizations which provided space for activities such as reading clubs and choir and drama rehearsals and performances. The nature of other major buildings depended on the local economy. More often than not the main source of income, apart from work on one's own lands, was employment on the local large estate. Thus, the buildings of the manor formed an important element of the local architecture. Frequently the estate owners or lessees had a mansion, surrounded by a park, orchards, and gardens, all enclosed in a high, walled fence.[57] Other manor buildings located on the estate or in the village proper might be mills, a distillery, a brewery, a brickyard, an oil press and a tavern. Gradually, in the last two decades of the century, the villagers began to operate similar enterprises.

Special features in some villages and towns were monasteries and convents, hospitals, synagogues, and ruins of old fortresses and other fortifications. One of the latter was Trajan's wall, which wended its way through some villages in Borshchiv county.[58] In every village there were crosses of freedom commemorating the end of compulsory labour in 1848, usually in the centre of the village, at the intersection of roads or out in the fields. They were the sites of annual memorial services. There might be a cross at the entrance to a village, or perhaps a portal or gate, to ward off evil and illness. Sometimes the gate led to a village square.

Naturally, the most numerous buildings were the houses and outbuildings of the peasants. These houses were usually detached, constructed in a typical Ukrainian style of clay mixed with straw, thatched in straw, and consisted of two rooms.[59] The interior and exterior were normally whitewashed, with some ornamentation on the woodwork and walls. At the back of the house were the peasants' gardens, orchards, and the outbuildings of their farmsteads. Typically Ukrainians enclosed the farmstead with a fence. Unlike other Slavic peoples, Ukrainians considered it a major disgrace for a householder not to have a fenced-in yard.[60]

Palace at Khorostkiv (XVIII century)

Church at Shmankivtsi, Chortkiv county (built 1895)

Zastinoche quarry

Strusiv market

Local Government and Justice

Southern Podillia in the 1880s had a variety of local government authorities. The two principal ones were the county and the commune, but there were also local school districts, county school districts, and county road districts, with their councils.

The commune was the administrative and social unit with which villagers had the most direct contact. A commune might consist of a town, a village, or two or more villages. The commune government was responsible for the protection of persons and property, the maintenance of commune roads and bridges, the administration of commune property, the observance of ordinances relating to servants, the issuance of building permits, and the establishment and maintenance of elementary schools (through local school districts), the attempt to mediate between disputants, firefighting and other safety measures, the care of the poor, and communal charities.[61] In 1890 there were 74 communes in Borshchiv county, 44 in Chortkiv, 50 in Husiatyn, 43 in Terebovlia, and 57 in Zalishchyky.[62] In market towns the commune authorities were responsible for supervising trade and for the accuracy of weights and measures, and they derived additional income from market fees and consumption taxes.[63] The commune had a direct impact on every peasant household through the taxes it imposed and because it required every landowner to perform up to six (later reduced to two) days' labour per year helping to maintain the commune roads.

In each commune there was a commune council, elected by voters who qualified in accordance with the amount of direct state tax they paid. In most communes there were three categories of voters, although the very smallest had only two. The system was weighted in favour of the more affluent. Regulations on the maintenance of lists of voters and the electoral process itself had many gaps, and there was no secret voting. Abuses were prevalent.[64] The principal official within the commune was the reeve (*viit*), who was often a prosperous peasant. Many reeves in the 1880s were illiterate, so another important personage was the scribe, who would otherwise have been a minor functionary. Reeves varied in quality, depending on their individual capabilities and honesty. Some were suspected of being under the influence of the local landowner or the local Jews, and were disliked accordingly. In all cases they possessed genuine authority within their communes.[65]

In theory, Austria's system of local self-government gave the communes some very real autonomy. In practice, especially as the inhabitants came to expect more from them, commune resources were not adequate. A special irritant throughout Galicia was that, by Sejm legislation, large estates were separate administrative units that did not pay appropriate local taxes even though they benefited from improvements in the villages, such as the upkeep of roads, and from schools.[66] Each commune possessed some communal property, income from which had once been intended to cover communal expenditures. Such communal property might be pasture, woodland, fishpond, quarry, or ploughland. There also were charitable trusts and bequests, often for specific purposes. Bilobozhnytsia (Chortkiv county) had 189 hectares of communal land.[67] In Husiatyn county in the 1890s, one commune possessed almost sixty hectares of communal land, and four well-endowed communes in Terebovlia county averaged about eighty hectares each. In Husiatyn county communally owned ploughland leased to the reeve and others in one locality brought annual sums ranging from 20 to 350 g into the commune treasury. On the other hand, thirteen communes in Zalishchyky county possessed, on average, about 0.75 of a hectare each.[68] The total real communal property in the five counties in the 1890s was as follows: Borshchiv 1872.7 hectares, Chortkiv 1265.7 ha, Husiatyn 786.6 ha, Terebovlia 1240.6 ha, and Zalishchyky 1720.4 ha, but the areas of individual communes' lands varied greatly.[69]

The administrative authority above the commune was the county (*Bezirkshauptmannschaft, povit*). Counties in Galicia had elected county councils (again, with a weighted franchise) and an executive committee. However, the real power lay in the hands of the County Officer (*Bezirkshauptmann, starosta*). That officer was appointed by the Ministry of the Interior in Vienna, upon recommendation of the Governor of Galicia. His responsibilities derived from authority delegated to him by the Land government and from duties imposed by Austrian statute. He was thus the direct representative in the county of both the Austrian and the Galician governments, and was assisted by a small number of subordinate officials.[70]

The County Officer had the power to issue regulations on many matters, which were valid only within his county. He was responsible for the preservation of peace and public order and the protection of property; supervised the county tax authorities; exercised some control over the local detachments of the gendarmerie and could call upon the military authorities for assistance; supervised the activities of the communes; carried out instructions from the Land government; collected data on behalf of the Viennese and Lviv authorities; and appointed electoral and census commissioners. With the assistance of the county road council and the county engineer he was responsible for the upkeep of roads. He could take administrative action against individuals. Appeals against his decisions could be made to the Governor in Lviv, the Minister of the Interior in Vienna, or the Administrative Courts. Most decisions were not contested or, if they were, the claimants were generally not successful. In Eastern Galicia most of the County Officers were Poles, sometimes Polish gentry. Polish was the language of administration, although bureaucrats in the Ukrainian-speaking areas were supposed to have knowledge of Ukrainian.[71]

Commune authorities were supposed to act as conciliators between parties to a civil conflict, which often involved disputes about the exact delineation of land. The courts of first instance were otherwise normally those of the judicial districts. Counties were usually divided into two judicial districts. In Southern Podillia, all of Chortkiv was one judicial district, but each of the other counties had two, one with its centre in the county capital and the other in another large town (Borshchiv and Melnytsia, Husiatyn and Kopychyntsi, Terebovlia and Budzaniv, Zalishchyky and Tovste). Below these courts was the more summary, and not always formalized, jurisdiction of the County Officer, the estate owner, and the commune government; above them was the circuit court at Ternopil and higher courts of appeal in Lviv and Vienna. Tax and landholding data were maintained in the judicial court towns, except for estates which enjoyed tabular status, whose landholding records were in Ternopil. Judges were supposedly independent of political pressures, but no doubt subject to social ones. In Galicia the judiciary tended to be Polish.[72]

Taxation

Direct taxes were levied by each of the four levels of government, but those imposed by the imperial authorities—direct state taxes—formed the basis for the other three. Reliable tax data for Southern Podillia have been all but impossible to obtain, but such data are available for direct taxes paid to the Austrian state in 1882 in each county, by category of tax:

Table 1
Number of Taxpayers and Amount of Taxes Paid, in Gulden, Direct Austrian State Taxes, 1882

	Land tax	House tax	Rental house tax	5 per cent levy on tax-exempt buildings	Business tax	Income tax	County Total
Borshchiv							
(a)	23,506	15,678	363	9	1,368	404	
(b)	77,115	28,029	3,397	45	12,928	17,455	138,969
Chortkiv							
(a)	13,680	8,621	593	14	616	317	
(b)	47,685	16,180	3,393	91	4,782	9,451	81,583
Husiatyn							
(a)	14,862	11,542	323	26	950	340	
(b)	64,953	20,666	4,196	190	7,930	13,393	111,328
Terebovlia							
(a)	15,678	9,650	349	12	878	264	
(b)	51,314	17,437	2,642	44	7,135	10,640	89,212

Zalishchyky							
(a)	17,707	10,689	214	14	1,031	313	
(b)	51,059	19,198	4,545	148	7,935	10,037	92,922

(a) number of taxpayers
(b) amount of taxes paid

Note: County totals do not include income taxes paid by state employees or the interest income of public trust-funds.

Source: *Oesterreichische Statistik*, vol. IX, no. 4, table VI.

It is apparent that few persons in each county paid income tax. Rather more paid the business tax (*Erwerbsteuer*) levied on manufacturing enterprises, traders, merchants, shopkeepers, and artists, and on such services as transportation and private instruction.[73] Neither of these taxes was normally paid by village agriculturalists. Peasants, like other people, did pay house tax and land tax. House tax was levied at varying rates, depending on the number of rooms the house contained. From the data contained in Table 1, it is clear that the overwhelming proportion of villagers paid the house tax at the standard rate for a one-room house, 1.70 g per annum.[74]

Land tax was paid in accordance with the assessed value of the land. For taxation purposes land was divided into the following categories: ploughland, meadow, woodland, pasturage, ponds and wetlands, and gardens. Each was taxed at a different rate; gardens and ploughland were the most highly taxed categories. On average, each payer of land tax in 1882 paid: Borshchiv 3.28 g, Chortkiv 3.49 g, Husiatyn 4.37 g, Terebovlia 3.27 g, and Zalishchyky 2.88 g.

We thus know the total amount of state land tax paid in each county and the number of persons who paid it. Because the latter included the owners of large estates who paid a considerable portion of the land tax because of the size of their holdings, the average amount paid by individual peasants in state land tax is somewhat smaller than the sums listed above. On the other hand, many peasant households, perhaps 50 per cent of them, paid two levies of land tax, on the husband's property and on the wife's. Probably these two factors come close to offsetting each other, so we may take the above figures as roughly the average amounts paid in state land tax by peasant families. To that must be added in each case the 1.70 g for house tax. So peasant households in Southern Podillia paid, on average, between 4.58 g (Zalishchyky county) and 6.07 g (Husiatyn county) in direct state taxes in 1882.[75]

The Galician, the county and the commune direct taxes were termed "supplements" to the direct state taxes.[76] On average, the total of these supplements was about 90-100 per cent of the direct state taxes.[77] In the early

1880s the peasant in Southern Podillia thus appears to have paid, on average and at most, between nine and twelve gulden per annum in direct taxes to all levels of government.[78] These totals do not include local school taxes, which in 1887 were at most 5 per cent of direct State taxes.[79] The direct tax burden on the peasants thus represented the value of about 1.5-2 metric centner of wheat at the Lviv market, or 17 to 24 days' cash pay during the grain harvest on some estate.[80]

In addition to the direct taxes, peasants had to pay a variety of unpopular tolls and some other charges. In a cash-poor society, the need to find cash to pay taxes was no doubt onerous, but the picture presented here is scarcely one of a peasantry groaning under a terrible tax burden. Indeed, complaints about the level of taxation were relatively rare after 1881 in the contemporary press. Overall one gains the impression that the Southern Podillian peasantry at the beginning of the 1880s was living a fairly tranquil life in what it regarded, on the whole, as reasonable circumstances. There were, of course, injustices and inequities, but the people worked hard, engaged in many communal activities, and appear to have had the time and inclination for enjoyment.

Notes

1. My terminology differs from that used by the Austrian Ministry of Agriculture in classifying the soil regions of Austria. In the Ministry's classification, from 1884 onward, "South Podillia" embraced Borshchiv, Chortkiv, Husiatyn, Zalishchyky, and the adjoining county of Buchach, while Terebovlia formed part of North Podillia. See *Statistisches Jahrbuch des k.k. Ackerbau-Ministeriums,* annual volumes. In view of the contiguity, topography, and transportation networks of the region, I believe my use of the term is justified.
2. For use of the term Austria, see R.A. Kann, *The Multinational Empire*, 1: 3, 17, 27-28; A.J. May, *The Hapsburg Monarchy, 1867-1914*, 43.
3. May, *The Hapsburg Monarchy*, 43-5; Kann, *The Multinational Empire*, 2: 130-3.
4. For Polish or Polonophile views of the partitions of Poland and their aftermath see W.F. Reddaway *et al.*, eds., *The Cambridge History of Poland*, II, chapters V, VII, VIII, and XV. For a brief discussion of the concept of Galicia see P.R. Magocsi, *Galicia: A Historical Survey and Bibliographic Guide*, xiv-xv.
5. For a convenient survey of early Ukrainian history, Kievan Rus', and Lithuanian and Polish domination see V. Kubijovyč, ed., *Ukraine: A Concise Encyclopaedia* (hereinafter, *Ukraine*), 1: 575-662.
6. In the late nineteenth century, only 1.7 per cent of the large landowners in Eastern Galicia were Ukrainian (H. Batowski, "Die Polen," 541).
7. Ibid., 529-47; May, *The Hapsburg Monarchy*, 52-3, 215-16, 226; Kann, *The Multinational Empire* 1: 231-232; S. Estreicher, "Galicia in the Period of Autonomy and Self-Government," 432-44; P. Wandycz, "The Poles in the Habsburg Monarchy," 84-94.

8. Eastern Galicia is here defined as Galicia, east of the river San.
9. See, in particular, I.L. Rudnytsky, "The Ukrainians in Galicia under Austrian Rule," 23-67; W. Bihl, "Die Ruthenen," 555-84.
10. S. Rudnitsky, *Ukraine: The Land and Its People*, 38; P. Lydolph, *Geography of the U.S.S.R.*; M.P. Chyzhov, *Ukrainskyi lisostep*, 29.
11. Rudnitsky, *Ukraine*, 41.
12. Chyzhov, *Ukrainskyi lisostep*, 25-6; Rudnitsky, *Ukraine*, 40-1.
13. Rudnitsky, *Ukraine*, 41.
14. P. Iudenych, *Po richkakh Ukrainy*, 196; Chyzhov, *Ukrainskyi lisostep*, 29.
15. Rudnitsky, *Ukraine*, 41-42. *Yar* is the Ukrainian word for ravine.
16. *Österreichisch-ungarische Monarchie in Wort und Bild*, 19: 52. This author was Emil von Habdank-Dunikowski, who travelled in the area in the 1880s.
17. Lydolph, *Geography of the U.S.S.R.*, 86; Chyzhov, *Ukrainskyi lisostep*, 73-9.
18. I. Vynnytsky, ed., *Terebovelska zemlia: Istorychno-memuarnyi zbirnyk*, 84-95.
19. *Istorychno-memuarnyi zbirnyk Chortkivskoi okruhy*, (hereinafter IMZCh), 713-6.
20. *Geograficheskii atlas dlia uchitelei srednei shkoly*, 107; Chyzhov, *Ukrainskyi lisostep*, 52.
21. Chyzhov, *Ukrainskyi lisostep*, 54-7; *Geograficheskii atlas*, 106-7. Details of weather conditions are given in the annual *Materyjaly do klimatografii Galicyi*. The meteorological station in Southern Podillia was at Iaholnytsia (Chortkiv county).
22. For example, the market town of Ulashkivtsi (Chortkiv county) had a spring which was said to cure eye disease (IMZCh, 241).
23. *Special-Orts-Repertorien der im oesterreichischen Reichsrathe vertretenen Königreiche und Länder*, XII, *passim* (hereinafter *Special-Orts-Repertorien*, 1880).
24. Kubijovyč, *Ukraine*, I: 260.
25. By 1900 Chortkiv, Chortkiv Staryi, and Vyhnanka formed an urban conglomerate of about 12,500 people. *Gemeindelexicon der im Reichsrathe vertretenen Königreiche und Länder*, XII: 132-4.
26. Interview with Mr. E. Michaels, 6 Oct. 1983.
27. See Appendix I.
28. *Nauka*, 1 Mar. 1884.
29. *Batkivshchyna*, 20 June 1884.
30. O. Makovei tells how the local reeve was annoyed with reminders from the county official about preventive health measures in the village (*Zalisia*, 58-60).
31. *Batkivshchyna*, 26 Jan. 1889.
32. *Hospodar*, January 1900.
33. See "The Stone Cross" by V. Stefanyk, in which he describes the leave-taking of settlers. See also R. Bilash, "Ukrainian Material Culture Change in East Central Alberta until 1930."
34. IMZCh, 7, 603, 637-8.
35. Ibid., 14-25. For a description of the treasure trove of Mykhalkiv (Borshchiv county), see P. Reinecke, "Die Gold Funde von Michalkow und Fokoru," 510-27.
36. *Sefer Borszczow*, 151.
37. IMZCh, 627-32, 762-3.
38. Archiwum Główne Akt Dawnych (hereinafter AGAD), Ministerium des Innern, File B50, Governor of Galicia to Ministry, 12 July 1891.

39. Ibid., 23 January 1888.
40. IMZCh, 440, 493.
41. Kubijovyč, *Ukraine*, 1: 256.
42. IMZCh, 772-3; interview with Mr. E. Michaels, 6 October 1983.
43. IMZCh, 642.
44. Ibid., 193.
45. Ibid., 440-1, 598; *Batkivshchyna*, 28 Feb. 1886.
46. *Batkivshchyna*, 11 Apr. 1890; see also 101-7 below.
47. IMZCh, 466.
48. Ibid., 610.
49. There are frequent references to the climate ("rauhes," "starke Winde," "strenger Winter") in I. Tittel, *Schematismus und Statistik des Grossgrundbesitzes*, but this may reflect upper-class views. See also *Geograficheskii atlas dlia uchitelei*; Chyzhov, *Ukrainskyi lisostep*; *Materyialy do klimatografii Galicyi*; J. Kleczyński, "Ekonomiczne stosunki Galicyi: stosunki włościańskie w Galicyi," 10.
50. V. Havrysh, *Moia Kanada i ia: spohady i rozpovidi pro ukrainskykh pioneriv u Kanadi*, 14-15, 64-5.
51. Stefanyk, "The Stone Cross," 21-2.
52. See Chapter III, below, for further details on road networks.
53. *Special-Orts-Repertorien*, 1880.
54. Havrysh, *Moia Kanada i ia*, 24-27, described the two "didychi" or large landowners in the vicinity of his village in Chortkiv county; IMZCh is replete with similar examples (180-2, 189, 190, 226, 230, and *passim*). For details regarding various features of large estates see K. Hempel, "Ekonomiczne stosunki Galicyi: stosunki większej własności ziemskiej w Galicyi," 92-189; T. Pilat, "Der landtäflicher Grundbesitz in Galizien," 287-308; F. Morawski, "Dzierżawy w obrębie własności tabularnej," 1-22; F. Bujak, *Galicya*, 1: 154-77, 261-76; Tittel, *Schematismus und Statistik*.
55. B. Wygoda, *Ustrój gospodarstw włościańskich w Galicyi*, 7-10; Havrysh, *Moia Kanada i ia*, 24; Kleczyński, "Ekonomiczne stosunki Galicyi," 13, 16.
56. IMZCh, 189, 196, 203, *passim*. These buildings were typical for the centre of villages in all ethnically Ukrainian territories. See F. Vovk, *Studii z ukrainskoi etnohrafii ta antropolohii*, 115.
57. See IMZCh, 372-3 for a description of the grounds of Count Stanisław Siemieński-Lewicki's estate in Khorostkiv.
58. Ibid., 673, 693, *passim*.
59. Vovk, *Studii z ukrainskoi*, 104-6; Kubijovyč, *Ukraine*, 1: 303-7. Most houses technically had one room and thus qualified for taxation at the one-room rate, but in effect had two rooms because of the position of the stove and the small entrance hall. See J. Lehr, "Ukrainian Houses in Alberta."
60. Vovk, *Studii z ukrainskoi*, 114; Kleczyński, "Ekonomiczne stosunki Galicyi," 23.
61. On local government, especially at the commune level, see W.J. Klabouch, "Die Lokalverwaltung in Cisleithanien," 2: 282-97; *Batkivshchyna*, 30 Sept. and 7 Oct. 1887; K. Grzybowski, *Galicja 1848-1914: historia ustroju politycznego na tle historii ustroju Austrii*, 238-71.
62. *Special-Orts-Repertorien*, 1890.

63. The main features of the budgets of Southern Podillian market towns in 1874 are known. The town of Terebovlia was clearly exceptional, for it owned extensive land and the propination rights thereto. It had revenues of 26,477 gulden and expenditures of 24,000 g. More typical were the following: Chortkiv: revenues 2,010 g (consumption taxes 350 g, supplements to direct taxes 634 g, market taxes and tolls 202 g, fines 50 g, sale of land 65 g), expenditures 2,021 g (administration 693 g, security and order 669 g, army costs 532 g, for the poor 5 g); Husiatyn: revenues 2833 g (consumption taxes 970 g, supplements to direct taxes 616 g, commune fees 930 g, fines 17 g), expenditures 2657 g (administration 796 g, security and order 461 g, school expenditures 279 g); Melnytsia: revenues 879 g (from commune property 261 g, consumption taxes 197 g, supplements to direct taxes 268 g), expenditures 880 g (administration 330 g, security 64 g, school 252 g); and Ustechko: revenues 481 g (from commune property 92 g, supplements to direct taxes 143 g, commune fees 246 g), expenditures 562 g (administration 442 g, security 86 g roads and bridges 34 g). See J. Kleczyński, "Życie gminne w Galicyi," 4: 222-9.
64. Klabouch, "Die Lokalverwaltung," 283-4; Kubijovyč, *Ukraine*, 1: 723.
65. For more on reeves and attitudes to them see also Chapters II and IX.
66. Galicia and Bukovyna were the only Austrian crownlands to permit tabular estates to remain apart from the commune. The estates thereby avoided being taxed for commune purposes; within their areas they were supposed to discharge the functions of a commune, but few did so effectively (Grzybowski, *Galicja 1848-1914*, 72; W. Schiff, "Bericht über die Tätigkeit des statistisches Seminares im Jahre 1896/97," 844-6.
67. *Batkivshchyna*, 5 Mar. 1885.
68. T. Pilat, "Grunta podlegające wspólnemu używaniu w Galicyi," 32-5, 42-3, 53.
69. Ibid., 42-3, where areas were given in morgs.
70. Klabouch, "Die Lokalverwaltung," 287-8; Kubijovyč, *Ukraine*, 1: 722-3; E.C. Hellbling, "Die Landesverwaltung in Cisleithanien," 150.
71. Grzybowski, *Galicja 1848-1914*, 206-8, 271-5; Klabouch, "Die Lokalverwaltung," 282-6; *Statistisches Jahrbuch der autonomen Landesverwaltung*, 1: xxiii, xxxv-xxxvii.
72. Kubijovyč, *Ukraine*, 2: 54. On records of landholdings see Pilat, "Der landtäflicher Grundbesitz," 289-90. On general legal matters in Austria see W. Ogris, "Die Rechtsentwicklung in Cisleithanien," 2: 555-71. On the summary powers of County Officers see Hellbling, "Die Landesverwaltung," 231 ff.
73. Business tax was assessed at various rates depending, in part, on the size of the locality in which the business was conducted; in villages of under 1,000 persons, traders and shopkeepers paid between 2.10 and 16.80 g per annum; *Oesterreichische Statistik* IX, no. 4, xxv.
74. For details on the house tax in 1882 see ibid., xxiv-xxv.
75. The total land tax payable to the State from Galicia was fixed in 1881 for the next fifteen years (ibid., xxiii). The house tax also remained constant till 1896. Therefore the direct state tax burden on South Podillian peasants did not increase. See *Chytalnia*, 21 July 1896, and *Svoboda*, 8 Apr. 1897 and 17 Mar. 1898, regarding decreased taxes in Southern Podillia. At the time of the 1881 tax

assessment revision, there had been protests against the low assessment on woodlands, which were predominantly in the hands of the large landowners (*Viche*, 25 Mar. 1881).

76. The Galician supplement to direct state taxes in 1883 and 1884 amounted to 27 per cent for general purposes and 31.5 per cent for the redemption fund. Between 1884 and 1893 the combined supplement rose from 58.5 to 68 per cent ("Zur Statistik der Umlagen der Selbstverwaltungskörper," tables 1 and 2). After 1893 the amount of the Galician supplement declined somewhat (*Podręcznik statystyki Galicyi*, VIII, pt. 2: 303). In the 1870s the combined Galician supplements amounted to over 80 per cent of direct state taxes (*Statistisches Jahrbuch über die direkten Steuern im Jahre 1887*, table XXXIII, addendum 2).

In the years 1884-8, supplements to direct state taxes were levied by the Southern Podillian counties as follows (expressed as percentages of direct state taxes):

County	**1884**	**1885**	**1886**	**1887**	**1888**
Borshchiv	10%	10%	10%	?	14%
Chortkiv	8%	20%	20%	7.5%	8%
Husiatyn	5%	5%	?	4%	4%
Terebovlia	17%	10%	10%	7%	7%
Zalishchyky	8%	6%	6%	5%	5%

No details are available for Southern Podillian county supplements to direct state taxes after 1888.

Source: *Oesterreichische Statistik*, XXXI, no. 2: table III.

Little is known about commune finances (J. Wysocki, "Die österreichische Finanzpolitik," 75). No information is available about the size of supplements to direct state taxes imposed by commune authorities in Southern Podillia. Supplements imposed by Galician communes in 1883 mostly fell in the range of 15-30 per cent (*Oesterreichische Statistik*, XXXI, no. 2: xliv-liii).

77. The average total supplement imposed by the Land, county, and commune authorities in Galicia in 1887 amounted to 86.6 per cent of direct state taxes (calculated from data in *Oesterreichische Statistik*, XXXI, no. 2, xliii). In 1893 the equivalent figure was 96.9 per cent ("Zur Statistik," table 5).

78. This calculation does not seem implausible in view of contemporary Austrian statisticians' calculations that in Galicia in 1887 the per capita cost of all direct taxes was 3.21 g (1.72 g to the state, 0.24 g to the commune, 1.25 g to the other two levels of government combined), *Oesterreichische Statistik*, XXXI, no. 2: xliii. As the average of 3.21 g includes business tax and income tax, neither of which the peasant paid, the villagers' per capita tax burden was considerably lower.

79. *Statistisches Jahrbuch über die direkten Steuern im Jahre 1887*, table XXXIII, appendix b2.

80. See Appendix II, and Chapter II below.

Chapter II

The People of Southern Podillia

Describing and analyzing peasant societies of the past is difficult because of the paucity both of data and descriptive materials.[1] Nevertheless, it is possible, despite significant gaps, to depict some salient features of Southern Podillian village life in the late nineteenth century.

Social Relationships in the Village

Late nineteenth-century Southern Podillia was a region of very marked social contrasts. Great mansions shared the countryside with the villages of the peasants and the largely Jewish market towns; large and very large estates adjoined the small plots of the peasantry. Countess Dunin-Borkowska owned several estates totalling 3,535 ha in Terebovlia county.[2] The annual land tax of landowner Kornel Hordyski in Kolyndiany was 590 g for 1,289 ha,[3] while at the same time 64 per cent of the households in that village were said to have landholdings of less than 1.5 ha.[4] In 1890 there were approximately 350 landowners who owned 285,055 ha of land in the Ternopil Court Circuit (to which the five counties belonged), while 396,820 ha remained for the remaining several hundred thousand inhabitants of that circuit.[5] In one village, two farms totalled 345 ha, whereas 230 ha remained for 120 people.[6]

The wealth of the large landowners (even though some were in fact in economic difficulties) was reflected in their political pre-eminence. Their power was feared; they received deference, but rarely respect and admiration. They lived separate from the people in every way. In their mansions their children were tutored privately while village children went to the local school.[7] Occasional religious and cultural festivities and political events brought them together, but on the whole their lives were worlds apart. The short stories of Vasyl Stefanyk abound with examples of the social distance between the classes. While the manor could provide work for the peasants to earn extra income, not everyone was prepared to take such work. This attitude was rooted in pre-1848 compulsory labour. Yet sometimes there were too many labourers available. Then, a crafty peasant might grovel before his squire in a show of great poverty:

> When he was on the way to the squire's place he had a very clear plan: on seeing him, he would take off his hat and approach him directly, like a stork walking on a marsh—carefully, lightly so as not to

> jar a single pebble. When he had drawn quite close to him, he would open his eyes wide and stare at the squire so as to make him think: "This one must really be poor." Then he would step up to him, take his hand, kiss it on both sides, apply his forehead to the squire's palm and move slightly back. Having done that, he would lower his shoulders, cast his hat on the ground behind him, wipe his palms with his sleeve and begin to speak.[8]

This performance may be exaggerated, but elements of that picture cannot be disregarded. The peasants played out rituals of this sort out of habit as much as real feeling. In their minds, they were realistic about the economic circumstances of their society and responded accordingly. On the other hand, there were some instances of genuine respect and admiration for large landowners by peasants. The decisive element seemed to be the behaviour of the manor lord and his family toward the villagers. If a nobleman or lessee were honest, treated the locals generously, were careful and progressive in the distribution of his wealth, he gained their regard no matter how extensive his wealth. A prime example of that in Southern Podillia was Prince Leon Sapieha and his wife Teresa, who owned enormous tracts of land in Borshchiv county. In several of the villages where they had mansions, they performed acts of charity which created fond memories of them among the former inhabitants. In Tsyhany Sapieha funded a child-care centre run by the Sisters of Mercy.[9] In Bilche and Kryvche they were the sponsors, along with the Shevchenko Scientific Society, of the excavation and cleaning of caves of geological interest.[10] Prince Sapieha was known to attend mass on Sunday in the Greek Catholic Church in Bilche, had donated a building in that village for a child-care facility, and had provided a building for a village bakery there.[11] One person declared: "Both of them were, from all points of view, humane and understanding."[12] Another respected noble, Count Borkowski in Korolivka, donated land for the village church and cemetery and covered 80 per cent of the costs of the church building.[13]

Normally, real respect was reserved for other strata of society. At the top of the social scale were the priest, teacher, cantor (*diak*) and other church officials, and any other professional people. These were the dynamic elements of village society who were frequently remembered as village leaders by former inhabitants of the region because they took the lead in organizing the villagers' religious and educational experiences. Next on the social scale were the wealthy peasants and artisans—people who engendered envy mingled with respect—for with their money and manual skills came a certain control over the less fortunate. Generally the next lowest on the scale—unless exceptionally capable and honest—were the political and administrative officials: the reeve or mayor, the county and commune officials (who were also often prosperous peasants or representatives of the large landowning class), and the commune scribe. Not only did their wealth and influence cause discomfort to their neighbours, but their power was feared. Lower still on the scale were the Jews of the village. Fellow peasants and the landless labourers, whether on the manor or the wealthier peasant holdings, were the people from whom they felt the least "social distance."[14]

The hierarchy presented here, garnered from contemporary accounts and later recollections, was probably not quite so rigid in practice. Factors such as family relationships, religious and linguistic differences, and size of landholdings necessarily entered the picture. Indicative of the existence of this social hierarchy was the fact that the press and memoirs reported mainly on the deeds of administrators, priests, teachers, and cantors. For example, "very active was the parish priest from 1883-1909, Fr. Hordiievsky. He founded a sobriety brotherhood, a savings association, a general store...."[15] In a similar vein, the cantor also held an honoured position:

> A good cantor is like the right hand of a good priest and may also do a lot of good for the people.... He teaches by example... if people see that he is a sober, reasonable man, reads books and newspapers, is respected, people will emulate him.[16]

The failings of prominent individuals were made public in letters to editors about priests who seemed indifferent or inadequate to their parishoners[17] or reeves who were turncoats (*khrun*), corrupt politically, and opposed to popular education or innovations in the village.[18] During elections, villagers who succumbed to the persuasion or bribery of the Polish nobility were identified in the press and berated for it.[19]

Publicity was also given to the achievements and failures of whole communes. A village such as Kalynivshchyna (Chortkiv county) was not considered successful because it looked neglected; there was too much consumption of alcohol associated with peoples' festivities; Poles dominated the commune council; and there was sloppy bookkeeping, especially of the tax registers.[20] Another village, Turylche (Borshchiv county), "looked wild, and had an empty church"; in that village people were sorry to have lost their tavern in a fire and were planning to rebuild it. By contrast, the village of Zalissia in the same county was exemplary: "the village is lovely with its pretty houses and other buildings: it does the heart good just to look at it." Moreover, in this village, the tavern was locked up, snow had not been cleared in front of it, and "not even the birds go near it."[21] There also were occasional statements of specific ideals for villages by various individuals. According to one Ukrainian children's journal, a successful community had a well-built and maintained church and belltower, a school with a garden and orchard which were

Prince Leon Sapieha

A family from Dobrovliany, Zalishchyky county, photographed at the Ternopil Exhibition, 1892

well-tended, a priest's house and farmstead which were in good repair, a commune council building, a reading club with its own loan society, a grain storage facility (*shpykhlir*), well cared-for yards and roads, an empty tavern, native artisans, and a population which respected its priest, hated evil, and observed Ukrainian customs.[22]

The rural nature of Southern Podillian settlements and the attachment of the inhabitants to the land, the social hierarchy in which the priests and intellectuals were the leading element, and the significance accorded to the commune were all attributes of Southern Podillian society which were noted by other contemporary writers, some of them non-Ukrainian. Although their writings dealt with Eastern Galicia or Ukrainians in Galicia, much of what they stated verified local experience which was conveyed in the press of the period. An Austrian observer noted that "the Ruthenians are mostly cultivators of the soil... cling to their inherited land... [and] only leave their birthplace under duress."[23] Another writer, dealing with a slightly later period, was impressed with the strength of the Ukrainians' link to agriculture, stating that they were "farmers by conviction" who "saw in agriculture the best and most honorable occupation."[24] A Ukrainian novelist, writing in Canada, had one of his characters who had come to Canada from Southern Podillia describe their philosophy of rural self-reliance: "Decent people help each other so long as each does his best to help himself and doesn't just sit around pretending the world owes him a living."[25] Being a *gazda*, a master of a farm, was a respected calling. According to V. Pakuliak, a villager from Ivankiv (Borshchiv county), "there was the sense of something decent, upright, and respectable in the full meaning of that word. To say to somebody that 'he wasn't a *gazda*' was a humiliation which everyone dreaded."[26]

For Umlauft, the Ukrainians in Eastern Galicia were "religious-minded... [and] faithful to the church," and he noted that the "people hang on to the church, the memorial of their nationality." He recognized the clergyman's important role as social leader of his commune and also the leadership roles of the Ukrainian intelligentsia. He saw the latter as "remaining true to its people with few exceptions and [having] done, next to the clergy, the most for their moral and material improvement."[27] A Canadian visitor to Eastern Galicia in 1898 commented on the material well-being, especially the neatness and good conditions, of the Ukrainian villages:

> One cannot avoid admiring the care and labour expended in that direction to make their habitations attractive. In very few cases did I observe a failure to whiten the outside of the cottages, and in not a single instance did I find cattle or fowl sheds annexed to the living apartments.... There were evidences of order and cleanliness that could not escape observation.... people in the neighborhood were not afflicted with appetites for strong drink... the village schoolhouse... next to the

> church was always the most extensive and best looking building in the community—large, airy, neat and clean.[28]

Other characteristics of Southern Podillian Ukrainian society were related to the people's view of themselves and of life itself. Individualism, liberty, equality, and popular government were valued in personal and public life.[29] To these should be added attachment to the commune, the parish, and the family.

The Family

The basic social and economic unit was the family. It was the primary production unit and fulfilled all society's needs. Sex roles were delineated, but the male did not have absolute power in the family. Women shared power and responsibility for the household, and were granted a relatively high position in this society. In these two important ways the Ukrainian family differed from that of neighbouring societies, especially the Polish and Russian.[30] In the Russian family, women were subordinate to the father, had little voice in the choice of their marriage partner, and were subordinate to their husbands after marriage. Among Podillian Ukrainians the custom of three generations of a family living under one roof was still widely in evidence in the late nineteenth century, but the nuclear family in a single dwelling was becoming more common. A sociological analysis of families who immigrated to Canada from Southern Podillia at the turn of the century concluded that the family structure in that region was in a transitional state, moving rapidly from "extended" to "nuclear."[31] Until the mid-seventeenth century the family had been a large patriarchal grouping (*rid*), which held all of its land and livestock communally. Four, five or more generations of direct kin lived together in a settlement (*dvoryshche*). Their duties were divided among all members by the oldest competent male and female in the family. Everything was held, worked, and used in common (including food and implements) except for dwellings and personal effects. The elders periodically redistributed all tasks and lands.[32] Gradually this arrangement eroded because of demographic and economic circumstances, so very few regions of the Ukrainian territories retained even a modified form of this family organization into the late nineteenth and early twentieth centuries. Typical, for Southern Podillia by 1900, was the family of three generations living in one dwelling (one of the married sons and his wife and young children together with the father and mother), and all of the other, extended, family living apart from them.[33]

Nevertheless, family and commune members' roles and activities were heavily influenced by these traditions. Women's work consisted of general management of the household: sowing and caring for the garden, harvesting its produce, and preserving food; daily food preparation; working the flax and hemp; spinning, weaving, and sewing of clothes; tending the cattle, poultry, and pigs (beekeeping was a male preserve); washing and mending clothes; and decorating the dwelling. Men's contribution was working in the fields and caring for the draught animals and farm equipment; providing fuel and looking after the implements; and providing outer clothing for the family, such as coats, hats, and boots. Many men and women combined work on the land with a trade or craft.[34] In each village there were artisans such as shoemakers, weavers, carpenters, blacksmiths, wheelwrights, cartwrights, tailors, furriers, and basket weavers. Both men and women took outside employment, mainly in agriculture, if the income from their own properties was insufficient. Men and women had joint tasks, especially at harvest time, when men reaped while women tied the sheaves. Women could own separate property and derive the earnings from it. Children learned early to do the work of their same sex parent.[35] Children's magazines extolled some of the societal values on family and communal duties. Boys and girls were to have "good health and enthusiasm for learning." Boys' learning should lead to their becoming "good farmers, wise artisans, or judges, lawyers or officials;" girls' learning should lead them to become the "best wives in the world."[36]

The Commune

The commune was both an administrative unit and a social organism. Unlike the *dvoryshche* of old, the late nineteenth-century village or commune was generally a cluster of several family groups. The actual importance of kinship ties was no longer so great, but they persisted. The tradition of defending the clan's honour sometimes led to squabbles and even lawsuits, which village conciliation courts tried to resolve.[37] Commune members co-operated in public and ceremonial events and in routine matters. The most impressive of the annual ceremonies was the communal procession to the village Cross of Freedom and the religious service there to commemorate the end of compulsory labour in 1848. Commune members also joined in organizing and celebrating the festivities associated with the church and agricultural calendars. A communal meal, general talk and gossip, and later music and dancing might round off such an event, which thus also served a socializing purpose.[38]

The same purpose was served by the working bee (*toloka*), which might include most or all of the villagers. Such bees were organized to help individual families with a complex task such as building a house, or to construct institutional buildings such as a church or school.[39] Smaller bees brought people of the commune together at some villager's yard to assist in such tasks as cornhusking, poultry plucking, pig killing, and manure hauling. Such a bee could end with singing and music.[40] The sharing of draught animals, wagons, and agricultural implements, usually in return for other favours, continued among villagers into the twentieth century.[41] Clan and community thus remained important. Ukrainian intelligentsia, toward the turn of the century, often invoked these feelings to arouse villagers to united action; "the commune is a big man" was a favourite expression in newspapers and in the speeches of political writers.[42]

Baptisms, weddings, and funerals were big occasions in the life of the village.[43] Weddings in Southern Podillia involved the whole village in the happy festivities surrounding this "rite of passage." The central figure was the bride, whose move to another clan was tinged with sorrow for her parents and family. Much of the ritual revolved around this. For example, when the groom came to take the bride, the women of the bride's clan locked the gate in front of him.[44] Religion, of course, was evident in the rituals and songs, but marriage was a secular celebration as well. In Podillia, generally, guests were invited by the bride and groom, but in Husiatyn county the couple's parents did this. Among the guests would be the reeve of the commune, who was expected to give the couple his blessing, and the manor lord, if he and the village "lived in harmony."[45] Agricultural symbolism pervaded various stages of the three days of celebration, for example, the bride's presentation of bread dipped in honey to each guest (along with a kiss), in return for which the guest placed money in a bowl of wheat. Singing, dancing, and the eating of festive foods, including special breads made from wheat flour, were the rule. A contemporary wrote that "the people delight in their old customs, but culture and progress in learning will soon alter these."[46]

Standard of Living

Standard of living is defined as the "degree of material comfort enjoyed by a person, class or community."[47] Financial elements which usually determine the standard of living are wages or other income, prices, capital, interest, and rents. On another level are such factors as the state of nutrition, housing, fuel or energy consumption, education, and health services. Although it is clear that some of these factors can be identified and measured, available documentary sources provide only fragmentary evidence on the financial factors, and data on some other factors are also elusive. Moreover, what "hard" evidence exists has often been incorrectly analyzed. A glaring example is literature that simplistically equates the size of landholding with income.[48] It is nevertheless possible to give some overview of the Southern Podillian standard of living.

Underlying all the factors constituting the standard of living in Southern Podillia was the existence of a dual economy, that is, a great deal of barter of goods and services operated parallel with a market economy where goods and services were bought and sold for currency.[49] This complicates both description and analysis of the standard of living, but in some ways it helps to clarify the picture. The main source of income was the small, family agricultural enterprise, but by 1880 there was some degree of differentiation of occupations, particularly in the market towns.[50] Industry was barely beginning to enter the five counties, but in Iaholnytsia (Chortkiv county) there was a large-scale industrial enterprise, the state tobacco factory, which employed over 200 people, many of them women engaged at piecework rates.[51] These industrial workers were still closely linked to their family farmsteads. This class of people has been labelled "semi-proletarian" or "semi-feudal" by Soviet and other Marxist historians.[52] This group, which in some ways resembled present-day *kolhosp* workers in the Soviet Union,[53] was not dependent for its material comfort on money wages alone, since most of their food, shelter, and other basic needs were met by the family farmstead, to which they returned every day.

Other peasants supplemented their activities on their own plots with other work. Some worked as day labourers on large estates, especially at harvest time. Complaints by large landowners about shortages of local labour, and their importation of harvest workers from the sub-Carpathian regions and Western Galicia in the late 1870s, indicate that Southern Podillians did not work as day labourers on local estates to any great extent then. However, some Southern Podillians went to work as seasonal labourers in the Russian Empire, where day wages were higher.[54] The principal way for peasants to supplement income from agriculture was to engage in a secondary occupation as artisans and craftsmen, as well as domestic industry workers. Domestic industry included spinning and weaving, woodcarving, basket making, and embroidery. Peasants also worked in brickyards and quarries, as shoemakers, tailors, cabinet makers and carpenters, blacksmiths, cartwrights, harness makers, potters, masons, butchers, oil pressers, coopers, thatchers, well diggers, fishermen, and casual forestry workers. All such occupations were seasonal "as everyone worked on the fields at harvest time." Even secondary occupations could change with the seasons. For example, along the Dnister, peasants who were fishermen turned to basket weaving in the winter.[55] Smuggling was another seasonal activity engaged in by Christian peasants and Jews in the border counties of Borshchiv and Husiatyn. Goods, people, and animals were smuggled across the Zbruch. Horse smuggling was even referred to as a "profession." It was often done with the connivance of Russian and Austrian officials.[56]

In the late 1870s the peasant family enterprise in Southern Podillia sought to secure the needs of the family rather than to make a profit. This type of enterprise most resembled Chaianov's "peasant economy" in that it depended almost totally on the work of its family members.[57] In Southern Podillia this economy went one step beyond Chaianov's peasant household in that even some peasants with small holdings hired workers.[58] They constituted a "post-subsistence peasant economy." Surpluses produced by the individual households were taken to market, sold to local traders, or bartered directly for needed goods or services.[59] A natural extension of this post-subsistence model of the individual farmstead was the post-subsistence commune or village. Thus, whatever need a village could not fulfill for its inhabitants might be met in a neighbouring village. For example, a master builder in one village might make himself available for the construction of houses and other buildings in neighbouring villages.

For agricultural labour, data relating to incomes in this post-subsistence economy are very difficult to obtain. No peasant budgets, such as those for the Russian peasantry in the late nineteenth century or Western Galician villagers around 1900, are available.[60] There are data available, however, for the year 1877 on wages paid to agricultural labour both on the small and large landholdings. The picture is complex. A small proportion of agricultural labour consisted of permanent farm servants—men, women, boys and girls hired on contract for one or more years. Farm servants received wages in cash and in kind. In Southern Podillia in 1877 (excluding Zalishchyky county, which apparently did not respond to the Land enquiry), male general farm servants received a sum in cash ranging from around 30 to 50 g per annum in Borshchiv, 60 g in Terebovlia, 72 g in Chortkiv, and up to 120 g in Husiatyn. A farm supervisor might make 240 g in cash. In addition, farm servants received produce valued at 10-21 g, plus accommodation, fuel, use of half a morg (0.28 of a hectare) of ploughland, and pasturage for two cows. They frequently received salt, and sometimes a coat and boots. (Higher rates in Husiatyn were due to the difficulty of getting steady workers.) Carters and stable men received less pay, both in cash and in kind; rates for boys and girls were lower still, especially in kind.[61]

Cash wages in Southern Podillia for male agricultural day labourers in the late 1870s at haying and harvest time generally ranged between 35 and 50 kr per nine to twelve or thirteen hour day, but almost 25 per cent of the reported instances were between 51 and 65 kr, and occasionally were higher. During the potato harvest, money wages for male casual labour mostly ranged between 25 and 45 kr per day. In winter, for a shorter working day (generally five to eight hours) and with lower demand for labour, most daily cash wages were between 20 and 30 kr, but some were as high as 50-60 kr. In spring, for ploughing and sowing, daily pay ranged from 15 to 45 kr, and was occasionally higher. Pay rates for female agricultural day labourers also varied considerably. In summer, the majority of female workers received between 26 and 40 kr per day, with the rest almost equally divided between those who were paid up to 25 kr and those who received more than 40 kr per day. For the potato harvest, most women were paid between 20 and 40 kr per day. In the winter, the majority received between 16 and 20 kr per day, but 10 per cent got less and 23 per cent more. In most cases pay for spring field work was in the range of 16 to 25 kr per day. Male and female workers hired for a specific purpose for a stated period of time, such as a week or a month for the distillery "campaign," would receive a higher wage, up to three g per day.[62]

Often, however, the day labourer's remuneration was not money.[63] A bewildering variety of pay in kind, allowances, and use of fields hinged on localized custom. This system persisted longer in Podillia than elsewhere.[64]

Payment in kind might take the form of every eighth or tenth or twelfth sheaf harvested or the number of sheaves might vary according to the crop (every tenth sheaf of wheat or rye and every twelfth sheaf of barley and peas). Workers would cut and bind the crop and "stook" the sheaves. In the hay harvest, day labourers might receive one-eighth to one-half of the harvest (the lower the quality of the harvest, the greater the worker's share). Similar arrangements applied to the potato harvest, where one-tenth was the worker's portion. Payment might be in a product which the landowner would have bought, such as three blocks of salt for every metric centner of grain harvested. Sometimes the day labourer became, in effect, a sharecropper, who received one-quarter or one-third of the maize harvest in return for seeding (with the landowner's seed) and harvesting it (if the worker supplied the seed, his share was one-half). At times, the day labourer worked so many days to earn the right to pasture one or two cows.[65] Also quite customary was the practice of the day labourer planting his own crop between the rows of maize. This last type of harvest, which belonged exclusively to the worker, was not part of the recorded economy at all.[66]

Because there was great variety in practice within Southern Podillia and because the value of payment in kind cannot be precisely known, no exact figures for the range of income derived from working for others are available. However, authorities as diverse as Pilat and Biegeleisen agreed that in a region which was cash poor and had many large owners who suffered from cash flow problems, the value of payment in kind was greater than the value of payment in cash for similar work.[67] Survival into the twentieth century of pre-modern modes of payment was thus to the advantage of the workers.

The presence of a diversity of types of remuneration and the absence of a standard measure make it difficult even to guess at the real worth of wages for agricultural day labourers. Some, but only some, light is cast upon this mystery by data obtained for the Galician Land Executive in 1876. The annual cost of the needs of an average family of five (two adults and three children) in 1876-7 was calculated for the various Galician counties, including those of Southern Podillia.[68] It was estimated that such a family, in Chortkiv county, required 11.5 bushels per annum (1 bushel = 1.23 hectolitres) of rye, worth 65 g, 5 bushels of barley worth 25 g, 4 bushels of maize worth 16 g, 17 bushels of potatoes worth 20 g, 180 cabbages worth 3 g, 3 bushels of beets worth 3 g, 307.5 litres of milk worth 16 g, 11.34 kg of fat worth 14 g, 40.5 kg of meat worth 20 g, 44.5 kg of salt worth 7 g, and 5 g worth of other victuals, for a total value of 194 g per annum.[69] Food consumed by a family of five in Husiatyn and Terebovlia counties was worth more, 252 g and 210 g respectively. The respective figures reported for Borshchiv and Zalishchyky counties were much lower at 78 and 77 g. While other indicators suggest that these were the poorest counties of Southern Podillia, some data were clearly missing and, in the case of Borshchiv, the value of food consumption was adjusted to 110 g by the author of the report.[70]

Food consumption was one of five main indicators used to calculate the cost of living for an average family. The overall configuration is given in Table 2.

Table 2
Average Cost of Family Necessities, 1876-7, in Gulden

County	Housing	Heating	Lighting	Food	Clothing	Total
Borshchiv	16	20	5	110	72	223
Chortkiv	11	20	3	194	52	280
Husiatyn	11	33	5	252	70	371
Terebovlia	12	30	8	210	95	355
Zalishchyky	13	22	2	77	70	184

Source: *Wiadomości statystyczne*, VII, 1, table XVI.

The statistician responsible for collating these data observed, plaintively but accurately, that estimating the cost of maintaining a family "belongs to the most difficult of social statistical exercises."[71] For example, it is not clear how much of the cost of clothing represented real expenditure on purchased items and how much was the money equivalent of home produced or bartered items. Likewise, it is not clear whether real or notional costs for upkeep on the family dwelling were reported, or whether the house tax was included.[72] Wood and straw were used in Southern Podillia for heating.[73] Straw was produced by most peasant small holdings and was often acquired by day labourers as payment in kind, but the cost of wood was most probably a real expense, as was the cost of lighting. Kerosene lamps were coming into extensive use in Chortkiv county, but were not reported elsewhere in Southern Podillia.[74] The peasants' landholdings plus their gardens produced the overwhelming bulk of their food supplies, so no cash expenditure was incurred except for salt. The amount of meat consumption in Chortkiv county is at variance with other testimony, but in that county smallholders raised pigs and sheep for their own tables.[75] It should also be noted that the above data do not include the cost of alcoholic drinks or tea and coffee. On average, a family's consumption of vodka and beer cost 18.25 g per annum; the addition of the cost of tea, coffee, rum, wine, sweet liqueurs, and mead would generally bring the total up to 25-30 g per year. Not included in any of the above estimates were the cost of tobacco (though many Southern Podillian peasants grew their own), or of special events such as wedding or funeral feasts.[76]

The 1876-7 investigation assumed that the Eastern Galician peasantry was self-sufficient in grain and other agricultural produce. Surpluses would be sold. For example, in Borshchiv county income from poultry paid for the costs of lighting, salt, and soap.[77] Other cash income specifically noted was from the sale of "old" cows, pigs, horses, oxen, and the tobacco and aniseed crops.[78] There was as yet no systematic raising of large animals for market by Southern Podillian peasants, but average quality cows were sold by peasants for 30-40 g in the fall of 1876 (a little less in Chortkiv county), with top quality animals fetching up to 60 g. Oxen were sold at 50-60 g, with top quality animals in the 70-80 g range (in Zalishchyky up to 100 g). Southern Podillian horses generally sold for 20-40 g, but the price ranged as high as 60-80 g, while poor quality animals were sold for as little as 5-8 g.[79]

On the basis of the 1877 data, the material condition of the Galician peasantry had probably improved in the previous decade, although responses from Borshchiv, Husiatyn, and Zalishchyky also contained some contrary indications. On the whole, peasants were better housed, in better heated dwellings, and wearing better clothes. Many were still regarded as improvident, because they lived well at harvest time, when taxes and previously incurred debts would be paid, but conserved too little for the late winter and spring months. The supply of food was dependent on the amplitude of each year's harvest, but while one harvest failure caused hardship, expert opinion held that it required several failures to bring ruin to a peasant family.[80]

There are some price indicators for the 1880s: a half-kilogram of tea cost 1.30 g, ordinary soap 27 kr per kg, bleach 1 g, starch 28 kr, fat pork 68 kr per kg, wheel grease 14 g per 100 kg, rice 16-17 g per 100 kg, and a packet of boot polish 24 kr. For school supplies, scribblers were between 58 kr and 1.40 g per 100, pencils 8-18 kr per dozen, chalk 20 kr per kg, slates 30-35 kr per 100.[81] Candles were 90 g per 100 kg and wine 40-50 kr per litre.[82] Salt cost 1 g per 100 kg.[83] In 1889 yeast was expensive at 1.40 g per kg.[84] The cheapest scythes were 20 kr and better quality ranged up to 40-50 kr each. Sickles cost 25-30 kr, and a cleaver 56 kr. Ploughs could be ordered from stores in Ternopil and Kolomyia at 7.60 g and 11 g for different models.[85] Some of those prices were wholesale, so there would be a markup by the time those commodities were sold in the villages. On the other hand, the price of goods at the great annual fair at Ulashkivtsi was often half the usual price, and competition among traders in the market towns tended to keep prices down.[86]

Most of the dietary requirements of the population were met from the production of individual households. Much of the usual diet was of plant origin and grown on the land of the individual householders or acquired in kind. Consequently, it is not possible to estimate its real cost. The main foods of Southern Podillians were: borsch; other soups made from chicken or other meat bones; cabbage soup; soups with millet, buckwheat or pearl barley groats; soups with vegetables such as broad beans, peas or onions; gruel or kasha made of cereal grains, corn, lentils or rice; *varenyky* (dumplings); cabbage rolls; potatoes; bread, usually made of rye sourdough; meat (mainly stewed chicken, or occasionally beef or mutton); and salt pork or fat. Most Podillians say meat was eaten only on holidays and Sundays, but this varied from family to family.[87] Eggs were not often eaten as a separate food.

Fish was also eaten from time to time either fresh or salted and pickled. Cottage cheese was made at home and stored for use mainly in fall and winter months. Other fall and winter foods were sauerkraut, dilled pickles, fermented beets, and dried vegetables and fruits. Mushrooms were picked and cooked from spring to fall. Fruits (plums, berries, cherries, apples, pears, and apricots) were eaten raw in season and dried in the winter, or as stewed compote. Noodles and dumplings made with eggs were often used in soups or alone, sprinkled with cottage cheese, milk or salt pork cracklings. Special "treats" in the diet were nuts, honey, and baked goods using fruit or poppyseed. Drinks were fruit juices, milk, buttermilk, sour milk, tea, coffee, beer, wine, vodka, and homemade liqueurs. Favourite flavourings were garlic, dill, and caraway seeds. Honey was used for sweetening.[88] The diet, although low in animal protein, was not lacking in good quality vegetable protein (broad beans, lentils, peas, rye bread, and the lowly potato),[89] nor in other dietary requirements for good health. (It is possible that more animal protein [from rabbits, birds, etc.] than has been reported did enter the diet.) Nonetheless, expenditures on nutrition, outside of plant seeds and labour, seem to have been very small indeed.

Housing expenses are equally difficult to assess. Most houses were built of beaten clay mixed with straw, and thatched with straw. For such houses the only purchased materials were the wood for framing doors and windows and glass for the windows.[90] These buildings lasted up to a century, if built properly,[91] and were relatively inexpensive to construct, approximately 40 g for a house for "an ordinary person" in 1900.[92] There were situations in which accommodation costs would be even lower, such as a father and eldest son living together, inheriting a house, or servants receiving free housing. As for the quality of such housing, ethnographic studies indicate that this style of house had been in use from time immemorial in this region. These houses were cool in summer, warm in winter, sturdy, and of the most affordable type. All but the very wealthiest people lived in them. The house, as well as most of the internal household amenities and chattels, were made of indigenous materials. Fuel and lighting, materials for furniture, household utensils, and clothing could be obtained locally through barter or purchase. Wood, often scarce, could be obtained from more distant locations. Only items such as matches, oil for lamps, boot polish, and wagon grease were brought into the region.

Thus, living standards in this society cannot be expressed accurately owing to the lack of good quality sources, but the average Southern Podillian household seems to have had reasonably adequate food and housing. How comfortable this standard of living was cannot be expressed with statistical accuracy, since the "unofficial" economy, that is, wages paid in kind and barter of goods and services, was still so widespread. However, there is testimony from inhabitants, former inhabitants, and travellers which may help us judge the quality of life in Southern Podillian villages. A memoirist from Mykhalkiv stated that "the economic position of the village was difficult, but the people's industriousness, innate versatility, and self-sufficiency helped the villagers in such a manner that they never lived in misery."[93] Archduke Rudolph, during his visit to Podillia in 1887, said that "these Eastern Galician peasants aren't as backward as they have been represented."[94] Another visitor to the region in the 1880s wrote:

> the villages we are passing show through their appearance the well-being of the villagers—pleasant looking clean houses with small flower gardens... well looking animals. All this proves that the black earth feeds its men.[95]

Population: Occupations and Mobility

The total population of Southern Podillia in 1880 was 362,575, rising to 429,908 by 1900. Rates of population increase were not the same in each of the counties (for details see Table 3).

About 65-70 per cent of the population in 1880 was Ukrainian; about 16-20 per cent were Poles and 14 per cent Jews.[96] According to the 1880 census, about 80 per cent of the total population was primarily dependent on agriculture and forestry for its livelihood.[97] The remaining 20 per cent of the population, largely in the small towns of the region, provided services to the rural areas. About 8.5 per cent were in the occupational category "industry and crafts," 4.5 per cent in commerce or transportation, and 3 per cent were non-agricultural day labourers. About 0.7 per cent were officials or other employees of the various levels of government, exclusive of the military, gendarmes, and revenue officers.

In 1880 there were 256 public security personnel in the five counties: Borshchiv 96, Chortkiv 61, Husiatyn 68, Terebovlia 17, and Zalishchyky 14. There was a military garrison of 545 men in Terebovlia and a detachment of 22 soldiers in Borshchiv county. There were 503 teachers in the five counties, of whom 463 were male and 40 female. There were 223 male clergy (all denominations included) and 12 nuns. There were nine lawyers, two in each county except Terebovlia, which had only one. As for architects and civil engineers, Husiatyn had three, while Chortkiv, Terebovlia, and Zalishchyky had one each. There were ten painters and sculptors in Husiatyn, and four in Chortkiv. Zalishchyky had the greatest number of people engaged primarily in commerce, indicating that this county had more traders and itinerant peddlers than elsewhere.[98]

Table 3
Population of Southern Podillia: 1880, 1890, 1900

(a) **Totals**	**1880**	**1890**	**1900**
Borshchiv	97,935	106,755	109,220
Chortkiv	57,257	64,741	71,981
Husiatyn	77,791	89,377	93,854
Terebovlia	63,235	71,823	77,212
Zalishchyky	66,357	72,598	77,641
Southern Podillia	362,575	405,294	429,908

(b) **Rate of Increase of Population**	**1880**	**1890**	**1900**
Borshchiv	100	109.0	111.5
Chortkiv	100	113.1	125.7
Husiatyn	100	114.9	120.6
Terebovlia	100	113.6	122.1
Zalishchyky	100	109.4	117.0
Southern Podillia	100	111.8	118.6

Source: Raw data in *Special-Orts-Repertorien*, 1880 and 1890; *Gemeindelexikon*.

The population may not have been monolithic in occupational distribution, but there was limited geographic mobility as of 1880, except for service in the army. The overwhelming majority of the people of Southern Podillia, consistent with their rural status, lived and died in the commune where they were born. By 1890, somewhat greater mobility began to be evident (see Table 4).

In 1880, the same number of men and women moved from one commune within the same county to another. However, about 10 per cent more men than women had moved from one county to another. Only Terebovlia county, in which there was a military garrison, had any significant number of persons from other parts of Austria. There were also "outsiders" in Borshchiv and Zalishchyky, which were just across the Dnister from Bukovyna, but very few in Husiatyn and Chortkiv. During the 1880s more mobility occurred. By 1890, the percentage of those living in the commune of their birth was lower than in 1880. Women, too, were beginning to move about more.[99] Traditional restraints

Table 4
Place of Birth of Inhabitants of Southern Podillia, 1880 and 1890
(as a percentage of total population)

County	1880 Born in commune of residence	1880 Born in another commune in county of residence	1880 Born in another county of Galicia	1890 Born in commune of residence	1890 Born in another commune in county of residence	1890 Born in another county of Galicia
Borshchiv	94.0	3.6	1.9	86.1	8.7	4.9
Chortkiv	92.0	3.7	4.0	82.8	7.9	8.5
Husiatyn	91.8	3.5	4.0	84.0	8.5	6.4
Terebovlia	92.9	2.6	2.7	84.5	8.1	6.9
Zalishchyky	93.4	2.5	3.6	85.5	6.8	6.6

Source: *Oesterreichische Statistik*, I, no. 3 and XXXII, no. 2.
Notes to Table 4:

For the sake of comparison it should be noted that in 1880, 89.4 per cent of the population of Galicia resided in the commune of their birth, and another 4.3 per cent in another commune in the county of their birth. In 1890, the percentages were 80.1 and 9.8 respectively. In 1890, 0.9 per cent of the inhabitants of Husiatyn county and 0.7 per cent of Borshchiv county—the two counties bordering on the Russian Empire—had been born outside of Austria.

upon movement were clearly weakening. Also, better methods of transportation, primarily the first railway line into the region, may have had some effect.[100]

The statistics do not differentiate between migration between the counties of Southern Podillia and in-migration from and out-migration to other parts of Galicia.[101] Most of the population movement in the 1880s seems to have been regional. The only exception to this was Chortkiv, which probably attracted people from other counties and even from outside the region, as it was becoming a transportation centre of some importance. But even as late as 1890 there had been relatively little out-migration to the two large metropolitan centres of Galicia, Lviv, and Cracow, or to Vienna.[102]

Although people thus tended to reside in the villages of their birth, this did not mean that they necessarily lived in ignorance of the wider world. Military service—not in fact universal, as the Austrian state could not afford to conscript all eligible males—took young men to far-off places and a small number made a career in the army before retiring to their home villages with some savings.[103] Large landowners needed to sell their grain and lumber outside the region, which necessitated transportation by wagon to the nearest railheads at Kolomyia, Chernivtsi, and Ternopil.[104] River-borne transport brought communities along the river into touch with the bargemen.[105]

Visits to the nearest market town took male villagers, and often women as well, outside their immediate surroundings. Great annual events, such as the St. Anne's cattle fair in Ternopil or the yearly pilgrimage to the holy shrine of the Blessed Virgin Mary at Zarvanytsia, Pidhaitsi county, attracted villagers from Southern Podillia in large numbers.[106] Within the region itself, the annual horse fair at Ulashkivtsi attracted people "from all over the world."[107] Horse-traders came from all parts of Galicia and Bukovyna, from European Russia, from other parts of Austria, and in smaller numbers from as far away as Western Europe and Central Asia.[108] For the villagers of the whole region it was a great event, a chance to see unusual sights and make small necessary purchases.[109] As Fernand Braudel has noted in another context, even in the pre-modern era villagers did travel and have contacts with the wider world to a greater extent than was once thought.

Notes

1. See S.H. Franklin, *The European Peasantry*, xiv-xv.
2. Tittel, *Schematismus und Statistik des Grossgrundbesitzes*, 217.
3. T. Pilat, *Skorowidz dóbr tabularnych w Galicji z wielkim ks. Krakowskiem*, 86-7.
4. T. Pilat, "Die Auswanderung aus den podolischen Bezirken nach Russland," 77. Ivan Franko decried the inequities in landholdings and suggested land reforms which would have eliminated the latifundia in East Galicia (Franko's "Zemelna vlastnist u Halychyni," 285-6, *passim*).
5. Pilat, "Die Auswanderung," 71.
6. IMZCh, 232. For sizes of landholdings in the five counties in 1900 and 1902 see Appendices I and IX.
7. In Makovei's *Zalisia*, the village priest's university-educated son was hired to tutor the son of the manor lord. Information also from interview of 6 October 1983 with Mr. E. Michaels.
8. V. Stefanyk, *The Stone Cross*, 71. See also W. Czumer, *Recollections About the Life of the First Ukrainian Settlers in Canada*, 29.
9. IMZCh, 579.
10. Ibid., 482.
11. Ibid., 614; *Batkivshchyna*, 15 Aug. 1884.
12. IMZCh, 617.
13. Ibid., 621; Czumer, *Recollections*, 28. On the other hand, the later Polish general, Józef Haller (who had an estate in Borshchiv county while stationed in the region

in the 1890s) and his wife "lived a decadent life" (IMZCh, 497).

14. There are frequent uncomplimentary references to "the rich peasants" of the village in Stefanyk's stories (Stefanyk, *The Stone Cross*, 43, 54, 69). For the concept of social distance see E.S. Bogardus, "Measuring Social Distance," 299-308.
15. IMZCh, 231.
16. *Batkivshchyna*, 1 Feb. 1884.
17. *Batkivshchyna* (10 July 1885) carried a letter from Terebovlia in which the writer complained that the priests were not very helpful to the population during the last elections; ibid. (24 Feb. 1890) had a letter from Zastinoche chastising the priest for distributing holy pictures with Polish script to Ukrainian school children; a correspondent from Zhezhava criticized the local priest for the high fees he charged (*Svoboda*, 10 Mar. 1898). These letters were outnumbered by those which praised local priests.
18. The reeve and councillors in Uvysla would not support the establishment of a commune grain storage facility and loan society (*Batkivshchyna*, 6 June 1884). Another letter, from Hovyliv, noted that the reeve was a *khrun* (ibid., 22 Jan. 1886). The reeve in Ustia Iepyskopske was opposed to the creation of a reading club there, so the gendarmes searched the homes of its founding members at night (ibid., 21 Mar. 1890). Another letter from that village complained about reeve Ivan Fochak, who had demanded that people who received aid from the state relief fund for victims of the crop failure in 1889 should pay him twenty kreuzer each for his effort to obtain this aid for them (ibid., 4 July 1890). In Pyshchatyntsi the reeve was a *khrun*, according to a correspondent from there (*Svoboda*, 1 Apr. 1897).
19. See *Batkivshchyna*, 21 June 1889, for one such example. See also Chapter IX below.
20. *Batkivshchyna*, 15 Jan. 1886.
21. *Batkivshchyna*, 22 Feb. 1889. See also ibid., 7 Mar. 1890, for an account of the progress of Kolodribka commune, and 13 Feb. 1895, on the successful commune of Kobylovoloky.
22. *Lastivka*, no. 2, 1878.
23. F. Umlauft, *Die Oesterreichisch-ungarische Monarchie*, 642.
24. S. Koenig, "The Ukrainians of East Galicia," 1935, 120.
25. I. Kiriak, *Sons of the Soil*, 47.
26. IMZCh, 589.
27. Umlauft, *Die Oesterreichisch-ungarische Monarchie*, 643. See also L. Kellner, P. Arnold, and A.L. Delisle, *Austria of the Austrians and Hungary of the Hungarians*, 25: "They are being roused from their lethargy now by their intelligent classes, and are likely to become dangerous to the Poles, so far the masters of the country."
28. W.T.R. Preston, "Report of Inspector of Agencies in Europe," 17.
29. Rudnitsky, *Ukraine: The Land and Its People*, 197.
30. Ibid., 197. For a different view, see Stefanyk, *The Stone Cross*, 45-7. See also D. Atkinson, "Society and the Sexes in the Russian Past," 30-3.
31. H. Muchin, "The Evolution of the Ukrainian Family and its Portrayal in Illya Kiriak's novel *Sons of the Soil*," 6. See also O. Kravets, *Simeinyi pobut i zvychai ukrainskoho narodu*, 19. He concurs with this position, stating, in addition, that the eldest son was expected to look after his parents until their death.

32. Muchin, "The Evolution of the Ukrainian Family," 11. See also R. Rozdolski, *Wspólnota gminna w b. Galicji wschodniej i jej zanik*, 5-6.
33. Muchin, "The Evolution of the Ukrainian Family," 5.
34. IMZCh, 846; *Batkivshchyna*, 15 Feb. 1884. The author's grandfather in Chortkiv county was a cantor and farmer, and her grandmother a midwife and seamstress. See also Vynnytsky, ed., *Terebovelska zemlia*, 363-8.
35. Kravets, *Simeinyi pobut i zvychai Ukrainskoho narodu*, 24-6, 43-4; Muchin, "The Evolution of the Ukrainian Family," 92-3. See also *Hospodar i promyshlennyk*, no. 6, 1887. (This semi-monthly newspaper was intended for agriculturalists).
36. *Lastivka*, no. 1, 1878.
37. IMZCh, 643.
38. Ibid., 203, 357-358 and 848.
39. Makovei, *Zalisia*, 290.
40. IMZCh, 643; *Batkivshchyna*, 24 Aug. 1886.
41. Interview with Mr. E. Michaels, 6 Oct. 1983.
42. See, for example, *Batkivshchyna*, 5 Jan. 1886; Stefanyk, *The Stone Cross*, 55. The strength of the commune tradition is apparent in Southern Podillian villagers' attempts to re-create it in Canada (Muchin, "The Evolution of the Family," 40-3; V.J. Kaye, *Early Ukrainian Settlements in Canada, 1895-1900*, 136, 165, 186, *passim*; J. Lehr, "The Pattern and Process of Ukrainian Rural Settlement in Western Canada, 1891-1914," esp. Chapter X).
43. "Exuberant" baptisms, weddings, and funeral rites were the cause of much indebtedness (L. Caro, "Lichwa na wsi w Galicyi w latach 1875-1891," 131).
44. M. Bilous, *Russkoe vesilie pislia zvychaiv i obychaiv narodnykh nad Prutom i na Podoliu*, 34.
45. Ibid., 14, 19.
46. Ibid., 34, 44. See also Vovk, *Studii z ukrainskoi*, 215-319.
47. J.B. Sykes, ed., *The Pocket Oxford Dictionary of Current English*, 89.
48. See Chapter VI below on landholding.
49. Soviet scholars call this the "Prussian route" to capitalism, that is, features of the feudal system co-existed with features of a capitalist economy. For some examples of this see V.K. Osechynsky, *Halychyna pid hnitom Avstro-Uhorshchyny*, 6-9; E. Niederhauser, "The Problems of Bourgeois Transformation in Eastern and South-Eastern Europe," 565.
50. *Oesterreichische Statistik*, I, no. 3: 242-305.
51. This may be inferred from data on the tobacco factories and their workers in *Oesterreichisches statistisches Handbuch*, I, 150.
52. V.K. Osechynsky, "Kolonialne stanovyshche Halychyny v skladi Avstro-Uhorshchyny," 40; J. Buszko, "Zum Wandel der Gesellschaftstruktur in Galizien und in der Bukowina," 9.
53. B. Kerblay, *Modern Soviet Society*, 85.
54. Hempel, "Ekonomiczne stosunki Galicyi," 127, 144-150; Kleczyński, "Ekonomiczne stosunki Galicyi: stosunki włościańskie w Galicyi," 39.
55. IMZCh, 262, 358, 364-5, 384, 420, 758-9, 769, 777, 790, 810; Vynnytsky, *Terebovelska zemlia*, 71.
56. IMZCh, 442, 498; *Sefer Borszczow*, *passim*; O. Remez, *Cherez kordon (z dnevnyka*

emihranta), passim; interview with J. Sokolyk, 19 July 1979; A. Birnboim, *From My Father's House*, 14, 17; Kleczyński, "Ekonomiczne stosunki Galicyi," 62.

57. B. Kerblay, "Chayanov and the Theory of Peasantry as a Specific Type of Economy," 150-1.
58. Kleczyński, "Ekonomiczne stosunki Galicyi," 35-57.
59. Evidence for this is scattered throughout the literature, including the memoirs and interviews of former inhabitants of the region. Note, especially, A. von Gorski, "Das Marktwesen," 855, where he speaks of the peddler moving about the countryside buying and selling goods. Adolf Lipp, *Verkehrs- und Handelsverhältnisse Galiziens*, 297, noted that the rural population raised a large number of pigs because they were easy to sell to a "passing trader." F. Bujak, *Galicya*, 1: 366-7, deals with the unsatisfactory marketing conditions for fruit, focusing on the "fruit handler" (*sadownik*) who "buys up the fruit very early, often in May"; W. Pruski, *Hodowla zwierząt gospodarskich w Galicji w latach 1772-1918*, 2: 94, 424 *passim*, mentions trade in butter and sheepskins. IMZCh, 307, 553, *passim*, has a *sadownik* from Skorodyntsi coming to Bilobozhnytsia to sell fruit and frequently refers to Jewish traders. Havrysh, *Moia Kanada i ia*, 64, described the local village tavern keeper, a Jew, Abramko, asking his mother to permit his elder brother to deliver some "goods like eggs, butter, etc. mostly bought in our village." Many newspaper items dealt with this issue. P. Chorney reported buying three chickens and a rooster from his neighbour (*Hospodar i promyshlennyk*, no. 12, 1880); Narodna Torhivlia, the trade co-operative founded by Ukrainians in Eastern Galicia, proposed to replace itinerant Jewish traders with its own itinerant agents (*Hospodar i promyshlennyk*, no. 1, 1885); there was a report on Jewish traders buying butter in the countryside (*Hospodar i promyshlennyk*, no. 1, 1886); people were reported to be trading their potatoes for whiskey at a distillery (*Batkivshchyna*, 4 July 1884); Jewish agents were buying eggs from village women for a pittance (*Batkivshchyna*, 3 Feb. 1889); workers were paid in kind in a lumber camp at Perehinske (*Batkivshchyna*, 15 Mar. 1889); people raised calves for Jewish cattle traders and split the profit when the calves were sold (*Batkivshchyna*, 21 Dec. 1889); one memoirist from Letiache (Zalishchyky county) mused about the Hutsul traders who came to his village almost daily with their wooden handicraft products and traded them only for grain (IMZCh, 842). See also Vynnytsky, *Terebovelska zemlia*, 71.
60. For example, see F.A. Shcherbina, *Krestianskie biudzhety*; F. Bujak, "Budżet chłopa," 171-99.
61. Hempel, "Ekonomiczne stosunki Galicyi," 127, 129, 133-7. In 1893 an estate of 320 ha in Zalishchyky county remunerated its eighteen male farm servants with a total of 704 g in cash and the equivalent of 1,335 g in kind, exclusive of customary gifts (*Oesterreichische Statistik*, XLIV, no. 1, 68; K.R. von Inama-Sternegg, "Die landwirtschaftlichen Arbeiter und deren Löhne," 389).
62. Hempel, "Ekonomiczne stosunki Galicyi," 127, 144-50, 154ff.; Kleczyński, "Ekonomiczne stosunki Galicyi," esp. 42-3.
63. Pilat, "Die Auswanderung," 79; Kleczyński, ibid., 40ff.
64. Pilat, "Die Auswanderung," 79-80; Inama-Sternegg, "Die landwirtschaftlichen Arbeiter," 407-8.

65. Hempel, "Ekonomiczne stosunki Galicyi," 150-3; *Oesterreichische Statistik*, XLIV, 1: 52; Pilat, "Die Auswanderung," 79-80; Inama-Sternegg, "Die landwirtschaftlichen Arbeiter," 407-8. In 1893 an estate of 320 ha in Zalishchyky county paid a total of 1,043 g in cash as well as produce to the value of 1,248 g to day labourers (*Oesterreichische Statistik*, XLIV, 1: 68).
66. Pilat, "Die Auswanderung," 80. On the concept of the unrecorded economy see J. McCallum, "15% of GNP goes underground," 67.
67. Pilat, "Die Auswanderung," 80; L.W. Biegeleisen, *Rozwój gospodarczy nowoczęsnej wsi Polskiej*, 1: 295.
68. A total of 944 questionnaires, each containing sixty questions pertaining to peasant agriculture, were sent out. Some were distributed by county executive committees, others went directly to correspondents of the Galician Agricultural Association, the three Galician Chambers of Commerce, and other "notables." Of these, 500 were returned, collated, and analyzed (T. Pilat, introduction to J. Kleczyński, "Ekonomiczne stosunki Galicyi: stosunki włościańskie w Galicyi," 1-4).
69. Ibid., table XV.
70. Ibid., 1, 4, table XV, 80. Some data for counties other than Chortkiv: both Husiatyn and Terebovlia reported consumption of wheat (2.5 bushels worth 22 g and 3.5 bushels worth 32 g respectively) and buckwheat (3 bushels worth 11 g and 4 bushels worth 16 g). Zalishchyky also reported the use of buckwheat (2 bushels worth 8 g). The "average" peasant family in Husiatyn used one bushel of buckwheat worth 7 g. Maize was used in all homes except those in Terebovlia. The use of legumes was reported only in Husiatyn (1.5 bushels worth 10 g) and Borshchiv (0.5 bushel worth 4 g). No data were reported from Borshchiv or Zalishchyky for cabbage, beets, milk, fat or meat. For Zalishchyky there were no data for salt. For Borshchiv it was stated that meat was eaten on holy days and at family festivities, but that the richer peasants would eat meat twice a week (ibid., 77). Meat consumption in Husiatyn was 30.37 kg worth 21 g per family, and in Terebovlia county 12.15 kg worth 6 g. Milk consumption in those two counties was somewhat lower than in Chortkiv, while fat consumption was much higher in Husiatyn (21.5 kg worth 24 g).
71. Kleczyński, "Ekonomiczne stosunki Galicyi," 72.
72. Ibid., 79.
73. Ibid., 79.
74. Ibid., 69.
75. Ibid., 66.
76. Ibid., 78, 80.
77. Ibid., 35.
78. Ibid., 33-4, 60.
79. Ibid., table XIV. See also S. Hryniuk, "Peasant Agriculture in East Galicia in the Late Nineteenth Century," footnote 22, 233.
80. Kleczyński, "Ekonomiczne stosunki Galicyi," 66-9, 72.
81. *Batkivshchyna*, 11 June 1886.
82. *Hospodar i promyshlennyk*, no. 1, 1885.
83. *Batkivshchyna*, 3 Aug. 1886. Salt was often smuggled in from Russia (ibid., 18 Apr. 1889).

84. *Batkivshchyna*, 29 Mar. 1889.
85. Ibid., 10 May 1889, 11 June 1886.
86. IMZCh, 245.
87. T. Pilat, "Grunta podlegające wspólnemu używaniu w Galicyi," 1-4 , table XV, 77, 80.
88. Interviews with former inhabitants; IMZCh, 467, 500, 841, *passim*. See also Kravets, *Simenyi pobut*; Vovk, *Studii z ukrainskoi*; O. Kolberg, "Ruś czerwona"; P. Humeniuk, *Hardships and Progress of Ukrainian Pioneers: Memoirs from Stuartburn Colony and other Points*, 38, 48, 49, *passim*; J. Cooper, "Ukrainian Cookery." See also N. Cybulski, *Próba badań nad żywieniem się ludu wiejskiego w Galicyi*. Rice was not indigenous to the region, so it was a purchased product. For an example of a recipe using rice see *Hospodar i promyshlennyk*, no. 2, 1885.
89. For the nutritive value of potatoes see R. Salamon, *The History and Social Influence of the Potato*, esp. 121-5. S. Szczepanowski (*Nędza Galicyi*, 48) and Bujak (*Galicya*, 1: 302) were among those who disparaged the potato. Its widespread use was certainly regarded by contemporary urban intellectuals as an indication of poverty.
90. Vovk, *Studii z ukrainskoi*, 94-5; "Clay Buildings," *Hospodar*, Feb. 1900.
91. Vovk, *Studii z ukrainskoi*, 95.
92. *Hospodar*, Feb. 1900.
93. IMZCh, 643.
94. *Batkivshchyna*, 22 July 1887.
95. E. von Habdank-Dunikowski in *Oesterreichisch-ungarische Monarchie*, 19: 156.
96. S. Hryniuk, "A Peasant Society in Transition," 94-101. The Polish administration of Galicia wished to show the highest possible number of Poles. Decennial censuses counted people by religion and by "language of usage." "Be careful not to be baptized Roman Catholic," *Batkivshchyna* warned its largely Greek Catholic readership on 29 Aug. 1890, for Roman Catholicism was identified by the authorities with Polishness. There was pressure, in Terebovlia county, on Greek Catholic Ukrainians to change rites (Vynnytsky, *Terebovelska zemlia*, 74, 270, 407). Data on language of usage were even more open to abuse by the predominantly Polish census takers. Under Austrian regulations, Jews were not allowed to list Yiddish as their language. In 1880 about one-third of Southern Podillia's 52,000 Jews listed themselves as German-speaking, about two-fifths as Ukrainian-speaking, and the remainder as Polish-speaking. By 1900 only slightly under 2,000 of the region's 52,600 Jews gave German as their language of usage, perhaps 3,000-4,000 gave Ukrainian, while the remainder, either voluntarily or under pressure, were registered as Polish-speaking, "despite the fact that village and small town Jews doubtless spoke better Ukrainian than Polish." In many instances, all Roman Catholics were automatically registered as Polish-speaking, even if the only Polish they used was very imperfect. The more zealous census-takers also listed all members of religiously mixed families as Polish. In Skorodyntsi (Chortkiv county), Ukrainians who spoke broken Polish only to "Mr. Gendarme" were registered as Polish-speaking (IMZCh, 11, 191, 355, 358, 399, 652, 681). See also E. Brix, *Die Umgangssprachen in Altösterreich zwischen Agitation und Assimilation*, esp. 367. For the religious affiliations of the population of Southern Podillia, as shown in the

official census data, see Appendix III.

97. *Oesterreichische Statistik*, I, no. 3.
98. Ibid., I, no. 3.
99. Ibid., and XXXII, no. 2.
100. See Chapter III for the coming of the railway to Chortkiv and Husiatyn.
101. On 31 Dec. 1890, of those born in each of the five counties and still living in Austria, the following percentages were no longer residing in the county of their birth: Borshchiv, 7.0; Chortkiv, 10.8; Husiatyn, 8.7; Terebovlia, 9.0; Zalishchyky, 11.1. The Galician average was 10.3; *Oesterreichische Statistik*, XXXII, no. 2.
102. Ibid.
103. G.E. Rothenberg, *The Army of Francis Joseph*, esp. 61, 128. An Austrian traveller through Southern Podillia encountered a talkative old man who had served eighteen years in the army and "who was not ignorant of the wider world" *Oesterreichisch-ungarische Monarchie*, 19: 55). "My father was in the army for three years... this gave him a great experience for life, he knew cities" (interview with J. Storoschuk, 20 June 1979). See also *Svoboda*, 1 Aug. 1898.
104. Hempel, "Ekonomiczne stosunki Galicyi," 175.
105. For details of river-borne traffic on the Dnister in 1882 see *Oesterreichisches statistisches Handbuch*, 1883, 176. Wood and wood products formed by far the largest percentage of goods transported on the Dnister; small quantities of grain and eggs accounted for most of the remainder.
106. IMZCh, 201; interview with Mr. W. Michalchyshyn, 30 Dec. 1983.
107. IMZCh, 244.
108. Habdank, *Oesterreichisch-ungarische Monarchie*, 19: 62. See also the recollections of the Ulashkivtsi fair by the Ukrainian author Bohdan Lepky (b. 1872) (IMZCh, 242-4).
109. Lepky wrote that from Easter onward his mother prepared shopping lists which she then discussed with his father before the whole family went to the fair. Ulashkivtsi was about 30-35 km by road from the Lepky home in Krehulets (IMZCh, 243).

Chapter III

Transportation and Communications

"The modernization of agriculture" in East Central Europe "was closely related to the rapidly growing export of agricultural products to industrial European markets."[1] By the early 1870s, railways had linked many areas of Galicia to Vienna, Bohemia, and Austrian Silesia (the most industrialized areas of Austria), as well as to Germany and other West European countries. Thus, they replaced roads, and to some extent waterways, as the principal carriers of goods and people over long distances. However, railways only reached Southern Podillia, one of the most isolated areas of the Habsburg territories, in the 1880s and 1890s. Nevertheless it was affected by early railway construction, first because the region's main highways became, in effect, access roads to the nearest railheads and then because railways reached into the region itself.[2] Developments in crop production and livestock breeding would not have been feasible without railways and the improved transportation and marketing opportunities these provided. Railways in Eastern Galicia, as elsewhere in Central Europe, were thus "an important starting point for the transformation of traditional economy."[3] Better communications also gave impetus to other developments.

The Road Network

In 1880, roads were still the natural mode of transportation for people and commerce in Southern Podillia. The closest railheads were at Ternopil, about thirty kilometres north of Terebovlia, and at Chernivtsi, some forty kilometres south of Zalishchyky. River-borne traffic on the Dnister consisted primarily of timber and lumber transported from other regions of Galicia to the Black Sea, and had little economic significance for Southern Podillia.[4] There were several types of roads in Southern Podillia, as in other parts of Austria. The best roads were the "imperial highways" (*Ärarialstrassen*), which had been built, and some of which were still maintained, by the state. In 1868 responsibility for the upkeep of certain Galician highways and roads previously maintained by the imperial authorities, including some in Southern Podillia, was transferred to the Land Executive.[5] Imperial highways were "macadamized," i.e., they had a base of crushed stone, with a gravel surface, and had to be between 6.3 and 9.5 metres wide, with actual width dependent on the maximum width of local wagons and the volume of traffic.[6]

The second category of road was Crownland roads (*Landstrassen*). Ukrainians sometimes described these as "the Polish roads," because they were badly neglected by the Polish-dominated Land authorities.[7] These roads were also supposed to be macadamized. The county and commune roads were under the general supervision of the Land Executive, which might give construction subsidies that did not exceed 50 per cent of the actual construction costs. County or commune authorities determined the type of construction base, width, gradient, and other details of roads under their jurisdiction. In practice, county roads ranged from macadamized roads to simple tracks; commune roads often scarcely deserved the name of road at all. Besides these four main categories of roads, there were also poorly maintained lesser commune or field roads not eligible for Land subsidies that merely connected outlying parts of a commune with the main village, as well as roads on the tabular estates, for which the estates were responsible.[8] These field and estate roads do not appear to have been included in any of the official statistics on road networks.

Southern Podillia was transected by an imperial highway, the "Podillian Highway." First built in the late eighteenth century,[9] it ran northward from Chernivtsi in Bukovyna, across a bridge over the Dnister at Zalishchyky, through Tovste, Chortkiv, Kopychyntsi, and Terebovlia, on to Ternopil, Zolochiv, and Lviv. It thus traversed four of the five counties of Southern Podillia and, prior to the coming of the railway, it was the region's main transportation artery and its chief link to the outside world. Another imperial highway, the "Pokutian Highway," branched off the Podillian Highway a few kilometres south of Tovste, ran to Ustechko and, after a ferry crossing of the Dnister, on to Horodenka and Kolomyia. Other imperial roads now under the jurisdiction of the Land Executive connected Chortkiv with Buchach to the west (and on to Stanyslaviv); Tovste with Buchach; Husiatyn with Kopychyntsi; and Buchach through the northwestern parts of Terebovlia county and the market town of Strusiv with the Podillian Highway.[10] Just to the east of Buchach the Chortkiv-Buchach road had a very steep 1:8 gradient that made it unsuitable for military wagon-trains.[11]

Major work was undertaken on the Podillian and Pokutian Highways in 1887-8 because of their military significance. Grading work was done and thousands of cubic metres of gravel were spread on them.[12] However, the necessary funds, 40,000 g, were not provided by the state to rebuild two sections of the Podillian Highway in Terebovlia county and one in neighbouring Ternopil county, where an 1886 military reconnaissance had found gradients of 1:12 or 1:13, which were "too steep."[13]

The Austrian Ministry of Commerce had road masters and inspectors on its staff to oversee the building and maintenance of imperial highways. State road keepers were responsible for the maintenance of these highways, and were usually distributed throughout the state road network at a rate of one per 4.14

MAP 2. COMMUNICATIONS IN SOUTHERN PODILLIA, 1875

kilometres of imperial highway. Zalishchyky and Ternopil had branch offices for state and Land road works and maintenance. The costs of maintenance of an imperial highway were borne by the state, except that snow clearance in a town or village was the responsibility of the commune.[14] In general, imperial highways were quite well maintained, and those in Galicia compared more than favourably with those in tsarist Ukraine.[15]

There is relatively little systematic information about the Galician Land roads, and very little data on county and commune roads.[16] By the 1870s a Land road connected some of the towns and villages of southern Borshchiv county, from Kryvche through Hermakivka, Melnytsia, Zvyniachka, and Babyntsi to the small market of Okopy in the southeastern corner of the region, from which it was possible to cross both the Dnister and the Zbruch by ferry. Kryvche, however, was connected only by a track to another Land road at Korolivka, about seven kilometres away, which ran from Zalishchyky through Kasperivtsi, Korolivka, and Borshchiv to Skala, and from there through Davydkivtsi to the Podillian Highway at Vyhnanka near Chortkiv. There were a few kilometres of "maintained" county roads from Husiatyn to Sukhodol and toward Kryvenke. Otherwise, there were only "unmaintained" roads, tracks, and paths.[17]

Most of the market towns[18] of Southern Podillia were situated on imperial or Land roads. Six of them—Zalishchyky, Tovste, Chortkiv, Kopychyntsi, Sukhostav, and Terebovlia—were on the Podillian Highway and one—Ustechko—on the Pokutian Highway. They, and the eleven others on the Land roads, were located at river crossings and at other road intersections. There was a bridge across the Zbruch at Husiatyn, which, with Skala and Okopy, were locations at which goods were legally exchanged between Austria and Russia. Of the market towns that were not on a main road, Khorostkiv was an ancient townsite that for centuries had been the central point of the very extensive landholdings of the Strus family. Although the estates later changed hands, their owner maintained a grand residence and large stables of fine horses in Khorostkiv.[19] Probizhna, on the headwaters of the Nichlava River, had three large estates nearby and was a meeting point for four secondary roads.[20] Budzaniv and Ianiv, both located at crossing points over the Seret, also had large estates nearby.[21] Ulashkivtsi, a market town located well away from any real road and the site of the famous annual fair, was likewise situated at a crossing point over the Seret. Ozeriany had the large landholdings of the Sapieha family in its general vicinity.[22] It clearly declined in importance after Bilche, the centre of the Sapieha estates in Southern Podillia, was granted market status in the 1880s. Horodok, on the northern bank of the Dnister where the Seret flowed into it, had once been a resting place for *chumak* caravans proceeding from the Black Sea to Halych.[23]

There were thus historical/geographical reasons for the existence of the market towns of Southern Podillia, even those where access by road was extremely difficult. Clearly the poor condition of many roads and tracks, with the exception of the imperial highways, did not prevent the movement of goods and people: large quantities of grain were regularly transported; traders moved around the villages buying animals, eggs, and grain, and selling their wares; "up to 100,000 people came to stock up for the whole year at the Ulashkivtsi fair;" and thousands from Southern Podillia went on pilgrimages to Zarvanytsia, in neighbouring Pidhaitsi county, and also to Pochaiv in the Russian Empire.[24]

Tolls were collected on most roads. Normally collection was undertaken by private entrepreneurs who contracted to collect the tolls for whichever level of government had the right to levy them. In the 1870s the tolls on imperial roads were 8 kr for a two-horse vehicle, 4 kr for a one-horse vehicle, 2 kr for an unhitched horse, and 1 kr each for cattle.[25] The Austrian parliament reduced these rates in 1890. The new rates, per eight kilometres, were 2 kr per animal hitched to a wagon, 1 kr per unhitched large farm animal, and 1/2 kr for a small farm animal. Tolls on bridges on imperial roads were abolished at this time.[26] There were some general complaints that tolls were too high, especially as it was claimed that there were few improvements, and that tollkeepers cheated users.[27] Some new tolls were authorized during the late eighties and early nineties, usually in conjunction with road building by county authorities. Thus the Borshchiv county council was given the right to collect tolls on the road from Ivankiv to Hermakivka, and on the longer route from Ozeriany to Ustia Iepyskopske; the Chortkiv county council collected on a stretch of road between Chortkiv and Vyhnanka; the Terebovlia county council collected for the road from Terebovlia to Budzaniv; and Zalishchyky county council collected for a stretch of county road near Ustechko.[28]

New roads were built in the 1880s and especially in the 1890s in the Southern Podillia counties, but statistical data are scanty.[29] The Land Executive provided subsidies in 1890 of 4,000 g to the Skalat county council and 3,000 g to Husiatyn toward the building of a road from Hrymaliv (Skalat county) to Khorostkiv (Husiatyn county) and then on to the Podillian Highway. The following year the Chortkiv county council received a subsidy of 3000 g toward the building of a county road from Iaholnytsia to Ulashkivtsi.[30] Generally, however, county and commune road building and maintenance were paid out of county and commune funds, including proceeds from tolls. Probably more onerous for the villagers than tolls were the contributions in kind (*prestation, sharvarok*) which they were required to make toward road construction and upkeep. Both work and materials could be required of them in amounts determined by the county or commune council. Early in this period compulsory road work could amount to as much as six days per annum for each landowner, but this was lowered in 1884 and reduced to two days per year in 1896. Because road work was assigned to all landowners equally, regardless of the size of their holdings, many small landowners harbored a sense of injustice.[31] There were also complaints that the roads, which the peasants were building and maintaining, were of far more benefit to the owners of large estates than to the peasants themselves, and that the estate owners, who were to supply materials as part of their obligations, were often failing to do so.[32]

During the last twenty years of the century, some progress was made in improving the Southern Podillian road network. By 1900 more of the market towns were linked to one another and to railway stations. A new iron road bridge across the Dnister at Zalishchyky was completed in 1887 and rebuilding was begun in 1892 on the bridge across the Zbruch at Husiatyn;[33] both were funded by the state government. Borshchiv and Chortkiv county authorities co-operated in building the county road from Ustia Iepyskopske through Bilche, Ozeriany, and Kolyndiany to Chortkiv.[34] The counties of Terebovlia and Zalishchyky, but not yet the other three, had paid road inspectors by 1895.[35] The approaches to railway stations, particularly in busy places, were gradually being improved.[36] Repairs to the Land-administered imperial road between Husiatyn and Kopychyntsi, which was of military importance, were impeded by the very heavy traffic, especially on market days, near the market place in Husiatyn.[37]

Mud was a great hazard on county and commune roads, particularly after spring and fall rains, and the roads were very dusty in summer.[38] Even roads under the direct administration of the Land were not necessarily in any better condition. On the road between Kopychyntsi and Husiatyn in the late eighties there were stretches that were "very neglected," with many potholes, long inclines with too few resting places, one bridge in a bad state of repair, and insufficient supplies of gravel to maintain the road surface. However, improvements continued to be made.[39] Villagers sometimes resented the building of a county or commune road because it would be of benefit only to estate owners; in such circumstances it was unlikely to be well-constructed.[40] However, certain communes, for example Kobylovoloky (Terebovlia county) and Khorostkiv and Kryvenke (both in Husiatyn county), were singled out for their exemplary roads.[41] Nevertheless, a Canadian official who visited Podillia and other parts of Galicia in the late 1890s reported that "except in respect of the great military highways, the roads are practically impassable during the fall and spring months."[42]

Steep gradients were another local hazard. Even as late as 1913 a writer cautioned that "in respect of very steep and sometimes extreme inclines, the highways and roads of Podillia are the worst."[43] The deep valleys and the general condition of the roads were not the only problems. Highway bandits were another. A salt merchant was murdered while making his way between Kopychyntsi and Khorostkiv in 1886.[44] There were complaints about robbers on the roads into the town of Terebovlia.[45] According to local lore there were some especially fearful places, such as a section of road near the village of Skoviatyn (Borshchiv county) called "the place of the gypsies" (*Tsyhanske*), which was said

Villagers from Hermakivka, Borshchiv county, photographed at the Ternopil Exhibition, 1892

Man and woman from Bile, Chortkiv county, photographed at the Ternopil Exhibition, 1892

to be a hiding place for bandits. Going to the Ulashkivtsi fair at night by wagon was dangerous because bandits were likely to be lurking in the Ozeriany forests.[46]

Despite these difficulties, people, goods, and animals continued to move around in large numbers. "Hundreds of loaded wagons of wheat" were reported at the Husiatyn railway station, which had opened in early 1885.[47] Tens of thousands of people, with thousands of wagons and animals, still attended the *iarmarok* at Ulashkivtsi. "People of quality," as well as traders and villagers, moved around. Prince Sapieha might arrive at an event despite the muddy state of the road; in 1888 the newly appointed Greek Catholic bishop of Stanyslaviv on a pastoral visit, spent a month on a circuitous itinerary, mainly through Chortkiv and Borshchiv counties, travelling mostly over commune roads; Crown Prince Rudolph's entourage rode extensively through Terebovlia, Zalishchyky, Borshchiv, and Buchach counties.[48]

At the other end of the social spectrum, peasants were exhorted by well-meaning intelligentsia in Lviv not to go to market too often.[49] However, they travelled for other purposes too, and sometimes to places much further afield. For example, 3,000 people, "mostly villagers," came from Eastern Galicia to an assembly (*viche*) in Lviv in 1888; two years earlier, people travelled from Melnytsia, Hermakivka, and Horoshova to a *viche* in Stanyslaviv.[50] In the 1890s the opening of reading clubs would regularly attract villagers from many communes, and itinerant teachers and agronomists also used local roads for their journeys. There were meetings of priests, teachers, and cantors. One cantors' meeting, in Melnytsia in 1886, attracted people from Ivanie Puste, Kudryntsi, and Panivtsi.[51] Two thousand people, including villagers from eight towns and villages up to twelve kilometres away, attended an anniversary ceremony in Kopychyntsi in 1898.[52] By the late nineties, meetings of several hundred people, often including many villagers, became quite common.[53]

However inadequate the roads, by 1900 there were more of them, and many that were more than mere tracks. They were much used, and brought the villages into closer contact with each other and with distant towns. Despite real improvements it is also true that the region's "inconvenient"[54] roads hampered the development of commerce in Southern Podillia. This problem was not overcome until railways had thoroughly penetrated the region and roads took on more of the character of feeders for the railways.

The Development of Railways in Southern Podillia

The first railway line into Galicia was constructed in the west in 1847. However, it was not until the second half of the 1850s that railway construction on any large scale was undertaken in the Land. The main line from Cracow to Lviv, begun in 1856, was completed in 1861. It belonged to the privately owned Galician Carl-Ludwig Railway Company, which had a stormy relationship with the Land authorities. Extensions of this railway included a line from Lviv through Ternopil to Pidvolochysk on the Austrian-Russian border in 1870-71, where a large grain market was centred and where a connection was established with the Russian line running to Odessa.[55] Other railways were built in the 1860s and 1870s, including one that opened up some regions of southeastern Galicia. This railway, 266 kilometres in length, ran from Lviv through Stanyslaviv and Kolomyia to Chernivtsi in Bukovyna; it was owned by the Lemberg-Czernowitz-Jassy Railway Company (controlled by a British syndicate). The line between Lviv and Chernivtsi was built in only sixteen months (opened 1866), and was later extended to the Romanian frontier (1869) and Jassy in Romania (1872).[56]

The Austrian state assisted railway construction in Galicia by various means, such as guarantees of gross income per kilometre, total net income, or net income per share capital.[57] Increased financial pressure on the state and on private entrepreneurs resulting from the 1873 crash on the Vienna stock exchange abruptly halted new investment in railway construction in Galicia. Many of the Galician railway companies had financial difficulties. Even before the crash, the Austrian Ministry of Commerce had temporarily sequestered the Lviv-Chernivtsi railway because of complaints about the disruption and uncertainty of traffic. It was released to its owners, but was finally brought under state administration in 1889, as were some other railways in Galicia.[58] In part, these difficulties stemmed from low volumes of traffic. Such problems, however, appeared not to affect greatly the Carl-Ludwig Railway, Galicia's largest and most significant. All trans-Galician traffic had to make use of its main line. The Carl-Ludwig Railway exploited this monopoly position and, as a Viennese newspaper reported, its "tariffs and the pressure which it puts on Galician users have earned it the hatred of Galicians."[59]

The railway construction of the late sixties and early seventies brought railways into the vicinity of Southern Podillia—at Ternopil, c. 30 kilometres north of Terebovlia, and at Chernivtsi, c. 40 kilometres south of Zalishchyky. The need to expand railways in Galicia was recognized by the early 1880s, and one of the projects considered was the building of a railway from Ternopil to Husiatyn. The Carl-Ludwig Railway was certain to bid for the concession. Even if it were not the successful bidder, the new line would connect at Ternopil to the main line under the control of that company. Breaking the monopoly of the Carl-Ludwig Railway was very important to political and business circles in Galicia. An alternate project, to build a Galician "Transversal" railway from Husiatyn in the east to Biała and Czechowice in West Galicia, there to connect with other Austrian railways, was therefore favoured by the Land Executive and the Lviv chamber of commerce. The military authorities also preferred this option, and this Transversal Railway project was approved by the Austrian Reichsrat in 1882.[60]

Portions of the Transversal Railway in fact consisted of extant stretches of line not owned by the Carl-Ludwig Railway, such as the line between Stryi and Stanyslaviv. In Eastern Galicia the railway had to be newly constructed from Stanyslaviv through Buchach and Chortkiv to Husiatyn, a distance of 144 kilometres. Work on the Transversal Railway was begun in October 1882 and completed, with the extension of the line to Husiatyn, only a few weeks behind schedule on 31 December 1884. The new main line consisted of 405 kilometres of new construction. The total cost, including stations, bridges, and viaducts, was 24,099,214 g, of which 1,100,000 g was provided by the Galician Land and the rest by the Austrian government.[61]

The new railway entered Southern Podillia to the west of Dzhuryn (Chortkiv county) and ran eastwards across the high plateau to Kalynivshchyna and then across a 30-metre-high viaduct over a gorge into Chortkiv. From there it climbed out of the Seret valley, crossed another viaduct to reach the high plateau near Hadynkivtsi, and went across several bridges to Kopychyntsi, then eastward, traversing a 600-metre-wide swamp, to Vasylkivtsi and finally to Husiatyn.[62]

The completion of the Transversal Railway broke the monopoly which the Carl-Ludwig Railway had long enjoyed in Galicia and the resulting competition brought about a long-overdue reduction of transportation rates for Eastern Galician agriculture and other produce.[63] It also brought the railway appreciably nearer to almost every corner of Southern Podillia.[64] Train travel was not particularly fast. In 1886 the twice-daily mixed passenger and goods trains from Husiatyn to Chortkiv took almost two hours to cover the distance of 38 km, and a total of six hours to travel the 144 km from Husiatyn to Stanyslaviv.[65] However, it was much faster than travel between such points had ever been before, and the railway could transport the region's agricultural produce more quickly and in greater volume than earlier transportation modes had permitted.

Southern Podillia was thus linked to the Galician and Austrian railway networks, with access to the large markets of Vienna, Prague, Lviv, and Germany. The extension of the railway fitted well into what has been described as "a political and strategic task of primary significance" of the Austro-Hungarian Monarchy as of other Empires, of building "systems of modern transport which would help unify these empires."[66] It also allowed Galician Ukrainian agriculturalists to send their produce into major European markets and thereby provided an incentive for them to raise production, especially of produce other than grain.[67] Of course it also opened the region to imports of manufactured goods, such as textiles and rope, which gradually displaced some domestic industries. Indeed, one newspaper charged that Galician railways had been built "to satisfy the needs of foreigners, to serve foreigners, and to give them greater profits."[68]

In 1892 the Carl-Ludwig Railway was absorbed into the Austrian State Railway network.[69] Although some other railway lines were still technically in

MAP 3. COMMUNICATIONS IN SOUTHERN PODILLIA, 1900

private hands, they were all administered by the state, and from 1892 onward one unified railway system operated in Galicia. Under the overall control (until 1896) of the General Directorate of the Austrian State Railways in Vienna, three railway directorates—at Cracow, Lviv, and Stanyslaviv—were responsible for the construction, maintenance, and operation of railways in Galicia. The railway directorate in Stanyslaviv had responsibility for the railways in southeast Galicia, including Southern Podillia, and Bukovyna, although in the late 1890s some construction of railways in Southern Podillia was in fact supervised out of Ternopil and Lviv. General policy on railways in Austria was considered by the State Railway Council. Government control over railways was exercised by the Ministry of Commerce until 1896, when an independent Ministry of Railways was established. It took over the functions of the General Railways Directorate; regional directorates reported to the ministry.

In the 1890s the Galician Sejm became more interested in railway development; a Land Railway Council was set up, and the Land Executive founded a railway bureau within its administrative organization.[70] To facilitate the economic development of areas bypassed by the main railway lines and their branches, Austrian legislation of 1880 made a distinction between main lines and "local railways," with different legal and tax arrangements. This legislation was not much utilized in the 1880s. In the early 1890s, however, the Sejm showed much interest in fostering and financing the construction of local railways. Among the projects initiated and completed in the 1890s were the various lines of the East Galician Local Railway.[71] Of these railway lines authorized in 1893-5, some were of primary significance for Southern Podillia. The first line constructed in the region ran from Ternopil to Terebovlia and on to Kopychyntsi, where it intersected with the Transversal line. Authorization for this line was given in 1895 and its seventy-three kilometre stretch was completed and opened for traffic in November 1896. Kopychyntsi station was also enlarged. Work was then begun on a 51 km line from a point on the Transversal railway west of Chortkiv, south through Iaholnytsia and Tovste to Zalishchyky; on a 43 km line from just east of Chortkiv through Ozeriany and Teresyn to Skala, with a 6.5 km spur from Teresyn to Borshchiv; and a little later on a 23.5 km stretch from Borshchiv south to Ivanie Puste. With the exception of the Borshchiv-Ivanie Puste line, these lines were opened for traffic in November 1898 (the Borshchiv-Ivanie Puste line was opened a month later). Zalishchyky's first rail connection was made in June 1898, when the railway reached it from the south (as the northern terminus of the Bukovynian local railway network). In 1899 a third line, the Pokutian section of the East Galician local railway network, was completed from Kolomyia through Horodenka to Zalishchyky. The line from Borky Velyki, east of Ternopil, to Skalat and Hrymaliv, completed in 1898, was also a branch of the East Galician network. Hrymaliv station, though in Skalat county, was the nearest railhead for a number of communes in eastern Terebovlia county and northern Husiatyn county.[72]

Passenger traffic was encouraged by excursion-rate fares for special events. Such cheap fares might be arranged through an organization, as, for example, when Prosvita invited "all" to come to Lviv on the occasion of Crown Prince Rudolph's visit in 1887, or through prominent individuals, as when people visiting Lviv in 1888 could notify a Sejm deputy to get discounted fares. New passenger tariffs in 1890 made third-class rail travel "very cheap."[73] Railways, even those still under private ownership, were made to serve as instruments of state policy through the intervention of the Austrian Railway Council. After the disastrous harvest of 1889, the railways reduced their freight rates on animal feed in Galicia and Bukovyna from January to June 1890, and their ability to bring in foodstuffs alleviated any threat of famine.[74] In 1894, in what was plainly an effort to boost animal husbandry, the railway lowered freight rates on fodder, fodder seed, and fertilizer; for fodder the new rate was 0.1 kr per 100 kg per km, for fodder seed and fertilizer it was 0.13 kr per 100 kg per km. To stimulate railway use on the still incomplete lines and help Southern Podillian agriculture, special low rates were announced in 1898 for the transportation of grain and potatoes out of Borshchiv and Zalishchyky counties.[75]

Expropriation of land for railway construction worried many villagers. In 1882 Prosvita published a booklet entitled "Land Expropriation for Railways," which gave basic advice. But questions continued; for example, an inquirer from Iaholnytsia was informed in 1897 that he should get the value of the land plus costs for the loss of the land's use. There were other hazards, too. Engine drivers were instructed in 1886 not to let sparks fly from locomotive chimneys when they passed houses.[76]

Railway construction brought some opportunities for tendering supplies and for work, which Ukrainians were urged to take. Although the major contractors were from outside the region, there was need for local supplies of rocks, gravel, sand, bricks, limestone, and other materials. The actual construction of railway lines probably brought a temporary boost to the local economies. However, the prospects of work for Southern Podillian villagers on railway construction in the 1880s and 1890s appear to have been meagre. In April 1898 the Austrian Minister of Railways declared that only Galicians were allowed to work on railway building. *Svoboda* commented that "perhaps fewer Italians will appear."[77]

More generally, people complained that railway employment was given to Poles rather than Ukrainians. Local people were willing to work on the railways but were not accepted. When the Stanyslaviv-Husiatyn line was being extensively improved in 1893, "many Mazurs came to work on it," but some Ukrainians were doubtless employed on construction and maintenance work.[78] Few, however, worked in clerical, technical, managerial or professional capacities.[79] Polish was replacing German as the official language of the railways in Galicia. Although railway personnel in Eastern Galicia were supposed to be able to give service in Ukrainian, it took time and effort to get

Ukrainian signs on railway stations. Official railway regulations were required to be translated into Ukrainian, but the Polish Galician authorities delayed. Ukrainians even had difficulty obtaining positions as watch guards because of the absence of translations of the regulations. In this way "the strict instructions of the ministry to the Railway Directorate in Stanyslaviv were disregarded for twelve years."[80]

Despite the language problem and discriminatory hiring practices, the railways brought great changes to Southern Podillia. The most obvious was in the number of people and volume of freight they carried. This can clearly be seen from data for successive years for the newly opened 73 km line from Kopychyntsi through Terebovlia to the big junction at Ternopil:

Table 5
Traffic on the Kopychyntsi-Ternopil Railway Line, 1897 and 1898

	No. of passengers	Income in gulden from passengers	Volume of freight (tons)	Income in gulden from freight
May 1897	4,943	2,079	3,908	6,095
May 1898	13,381	7,387	7,304	20,010
Jan-May 1897	17,397	n/a	13,834	n/a
Jan-May 1898	47,769	n/a	25,898	n/a

Source: *Verordnungsblatt für Eisenbahnen und Schiffahrt*, 80/1897 and 77/1898

The first full year of operation for the Kopychyntsi-Ternopil line was 1897. It is clear that although this line connected two towns that were already on railways, it met a great local need. The 87 per cent increase in the volume of freight carried on this line between 1897 and 1898 indicates that filling the gap in the previous transportation network had an economic impact on the region. As there appear to have been no general freight tariff increases, it may be presumed that some goods were being carried over greater distances. The great increase in passenger traffic is even more striking; people were obviously very willing to utilize the more rapid means of travel.[81]

Not everyone benefited from the coming of the railways. Crop and animal data indicate that until the end of the century domestic industries in Borshchiv and Zalishchyky counties were less affected than those in the other three Southern Podillian counties. The railway lines had a particular and obvious effect on the carters and wagoners. Demand for their services declined as the distances to the nearest railhead were reduced,[82] and this decline was, of course, particularly noticeable in places near the railways. Nevertheless, the railways' overall effect was very beneficial to the economy of the region. Animals could be transported without losing condition; grain and other produce could be shipped more quickly and efficiently, which was particularly important for the fruit-producing areas of Borshchiv and Zalishchyky counties. The railways were also an essential precondition for the dairying industry, which began to flourish throughout much of southeastern Galicia around the turn of the century. Secondary industries also began to develop, such as the egg-packing and jam-making plants in Husiatyn, and a new tobacco factory at Ozeriany.[83]

The railways also brought into the region a new group of managerial and professional men, with their dependents and assorted needs. Professional engineers and surveyors were brought in during the railways' construction phases, and some remained in the track maintenance section offices, first at Chortkiv and Husiatyn, then at Terebovlia and Zalishchyky. Some were long-service railway men, such as chief engineer Victor Laba of the Terebovlia section office in 1898, who had been an assistant engineer with the Carl-Ludwig Railway at Zboriv, East Galicia, in 1889.[84] In 1898 some of the station masters in the larger places, such as Ferdinand Herzog at Chortkiv and Daniel Dryliński at Husiatyn, were also professional engineers. Others were railwaymen of long standing who had been promoted through the ranks.[85]

The effect of the railways on Southern Podillian towns was quite disparate. The two large market towns on the Russian border, Husiatyn and Skala, experienced population decreases in the 1890s, suggesting a reduced trade with Russia. In Husiatyn's case, this was despite its status as the county seat and its continued importance as a local market centre and railhead.[86] Here, as in many other regional market towns, it was the Jewish population that decreased in absolute numbers, no doubt because of emigration owing to increasing competition from Ukrainian co-operative marketing agencies and village shops that were often associated with reading clubs.

Okopy, the small market centre in the southeasternmost corner of the region, and also on the Russian border, lost its market status altogether in 1896. So did Sukhostav (Husiatyn county), which was quite near the railway but was bypassed by it. Ozeriany (Borshchiv county) declined in size, although the railway reached it in 1898. The cause of that decline was competition from Bilche, the centre of the Sapieha estates, which acquired market status in the 1880s and became better connected with the county by improved roads in the 1890s. On the other hand, reasons for the decline in population of Melnytsia, a county court seat and very close to the railway after 1898, or Iaholnytsia, on the railway in 1898 and with a large tobacco factory, are not clear.[87]

The absence of the railway was no necessary impediment to continued growth. Probizhna (Husiatyn county) experienced growth, probably because of improved roads, including one to the railway station at Hadynkivtsi. Budzaniv and Ianiv (Terebovlia county) were not on the railway, but they also grew. By 1900 both were on an improved county road that linked them to Terebovlia and Chortkiv. Khorostkiv prospered despite the fact that the railway station which bore its name was some kilometres from the town; it was the centre of some particularly fine agricultural land and was well known for its stables, as well as for its crafts and cultural life.

Some places that were not market towns undoubtedly grew because they had railway stations as of 1884. Vasylkivtsi and Hadynkivtsi (Husiatyn county) increased from 1,967 to 2,618 and from 1,113 to 1,568 inhabitants respectively, and Bile (Chortkiv county) from 3,289 to 4,083 between 1880 and 1900, although it was some distance from its railway station. The biggest increases, however, were recorded by Kopychyntsi, a county court seat which the railway reached in 1884 and which became a railway junction in 1896; Terebovlia, a county seat and garrison town reached by the railway in 1896; and Chortkiv, which was emerging as a focal point for the whole region. On the Podillian Highway and with a bridge across the Seret, Chortkiv had long been a market and road junction. The railway first reached it in 1884, and in 1898 it became the main regional railway junction, with a line south to Zalishchyky and another one southeast into Borshchiv county. In the 1880s it also acquired a military garrison.[88] The population of Chortkiv itself grew from 3,524 in 1880 to 4,531 in 1890 and 5,099 in 1900; that of its sister "village," Vyhnanka, where the railway workshops were located, from 3,181 to 4,017 and then 5,212; and that of Chortkiv Staryi from 1,376 to 1,639 to 2,127 by 1900. The combined population of Chortkiv and its satellite villages was thus almost 12,500 by 1900.[89]

Posts and Telegraphs

Austria was the first continental European country to adopt the new adhesive postage stamps, in 1843. Postal services had existed before, but a vast growth took place in the nineteenth century as populations rose, transportation became more rapid, and the state took on the organization of the mail services instead of leaving them in the hands of private contractors.[90] By 1880 Southern Podillia too had its network of postal and telegraph services. The Podillian Highway was the main artery for the mails. There were postal stables and stage points at Zalishchyky, Tovste, Chortkiv, Kopychyntsi (with "12 pairs of post-horses"), and Terebovlia,[91] and a total of twenty-six post offices, mostly in market towns. As befitted its size, there were nine post offices in Borshchiv county, at Borshchiv, Korolivka, Ozeriany, Skala, Kryvche, Melnytsia, Ustia Iepyskopske, Okopy, and Kozachivka; four in Chortkiv county at Chortkiv, Dzhuryn, Ulashkivtsi, and Iaholnytsia; three in Husiatyn county, at Horodnytsia, Husiatyn and Kopychyntsi; six in Terebovlia county, at Budzaniv, Ianiv, Ilavche, Khmelivka, Strusiv, and

Terebovlia; and four in Zalishchyky county, at Duplyshka, Ustechko, Tovste, and Zalishchyky.[92] By 1890 the number of post offices in Southern Podillia had risen to thirty-three, with four new ones in Husiatyn county, at Khorostkiv, Probizhna, Sukhostav, and Vasylkivtsi; three in Zalishchyky county, at Kasperivtsi, Koshylivtsi, and Synkiv; one in Chortkiv county, at Kolyndiany, and one in Borshchiv county, at Kudryntsi. The post office at Okopy, only 3 km from Kozachivka, had been closed.[93]

In the decade of the 1890s there was a great expansion of postal services in Galicia.[94] By 1900 there were 50 post offices in Southern Podillia (Borshchiv county 15; Chortkiv 9; Husiatyn 12; Terebovlia 6; and Zalishchyky 8). In addition, six villages were designated places from which mail would be distributed, but with no facilities for sending mail. There were main imperial post offices in the towns of Chortkiv and Zalishchyky.[95] The volume of postal business in Southern Podillia cannot be ascertained, but the region probably shared the general upsurge in the use of the mails, which included the delivery of newspapers. Ukrainians, including former Austrian army non-commissioned officers, were among the region's postal officials. Sometimes they may have tried to conceal their background, for there were complaints that the Ukrainian postmaster in Terebovlia spoke to people only in Polish.[96] Mail deliveries over country roads appear to have been made "almost daily," so rural mail deliverymen had to have good horses.[97] In 1882 Austria established a post office savings bank, with numerous local branches at which people could deposit even very small amounts of savings. Eighteen branches of the post office savings bank were opened in Southern Podillia on 12 January 1883. Probably as more post offices were opened in Southern Podillia there were also more savings bank branches.[98]

Another modern development, the electric telegraph, reached Southern Podillia prior to 1880. In that year the region had seventeen telegraph offices. Seven were in Borshchiv county, at Borshchiv, Korolivka, Ozeriany, Skala, Kozachivka, Melnytsia, and Ustia Iepyskopske; three in Chortkiv county, at Chortkiv, Ulashkivtsi, and Iaholnytsia; three in Husiatyn county, at Husiatyn, Kopychyntsi, and Khorostkiv; two in Terebovlia county, at Strusiv and Terebovlia; and two in Zalishchyky county, at Tovste and Zalishchyky.[99] Only a modest increase in the number of telegraph offices took place between 1880 and 1890; by then three new ones had been opened in Husiatyn county, at Hadynkivtsi, Probizhna, and Vasylkivtsi, plus one at Kryvche in Borshchiv county, and one at Dzhuryn in Chortkiv county.[100]

As with post offices, there was a substantial increase in Galicia in the 1890s in the number of telegraph offices, and the official statistics clearly differentiated between state and railway telegraph offices.[101] This differentiation makes it difficult to determine the increase in the number of telegraph offices in Southern Podillia by 1900. The 1900 *Gemeindelexicon* appears to list only the state offices (ten in Borshchiv county, five in Chortkiv, four in Husiatyn, four in Terebovlia, and five in Zalishchyky, for a total of twenty-eight in Southern Podillia).[102] In addition, there would have been telegraph offices at railway stations in villages not served by the state telegraph network.[103] State telegrams cost 30 kr per 10 words in the early twentieth century, while telegrams sent from a railway station were slightly more expensive. Even as late as 1913, Ukrainians had to be reminded that only Latin lettering could be used in telegrams.[104] By 1900 Southern Podillia was well covered by the state network of post offices and postal deliveries. Most of the region was also within relatively easy access of a telegraph office, the exceptions being the area between Melnytsia and Kozachivka/Okopy in southeast Borshchiv county and the western parts of Terebovlia and Zalishchyky counties.

* * *

The coming and extension of the railways in Southern Podillia, as elsewhere, displaced the roads from their previous predominance. Roads, in fact, took on the new role of giving access to the railways.[105] The attention devoted to the construction of county and commune roads rather than trunk highways fits into this pattern. In Southern Podillia some of this development took place only in the 1890s. Nevertheless, by 1900 there was a substantial and integrated transportation and communication system in the region,[106] one that made for easier and more comfortable travel for people and speedier and less costly transportation for the region's agricultural produce.[107]

Notes

1. I.T. Berend and G. Ranki, *Economic Development in East-Central Europe in the 19th and 20th Centuries*, 57.
2. H.J. Habakkuk and M. Postan, eds., *The Cambridge Economic History of Europe*, 6: 212-13, 236-7, 240-5.
3. Berend and Ranki, *Economic Development in East-Central Europe*, 79.
4. For river-borne traffic on the Dnister see *Oesterreichisches statistisches Handbuch*, 2: 176; *Oesterreichische Statistik*, XLII, no. 3, xxvi-xxviii. In 1893, 439,513 mc of wood was transported out of Austria on the Dnister, but only 3,016 mc of grain and beans. See also IMZCh, 384.
5. L. von Bilinski, "Das Verkehrswesen," 881.
6. United States, *House Misc. Docs.*, 2.
7. IMZCh, 332, 465, 483, 491; Rudnitsky, *Ukraine*, 298.
8. Bilinski, "Das Verkehrswesen," 881-2; *Oesterreichische Statistik*, XLII, no. 3, vii-viii.
9. Bilinski, 880.
10. Austria, Militär-geografisches Institut, *Galizien* (this map, published in 1872 and

located in the Library of Congress Map Library, is there incorrectly cited as a map dated 1868).

11. AGAD, Ministerium des Innern, file B 9, "Bau der Strassen und Chausseen, 1888-89," "Übersicht über die Karpaten Routen ...," undated but based on "technical studies of 1888."
12. Ibid., Governor of Galicia to Minister of Interior, 24 Feb. 1888. A total of 138,000 g had been appropriated for this purpose for 1887 and 1888. Major road work continued into the early nineties (ibid., Lviv to Vienna, 13 Oct. and 5 Dec. 1889).
13. Ibid., Lviv to Vienna, 24 Feb. 1889, and file comments thereto. The situation was deemed "not very unfavourable," for only short distances had steep gradients.
14. United States, *House Misc. Docs.*, 4; *Gemeindelexicon* 1900, 762.
15. S. Rudnitsky, *Ukraine*, 298.
16. "Bericht über die Tätigkeit des statistischen Seminars und der anschliessenden statistischen Übungen an der Universität Wien im Wintersemester 1899-1900," 68. K. Bachinger, "Das Verkehrswesen," 278-322, contains very little information on roads. Galician laws and regulations on road building and maintenance are summarized in K. Grzybowski, *Galicja 1848-1914*, 274, 284; and *Svoboda*, 7 Jan. 1897.
17. Austria, Militär-geografisches Institut, *Galizien.*
18. Market status was officially conferred upon suitable communes by the imperial and, after 1859, by the county authorities (A. von Gorski, "Das Marktwesen," 855).
19. IMZCh, 370-80.
20. Ibid., 472-5.
21. T. Pilat, *Skorowidz*, 22-3, 72-3.
22. IMZCh, 602-3.
23. Ibid., 776-7.
24. Ibid., 245, 384.
25. United States, *House Misc. Docs.*, 7. Unfortunately, no distances were given.
26. *Batkivshchyna*, 23 May 1890. I have been unable to ascertain what tolls were charged on other types of roads, but they were probably similar.
27. See, for example, *Batkivshchyna*, 26 Jan. 1889; *Chytalnia*, 21 April 1896. On the other hand, complaints were not very frequent. For a matter-of-fact account of some tolls in Borshchiv county see IMZCh, 483.
28. *Batkivshchyna*, 9 Nov. 1889; *Halychanyn*, 31 Oct. 1893.
29. There was clearly a thrust towards the construction of county roads. See Galicia, *Podręcznik statystyki*, VII, pt. 2: 207; *Oesterreichische Statistik*, XLII, no. 3, ix-x; "Bericht über die Tätigkeit des statistischen Seminars... 1899-1900," 686. The estimated average cost per kilometre of road construction in Galicia at the end of the nineteenth century was 5460 g for Land roads, 3000 g for county roads, and 1500 g for commune roads (Bilinski, "Das Verkehrswesen," 881).
30. *Dilo*, 17 Jan. 1890, *Batkivshchyna*, 7 Feb. 1890, and 24 July 1891.
31. W. Najdus, *Szkice z historii Galicji*, 128-9; *Svoboda*, 29 Apr. 1897. Compulsory road work was abolished after World War I, and county roads often deteriorated thereafter (IMZCh, 688).
32. *Dilo*, 28 May 1890; *Batkivshchyna*, 14 June and 6 Sept. 1889, 28 Apr. 1895, 28 Nov. 1896.

33. AGAD, Ministerium des Innern, file B 50, "Brückenbau 1888-1893," Lviv to Vienna, 23 Jan. 1888, 12 July 1891, 1 Jan. 1892, Vienna to Lviv, 15 Jan. 1892. There was also a wooden bridge across the Zbruch at Shydlivtsi, Husiatyn county, IMZCh, 441.
34. IMZCh, 492.
35. B. Czołowski, "Urzędnicy galicyjskich wydziałów powiatowych w 1894," 34-7.
36. Cf. AGAD, Ministerium des Innern, file B 11, "Bau der Strassen und Chausseen, 1893-95," Lviv to Vienna, 27 Mar. 1894.
37. AGAD, Ministerium des Innern, file B 10, "Karpaten Routen," Governor Badeni to Vienna, 31 Jan. 1890.
38. *Batkivshchyna*, 15 Aug. 1884; IMZCh, 332, 437, 491, 840; Rudnitsky, *Ukraine*, 297-8.
39. AGAD, Ministerium des Innern, file B 9, "Übersicht über die Karpaten Routen." There was a later dispute about who was to pay for the repairs, ibid., file B 11, "Bau der Strassen und Chausseen, 1893-95," Lviv to Vienna, 14 Jan. 1893, and Vienna memorandum of 9 Mar. 1893.
40. *Dilo*, 28 May 1890. The correspondent exhorted villagers not to allow the building of roads such as the one from Melnytsia to Kudryntsi, Borshchiv county.
41. *Batkivshchyna*, 13 Feb. 1895, and 7 Mar. 1890; IMZCh, 462.
42. Preston, "Report of Inspector of Agencies in Europe," 17-18. But see, for example, W. L. Morton, *Manitoba—A History*, 401, and Humeniuk, *Hardships and Progress*, 88, for bad conditions of rural roads in Manitoba, Canada, in the first half of the twentieth century.
43. M. Orlowicz, *Co zwiedzać w Galicji? (Wskazówki dla turystow)*, 41. Tourism was also hampered by the general state of Southern Podillian roads (IMZCh, 831).
44. *Batkivshchyna*, 25 June 1886.
45. Ibid., 26 Jan. 1889.
46. IMZCh, 624, 243.
47. AGAD, Ministerium des Innern, File B 10, Lviv to Vienna, 31 Jan. 1890.
48. *Batkivshchyna*, 28 Sept. 1888; *Oesterreichisch-ungarische Monarchie*, 50-64; *Batkivshchyna*, 15 Aug. 1884; IMZCh, 332, 437, 491, 840; Rudnitsky, *Ukraine*, 297-8.
49. *Chytalnia*, 21 April 1896.
50. *Batkivshchyna*, 18 Oct. 1888, 7 Jan. 1887; in the latter case a journey of 55-70 km to the nearest railway station was involved..
51. *Batkivshchyna*, 18 June 1886.
52. *Svoboda*, 2 June 1898.
53. See, for example, ibid., 3 and 24 Mar. 1898.
54. IMZCh, 483.
55. I. Konta, "Geschichte der Eisenbahnen Oesterreichs," 30-3; Eisenbahn-Ministerium, *Statistik der... Lokomotiveisenbahnen*; Bachinger, "Das Verkehrswesen," 288-9; W. Hoffman, ed., *Taschenbuch für den Oesterreich. Eisenbahn-Betriebs-Beamten für das Jahr 1896*, 35; S. Inglot, *Historia chłopów polskich*, 14.
56. Konta, "Geschichte der Eisenbahnen Oesterreichs," 33-7, 78-84, 134-9; Bachinger, "Das Verkehrswesen," 287-9; Eisenbahn-Ministerium, *Statistik der... Lokomotiveisenbahnen*.

57. Bachinger, "Das Verkehrswesen," 294, fn. 33.
58. Konta, "Geschichte der Eisenbahnen Oesterreichs," 205-6, 302-3, 387; Bachinger, "Das Verkehrswesen," 291-4.
59. *Parlamentär*, 27 June 1880. Complaints about the high freight rates of the Carl-Ludwig Railway continued throughout the 1880s. According to a Ukrainian deputy in the Sejm, "the company cares nothing about Galicia's interests" (*Batkivshchyna*, 25 Oct. 1889). There were many other complaints from bodies such as the Sejm, chambers of commerce, and the agricultural associations in Galicia (I. Konta, *Eisenbahn-Jahrbuch der Oesterreichisch-ungarischen Monarchie*, XXI, 417). In 1888 the Carl-Ludwig Railway had an operating profit of 3,836,027 g on a gross income of 9,276,304 g (Konta, *Eisenbahn-Jahrbuch*, 428).
60. *Parlamentär*, 9 and 23 Jan., 20 Mar. 1881, 27 July 1882; Konta, "Geschichte der Eisenbahnen Oesterreichs," 228-333; Bachinger, "Das Verkehrswesen," 297. For a petition of July 13, 1880, from the Chortkiv county executive committee for the building of the Transversal Railway, see Galicia, *Stenograficzne sprawozdanie sejmu krajowego królestwa Galicyi i Lodomeryi wraz z wielkiem Księstwem Krakowskiem*, z 3 sesyi 4-tego perjodu w roku 1880, 533.
61. Konta, "Geschichte der Eisenbahnen Oesterreichs," 334. The line between Buchach and Kopychyntsi was opened for all traffic on 31 Dec. 1884; on the same date the Kopychyntsi-Husiatyn line was opened for freight traffic, with passenger traffic following on 1 Feb. 1885 (ibid., 333).
62. Ibid., 337.
63. Ibid., 334.
64. The town of Zalishchyky was about equidistant from Chortkiv and Chernivtsi, but every other commune was now much closer to a railhead than before.
65. *Iliustrovanyi kaliendar tovarystva "Prosvita" 1886*, xxviii.
66. Berend and Ranki, *Economic Development in East-Central Europe*, 70. For the role of railways in the economic development of the Hapsburg Monarchy see ibid., 71-2, *passim*; D. Warriner, ed., *Contrasts in Emerging Societies: Readings in the Social and Economic History of South-Eastern Europe in the Nineteenth Century*, 11-12, 17, 19, 33-4; H. Benedikt, *Die wirtschaftliche Entwicklung in der Franz-Jozefzeit*, 134, 180. See also *Oesterreichisch-ungarische Monarchie*, 19: 244-50, for the effect of railways on the Galician forest industry.
67. *Hospodar i promyshlennyk*, no. 1, 1885.
68. *Batkivshchyna*, 12 Apr. 1889. For the decline of weaving due to the importation of textiles see ibid., 15 Feb. 1884. The number of weavers in Galicia declined from c. 30,000 in 1889 to c. 16,000 in 1902 (S. Anczyc, *O przemysłe tkackim w Galicyi*, 14, 17, 19). The expansion of railways and roads had cut into "monopolies" previously enjoyed by local farmers and thus also into their incomes, especially in Southern Podillia (*Nauka*, 31 Jan. 1889).
69. *Batkivshchyna*, 14 Dec. 1891; Konta, *Eisenbahn-Jahrbuch*, 417-8.
70. *Eisenbahn-Schematismus für Oesterreich-Ungarn*, XXIV (Vienna 1898), 283, 298, 310; Bachinger, "Das Verkehrswesen," 296; J. Rutkowski, *Historia gospodarcza Polski*, 318-9; Berend and Ranki, *Economic Development in East-Central Europe*, 84-5; J. von Raczynski, "Die galizische Landwirtschaft der Gegenwart," 72.
71. Bachinger, "Das Verkehrswesen," 298; Berend and Ranki, *Economic Development*

in East-Central Europe, 72; Rutkowski, *Historia gospodarcza Polski*, II, 319; Konta, "Geschichte der Eisenbahnen Oesterreichs," 413-4; P.F. Kupka, "Das Lokalbahnwesen," 498-9, 504-5. The Austrian state contributed 17.5 per cent of the cost of the Galician local railways in the 1890s, with the remainder being raised by the Sejm; Kupka, "Das Lokalbahnwesen," 498. In 1890 there had been 440 km of local railways in Galicia; by 1900 there were 962 km (Galicia, *Podręcznik statystyki Galicyi*, VII, pt. 1, 210.

72. *Verordnungs-Blatt des k.k. Handels-Ministerium für Eisenbahnen und Schiffahrt* 50/1891, 7/1893, 68/1894, 83/1894, 84/1895, 132/1895, 133/1895, and 143/1896, and *Verordnungsblatt für Eisenbahnen und Schiffahrt* 80/1897, 141/1898, and 148/1898; *Statistik der Lokomotiveisenbahnen*; A.von Strigl, *Die österreichischen Staatsbahnen, 1896-1908*, 38-9; Kupka, "Das Lokalbahnwesen," 512-15; *Chytalnia*, 23 Jan. 1893; Galicia, *Podręcznik statystyki Galicyi*, VII, pt. 1: 210-11.
73. *Batkivshchyna*, 17 June 1887, 5 Oct. 1888, 16 Aug. 1889, 23 May 1890.
74. *Batkivshchyna*, 13 Jan. and 1 Aug. 1890. Railway construction as a public works relief measure, following the bad 1889 harvest, was suggested by *Batkivshchyna* on 2 Nov. 1889, but this idea was ahead of its time in Galicia.
75. *Chytalnia*, 6 Apr. 1894; *Svoboda*, 31 Mar. 1898. State policy could also work to the detriment of Galician producers. The costs of transportation of pigs was kept high in order to protect the interests of Bohemian hog producers. Transportation costs for pigs and cattle in the late 1890s were:

	Per Head	
Distance	**Pigs**	**Cattle**
up to 50 km	1.50 g	0.90 g
for the next 100 km	1.40 g	0.85 g
for the next 150 km	1.30 g	0.80 g
any further distance	1.20 g	0.75 g

Source: *Svoboda*, 3 June 1897.

76. *Svoboda*, 13 May 1897; *Batkivshchyna*, 16 Dec. 1886.
77. *Svoboda*, 21 Apr. 1898.
78. *Batkivshchyna*, 26 Jan. 1889; *Chytalnia*, 20 May 1893. See also *Batkivshchyna*, 28 Jan. 1895; IMZCh, 332; K. Murzynowska, "Polska emigracja zarobkowa przed 1914 r.," 755.
79. See the names of railway personnel in Southern Podillia that appear in *Eisenbahn-Schematismus*, esp. XV (1889) and XXIV (1898). Podillia.
80. P. Mechtler, "Striflichter auf des Nationalitätenproblem bei den österreichischen Eisenbahnen," 435. See also ibid., 426, 437-8. The reference to Ukrainian signs on railways is from a report of the achievements of Narodna Rada in 1896 (*Svoboda*, 8 July 1897).
81. Unfortunately, I have been unable to find similar data for other purely Podillian stretches of railway line. For traffic volumes, income, and expenditures on the East Galician local railways in 1900 see Galicia, *Podręcznik statystyki Galicyi*, VII, pt.

2: 210-11.

82. See, for example, IMZCh, 384.
83. Bujak, *Galicya*, 1: 364; A. Birnboim, *From My Father's House*, 17; *Oesterreichische Statistik*, LXXV, pt. 11; W. Pruski, *Hodowla zwierząt gospodarskich w Galicji w latach 1772-1918*, 2: 449.
84. *Eisenbahn-Schematismus*, XXIV: 313, 322; see also XV: 137, 273.
85. Ibid., 24: 315, 318; 15: 133, 266, 267.
86. Husiatyn was much damaged by a fire on 14 July 1893, "with 3,000 people, mostly Jews, left homeless" (*Chytalnia*, 20 July 1893). Political relations between Austria and Russia deteriorated in the late 1880s and remained poor until 1897 (May, *The Hapsburg Monarchy, 1867-1914*, 291-4, 297, 301-3).
87. Population data are from *Special-Orts-Repertorien* (1880 and 1890), and *Gemeindelexicon* 1900.
88. Military garrisons in 1900 were located at Chortkiv (661 personnel), Zalishchyky (627), and Terebovlia (874), with smaller detachments at Strusiv (143, quartered on the estate, not in the town) and Vyhnanka (71) (*Gemeindelexicon*, 132, 134, 716, 718, 762). In 1890 the garrisons had been at Chortkiv (261 personnel), Terebovlia (486), and Strusiv (150) (*Special-Orts-Repertorien* 1890, 113, 615).
89. Chortkiv in 1900 also had a military hospital, the county health insurance office (*Krankenkasse*), a main tax office, a land tax assessment revision record office, medicinal baths, an extended care institution, six credit unions, a county agricultural association, a monastery, a convent, and an orphanage (*Gemeindelexicon*, 1900, 132). It appears to have been quite a thriving place.
90. Bachinger, "Das Verkehrswesen," 316.
91. For Kopychyntsi see IMZCh, 282. In 1900 there were still postal stables at Chortkiv, Tovste, and Zalishchyky (*Gemeindelexicon*, 1900). I have found no direct evidence of postal stables at Terebovlia, but it is improbable that there would not have been such stables there. Probably there was a postal stage coach service along the Podillian Highway (see Bachinger, *Das Verkehrswesen*, 316), but I have found no direct evidence for this.
92. *Special-Orts-Repertorien*, 1880. In 1880 the Korolivka post office was said to be in the adjoining small village of the same name in Zalishchyky county (ibid.), but later sources locate it in the market town of Korolivka (Borshchiv county) (ibid., 1890; *Gemeindelexicon*, 1900).
93. *Special-Orts-Repertorien*, 1890. The opening of the post offices in Koshylivtsi and Synkiv was reported in *Batkivshchyna*, 4 Sept. 1885. One of the region's largest towns, Khorostkiv, obtained a post office only in the 1880s. On the other hand, the geographical distribution of post offices prior to 1880 shows an attempt to cover the countryside with mail services.
94. Galicia, *Podręcznik statystyki*, VII, 2: 213.
95. *Gemeindelexicon*, 1900; IMZCh, 492.
96. *Batkivshchyna*, 10 Apr. 1885; IMZCh, 330, 406, 509.
97. Interview with Mrs. L. Salamandyk, Vita, Manitoba, 19 June, 1979 (her father carried mail at Synkiv, Zalishchyky county).
98. E. März and S. Socher, "Währung und Banken in Cisleithanien," 1: 351; *Russkaia rada*, 30 Dec. 1882. (That newspaper report refers to a post office savings bank at

Loshniv, Terebovlia county, but it is not listed in the decennial register of villages.)

99. *Special-Orts-Repertorien*, 1880. Telegraph offices clearly denote that electric power was being brought into the region, but there is no sign of its general use there in the nineteenth century. However, Chortkiv had electric street lighting prior to the First World War (IMZCh, 84). For the early use of the electric telegraph see Habakkuk and Postan, *The Cambridge Economic History of Europe*, 231, 234.
100. *Special-Orts-Repertorien*, 1890. The offices at Dzhuryn, Hadynkivtsi, and Vasylkivtsi were probably "railway telegraph offices."
101. Galicia, *Podręcznik statystyki*, VII, 2: 213. Ukrainians were advised to use telegrams to send protests to various levels of government (*Batkivshchyna*, 18 April 1889; *Hromadskyi holos*, 1 Jan. 1898).
102. *Gemeindelexicon*, 1900.
103. Until 1896 the Ministry of Commerce had responsibility for post, telegraph, and railways. With the establishment of a separate Ministry of Railways there was a need to differentiate between "state" telegraph offices and the business they generated, which remained under the jurisdiction of the Ministry of Commerce, and telegrams sent via the "railway telegraph offices," which were really a by-product of the railways' own need for efficient communications and traffic control.
104. *Kalendar Misionara 1913*, 133.
105. Habakkuk and Postan, *The Cambridge Economic History of Europe*, 213; Bachinger, "Das Verkehrswesen," 307.
106. A practical example of this integration is provided by the instructions of the Stanyslaviv co-operative pig marketing agency. Members, some of whom were from Southern Podillia, were to notify the Stanyslaviv office by telegram whenever they sent a shipment of pigs by rail (*Svoboda*, 22 Dec. 1898).
107. The big gap that still remained was the absence of telephones. In 1900 there were still only twenty-one communities in Galicia that had telephone service; these included the town of Ternopil in Northern Podillia (*Podręcznik statystyki*, VII, 2: 212). By 1909 even southeastern Borshchiv county had telephone service (IMZCh, 492).

Chapter IV

Formal Education

It has been said that

> the main difference between more and less developed countries is that the former possess more knowledge than the latter.... In order to be used for practical purposes, knowledge must, however, also expand in breadth so that more and more people come to possess adequate parts of the existing knowledge.[1]

This chapter deals with the ways in which the public school system—in many ways the necessary prerequisite for the spread of knowledge—developed in Southern Podillia in the late nineteenth century.

Historical Background

Studies of education in Eastern Galicia have tended to overlook many developments of significance to a rural population. They focused instead on the high illiteracy rate and, when written by Ukrainians, on the injustices done to Ukrainians by the Polish conservatives who dominated the Sejm and the Galician Land School Council (the agency that supervised the school system). Such injustices took many forms.[2] However, the function of the village school and its role in society have not been extensively explored. The growth of the elementary education system in Southern Podillia will be primarily examined here.

At the time of the incorporation of Eastern Galicia into the Habsburg domains in 1772, public schooling was at a low ebb. The Greek Catholic (Uniate) clergy had been the main educators in the East Galician villages, but their own standard of learning was low. Both Empress Maria Theresa (1717-80) and Emperor Joseph II (1741-90) recognized the importance of the Uniate clergy as intellectual leaders of their society, and provided opportunities for the enhancement of their educational competence. Joseph II determined that there was to be a national education to form Austrian citizens and that each village was to have a "trivial" or primary school which would be maintained by the commune or manor. It was to offer instruction in the local language. Each district was to have a higher school funded by a Land educational fund, with a "normal" or high school and teacher training school in the Land capital. There was to be compulsory education for children 5-12 years of age.[3] The village school was to teach religion, reading, writing, and arithmetic. Teachers were bound to teach only the assigned curriculum. They were to cultivate the development of obedient, hard-working people, and not much else. Establishment of village schools was placed under the control of the Bishops' Consistories, with the maintenance and payment of teachers the responsibility of the local manor. These responsibilities were often disregarded, and teachers were frequently in short supply and of poor quality. In fact, compulsory education was not realized in Galicia, nor elsewhere in the Crownlands.

During the nineteenth century there was a steady increase in the number of village schools in Galicia. In the Ukrainian areas after 1818, by imperial edict, they were to use Ukrainian as the language of instruction. Nevertheless, many villages remained without schools until the 1880s.[4] The educational system continued to be church-administered, which was most compatible with the political system. After the transformation of Austria into a constitutional monarchy in 1867 and the granting of substantial autonomy to Galicia, significant changes in education began there.[5] In the spirit of the new political system, a new school law was passed in 1869 for the entire empire, which gave certain major responsibilities for elementary education to the Land authorities. Article 21 of the Imperial School Law of 14 May 1869 stated that compulsory education would be in effect from the end of the sixth to the end of the fourteenth year in all of Austria, except in those crownlands to which Article 75 of that Law gave the power to change the length of compulsory schooling by Land legislation. Among such crownlands was Galicia.[6]

Elementary Education in Galicia

The Galician Education Law of 2 May 1873 called for widespread elementary school education for all citizens, but the Sejm, by Article 40 of this law, chose to require compulsory education for only six years, from the end of the sixth to the end of the twelfth year of age. Children aged 13-15 were to attend "continuation school" for four or six hours per week. In fact, compulsory education could not be enforced because many communes lacked schools. The establishment and maintenance of elementary schools was the responsibility of local school districts, which consisted of one commune or a group of communes. The requirement that there be a school within four kilometres of every centre of population would only be met if communities were ready to make the necessary provision, or if the authorities exerted sufficient pressure on them to do so, sometimes with the additional inducement of subsidies. Initially, the Galician authorities showed little inclination to enforce the provisions of their own law.[7] In each crownland a Land School Council was established as the highest authority for the administration of the educational system. However, control over curricula was retained by the Viennese authorities. The Galician School Council was a bureaucratic body made up of nominated officials, not pedagogic specialists responsive to local conditions, as had been envisaged. It had the power to establish the language of instruction in every school in Galicia.[8]

In the period 1869-81, the number of elementary schools in Galicia rose from 2,476 to 2,925. This increase is remarkable in view of the economic difficulties experienced in Galicia and Austria after the early 1870s and the devastating cholera epidemic of 1873. Most of the newly established schools were one-teacher schools, called "one-class" schools in the data, although more than one grade would be taught there (2,693 of the 2,925 elementary schools in Galicia in 1881 were one-teacher schools). Basic education was thus spreading to the villages. Seventy new schools were built in Eastern Galicia alone between 1871 and 1874.[9] The number of schools being established continued to rise in the 1880s. Between 1883 and 1891 a further 1,224 schools were organized, bringing the total for Galicia to 4,149.[10] Not surprisingly, the number of those who were literate increased between 1880 and 1890.[11]

Qualitative changes in elementary education after 1880, by no means all beneficial, resulted from a new composition and policy of the Land School Council. The Polish conservative majority in the Sejm became much more influential in the policy making of the Land School Council through its more numerous representation on that body. One man, Michał Bobrzyński, became increasingly powerful in Galician educational affairs after 1888. Owing to his influence and that of his colleagues in the Polish circle in Vienna, the office of permanent vice-president of the council was created, and Bobrzyński—a spokesman for the conservative viewpoint—held this position from 1892 to 1901.[12] This Polish conservative position very much reflected the interests of the landowning gentry. It sought to expand greatly the availability of elementary education in the Land, but to restrict the actual amount of education in the villages to whatever the one-teacher school could provide.[13] Peasants were to be made just literate, but further schooling was to be avoided for fear that a more advanced education would lead to the peasants getting ideas above their station in life. Thus, the social structure of Galicia, and the power of the owners of large estates, would be preserved. The educational system would, therefore, maintain an ignorant mass of unthinking, but literate, individuals who would provide a pool of cheap labour for the estates of the great landowners.[14]

As it turned out, these expectations were not met. In part, this was due to the tireless work of voluntary organizations in the field of popular education and the Ukrainian press. In part it was due to the expansion of the school system beyond the confines which the Land School Council had in mind.

Elementary Education in Southern Podillia

Developments in Southern Podillia in many ways paralleled those elsewhere in

Galicia, although the rate of progress in some of the counties between 1880 and 1900 was faster than in many other places. The number of schools increased greatly between 1880 and 1900, particularly in Borshchiv county, which made education more accessible. The number of children attending school increased significantly between 1890 and 1900, and the increase in the number of girls attending school is particularly notable.[15]

By 1890 most towns and villages had an elementary school or had joined with other communes in a local school district. By 1900, only thirty-three small villages in all of Southern Podillia, mostly in Borshchiv and Zalishchyky counties, out of a total of 269 towns and villages in the region, were not part of a local school district. The number of children of school age who were without access to an elementary school was thus relatively small. Probably not all those who were registered attended regularly. Nevertheless the trend toward universal elementary education was impressive. Further, the general attendance data show that Ukrainian children were attending school in significant numbers. Equally important was the increase in the number of schools with more than one teacher. Even a school with one teacher had to cover at least four grades of the elementary school curriculum. The law of 1873, in fact, provided detailed schedules showing how the total curriculum was to be covered in schools with varying numbers of teachers.[16] One-teacher schools in the villages were quite effective.[17] Nevertheless, in view of the greater number of school children and overcrowding in the schools, the trend toward multi-teacher schools (see Table 6) represented significant progress. It is noteworthy that this progress was more marked in Southern Podillia than in Galicia generally, for in 1900, 60.5 per cent of Galicia's elementary schools were still one-teacher schools, while in Southern Podillia, despite the lag in Zalishchyky county, it was 46.4 per cent.

Table 6
Elementary Schools in Southern Podillia

		Type of School (class; i.e. number of teachers)								
	Number of Schools	**1**	**2**	**3**	**4**	**5**	**6**	**7**	**Boys**	**Girls**
1890	208	168	25	6	5	4	-	-	15,816	11,743
1900	224	104	86	13	10	3	7	1	23,385	18,742

Source: *Oesterreichische Statistik*, XXXV, no. 1, and LXII, no. 2; *Schematismus der allgemeinen Volksschulen*, 1890 and 1900.

In all five counties the schools in the county seat were the largest. In such towns there were separate schools for boys and girls. Otherwise, progress in the different counties varied. In 1890 the most developed elementary school systems were in Terebovlia and Husiatyn counties. Terebovlia was the most advanced, but even there one-teacher schools still predominated in 1890 (71 per cent). Six villages had two-teacher schools; two other villages (Kobylovoloky and Loshniv), as well as the market town of Budzaniv, had three-teacher schools; Strusiv had a four-teacher school; and there were separate five-teacher schools for boys and girls in Terebovlia. By 1900 the two schools in the town of Terebovlia each had six teachers, and there were two four-teacher schools in Strusiv, as well as one each in the market town of Ianiv and the village of Loshniv. Another village, Mohylnytsia, had a three-teacher school. Only eighteen villages still had one-teacher schools, while sixteen had two teachers each. Husiatyn in 1890 had more two-teacher schools—thirteen—than any other county in the region, but one-teacher schools still predominated (60 per cent). There were two three-teacher schools (in the market town of Khorostkiv and in the village of Chornokintsi Velyki), and two four-teacher schools (in Husiatyn and, for boys only, in Kopychyntsi). By 1900 only fourteen village schools still had only one teacher each. Almost half the county's schools (21 out of 43) were two-teacher schools. Two more villages, Kotsiubyntsi and Vasylkivtsi, had acquired three-teacher schools, and one village, Horodnytsia, even had a four-teacher school. Khorostkiv also had a four-teacher school, where special agricultural instruction was offered. Kopychyntsi had a six-teacher school for boys and a four-teacher school for girls; in the town of Husiatyn there was also a six-teacher boys' school and a five-teacher girls' school.

Zalishchyky was the county in which least progress was made. It had twenty-seven elementary schools in 1880; by 1890 there were forty-four public schools and one private elementary school run by the Sisters of Mercy in Nyrkiv. This growth in numbers denotes considerable effort, but in 1890 the public schools were overwhelmingly one-teacher schools (93 per cent). In addition there was a two-teacher school for girls and a four-teacher school for boys in the town of Zalishchyky, and a two-teacher school in the market town of Tovste. By 1900 the number of public elementary schools declined from forty-four to thirty-eight, and thirteen villages were not part of any local school district. The number of private schools rose from one to four (two new elementary schools for Jewish boys schools in Zalishchyky and another in Tovste, all supported by the Baron Hirsch foundation). Zalishchyky was the only county in Southern Podillia in which one-teacher schools were still preponderant in 1900. Only three villages, Novosilka Kostiukova, Uhrynkivtsi, and Vyniatyntsi, had two-teacher public schools. The remaining larger elementary schools were in Tovste and the town of Zalishchyky, but the latter also had Southern Podillia's only seven-teacher public school. The increase in school enrolment was the smallest in the region during the decade 1890-1900 (29.5 per cent), with about one-half of this increase attributable specifically to the increased elementary school attendance of Jewish boys in Tovste and Zalishchyky.

Zalishchyky presented the most negative picture, but developments in Borshchiv and Chortkiv counties denoted very marked progress. In 1880, the 74 small towns and villages of Borshchiv had between them only 27 public elementary schools. By 1890, this county had 47 public schools, almost all of which were one-teacher village schools, as well as one private girls' school. As of 1900, Borshchiv county had 56 public elementary schools as well as one private Jewish boys' school. School attendance increased 68.4 per cent in the decade after 1890. The number of one-teacher schools dropped from 44 to 30; those with two teachers rose from 1 to 19. In 1900 there were three-teacher schools in Ivankiv, Korolivka (where there were two), Ustia Iepyskopske, and Bilche, and a four-teacher school in Ozeriany. The school in the town of Borshchiv went from a three-teacher school in 1890 to a five-teacher school in 1900, while the school in Skala went from four to five teachers. In addition to these dramatic changes, the school at Ozeriany offered special agricultural instruction. Nevertheless, in 1900 there were still eleven small villages that were not part of a local school district. The number of public elementary schools in Chortkiv county increased from twenty-three in 1880 to thirty-one in 1890. All but four were one-teacher schools. The only larger schools were in the villages of Bile, Iaholnytsia, and Zvyniache, each with two teachers, and the five-teacher school in the town of Chortkiv. By 1900 there were thirty-nine public elementary schools, only eight of which were still one-teacher schools. The town of Chortkiv had two six-teacher schools, one for boys and one for girls. There were twenty-seven two-teacher schools, as well as one with three and one with four teachers, in the county. School attendance increased by 80.7 per cent between 1890 and 1900, the highest rate of increase in Southern Podillia.

Overall, in Southern Podillia opportunities for elementary education increased significantly between 1880 and 1900, as more and more local school districts were established and schools were built. This increase in educational opportunities was most marked in Borshchiv and Chortkiv counties. The number of children attending school, both in the small towns and in the villages, increased significantly. It is also clear that a greater proportion of Southern Podillian children were attending school by 1900. The school population amounted to 6.8 per cent of the total population of the five counties in 1890 and 9.8 per cent in 1900. Moreover, the schools they were attending were no longer overwhelmingly one-teacher schools, for everywhere, except in Zalishchyky county, there was a significant trend toward multi-teacher schools.

Financing and Administering the School System

The basic administrative unit for elementary school education was the local school district. Normally this covered the area of one commune and its adjoining estate, but it might encompass two or more communes and estates. By 1890 there were 201 local school districts in Southern Podillia; during the next ten years nine more were formed in Borshchiv county and a further six in Chortkiv county, although there was a decrease of seven in Zalishchyky and one in Husiatyn.

The building and maintenance of a school could impose a considerable burden on a commune and its local school district. Construction costs alone could be quite high. It was reported, with some pride, from Kolodribka in 1884 that 1,200 g had been collected toward the new school, but in fact the school and its teacher's residence had cost 3,500 g by the time they were completed in 1888.[18] The school in Shchytivtsi (Zalishchyky county) cost 6,000 g to build in the late 1890s.[19] On one occasion the emperor sent a gift of 100 g toward school costs.[20]

Information about the financing of elementary schools is fragmentary at best, with the exception of some data for the year 1890.[21] Elementary education itself was free, but parents were responsible for the cost of books and scribblers. Local school districts helped and the state might contribute when parents were unable to cover such costs. The Prosvita society also contributed books and there are some recorded occasions, for example at Sapohiv (Borshchiv county), where the county school council also gave assistance.[22]

The single largest ongoing expenditure for local school districts was the salary of the teacher or teachers. Except in very rare instances, they did not pay the teachers directly, for until 1894 teachers' salaries were normally paid by the county school council, partly from its own funds and partly from money contributed by the local school districts. In 1890 the local school districts of Borshchiv county contributed about 67 per cent of the total cost of teachers' salaries in that county, Husiatyn about 64 per cent and Zalishchyky about 69 per cent, but in Chortkiv their share was nearly 75 per cent, while in Terebovlia county they paid for only 53 per cent of the total cost.[23] Clearly, different practices prevailed in the different jurisdictions. The 1890 data also show that considerable sums (5,465 g) were being expended by local school districts in Borshchiv county on construction or renovation, with lesser amounts being spent in the other counties. In every county, but particularly in Zalishchyky, some local school districts rented the school building. Other major expenses were for heating, lighting, and cleaning the schools, which absorbed a greater proportion of school district funds in Southern Podillia than in Galicia as a whole. Other local school district expenditures were for maintenance and repairs, the purchase of equipment, schoolbooks and supplies "for the needy," administration, subsidies for teachers' accommodation, and travel expenses of instructors of religion.[24]

Local school districts obtained much of their revenue from taxes—a percentage of the direct state taxes, determined locally but within fixed maxima—and people frequently complained that the estates were not paying their fair share. Other sources of revenue were school trust funds, voluntary contributions, and fines for truancy.[25] Despite the expense involved, the opening of a new school could be an occasion for celebration. In 1889 the new two-teacher school in Laskivtsi (Terebovlia county) was blessed by the priest in the presence of many people, including the reeve.[26] Some villagers obviously took much pride in their school. A report from Kolodribka in 1890 noted with satisfaction that the village had had a school since 1865 and that "now we have educated people"; the priest, Fr. A. Kapustynsky, worked hard for the school as well as for the church and the reading hall.[27] Much depended on the quality of the teacher, and Kolodribka made a point of thanking a teacher when he left its school in 1890.[28] There were occasional complaints about the expulsion of children from school or that the local school council was run by Poles,[29] or was headed by a local large landowner and few people bothered to attend its meetings.[30] On the other hand, the work of a Ukrainian school inspector was regarded as very helpful by a correspondent from Ivanie Puste (Borshchiv county).[31]

Until 1894 county school districts were administratively superimposed on the local school districts. They were responsible for payments to teachers, for providing some educational materials and funds for teachers' and students' school libraries, for organizing county teachers' conferences, and for the general supervision of local schools. With the passing of the Galician Law of 24 April 1894, all the assets and most of the responsibilities of the county school districts passed into the hands of the Land School Council.[32] County school districts in Southern Podillia were not noticed much in the press. A single editorial took the county school council to task for requesting that the Borshchiv local school council correspond with it in Polish—they could write in Ukrainian but had to use the Latin alphabet.[33] The Land School Council and its administrative and inspector staffs were charged with the overall supervision of all elementary schools in the Land. This mandate included approval of textbooks used in the schools. The Prosvita society prepared some of the textbooks to be used in Ukrainian language and mixed language (*utraquist*) schools.[34]

The Teachers and the Curriculum

According to established formulae, if the number of children in a school exceeded eighty, there were to be two teachers, and three teachers when the number exceeded 160.[35] These staffing targets were rarely attained in Southern Podillia.[36]

The task of the teacher in one- and two-teacher schools was a difficult one.

It was eased somewhat because, in practice, children in most localities attended school for a half-day only—the older ones in the morning from 7 a.m., and the younger ones in the afternoons until 6 p.m.[37] This made for a long work day for the teacher, but eased the task of trying to offer instruction simultaneously to children of widely disparate ages. Children in Southern Podillia, where both the Julian and Gregorian calendars were in use, went to school for forty-six weeks per year (fewer in Husiatyn and Terebovlia counties), but there were many breaks. There was no school on Sundays, and Thursday afternoons were free, too. All Catholic holy days, of both rites, were school holidays, as were 28 June, in memory of Emperor Ferdinand, and the birthdays of Emperor Franz Josef and Empress Elizabeth. Religious authorities could name other school holidays in individual localities, such as the day of the local church's patron saint, and there might be days when school had to finish by noon for special church services.[38]

Local school districts increasingly provided accommodation for the school principal or sole teacher, and quite often for other teachers too. In 1890, 191 local school districts provided such residences for the principal or sole teacher, and 11 provided them for other teachers also; in 1900, 204 principal or sole teachers received such accommodation, and 29 local school districts also made provision for other teachers.[39]

In 1900, excluding teachers of religion, there were 462 teachers in the public elementary schools of Southern Podillia. Of the 257 male teachers, the majority were married, and their salaries were most frequently in the range of 300-600 g per annum, though many earned more. The majority had been in the teaching profession more than ten years. The 205 female teachers were, for the most part, single (four were nuns), had been teaching for fewer than ten years, and while the majority also had an annual remuneration in the 300-600 g range, many earned less. About one-half of the male teachers were Greek Catholic (127) and one-half Roman Catholic (128), while two did not specify beliefs; among the women, 156 were Roman Catholic and only 34 Greek Catholic, five Jewish, and one "unclassified." No religious affiliation was given for the nine women teachers of vocational subjects. Using religious belief as an indicator of national identification, there was clearly a preponderance of Poles on the teaching staff of the Southern Podillian elementary schools.[40]

The county and the Land educational authorities showed ongoing concern for the professional development of teachers. They organized conferences for teachers, and funds were appropriated for this purpose. Funds were also provided for teachers' libraries, reference books and other materials to support their instructional activities.[41] The number of such libraries in Southern Podillia was 139 in 1890 and 173 in 1900; by the latter year almost all the schools in Borshchiv and Terebovlia counties had such libraries. The number of books they contained increased from 3,323 in 1890 to 7,438 in 1900, with the greatest increases in Borshchiv and Chortkiv counties, and Zalishchyky, again, lagging far behind.[42]

Libraries were also provided for many of the schools—115 in 1890 and 131 in 1900. By 1900 all but one of the schools in Terebovlia county had a school library, as did the majority of schools in Chortkiv and Husiatyn counties, although in the last-named there had actually been a decline in their number during the previous decade. The number of volumes in the school libraries, though pitifully small given the number of school children, also increased during the decade, from 4,028 to 6,373, with the largest increases in Chortkiv and Terebovlia counties.[43] The Ukrainian enlightenment societies at times gave books for use in school libraries.

The role of the village school continued, throughout the period, to be the imparting of basic education to the citizenry. Language arts (reading and writing), arithmetic, religion—taught not by the secular teacher but by priests of the local religious faiths, excluding the Jewish—and singing formed the core of the curriculum in grades one and two. A second Land language was introduced in grade two. In grades three and four the children were introduced to natural sciences, geography, history, drawing, geometry, and physical education for boys.[44] Besides the basic curriculum, a growing number of courses were offered in such technical or vocational subjects as horticulture, beekeeping, silkworm raising, and agriculture, and for girls from grade three upward, domestic science. This was consistent with Austrian educational theory, which held that the education of children should be adapted to the needs and demands of the local population and resources, and that technical education should be expanded throughout the state.[45] By 1890 most of the schools in Southern Podillia had school gardens that were used for instructional purposes. The number of schools offering domestic science rose significantly, from 81 to 150 between 1890 and 1900, with the most marked growth in the three counties (Borshchiv, Chortkiv, and Zalishchyky) where such instruction had been lagging.[46] Domestic science courses covered such topics as the origins, quality, and cost of food, utensils, and housing materials. Sewing, with related crafts, and, in the upper grades, care of the sick were also included.[47]

There are several other indicators that modern educational opportunities were being provided in the five counties. By 1900 Borshchiv county had five public schools with physics laboratories, one with a chemistry laboratory, and one with a special room for drafting and drawing. Several more schools had specific physical education facilities, craft workshops, and agricultural courses.[48] In particular, Borshchiv, Husiatyn, and Terebovlia counties each had one school offering special agricultural courses at the public elementary school level.[49] In addition, an agricultural school, maintained by the Land, was founded at Iaholnytsia (Chortkiv county) in 1885. It provided specialist agricultural education to boys aged sixteen and over. By 1892 it had six teachers and offered a three-year program (two years in school, followed by a one-year internship) designed to fit its graduates for careers such as overseers or managers on farms or to run their own holdings. It also offered short courses at no fee.[50] An Institute of Pomology, which was opened at Zalishchyky in 1900, offered a two-year course; this was an important development for the extensive orchard culture of Southern Podillia.[51] There also was a school at Tovste that provided training in ceramics.[52] Efforts to establish a Teacher Training College in the region finally led to the opening of one for men in Zalishchyky. It offered a one-year preparatory course, followed by a four-year training program. In the 1900-1 academic year, it had eleven instructors and a total of 127 students in the first three years of what was, in effect, a five-year program. Instruction was given in both Polish and Ukrainian; the student body consisted of sixty-seven who claimed Ukrainian and sixty who claimed Polish as their mother tongues. Ninety were scholarship students.[53]

The Language of Instruction

Even in the village schools of Southern Podillia, children had to begin learning a second Galician language in grade two. With one exception, this second language was either Polish or Ukrainian. In upper grades of town schools, a third language (normally German, unless this had been the "second" language) was also introduced. A Polish authority, J. Bużek, regarded the people of Eastern Galicia as the most fortunate of all Austrian peoples for being given the opportunity to learn so many languages.[54] The complaints of Ukrainians were not about the opportunity to learn languages, but about the issue of the language of instruction in schools in the predominantly Ukrainian areas. There is no doubt that the provisions of Austria's fundamental law guaranteeing "the equal rights of all languages customarily spoken in the Land in the schools" were not being observed.[55]

The language of instruction in the elementary schools was determined by the Galician Land School Council (see Table 7). The Jewish boys' schools that were established in the 1890s, as well as other private elementary schools, used Polish as the language of instruction.

The numbers shown in Table 7 disguise the fact that the larger schools and the urban schools (often these categories were synonymous) used Polish as the language of instruction, though some "parallel" classes for Ukrainians might be offered in town schools. (This fact is not indicated in Table 7.) The Husiatyn Boys' School, in 1900, for example, was classified as having five classes in which Polish was the language of instruction, and only two parallel classes in which Ukrainian was the teaching medium;[56] Tovste's four-teacher public elementary school had only one parallel class.[57] Of the 42 schools in Borshchiv county that used Ukrainian as the language of instruction in 1900, 26 were one-teacher schools, 13 were two-teacher schools, and three were three-teacher schools. Of the 12 Polish language schools, four had one teacher, three had two,

Table 7
Languages of Instruction in the Elementary Schools of Southern Podillia

	Number of Schools using Ukrainian, Polish or both as languages of instruction					
	1890			1900		
County	**Ukr.**	**Pol.**	**Ukr. & Pol.**	**Ukr.**	**Pol.**	**Ukr. & Pol.**
Borshchiv	32	9	7	42	12	3
Chortkiv	22	8	1	16	19	3
Husiatyn	34	9	0	16	11	16
Terebovlia	17	16	8	21	22	0
Zalishchyky	35	5	5	32	9	1

Source: *Schematismus der allgemeinen Volksschulen*, 1890 and 1900 (one small village school in Chortkiv county used German in 1900).

two were three-teacher schools, one was a four-teacher school, and two were five-teacher schools.[58] In Terebovlia county in 1900, both the six-teacher schools and all of the four-teacher schools used Polish as the language of instruction.[59] The overall effect of the systematic favouring of Polish can best be seen in the data contained in Table 8.

Table 8
Language in which Children were Taught, 1890 and 1900

	Percentage of children in schools in which the language of instruction was:					
	Polish		**Ukrainian**		**Polish and Ukrainian**	
County	1890	1900	1890	1900	1890	1900
Borshchiv	22.9	30.3	58.8	64.6	18.2	5.1
Chortkiv	40.4	55.4	59.6	35.9	-	8.3
Husiatyn	25.3	30.9	74.7	28.7	-	40.4
Terebovlia	47.6	56.0	34.0	44.0	18.4	-
Zalishchyky	20.7	27.1	71.5	70.3	7.8	2.6

Source: *Schematismus der Allgemeinen Volksschulen*, 1890 and 1900 (Chortkiv in 1900 had one German-language school with 32 children; the mixed-language school shown for 1890 in Chortkiv is here classified as Polish).

Clearly, there was in Southern Podillia a trend toward greater use of Polish as the language of instruction. The decline in the percentage of children who were taught in schools where only Ukrainian was the language of instruction was greatest in Husiatyn and Chortkiv. In Borshchiv and Terebovlia counties there was, in fact, an increase in the number of children in this category between 1890 and 1900, but it was more apparent than real, because of the decline in these counties in the number of children attending schools where both languages were used as languages of instruction (again, excluding parallel classes). Given these overall trends, it is remarkable that there were so very few references in the Ukrainian press, before 1900, to the issue of language of instruction in the Southern Podillian elementary schools.[60]

Problems and Progress

Serious deficiencies remained in the education system and in the opportunities it provided for children in Southern Podillia. There were too few teachers;[61] overcrowding of schools was also sometimes a problem. Even more serious was the fact that the system, except with extreme difficulty, did not allow for regular progression from elementary to secondary and higher levels of education for village and small-town children.

Austrian public elementary schools were, de jure, of two types, the *allgemeine Volksschulen* (elementary schools), and the *Bürgerschulen* (elementary schools in the larger towns that offered a more advanced variety of elementary education). There were no *Bürgerschulen* in Southern Podillia before 1900.[62] In practice, the *Volksschulen* were divided into two categories, the village elementary schools, with 1-3 teachers, and elementary schools "of the urban type" (higher elementary schools), with four or more teachers, which offered a level of education between the village school and the *Bürgerschule*.[63] In 1890 there were only nine such higher standing schools in the towns of Southern Podillia; in 1900 there were twenty-one (see Table 6). However, this improvement in the number of higher elementary schools was counterbalanced by a regression in the level of education offered in the village schools of Galicia in the 1890s. Austrian legislation had called for the same curriculum to be taught in elementary schools throughout the country. In 1883 a "reform" was proposed in the Sejm for Galicia, and it was passed into law by that body in 1885. Different curricula were to be introduced for elementary schools in the villages and towns because the normal curriculum was "socially inappropriate" for village children (whether Polish or Ukrainian) in Galicia. In essence, village children in Galicia were to be educated only to a level considered fit for their rural situations. Curricula and course materials for the village schools were to stress the needs—as perceived by the Sejm and the Land School Council—of a rural population; town schools on the other hand were to have a curriculum to prepare children for occupations in trade and industry.[64] The authorities in Vienna were

School at Ilavche, Terebovlia county, photographed by the author, May 1990 (above)

Lev Iasinchuk (right)

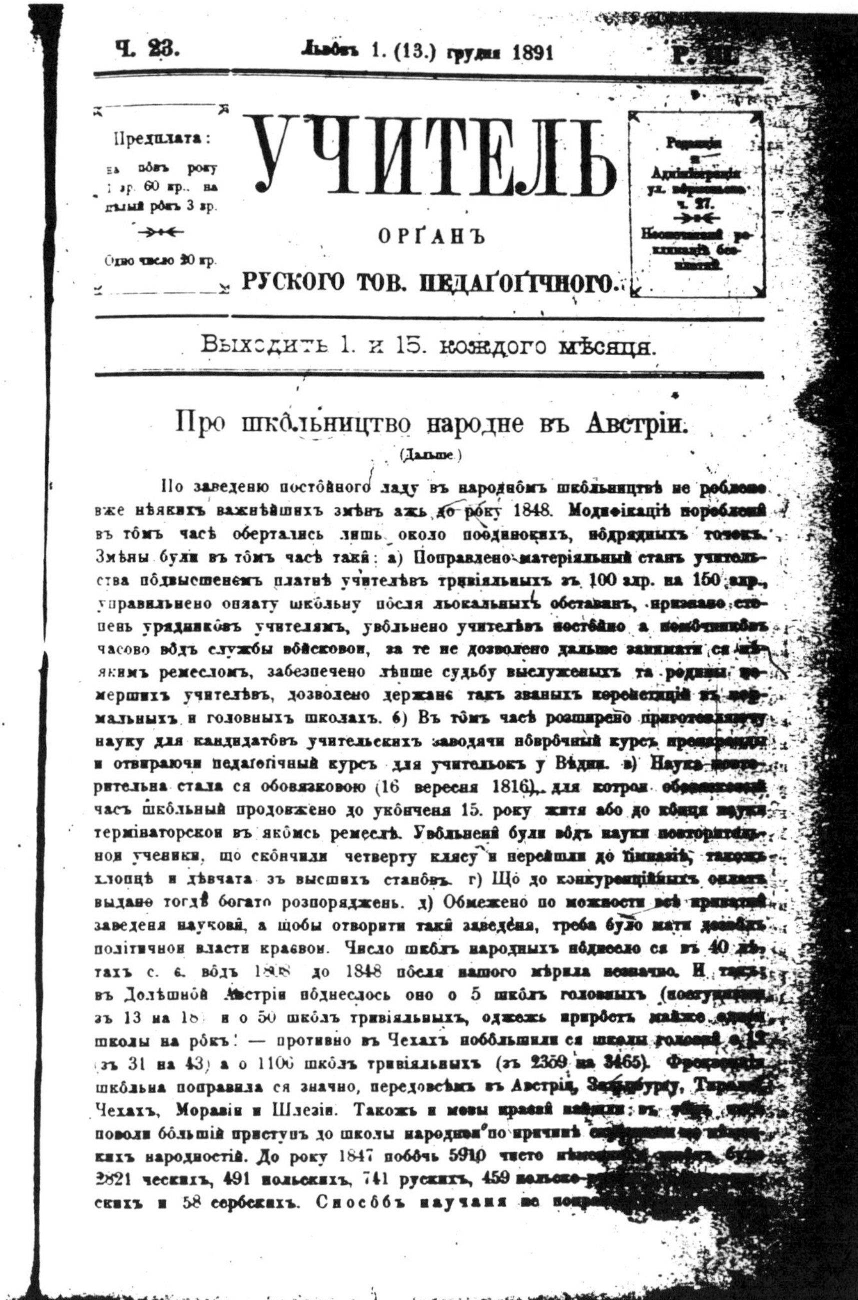

Ч. 23. Львôвъ 1. (13.) грудня 1891 Р. [illegible]

Предплата: за пôвъ року 1 зр. 60 кр., на цѣлый рôкъ 3 зр. Одно число 20 кр.

УЧИТЕЛЬ

ОРҐАНЪ РУСКОГО ТОВ. ПЕДАҐОҐІЧНОГО.

Редакція и Адміністрація ул. [illegible] ч. 27. Несоотвѣтственный [illegible]

Выходить 1. и 15. кождого мѣсяця.

Про школьництво народне въ Австріи.

(Дальше.)

По заведеню постôйного ладу въ народнôмъ школьництвѣ не роблено вже нѣякихъ важнѣйшихъ змѣнъ ажъ до року 1848. Модифікаціѣ пороблені въ тôмъ часѣ обертали ся лишь около поодинокихъ, пôдрядныхъ точокъ. Змѣны були въ тôмъ часѣ такі: а) Поправлено матеріяльный станъ учительства пôдвысшенемъ платнѣ учителѣвъ тривіяльныхъ зъ 100 злр. на 150 злр., управильнено оплату школьну пôсля льокальныхъ обставинъ, признано степень урядникôвъ учителямъ, увôльнено учителѣвъ постôйно а помôчникôвъ часово вôдъ службы вôйсковои, за те не дозволено дальше занимати ся [illegible] якимъ ремесломъ, забезпечено лѣпше судьбу выслуженыхъ та родины [illegible] померших учителѣвъ, дозволено держанє такъ званыхъ корепетицій въ нормальныхъ и головныхъ школахъ. б) Въ тôмъ часѣ розширено приготовляючу науку для кандидатôвъ учительскихъ заводячи пôврôчный курсъ [illegible] и отвираючи педагоґічный курсъ для учительокъ у Вѣдни. в) Наука повторительна стала ся обовязковою (16 вересня 1816), для котрои обовязковый часъ шкôльный продовжено до укôнченя 15. року житя або до конця науки терміваторскои въ якôмсь ремеслѣ. Увôльнені були вôдъ науки повторительнои ученики, що скôнчили четверту клясу и перейшли до ґимназіѣ, также хлопцѣ и дѣвчата зъ высшихъ станôвъ. г) Що до конкуренційныхъ оплатъ выдано тогдѣ богато розпоряджень. д) Обмежено по можности всѣ приватні заведеня науковú, а щобы отворити такі заведѣня, треба було мати дозволъ політичнои власти краєвои. Число школъ народныхъ пôднесло ся въ 40 лѣтахъ с. є. вôдъ 1808 до 1848 пôсля нашого мѣрила незначно. И такъ въ Долѣшнôй Австріи пôднеслось оно о 5 школъ головныхъ (поступенно зъ 13 на 18) и о 50 школъ тривіяльныхъ, оджежь прирôстъ майже одной школы на рôкъ! — противно въ Чехахъ побôльшили ся школы головні о 12 (зъ 31 на 43) а о 1106 школъ тривіяльныхъ (зъ 2359 на 3465). Фреквенція шкôльна поправила ся значно, передовсѣмъ въ Австріи, Зальцбургу, Тиролю, Чехахъ, Моравіи и Шлезіи. Такожъ и мовы краєвî найшли въ [illegible] поволи бôльшій приступъ до школы народнои по причинѣ [illegible] кихъ народностій. До року 1847 побôчь 5910 чисто [illegible] було 2821 ческихъ, 491 польскихъ, 741 рускихъ, 459 польско-[illegible] скихъ и 58 сербскихъ. Способъ научаня не попра[illegible]

Front page of *Uchytel*, 13 December 1891

sufficiently concerned about this item of Galician legislation to withhold their consent until 1893. With its implementation in 1894, the "ladder of schooling" was made even more difficult to climb.

Despite these difficulties, and the absence of any secondary school in Southern Podillia (agitation for the establishment of a public *gymnasium* in Chortkiv was unsuccessful[65]), some village and town children from the region did attend *gymnasia* and other types of secondary schools, entrance to which was by examination. Lev Iasinchuk (b. 1882) has recorded how well he was taught, in both Ukrainian and Polish, by a Polish teacher in the village school at Bilobozhnytsia, and how his knowledge of Polish grammar "stood me in good stead later in [the] Gymnasium" at Buchach.[66] Memoir writers also noted that "the people of Zvyniach sent their children to *gymnasium* or teachers' seminaries,"[67] and—from Bychkivtsi (Chortkiv county)—"some villagers sent their children to higher and middle schools." One became a priest and three went on to become teachers.[68] Many individual examples are recorded of Ukrainian villagers, some of them priests' sons, from villages such as Hovyliv Velykyi, Hadynkivtsi, Mshanets, Chornokintsi Mali, and Sydoriv (Husiatyn county), Bilobozhnytsia, Dzhuryn, and Zvyniach (Chortkiv county), Kobylovoloky (Terebovlia county), and Lysivtsi (Zalishchyky county), as well as from towns such as Chortkiv and Kopychyntsi, going to *gymnasia* in Galicia and, in one case, in Kitsman in Bukovyna. They went on to become lawyers, teachers, priests (in one case, bishop), journalists, opera singers and academics.[69]

Opportunities for higher education, and the career prospects that this held out, were thus not completely closed, even for village children.[70] Sometimes village priests provided encouragement and financial assistance to enable a village youngster to proceed to secondary education.[71] At other times cantors provided extra lessons to those anxious to go on, as well as to other children, thereby continuing an old tradition.[72] Probably some teachers gave supplementary instruction to gifted village children in order to prepare them for the entrance examination. Some villagers sent their children to a nearby town to take advantage of the higher level of education offered there.[73] In time, assistance to village children became more systematized. The Ruthenian Pedagogical Association began to give preparatory courses to village children to assist them in gaining entry to secondary schools, and *bursy* (residential accommodation facilities which also provided educational and cultural enrichment) were established by the association just after the turn of the century in the towns of Chortkiv, Kopychyntsi, and Zalishchyky. A fourth one was founded privately at Terebovlia.[74]

How many village children were able, by such means and their own ingenuity, to escape from the confines which the Land authorities wished to place on village education cannot be known. On the other hand, not all children were being sent to school. The 1873 law on compulsory schooling initially was not taken very seriously, but as time went on more attempts were made to ensure school attendance in Southern Podillia. The authorities of all five counties endeavoured, in the 1890s, to enforce the school attendance laws, but they adopted very different practices of prosecution and punishment for truancy. In Borshchiv, in 1890, very few parents were convicted for their childrens' absenteeism, but those who were fined were, on average, fined heavily (10.78 g). In the same county, in 1895, the number of convictions had increased dramatically, indicating a concerted drive by the authorities to increase school attendance once more schools were operational, but the average fine paid by a total of 481 parents was just over 1 g. In Chortkiv, the number of convictions declined considerably between 1890 and 1895, but those convicted in the latter year paid an average of 7.43 g each. In Husiatyn, in 1895, the average fine, at 36.85 g, was the highest in Galicia. Sometimes offenders were jailed. The proceeds from truancy fines went to the local school districts.[75]

Doubtless absenteeism was of far greater proportions than the conviction data indicate, but the data do show that by the 1890s the authorities were trying to enforce school attendance, sometimes by heavy exemplary fines, as in Husiatyn in 1895, or sometimes by greatly increased numbers of prosecutions leading to convictions, as in Borshchiv county in the same year. Overall, given the number of children who did not attend school, the number of convictions was small. The press was almost silent on this issue; only one letter complained about the seizure and sale of a man's coat to pay the fine.[76]

If a complaint about the enforcement of the truancy law represents one side of the picture, the other is provided by the vignette of the boy, no longer going to school, who was reading while pasturing the horses.[77] In general, during the period 1880-1900 in Southern Podillia there was a very considerable increase in the numbers of public elementary schools and in the numbers of children who attended them. The number of teachers rose in Southern Podillia, as indicated by the increase in the number of schools with more than one teacher. More books were being provided for the teachers' reference, and so was better accommodation. More books were also being provided for student use in the school libraries. Advanced subjects appeared in the larger schools in the towns, and more technical education was being provided in a handful of rural locations. Whatever the continuing deficiencies, significant progress had been made.

The Question of Literacy

Galicia in general, and parts of Eastern Galicia in particular, were, in 1880, areas with very high illiteracy rates.[78] It would have been surprising if literacy rates did not increase during a period of general progress in educational matters. However, owing to the survival of people who had grown to adulthood before large-scale public schooling began in Southern Podillia, the number and percentage of illiterates remained very high even in 1900.

Table 9
Literacy in Southern Podillia, 1880-1900,
(as a percentage of total population)

	Male			Female		
County	**1880**	**1890**	**1900**	**1880**	**1890**	**1900**
Borshchiv	8.4	10.3	20.8	4.8	5.7	13.4
Chortkiv	15.4	19.2	35.0	8.1	9.7	26.5
Husiatyn	13.0	22.5	33.3	6.8	12.4	22.3
Terebovlia	20.0	34.3	45.2	11.9	24.5	33.1
Zalishchyky	7.7	12.8	20.2	4.1	7.2	12.8

Source: Calculated from raw data in *Oesterreichische Statistik*, vols. I, no. 2, XXXII, no. 1; LXIII, no. 2.

Note: "Literate" includes both those who could read and write, and those who could only read. The latter constituted generally between 10 and 15 per cent of the total of literates.

A number of points need to be noted about the data presented in Table 9. First, the percentages are of the total male and female population of the five counties. They are thus percentages of totals that include an automatic, natural increase in the number of illiterates—all children six years of age and younger, who were not yet attending school. Lower numbers and percentages of illiterates have been found when the official data used for comparative purposes included only those persons of school age and older, but even with this aberration, the numbers and trends are significant. The data illustrate the effect of the better and longer established school systems of Husiatyn and Terebovlia counties on rates of literacy. They also show the significant progress made in Borshchiv and Chortkiv counties between 1890 and 1900, and that the schools of Zalishchyky county fell somewhat behind those of the rest of the region. That fewer females were literate is scarcely surprising, given the traditions of a rural region, but starting from a lower base, the rate of increase in female literacy was actually greater than among males. Between 1880 and 1890, the rate of growth of literacy in Husiatyn and Terebovlia counties was greater than in either Galicia or Austria, and this rate continued to be high in the 1890s. However, only Terebovlia saw an absolute decline in the number of illiterates between 1880 and 1890, though there were declines (slight in Zalishchyky) in all the counties between 1890 and 1900, despite the constant recruitment to the pool of illiterates through new births.

Given peasant customs and suspicions of officials, it is even possible that the official data overstated somewhat the extent of illiteracy. The editor of

Batkivshchyna, who had good knowledge of the traits of his readership, addressed their probable fears when he chided them before the 1890 census:

> It often happens at census time that people are asked whether they know how to read and write, and they say "no." Maybe they do this out of fear that they'll have to pay some sort of taxes. No, my dear people, a tax on knowledge hasn't been invented yet, and it brings honour to the Ruthenian people when greater numbers of literate people are recorded.[79]

Ivan Franko, in 1892, despaired of the slow growth of literacy in Galicia.[80] However, the data plainly show both an upward trend and that the ascription of 90 per cent illiteracy to Ukrainian peasants in Galicia at the end of the nineteenth century,[81] certainly as far as Southern Podillia is concerned, is erroneous. Austrian data for 1900 show the following percentages of the population of school age and older as literate: Borshchiv county, males 24.9 per cent, females 16.0 per cent; Chortkiv, 41.8 per cent and 26.25 per cent. Husiatyn, 40.15 per cent and 26.9 per cent; Terebovlia, 53.95 per cent and 37.4 per cent; Zalishchyky, 24.15 per cent and 15.1 per cent. There is no reason to think that Ukrainian literacy rates in Southern Podillia differed greatly from the region's general literacy rates.[82]

Although illiteracy was thus still unacceptably high, the sustained endeavours of the previous years deserve to be properly appreciated. Schooling in Southern Podillia appears to have been particularly effective for those who received their education in the 1890s, and the people of the region who were literate may well have been literate in more than one language. Canadian immigration agent Paul Wood responded to allegations in 1900 that Ukrainian settlers in the Dauphin area of Manitoba, the majority of whom came from Southern Podillia, were almost totally illiterate:

> Sir;—Kindly allow me space to correct a statement published by you in your last issue. So nearly as I can estimate after nearly four years observation, fully 35 per cent of the male adult Galicians can read and write in their own language, and many of these also can read and write Polish. Of the children who were attending school [for] any length [of time] at home in the old country before leaving for Canada, nearly all can read and write. Education there is conducted by the state on excellent lines, and attendance is compulsory though often shirked. Naturally, a year or two without schooling throws any child back. Thus barring the children born in Canada, I estimate that fully fifty per cent of Galician children can read and write. Regarding the women, I have no data. I may state that in many instances, I have found Galicians

preferring to sign receipts and other documents with a cross mark, who afterwards, I found out, could both read and write.[83]

Notes

1. T. Kristensen, *Development in Rich and Poor Countries*, 5.
2. V. Swidomyj, "Das galizische Volksschulwesen in Ziffern," 589-6; Z. Dulczewski, *Walka o szkole na wsi Galicyjskiej*, 65-86; S. Inglot et al., eds., *Historia chłopów polskich*, 2: 595; A. Sirka, *The Nationality Question in Austrian Education: The Case of the Ukrainians in Galicia 1867-1914*, 79.
3. S. Persky, *Populiarna istoriia tovarystva "Prosvity" v Lvovi*, 5; C.A. Macartney, *Maria Theresa and the House of Austria*, 125-6; T.C.W. Blanning, *Joseph II and Enlightened Despotism*; Sirka, *The Nationality Question*, 5.
4. For data on the number of elementary schools in Galicia and number of children attending, see *Rocznik statystyki Galicyi*, 2: 97.
5. W.F. Reddaway et al. eds., *The Cambridge History of Poland*, II, 432-44; Sirka, *The Nationality Question*, 35-50; E. Crankshaw, *The Fall of the House of Hapsburg*, 252; R.A. Kann, *The Multinational Empire*, 1: 324-6.
6. Austria, *Reichsgesetzblatt*, Vienna, 1869, no. 62.
7. J. Bużek, *Studya z zakresu administracyi i wychowania publicznego*, 42, 148; S.H. Badeni, "Schulpflicht und Schulbesuch in Oesterreich," 281.
8. W. Bartel, "Zur Geschichte des Galizischen Landesschulrates, 1867-1918," 348-50.
9. Inglot, *Historia chłopów polskich*, 594.
10. Ibid., 595.
11. H. Rauchberg, "Der Bildungsgrad der Bevölkerung Oesterreichs nach Altersstufen," 270.
12. Bobrzyński's career in Galician school and general politics is described in Bartel, "Zur Geschichte des Galizischen Landesschulrates," 353-4; a less favourable view of Bobrzyński is taken by Sirka, *The Nationality Question*, 80.
13. Inglot, *Historia chłopów polskich*, 595; Sirka, *The Nationality Question*, 79.
14. Sirka, *The Nationality Question*, 79-80; Inglot, *Historia chłopów polskich*, 595; Dulczewski, *Walka o szkole na wsi Galicyjskiej*, 66.
15. Unless otherwise noted, this section is based on data in *Oesterreichische Statistik*, XXXV, no. 1 and LXII, no. 2, and in *Schematismus der allgemeinen Volksschulen*, 1890 and 1900.
16. For details of curriculum organization see M. Baranowski, *Pogląd na rozwój szkolnictwa ludowego w Galicyi od 1772 do 1895 roku*, 12-4.
17. Except in Terebovlia county, higher "read and write" rates were recorded in 1900 for villages of 500 people or fewer than for places with populations of 501-5,000. Data, by category of community size, are in *Oesterreichische Statistik*, LXIII, no. 2. The low "read and write" rate in small towns in 1900 is probably due to the previous very low public elementary school attendance by Jewish boys. It was for this reason that Jewish elementary schools for boys began to be established in the 1890s with funds provided by the Baron Hirsch foundation (S. Gruiński, *Materyały do kwestyi żydowskiej w Galicyi*, 35). In 1900 the town of Zalishchyky, with its

very considerable Jewish population and two Baron Hirsch schools, recorded the highest "read and write" rate, at 46 per cent. The rates for Husiatyn and Kopychyntsi, also with sizable Jewish populations but without Baron Hirsch schools, were considerably lower, *Oesterreichische Statistik*, vol. LXIII, no. 2.

18. *Batkivshchyna*, 27 June 1884 and 28 Mar. 1890.
19. *Hromadskyi holos*, 15 Mar. 1899.
20. *Chytalnia*, 20 Feb. 1893. The Sejm or the county education council at times made grants or advances for the building of schools. For the request from the town of Borshchiv to the Sejm for 2,000 gulden in 1880 see *Stenograficzne sprawozdanie*, 350.
21. See *Oesterreichische Statistik*, XLII, no. 1, table cvii; and Appendix IV below.
22. Bużek, *Studya z zakresu administracyi*, 1: 175-6; *Oesterreichische Statistik*, vols. XLII, no. 1, clxiii, and LXII, no. 1, table A7; *Hospodar i promyshlennyk*, no. 7, 1884.
23. *Oesterreichische Statistik*, XLII, no. 1, clxiii-clxvi and table cviii.
24. Ibid.; see also Appendix IV below.
25. According to the Land Law of 2 May 1873, owners of tabular estates might be required to pay to local school districts a supplementary tax of up to 4 per cent of their direct state taxes, while villagers paid a supplement of up to 12 per cent toward local school expenses (Dulczewski, *Walka o szkole*, 64; *Oesterreichische Statistik*, XLII, no. 1, clxiii).
26. *Batkivshchyna*, 31 Jan. 1890.
27. Ibid., 28 Mar. 1890.
28. Ibid., 21 Nov. 1890.
29. *Hromadskyi holos*, 15 Mar. 1899.
30. *Svoboda*, 3 Mar. 1898.
31. *Batkivshchyna*, 4 July 1890.
32. *Oesterreichische Statistik*, XLII, no. 1, clxiii; Bużek, *Studya z zakresu administracyi*, 1: 313, 320-1. County school districts embraced two counties: Borshchiv and Zalishchyky counties formed one county school district, as did Husiatyn and Terebovlia; Chortkiv was linked with the adjoining county, Buchach.
33. *Batkivshchyna*, 29 July 1887.
34. Baranowski, *Pogląd na rozwój szkolnictwa*, 21-2.
35. Bużek, *Studya z zakresu administracyi*, 1: 46-7.
36. The 1890 *Schematismus der allgemeinen Volksschulen* gives the names of teachers in the individual schools, as well as the number of children attending these schools.
37. Bużek, *Studya z zakresu administracyi*, 1: 157, 161; *Oesterreichische Statistik*, XXXV, no. 1.
38. Bużek, *Studya z zakresu administracyi*, 1: 151-3; *Oesterreichische Statistik*, XXXV, no. 1.
39. *Oesterreichische Statistik*, XXXV, no. 1 and LXII, no. 2. Some criticized teachers' residential arrangements and professional development (L. Iasinchuk, *50 lit Ridnoi Shkoly, 1881-1931*, 10; *Narod*, nos. 7 and 8, 1892).
40. *Oesterreichische Statistik*, LXII, no. 2. Ukrainians were generally underrepresented in teaching, as in every other profession; see Sirka, *The Nationality Question*, 31-2, 85-7, 205. On the basis of names listed in the 1890 *Schematismus der allgemeinen*

Volksschulen, it may be inferred that there were considerably more Polish than Ukrainian teachers in the Southern Podillian schools. In Zvyniach, however, most of the teachers were Ukrainians (IMZCh, 186). There were many other reported instances of Ukrainian teachers; Bilche's teachers were Polish, Jewish, and Ukrainian (IMZCh, 617). Complaints about discrimination by Polish teachers against Ukrainian children arose mainly in the twentieth century (Sirka, *The Nationality Question*, 81-2; W. Batschynskyj, "Das ukrainische Schulwesen in Galizien," 83-4; Swidomyj, "Das galizische Volksschulwesen," 592-5). On the other hand, Iasinchuk's teacher, a Pole, was "a quiet person, approachable. He always spoke to the children and villagers in Ukrainian" and he was a good teacher, too (IMZCh, 209).

41. *Oesterreichische Statistik*, XLII, no. 1, table cvii.
42. *Oesterreichische Statistik*, XXXV, no. 1 and LXII, no. 2. For negative views of teachers' libraries in Galicia see S. Sempołowska, "Niedola młodzieży w szkole Galicyjskiej," in N. Falski, ed., *S. Sempołowska: Pisma pedagogiczne i oświatowe*, 61; K. Wojciechowski, *Oświata ludowa 1863-1905*, 12.
43. *Oesterreichische Statistik*, XXXV, no. 1 and LXII, no. 2.
44. Baranowski, *Pogląd na rozwój szkolnictwa*, esp. 12, 15; Great Britain, Board of Education, *Report on Technical and Commercial Education in East Prussia, Poland, Galicia, Silesia and Bohemia*, 32; Bużek, *Studya z zakresu administracyi*, 1: 72, 112.
45. Great Britain, *Report on Technical and Commercial Education*, 6.
46. *Oesterreichische Statistik*, XXXV, no. 1 and LXII, no. 2.
47. Bużek, *Studya z zakresu administracyi*, 1: 45, 83.
48. *Oesterreichische Statistik*, LXII, no. 2.
49. Respectively at Ozeriany, Khorostkiv, and Loshniv (*Oesterreichische Statistik*, LXIII, no. 4, 178).
50. *Batkivshchyna*, 23 Jan. 1885; *Chytalnia*, 6 May and 6 Nov. 1895; *Svoboda*, 3 Mar. 1898; *Oesterreichische Statistik*, XLIII, no. 4, 178.
51. *Oesterreichische Statistik*, LXX, no. 3, table 20.
52. *Chytalnia*, 6 Nov. 1895.
53. *Oesterreichische Statistik*, LXX, no. 3, table 15. See also *Chytalnia*, 24 Nov. 1895. Of the 127 students in the 1900-1 academic year, 114 were listed as Catholic, without differentiation of rite, and 13 as Jewish.
54. Bużek, *Studya z zakresu administracyi*, 1: 45.
55. For the text of Article XIX of the fundamental law no. 142 of 1867 in English translation see Kann, *The Multinational Empire*, 1: 405. The article also indicated that there should be "no compulsion of learning a second language of the Land" in public educational institutions. Sirka is undoubtedly correct when she states that "what type of school and which language of instruction was to be established where became very much a question of politics rather than of necessity" (Sirka, *The Nationality Question*, 77; see also 55-8, 178-9).
56. *Schematismus der allgemeinen Volksschulen*, 1900, 626.
57. Ibid., 737.
58. Ibid., 591-3.
59. Ibid., 730-1.

60. On Polish influence in elementary schools see *Batkivshchyna*, 12 Feb. 1886; and *Hromadskyi holos*, 15 Mar. 1899. There were also two complaints that Roman Catholic nuns, who had recently opened child-care facilities for children of working women, were intending to polonize Ukrainian children (*Prolom*, 11 Dec. 1881; *Batkivshchyna*, 18 Oct. 1888).
61. See Bużek, (*Studya z zakresu administracyi*, I, 196), who singles out Bile (Chortkiv county) in 1901-2 for special comment.
62. *Schematismus der allgemeinen Volksschulen*, 1900.
63. Sirka, *The Nationality Question*, 76-8.
64. Baranowski, *Pogląd na rozwój szkolnictwa*, 6-8, 14-24; Iasinchuk, *50 lit Ridnoi Shkoly*, 10; Inglot, *Historia chłopów polskich*, 594-7.
65. See, for example, *Batkivshchyna*, 25 Feb. 1887, 22 Mar., and 25 Oct. 1889. A *gymnasium* was finally opened in Kopychyntsi in 1906 (Iasinchuk, *50 lit Ridnoi Shkoly*, 102), and a private Ukrainian *gymnasium* in Chortkiv in 1911 (Sirka, *The Nationality Question*, 160).
66. IMZCh, 209.
67. Ibid., 186.
68. Ibid., 189.
69. The examples are of persons who (judging by the dates of their births) received at least some of their education before 1900 (ibid., 39, 43-9, 82, 89, 135, 232, *passim*).
70. This situation clearly worried the gentry-dominated Sejm, which in 1906 passed a law forbidding Galician villagers from sending their children to town schools (Iasinchuk, *50 lit Ridnoi Shkoly*, 10).
71. IMZCh, 580, 651.
72. The author's grandfather, a cantor, gave such supplementary instruction in Skorodyntsi (Chortkiv county) in the early 1900s. See also IMZCh, 209.
73. This may be inferred from Iasinchuk, *50 lit Ridnoi Shkoly*, 102.
74. Ibid., 32-41. See also IMZCh, 120.
75. *Oesterreichische Statistik*, XXXV, no. 1 and LI, no. 1; Badeni, "Schulpflicht und Schulbesuch," 281-309, esp. 308.
76. *Halychanyn*, 18 Jan. 1893.
77. IMZCh, 210.
78. In 1880 illiteracy among males in Borshchiv was 91.6 per cent, in Chortkiv 84.6 per cent, in Husiatyn 87 per cent, in Terebovlia 80 per cent, and in Zalishchyky 92.3 per cent. By way of comparison, data for some other counties of Galicia may be cited: Bohorodchany 95.1 per cent, Buchach 86.1 per cent, Horodenka 93.6 per cent, Kosiv 93.6 per cent, Lisko 95.7 per cent, Pidhaitsi 84.4 per cent, Ternopil 78.0 per cent, Turka 94.9 per cent, Zbarazh 96.9 per cent. Illiteracy among females was even greater: Borshchiv 95.6 per cent, Chortkiv 91.9 per cent, Husiatyn 93.1 per cent, Terebovlia 88.1 per cent, Zalishchyky 95.9 per cent, Bohorodchany 97.9 per cent, Buchach 92.4 per cent, Horodenka 96.7 per cent, Kosiv 97.1 per cent, Lisko 97.0 per cent, Pidhaitsi 92.3 per cent, Ternopil 84.6 per cent, and Turka 98.0 per cent (*Oesterreichische Statistik*, V, no. 3).
79. *Batkivshchyna*, 29 Aug. 1890.
80. *Narod*, nos. 7 and 8, 1892.
81. J.-P. Himka, "Polish and Ukrainian Socialism: Austria, 1867-1890," 93.

82. See *Oesterreichische Statistik*, vol. LXIII, no. 2, lxii-lxiv. Ukrainians in Southern Podillia were perhaps underrepresented in the school attendance of girls. Of the 18,637 girls attending public elementary schools in 1900, 56.6 per cent were stated to be Greek Catholic, 27.3 per cent Roman Catholic, and 16.0 per cent Jewish; of the 22,577 boys attending public elementary school, 65.8 per cent were Greek Catholic, 27.9 per cent Roman Catholic, and 6.2 per cent Jewish (ibid., LXII, no. 2, table A8). Most of the almost 900 children attending private elementary schools were Jewish boys in Borshchiv and Zalishchyky counties (ibid., table B11).
83. Cited from the *Dauphin Weekly Herald* in V.J. Kaye-Kysilevsky, "The Descendants of the Boyars of Halych on the Prairies of the Canadian West," 363. See also M. Ewanchuk, *Spruce, Swamp and Stone: A History of the Pioneer Ukrainian Settlements in the Gimli Area*, 77.

Chapter V

Popular Education

Public education, although clearly very important, was not the only force bringing literacy, information, and knowledge into Southern Podillia. Popular education, here defined as any activity of an instructional nature, also played a very large role. Activities of the three principal media of popular education—enlightenment societies, the press, and reading clubs—intersected in many ways, and were intended to do so. They were all directed primarily to adults, but younger people also were touched by them. Although parish priests provided the main instigating impetus, and in many ways continued to be very important in popular education work, it took on an increasingly secular character.

The Background

Prior to 1848 the printed word had little place in the lives of Galician peasants. Only a few of them, generally taught by cantors, could read. Normally, the literate persons in the East Galician villages were the priests, cantors, teachers, and perhaps some persons connected with the manorial estates. Reading materials consisted of prayer books, hymnals, the Epistles, Psalters, and works concerning religious observances, using Church Slavonic script and etymological orthography.

The earliest, relatively modern, popular education work in Eastern Galicia was undertaken by the brotherhoods or church brotherhoods. Their roots went back at least to the medieval Galician-Volhynian state. They were among the very few legal, voluntary associations for charitable and educational work in ethnically Ukrainian territories before the middle of the nineteenth century and they "served as organizers of the Ukrainian nation."[1] Brotherhoods were associations of men; women's groups were organized as sisterhoods. Under Polish rule prior to 1772, and later under Austrian rule, brotherhoods in rural areas, though secular organizations, were closely associated with the Uniate parishes and were usually influenced by the parish priest, although they might also serve to keep in check some local priest's overly autocratic tendencies. They helped the priest to look after the affairs of the parish, and in the absence of any organ of local government, functioned to some extent as such. They planned and implemented the ceremonial events associated with church activities, and they sustained and nurtured the faith, language, and traditions of the Ukrainian population. Their educational work in the countryside consisted mainly of ensuring that a few people could read the Holy Books, and perhaps a very few could also write. In larger towns some brotherhoods had their own printing presses and libraries. The most notable was the Lviv brotherhood's Stauropegial Press, founded in 1586.[2]

After 1848, with the establishment of the communes as administrative units, the civic administrative functions which the brotherhoods had performed ceased, but their parish and educational tasks did not. They were also called upon to adjust their practices to the emergent market economy and to teach their members sound agricultural practices.[3] Many subscribed to the newly founded periodical press.[4] Others established reading clubs or sponsored sobriety campaigns for their parishes, among them the village of Kobylovoloky (Terebovlia county), whose brotherhood had over 1,000 members in 1874.[5] In the 1860s and 1870s they had to compete increasingly with the new secular enlightenment societies, whose beliefs and loyalties attracted the villagers. Still, brotherhoods did not disappear. In the early 1870s *Slovo* (The Word) was still urging brotherhoods to undertake more popular education initiatives. Between 1884 and 1886, nineteen church brotherhoods were members of Narodna Torhivlia (People's Commerce), an agricultural-commercial co-operative organization in Eastern Galicia.[6] Increasingly, however, they confined themselves to parish and church-related activities, and others took their place in the field of popular education.

From the 1850s onwards, church brotherhoods were also often associated with the sobriety movements, which combatted drunkenness among the Ukrainian peasantry of Eastern Galicia. Separate "sobriety brotherhoods" were also formed. That movement was given a fresh impetus by the publication in 1869 of a brochure by Fr. Stepan Kachala entitled "What is destroying us and what can help us." Kachala discerned too much laziness, drunkenness, and wastefulness among East Galician peasants, and set out the virtues of hard work, sobriety, and thrift as antidotes that would bring about a better life. The sobriety campaigns of the 1870s brought many people together in a common cause, and reinforced, at least for a time, the brotherhood's message of parish co-operation and mutual aid.[7] A tradition of self-help had been established in the villages and this tradition endured even when outside helping agencies did appear on the scene.

The earliest enlightenment society in Eastern Galicia was the Association of Galician Greek Catholic Priests, established in Przemyśl in 1816.[8] It sought to introduce education "in the ordinary language used in the village, and in the most straightforward style."[9] It encouraged parishes to found private schools, prepared some textbooks in Ukrainian, and published a few other books on such subjects as agriculture and health. The idea of reaching out to the general population ran into great problems, however, and great difficulties were posed by the related question of what language and what alphabet were to be used in the work of enlightenment.

In 1848 in Lviv, a "Congress of Scholars" convened by the Supreme Ruthenian Council established an enlightenment society, the "Halytsko-Ruska Matytsia."[10] Some of its planned activities were publication of popular literature (including a general reference work on agriculture and a history of Galicia in the vernacular), establishment of reading clubs, founding of an agricultural association, preservation of Ukrainian historic monuments, and translation of prayer books into the vernacular.[11] The actual achievements of this society fell far short of their mark. Not enough members supported the notion of using the vernacular for the society to realize its publication goals. Moreover, the reactionary faction of the society gradually became dominant and rejected the innovative ideas espoused at the founding meetings. The reading club Narodnyi Dim (National Home) established in Lviv and the periodical *Zoria Halytska* (Galician Star), both offshoots of the 1848 "Spring of the Ukrainian Nation," came to be controlled by the conservative Old Ruthenian group in the leadership. The popular educational function was set aside in favour of activities of more interest to the secular intelligentsia and the urban clergy.[12]

Some Greek Catholic clergy did continue with popular education work. One of them, Fr. Ivan Naumovych, was instrumental in founding three newspapers in the 1860s.[13] Some younger men, influenced by ideas from Dnieper Ukraine, founded *hromady* in several Eastern Galician county seats, linked to a headquarters in Lviv, to spread populist educational and nationalist ideas with readings, lectures, singing, and theatrical performances. They published several short-lived periodicals in the 1860s, and in 1864 established the first Ukrainian theatrical company. All this was done despite the opposition of their mentors in the Lviv Matytsia. However, they never really reached the countryside.[14] The unity of the intelligentsia with the people was a long time coming in Eastern Galicia.[15]

The Language Question

Reading materials available to literate Ukrainians up to the 1830s were in Church Slavonic, a language with a long tradition and with its own particular script and orthography. Some intellectuals recognized that any attempt to reach out to the people would be more likely to succeed if it made use of the language actually spoken by the people. The written version of this language should have a simpler, phonic orthography.[16] For the remainder of the century, and indeed beyond, there were agonized debates about whether this route should be followed, and if so, what the best way might be. The idea of abrogating the monopoly of the "ecclesiastical language" on the printed word aroused strong initial opposition among many in the Greek Catholic Church hierarchy. Later, various streams of the intelligentsia, for different reasons, also clung to "the language of old chronicles and religious texts," which seemed to be the basis for "an acceptable literary language," and which they believed they held in common with all eastern Slavs. Others, however, accepted as a basic principle that it would be most natural, and most conducive to the creative spirit, for the written language to reflect as closely as possible the spoken language of Galicia's Ukrainian people.[17]

The language issue was fought out during the second half of the nineteenth century. A uniform spelling and grammar for the Ukrainian language, with a phonic orthography, gradually became established. Printed materials in this medium, such as textbooks and popular literature, began to appear in some number, in part stimulated by the influx into Eastern Galicia of the works and ideas of Taras Shevchenko and other Ukrainian writers from the tsarist empire, with their populist orientation. However, even late in the century some publications aimed at a general readership still used a non-phonic or only semi-phonic (*iazychiie*) orthography, while toward the end of the century some publications began to appear in Russian.[18]

The National Movement

Struggles over language issues formed one very important element in the divisions which occurred in the Ukrainian national movement in Galicia during the last four decades of the nineteenth century. These lines of division were by no means always clear; the views of some prominent individuals underwent changes over time; and attention to particular political issues of the day necessitated compromises and tactical responses. The earliest, and at first the predominant modern group that fostered a specifically Ukrainian identity was the conservative reformers ("Old Ruthenians"). They were proud of being Greek Catholics; they were loyal to the Habsburg monarchy and the ruling Habsburg emperor, Franz Josef; they were opposed to the Poles and Polish influence; they strove for equal rights for Ukrainians in Galicia and for better schools for their people. On the language issue they thought, for the most part, that the written language should be standardized on the basis of the Galician version (or recension) of Church Slavonic. Greek Catholic clergy formed an important element in this movement, which often gave the impression of being primarily concerned with the Ruthenians in Galicia, rather than with Ukrainians as a whole.[19]

From the late 1860s onward, some members of the younger generation, impatient with the apparent lack of achievement by the Old Ruthenians, gradually formed their own movement. Although at one time termed "Young Ruthenians," they have become known as the "Populists" (*narodovtsi*) or "Ukrainophiles." Influenced by the populism of Taras Shevchenko's writings, they embraced a more democratic spirit than did the Old Ruthenians. Also, they sought, and ultimately attained, a literary language that was based on the peasant vernacular. More explicitly than the Old Ruthenians, the Ukrainophiles looked beyond the borders of Galicia and hoped for a time when reforms in the Russian Empire would permit freer interaction with the oppressed Ukrainian national movement in Dnieper Ukraine. However, for the present, they, like the Old Ruthenians, endeavoured to promote the national cause within the Austrian system. In the last two decades of the century the Ukrainophiles tended to attract more of the secular intelligentsia; otherwise they perhaps differed from the Old Ruthenians more in temperament than on issues, and over the years there was considerable collaboration between the two.[20]

In the 1880s a more radical grouping also emerged, first within the Ukrainophile movement, but later separate from it. It quickly became noted for its anti-clericalism and its social-democratic sentiments. This Radical party was formally established in 1890; Ivan Franko was one of its most prominent founders and members. Its differences with the populist Ukrainophiles grew, and it accused them of being under the sway of the clergy.[21]

Some other Galician Ukrainian intellectuals, and a small number of Greek Catholic clergymen, were attracted to a movement that came to be known as "Russophilism," which has been called "the national movement of those Galician Ruthenians who identified themselves as part of the Russian nation."[22] People were attracted to Russophilism for a variety of reasons. Some of these were religious and cultural: the common rite and similar rituals of Greek Catholicism and Russian Orthodoxy; the Cyrillic alphabet shared by the Ukrainian and Russian languages; and the similarity of Church Slavonic to the Russian language. Some were political or cultural-political: the attraction of a seemingly strong neighbouring political force, especially one opposed to the Poles; the appeal of Slavophilism (brotherhood of Slavic peoples under the leadership of the Russian people); and the desire to identify oneself with a well-established kindred culture in order to avoid the stigma of belonging merely to a peasant culture.[23] Some Old Ruthenians espoused aspects of Russophilism and, in the late 1890s, the Russophiles took control of some Old Ruthenian publications and organizations.[24] By the end of the nineteenth century, therefore, there were four groups or parties vying for support from the Ukrainian peasantry for their particular concepts of national identity. Popular education was the medium for carrying these concepts to the masses.

Ukrainian Enlightenment Societies in the Late Nineteenth Century

Enlightenment societies to promote the cause of popular education had been formed among other Slavic peoples, such as the Czechs and Serbs, before any modern enlightenment societies emerged among the Ukrainians of Eastern Galicia. Under the new Austrian fundamental law, which allowed greater freedom of association, Ukrainians, led by a young and mainly secular intelligentsia, formed a new society named Prosvita (enlightenment) in 1868. Its goal was "to promote popular education—moral, practical, and political."[25] The conjunction of the founding of Prosvita and the introduction of universal, free, and in theory compulsory, elementary education was important, since formal and informal education reinforced each other.

Prosvita began with sixty-six members in 1868. At first it grew slowly (to 174 members in 1873), then more rapidly (to 1,277 in 1878). Thereafter, membership in the Lviv "maternal" society alone increased to 3,657 in 1888 and to 11,323 in 1898.[26] The early membership was small because, initially, membership fees were very high and an early focus on conducting scholarly ethnographic research attracted mainly the intelligentsia. Once again it seemed that "the intelligentsia was to work for the people, over the people, but not with the people."[27] Changes in Prosvita's statute in 1870 and 1876, partly stimulated by the emergence of another enlightenment society, changed this situation. Aims were revised and membership fees reduced very considerably. That reduction in membership fees facilitated the formation of village reading clubs that belonged to Prosvita. The 1876 revision was also significant because it permitted the formation of affiliate Prosvita societies in the county seats. These were an intermediate tier in a three-tier system—Prosvita in Lviv, the affiliates, and village reading clubs. After 1876 villagers who were members of reading clubs associated with Prosvita could increasingly call upon the executives of the affiliates for guidance, literature, and speakers, instead of referring everything to the central executive in Lviv. There were three such affiliates in 1880, four in 1890, and twenty in 1900.[28]

The original Prosvita organizers chose two methods to spread popular education: 1) collection and publication of ethnographic materials on Ukrainian society, and 2) publication and dissemination of popular literature in vernacular Ukrainian. In 1869 Prosvita published its first item of popular literature, *Zoria, Reader for Village People*, in 2000 copies. It sold out in two weeks. "The whole village knows the contents of *Zoria* (The Star)," and "the children have received *Zoria* with unusual enthusiasm," wrote Fr. Naumovych to the Prosvita executive in 1869.[29] Its popularity convinced Prosvita activists to drop ethnographic efforts temporarily, and to concentrate on popular literature. Prosvita published three more booklets in 1869, with runs of 3000-4000 each, which also sold out rapidly. Mailing each member a Prosvita booklet monthly, as part of his or her regular membership benefits, began in 1877 and continued until 1914. The association published and disseminated 224 booklets between 1869 and 1898:

1869-1878	50 books	447,700 copies
1879-1888	64 books	265,255 copies
1889-1898	110 books	679,200 copies

Between 1877 and 1914, Prosvita published a total of 348 titles in 2,941,115 copies, of which 305 titles in 2,551,265 copies were mailed to members.[30] This total indicates how much more interest there was in Prosvita than the available membership figures alone denote.[31] The popular literature program was one of the most impressive of Prosvita's achievements.

Among the booklets published by Prosvita were those which particularly sought to provide practical knowledge to rural people. Some early publications were entitled *Practical Education for a Peasant Farmer* by I. Bilai (1873), and *The Calendar of the Beekeeper* (1879).[32] Prior to 1893, titles of Prosvita brochures included *Horned Cattle, Hedges and Forests, Small Domestic Fowl, Pig Raising, Cultivation of Barley and Oats, Facts about the Soil, About Field Pests, About Land Books*, and *Flax and Hemp*.[33] Later publications included Dr. Oleskiv's *About Free Lands*,[34] *Gardens, Orchards and Dairying*,[35] and a booklet entitled *How to Care for the Sick* by J. Nevestiuk. All used relatively simple language, and all were inexpensive (Nevestiuk's pamphlet, one of the longer ones with seventy-six pages, was advertised in 1897 at 20 kr).[36] As early as 1877, Prosvita's Ternopil affiliate published *The Beehive*, which was widely used in the Podillian counties along the Zbruch and frequently reprinted.[37]

Prosvita activists undertook to publish other genres, including a new reader and spelling book (*Bukvar*) for elementary schools.[38] The society also published almanacs (*kaliendary*) every year from 1870 onward except for 1871 and 1883-9; a belles-lettres periodical, *Pysmo z Prosvity* (Letter from Prosvita, 1877-9 and 1893-6); and *Chytalnia* (Reading Club), primarily an agricultural-economic journal. Other Prosvita publications prior to 1900 included a series of portraits of Ukrainian writers and activists; maps of Galicia and Bukovyna; various instructions, formularies, and guide books for organizing communal reading clubs, independent credit unions, grain-storage facilities, and libraries; as well as statutes, judicial procedures, circulars, and occasional pamphlets—all in thousands of copies.[39] In short, Prosvita performed a prodigious enlightenment task by providing villagers at low cost, or free of charge, a full range of printed materials in their own language, ranging from the seriously educational to the largely ornamental.

There were legal impediments to involvement by an enlightenment society in matters that were overtly political. However, through interlocking memberships on executives and boards of directors, and through the movement of persons from the society to the writing staff of a newspaper and back again, Prosvita was instrumental in the founding and continuation of such populist newspapers as *Dilo* (Deed), *Batkivshchyna* (Fatherland), and *Svoboda* (Freedom). Prosvita's activist members provided ideas and wrote editorials and articles. Before they broke completely with the populists, Mykhailo Pavlyk served briefly as editor of *Batkivshchyna*, and Ivan Franko wrote a celebrated "Twelve Commandments for Electors."[40] In 1885 some Prosvita members formed a separate Ukrainophile political organization, Narodna Rada (People's

Council), to function as a political lobby group for Ukrainian causes in Galicia.[41] Prosvita was thus not only an enlightenment society, but a veritable network of activities. It was one wing of the Ukrainian national movement, with political as well as educational aims. Indeed, the two cannot be separated, for one of the principal goals of the educational activities was to raise the political consciousness of the Ukrainian population of Galicia and obtain its support for populist national objectives.[42] However, Prosvita's educational work never neglected its aim of bringing literacy and practical knowledge to the villages. Disseminating its publications was a problem, given the transportation and communication networks of Eastern Galicia in the last quarter of the nineteenth century. In its first ten years, and to some extent thereafter, putting Prosvita's publications in the hands of villagers depended largely on the good will of individuals who belonged to the association or supported its ideals. Marketing of the booklets was done through various means available to the Lviv executive and whatever affiliate executives were formed. This is when the earlier *hromada* structure served as a ready network of adherents who would distribute Prosvita's publications. The most logical marketing agents for Prosvita were shopkeepers and booksellers, who could hawk them on market days, at fairs, at religious pilgrimage locations, and at other large gatherings of people.[43] In the mid-1870s a shopkeeper in Zalishchyky acted as agent for Prosvita publications.[44] They also sent free publications to army, hospital, prison, and other libraries, and to church brotherhoods.[45] Reading clubs that became members received donations of books from Prosvita. The society also repeatedly urged political administrators and school inspectors at the county level to buy Prosvita publications and to give them out as awards for merit to villagers and their children.[46]

Between 1875 and 1877 Prosvita had seventy-five agents in Eastern Galicia. The majority, forty, were priests. The others were shopkeepers, booksellers, cantors, and teachers. Other enlightenment organizations' branches also sold Prosvita works.[47] After 1877, when the change in the statute provided for monthly booklets for members, the distribution problems were considerably eased. However, Prosvita continued to send its publications to new reading clubs and libraries. The proud boast, made by a Prosvita member in 1921, does not seem wide of the mark: "There does not exist, in Galician Ukraine, a single Ukrainian organization whose beginning is not connected, by stronger or weaker ties, with Prosvita."[48]

Prosvita was not, however, the only major Ukrainian enlightenment society in Eastern Galicia. The Old Ruthenians established the Mykhailo Kachkovsky Society in 1874 as a counter to Prosvita.[49] Prosvita and the Kachkovsky Society shared many of the same aims.[50] The two societies worked on parallel lines, though each had its own political agenda. Like Prosvita, the Kachkovsky Society was interested in bringing about improvements in literacy and in the economic well-being of Galicia's Ukrainian peasantry. It too promoted lectures, reading clubs, grain-storage facilities, and educational opportunities in Eastern Galicia. It distributed seeds to its members, who were asked to pass some on to their neighbours after the next harvest. It also published educational booklets each month, which cost a mere 10 kr, as well as almanacs, histories and agricultural pamphlets.[51] Among its early publications were titles such as *Cultivation of Hops*, *About the Profitable Use of Wastelands*, and *Cultivation of Corn*.[52] Later, it published inter alia Dr. Oleskiv's *On Emigration*,[53] showing that an author could be published in the same year by both Prosvita and the Kachkovsky Society. Indeed, in the mid-1880s the possibility of joint publication by the two societies was considered.[54]

Fr. Naumovych had been a moving spirit in the founding of the Kachkovsky Society, and wrote educational booklets for it in a series called "Russkaia Chytalnia" (Ruthenian Reading Club).[55] His arrest for treason and conviction for disturbing public order (1882), his imprisonment, emigration to the tsarist empire, and later conversion to Russian Orthodoxy deprived the Old Ruthenian camp and the Kachkovsky Society of a driving force and a very talented writer who "accustomed the peasants to steady reading."[56] In Southern Podillia, Fr. Naumovych's influence appears to have been greatest in the northern districts, which adjoined Skalat county where Naumovych had his parish.[57]

The newspapers *Slovo*, *Russkaia rada* (Ruthenian Council), and *Nauka* (Learning), already established by 1871, came to have the same sort of relationship to the Old Ruthenians as *Batkivshchyna* and others did to the Ukrainophile populists and Prosvita. The Kachkovsky Society also established other periodicals, such as the short-lived *Khliborob* (The Farmer) for agriculturalists (1879).[58] It also sponsored agricultural courses and trade shows, such as the one in Kolomyia in September 1880.[59] By 1890 it had 4,136 members, who paid annual dues of one g each.[60] Like Prosvita, the Kachkovsky Society was organized in three tiers, with headquarters in Lviv, affiliates in county seats, and reading clubs in the villages, but it had rather more organized affiliates in 1890, sixteen.[61] The Kachkovsky Society initially printed more publications than Prosvita did. While its early publications were in the vernacular, using phonic orthography, later they were partially *iazychiie*, which perhaps inhibited their readership.[62] Initially, too, the Kachkovsky Society had greater success establishing or affiliating reading clubs, and Prosvita's reduction in membership fees in the 1870s was, in part, a reaction to the competition, as was Prosvita's provision of booklets to its members.[63] Clearly there was rivalry between the two societies. If the Old Ruthenians published instructions on how to found village institutions, the Ukrainophiles followed suit;[64] if the latter founded artisans' associations, so did the former.[65] Later, there were squabbles about which society had the larger membership.[66]

There were, however, also attempts to collaborate and to present a united front. The Ukrainophile press advertised its rivals' publications and vice versa, and each announced the general meetings of the other's society and carried reports on them.[67] Reading clubs sometimes were members of both societies. Representatives of both societies attended, and were equally acknowledged, at important Ukrainian events in Eastern Galicia, such as the 1880 visit of the emperor to Narodnyi Dim in Lviv.[68]

Prosvita and the Kachkovsky Society were not the only enlightenment societies. Others, however, were much more specialized. Some were more in the nature of incipient professional associations, such as the Ruthenian Pedagogical Association (1881), a Prosvita offshoot.[69] Another society, Narodnyi Dim, by the late nineteenth century was an association with much wealth, but not as profound an influence as the two main enlightenment societies.[70] Two agencies that provided specialized education in the countryside were Narodna Torhivlia (People's Commerce) and the Galician Agricultural Association. For a time in the 1880s, Narodna Torhivlia was associated with the agricultural newspaper *Hospodar i promyshlennyk* (Farmer and Craftsman), but its real cause was the promotion of rural co-operatives.[71] The Galician Agricultural Association was a semi-government agency, supported by public funds, which for many years had been concerned with the well-being of large landowners, but entered the field of popular education in the last two decades of the century. It tried to bring agricultural education to the peasants and organize peasant societies. Although it was under Polish gentry domination, in the 1890s it appears to have tried to reach out to Ukrainian villagers, too.[72]

There is every indication that Prosvita and the Kachkovsky Society reached their target audiences in Southern Podillia. Books were read in the villages of Southern Podillia even before there were reading halls, and evidently also "read aloud," so that they reached a wider audience than the literate.[73] Books, newspapers, and reading halls reinforced the education received in elementary schools (children too "get more taste for reading and learning and do not forget what they learned at school"),[74] and provided new knowledge. The rivalry between Prosvita and the Kachkovsky Society redounded to the advantage of practical education in the countryside. Probably more materials were published than if there had been only one organization. More efforts were made to reach out to the villages simply because of the competitive situation, and under these conditions villagers could benefit from the activities of the enlightenment societies to a greater extent. Many reading clubs belonged to both societies, and received books and other materials from each. During the period 1880-1900, Prosvita appears to have prevailed, at least in the Southern Podillian villages: in Borshchiv county many reading clubs, initially members of the Kachkovsky Society, changed their affiliation to Prosvita.[75]

Both Kachkovsky and Prosvita in their publications encouraged their member reading clubs to found co-operative shops, savings and loan societies, and grain storage facilities. After the change in its statute in 1891 provided for more emphasis on community development work, Prosvita's reading clubs increasingly came to house such facilities. A precipitating factor in the growth of village loan societies was the collapse of some major credit associations in the 1880s, specifically the Rustical Bank (1884) and the *Obshche rolniche-kredytove zavedenie* (General Agricultural Credit Association) (1886).[76] These associations had loaned money to peasants and when they collapsed, the loans were called in, which caused great hardship for many of their clients, and in some cases forced auctions of land.[77] Thereafter, peasants were not eager to trust their financial affairs to organizations other than ones they themselves could control. There had been loan societies associated with reading clubs prior to the mid-1880s, such as those in Kolodribka, Trybukhivtsi, and Tovstenke,[78] but in the late 1880s and 1890s many more were formed in the reading clubs of Southern Podillia, for example in Kudryntsi in 1894 and Sukhostav in 1898.[79]

Village shops associated with reading clubs were established throughout the countryside as well, assisted by the enlightenment societies. An additional factor that encouraged the growth in their numbers was the founding of Narodna Torhivlia, many of whose activities were directed by Prosvita and Kachkovsky society members. It supplied village shops with wholesale goods at a discount to members. New shops emerged in the 1880s and 1890s throughout the region, for example, in Samolusky, Skala, Zazdrist, and Shuparka.[80] Kozachchyna (Borshchiv county) bought a tavern from Prince Leo Sapieha and converted it to a shop.[81] By the end of 1898, Narodna Torhivlia boasted that 549 village shops in Galicia were working with it and there were fifteen warehouses, one in each of its affiliate towns.[82] Grain storage facilities were not a new phenomenon in Southern Podillia, but after 1880 they were associated more frequently with reading clubs. There were reports of new ones being started up in the 1890s, for example in Tovstenke, Romanivka, Bychkivtsi, and Ulashkivtsi.[83] In Romanivka, the grain-storage facility served 105 people.[84]

Another activity that arose from the new economic awareness in the countryside, and was connected to the enlightenment societies, was the insuring of buildings. By law, all schools, churches, and parish buildings had to be insured. Various insurance companies within and outside Galicia had been utilized for this purpose, but in 1892 a Ukrainian insurance organization, Dnister, was founded. Many of the founders were associated with Prosvita. Within a very short time, Dnister agents were active in all counties, and insurance on private buildings became more widespread.[85] By the end of its first year, Dnister had sold 15,505 policies in Galicia.[86] Hleshchava (Terebovlia county) claimed that the "blue marker" on a building denoting its Dnister insurance coverage was on half the houses of that village.[87]

The enlightenment societies not only spurred existing organizations into greater activity, but also indirectly contributed to the emergence of several new economic organizations, such as Dnister's Credit Association[88] and Silskyi

Число 21. Львів дня 25. мая (7. червня) 1900. Річник IV.

Виходить що тижня в четвер. Редакція і адміністрація: Львів, ул. Бічна-Крижова ч. 5. — Рекламації вільні від оплати.

СВОБОДА

Передплата на цілий рік стоїть 4 корони. За авонси платить ся 20 сотиків від стрічки. Надісланих рукописів не звертає ся.

Політичне, просьвітне і господарске письмо для народу.

Видавець і одвічальний редактор: Д-р Володимир Охримович.

Робім довірочні збори!

Звичайно веде ся у нас осьвідомлюванє народу на публичних повітових вічах, на які кождий може прийти і на них слово забирати та про які треба дати знати що найменче три дни наперед до староства, котре звичайно висилає на збори свого комісаря. Та єще инший рід зборів, про які якось між нашими селянами мало-де чути, а які є дуже важні та могли би нашому народови віддати немалу прислугу. Той другий рід зборів — се „довірочні збори". На такі збори вільно явити ся тільки тому, кого письменно запрошено. Про довірочні збори нігде наперед публично не оголошує ся, ані до староства про них не треба давати знати. Такі „довірочні збори" є дозволені параграфом 2-им закону о зборах з 15 падолиста 1867 р. (Вістник державних законів ч. 135). В тім параграфі сказано, що до староства треба тільки тоді давати знати про збори, коли ті збори не є довірочні то значить не є обмежені на самі запрошені особи.

Як хто хоче такі „довірочні збори" урядити, то мусить розіслати письменні запрошеня особисто до кождого з тих людей, яких хоче мати на зборах. На тім запрошеню має бути написано так: „До п. (...імя і прізвище запрошеного...) в (...назва місця...) Сим маю честь запросити Вас на довірочні збори, які відбудуть ся на основі § 2-ого закону о зборах з 15 падолиста 1867 В. з. д. Ч. 135. дня (... день місяць і рік...) о годині (... цифра) в домі (...імя властителя...) під числом (...цифра...) (Дата-себ-то місцевість і день виставленого запрошеня) (Підпис того, що запрошує)."

Як видите з того, в запрошеню мусить бути виразно сказано, що збори будуть довірочні. Мусить бути докладно означене місце, день і година збору і мусить бути дата виставленя і власноручний підпис того, що запрошує. Крім того той, що скликує довірочні збори, мусить мати спис всіх запрошених на аркуші паперу і мусить знати особисто кождого запрошеного гостя а як кількох скликує довірочні збори, то кождий з них повинен знати свою пайку запрошених так, щоби не було ні одного такого запрошеного, котрого би бодай оден із запрошуючих не знав. На довірочнім зборі не сьміє бути ніхто, хто би не мав при собі запрошеня від аранжерів (себ то запрошуючих) збору. Тому, заким збори зачнуть ся, коли ще льокаль зборів порожний, повинен хтось із запрошуючих стануть при вході і пускати тільки тих, що покажуть важне запрошене. Так само в часї зборів мусить хтось при дверех стояти, аби хто незапрошений не вкрутив ся. Хоч про довірочні збори до староства не дає ся знати, ані староство не має права до них свого комісаря висилати — то всеж буває так, що часом староство довідає ся про такі збори і вишле там свого комісаря, аби вилапати, чи збори не публичні. Такий комісар мусить бути в урядовім мундурі і тільки тоді пускає ся його до середини. Він має право, казати собі предложити лісту запрошених і може потім контролювати, чи всі мають запрошеня та чи запрошуючі знають запрошених і чи нема кого, запрошеного хтоби не був на лісті або був без запрошеня. Запрошень ані ліст комісареви до рук не треба давати але тільки показати, най подивить ся. Крім комісаря нікого більше на збори не пускає ся ані жандарма ані нікого більше і для того підчас ревізиї комісаря треба двері добре пильнувати. Як комісар своє діло зробить, а нічого неправильного не знайде, мусить сейчас вийти а не сьміє лишати ся і слухати, що будуть говорити і радити. Якже знайде кого без запрошеня, або такого, що його ніхто не знає, то може збори розвязати. Інакше зборів розвязувати не сьміє!

Отже на таких довірочних зборах, де самі свої, можна щиро і отверто говорити, можна всю правду висказати, бо нема комісаря, що гамував би кожде острійше слово. Такі збори мають велику вагу — і наші селяне повинні в кождім селї часто їх устроювати. Збори такі можна скликати або ліпше спросити до чиєї небудь хати (але не до читальні!). Той що спрошує, може переказати людям, над чим буде рада і може назначити головних бесїдників (референтів). Можна на довірочні збори запрошувати письменно і людей з кількох сіл або і з цілого краю.

Ми заохочуємо наших селян, аби пробували самі скликувати такі довірочні збори, бо з них ще більша користь, як із віч. А як селяне з'організують ся через довірочні збори то їх і саме пекло не переможе, а не то польські пани та старости.

Тому, братя селяне! Користайте з законів! Збирайте ся на довірочні збори і там радьте о всїх справах, що вас обходять: радьте над порядками в громадї, повітї, краю і державі, радьте над поліпшенем Вашої долї над тим, що Вас кривдить і чого Вам треба. Завяжіть в кождій громадї комітет і той най робить довірочні збори. Радьте ся! організуйте ся! агітуйте самі, бо аж тодї стане твердо хлопська справа, як самі хлопи будуть собі провідниками! Не спіть! не дрімайте! рук не закладайте! бо в організациї, в карности і в єдности ваша сила і ваша побіда!

Голоси селян о »Русскомъ Словѣ.«

II. (Письмо Івана Семчія з Ловіннн).

Прошу Сьвітлої Редакциї помістити в Свободї мій відклик на письмо якогось Ілії Боруха в „Руском Слові" ч. 20. з 11/5 1900., бо чоловік аж дрожить, коли прочитає таку мерзку брехню на чоловіка, котрий з тілом і з душею офірує ся за нарід, а той нарід, як Юда Іскаріот, не тільки, щоби продав свого учителя, але за его жертву ще его публично ганьбить. Хто в нашої околиці не знає отця Пеленьского, який то труженик на ниві народної просьвіти!? Хто его знає, той може безпечно плюнути в очи якомусь там Ілії Боруховн „селянинови з над Дністра" за его плюгаву писанину „до братів селян". Він каже, що він нам рідний брат з діда прадіда; він просить нас, щоби ми не слухали „лживих пророків!" Певно, що не будем слухати, але таких, як він сам і як „Русское Слово". А що до о. Пеленьского з Книгинич, тоби сьмо жадали від пана Боруха, може би наперед переконав ся о роботї о. Пеленьского, може би пійшов по его місиях, як духовних так сьвіцких, та вдарив ся в груди, що до „Русского Слова" писати не буде.

Пане Борух! Ви відки взяли ся такий великий противник фонетики?! Чи Ви були коли на утрені в церкві, як сьпівають „всякоє диханіе да хвалить Господа"? Так і всякоє писаніє може ся писати на хвалу Божу, чи є в нім „Ъ" чи нема. А чому Ви пане Борух не орете тим плугом, що Ваш пра-прадід орав, але орете новим теперішним? То також лживий „пророк", що его вигадав — а Ви ним орете! То не справедливо: сами себе посуджуєте, бо старого ся тримаєте, а за нове хватаєте.

А що Ви, п. Борух, такі дурниці пишете о „кирилиці", о св. Кирилі і Методию? Видко, що „Русское Слово" вже цілком затуманило Вам голову! Ви гадаєте що „Рус. Слово" пише „кирилицею"? Та Ви хиба не бачили церковних книг і церковного письма! Отже тото письмо, в церковних книгах, острокінчасте і ломане, називає ся „кирилиця", а тото письмо, яким друкує ся „Русское Слово" більше заокруглене то є „гражданка". „Русское Слово" все хвалить ся, що воно твердо тримає ся старого і ганьбить українців, що вони „запродали азбуку". А чого-ж „Русское Слово" змінило і зрадило стару азбуку? чого оно не друкує ся кирилицею лише гражданкою? „Русское Слово" все говорить на „куцую" фонетику, все ганьбить українців що викинули ъ, ы, ѣ, а чого-ж „Русское Слово" тай всї москвофіли повикидали в своїх книжках старорускі букви ѯ, ѱ, ѵ, ѕ, ѧ, ѡ, ѫ, ѹ, є? Та-ж тоті всї букви належать до руской азбуки! А чи видно їх в „Русскомъ Словѣ"?

Коли Ви такі тверді, то дивно чому „Русское Слово" не пише язиком московским, як от „Тарас Бульба;" бо то якось не добре, щоби бути „таким твердим в писку" а мягким наріччем писати. Як з того всього видко, то Ви найгірше баламутите нарід! Кажете, що Шевченко не писав, щоби нарід ділив ся на партиї! То правда — але Шевченко писав також, щоби серед народу не було здрадників. Скажіть, за котрий нарід страдав Шевченко, — за Москву чи за Україну? Скажіть сами, хто его переслідував, — чи не пажерлива Москва, до котрої ви нас манпте, бо-сьте сами сьліпі, а нас хочете водити за ніс. Отдайте ся ліпше до операциї, най вам з очей здоймуть московску полуду! А чи не за Вас то, чи не за москвофілів, писав Шевченко:

А тим часом перевертнї
Нехай підростають
Та поможуть Москалеви
Господарювати,
Та з матери полатану
Сорочку здіймати!....
Помагайте недолюдки,
Матір катувати!

Front page of *Svoboda*, 7 June 1900

НАРОДНА ТОРГОВЛЯ

у Львовѣ (въ каменици Народного Дому),

въ Станиславовѣ, Перемышли, Тернополи, Дрогобычи и Коломыи

поручае:

Для Пч. Братствъ церковныхъ.

Свѣтло церковне просто зъ фабрики въ скринкахъ, почавши вôдъ 30 кільо I-а по 94, II. по 86 кр. за 1 кільо, окрôмъ транспорту. Скринка не зачисляе ся. (Замовляти просимо черезъ центральный Зарядъ у Львовѣ.)

Вôскъ чистый по 1 зр. 60 кр. за кільо.

Кадило королѣвске по 80 кр.; бурштинъ по 90 кр.; ладанъ по 1 зр. 20 кр. за кільо.

Вино по 50, 60, 70 кр. за літру и высше въ барылкахъ 4-літровыхъ. (Барылка зачисляе ся 50 кр., за звернену платимо 45 кр.)

Для Пч. Зарядôвъ шкôльныхъ.

Зошиты (скриптуры), сотка по 58 и 140 кр.

Оловцѣ, тузинъ по 8 и 18 кр.

Пера, пуделко почавши вôдъ 23 кр.

Крейда, кільо 20 кр.

Писальцѣ, сотка по 30 и 35 кр.

Таблички, тузинъ по 50, 60, 70, 89, 90, 100 и 110 кр.

Ручки, тузинъ 4 кр. и высше.

Губки, одно дека 10 кр.

и всякї иншї приборы до писаня.

Для Пч. Господарѣвъ.

Косы, по 25, 36 и 40 кр. за штуку.

Серпы, по 30 кр.

Рѣзаки до простыхъ скринокъ, по 56 кр. за штуку.

Для крамницъ.

Чай звычайный, за фунтъ 1 зр. 30 кр.

Чай караванный въ пачкахъ „Народнои Торговлѣ": 1/4 фунта по 60, 70, 80, 90 и 100 кр.; 1/8 фунта за половину повысшои цѣны. Опустъ 15%.

Мыло звычайне, за кільо 27 кр.

Фарбка табличкова до бѣлизны, кільо по 1 зр.

Солонина, кільо 68 кр.

Рыжъ, при замовленю 50 кільо по 16 до 17 зр. вôдъ 100 кільо. (Высылае ся зъ Перемышля.)

Шниръ до чобôтъ въ пачкахъ по 16, 12, 8 и 6 штукъ; за пачку 24 кр.

Шварцъ Nr. I. по 1 зр., II. по 1 зр. 20 кр., II 1/2 по 1 зр. 50 кр., а Nr. III. по 2 зр. Опустъ 10%.

Крохмаль, кільо по 28 кр.

Мастило до возôвъ, при замовленю 50 кільо 12 зр.; при меншôмъ 14 зр. вôдъ 100 кільо. (2—17)

Выдае и вôдповѣдае за редакцію Василь Нагôрный. — Зъ друкарнѣ Товариства им. Шевченка.

Advertisement for Narodnia Torhivlia (*Batkivshchyna*, 25 June 1886)

Hospodar (Village Farmer) in the late 1890s.[89] In 1896 Prosvita hired its own agronomist, Vasyl Korol, who travelled throughout the rural areas, wherever there were Prosvita reading clubs, to give lectures on agronomic themes, to assist farmers with any specific agricultural problems raised at these visits, and to give them general advice. Korol visited nineteen communes in Borshchiv in the first year.[90] The enlightenment societies and their offshoots thus made major direct contributions to economic progress in Southern Podillia.

The Press

There is an obvious connection between the growth of a more literate public and the growth of a readership for periodicals, newspapers, and books. The number and secular orientation of the Ukrainian-language press in Galicia grew considerably after 1880, even though some publications were short-lived. However, there are no reliable data on the circulation of the press and only fragmentary information about its distribution.

With the fading of hopes unleashed by the 1848 social and constitutional reforms and the return of absolutism in Austria, the activity of the Ukrainian press had remained low-key. Most of the ten new titles that appeared in the 1850s survived less than one year each; only two continued into the 1860s.[91] There was a renewed spurt of activity in the somewhat freer 1860s, and by 1870 the number of Ukrainian periodicals had increased to twelve, ten of which were published in Lviv, and one each in Kolomyia and Budapest. Nevertheless, a real "community" press in the Ukrainian language was still in its embryonic stage in 1870, and only the Old Ruthenian *Slovo*, which began publication in 1861, really aspired to this status.[92] The other periodicals catered mainly to urban intellectuals. By 1880 there were ten Ukrainian periodicals published in Lviv, two in Stanyslaviv, one in Kolomyia, and one in Vienna.

The really dramatic change in the periodical press, both in number of titles in print and in variety of content, took place in the period 1880 to 1900. The education of Eastern Galician Ukrainian peasants was linked directly to both these phenomena. The Ukrainian-language press, particularly in its didactic capacity, contributed significantly to the development of a more forward-looking Ukrainian peasantry. Quantitatively, there were fluctuations, as some periodicals ceased publication and others began, and as some changed from weekly publication to bi- or tri-weekly or, in the case of *Dilo*, to daily. The Ukrainian press in Austria-Hungary increased from 14 titles in 1880 to 26 in 1890 and 38 in 1900. In 1890, 17 of the titles were published in Lviv, 2 in Przemyśl, and one each in Kolomyia and Berezhany, for a total of 21 in Galicia. In addition, 2 were published in Chernivtsi and 3 in Vienna. In 1900, 32 Ukrainian-language newspapers and periodicals were published in Galicia itself (19 in Lviv), 3 in Bukovyna, 2 in Hungary, and one in Vienna.

Not all periodicals had a pronounced political orientation, but the growing competition for support between Old Ruthenians and Ukrainophiles in the 1870s and 1880s helped to stimulate the growth in the number of publications. In the 1890s the Radical press further augmented the numbers. Initially, the Old Ruthenians, with their superior resources, had the upper hand. Fr. I. Naumovych was instrumental in founding not only *Slovo* but also, in 1869-70, *Russkaia rada* (designed for the peasantry) and *Nauka*.[93] Through their control of the Stauropegial Press in Lviv and the enlightenment society Halytsko-Ruska Matytsia, they played a major role in sponsoring other publications. The Ukrainophiles, too, endeavoured to publish popular literature and periodical press titles. Whatever its effects on national feeling may have been, competition between the major groups led to the publication of more journals, including weekly newspapers, which strove to bring secular knowledge to Eastern Galician villages and thus served as a "liberating force" in the transition from a traditional to a more modern society. All newspapers were subject to censorship, but none incurred the wrath of the authorities as often as the radical press of the 1890s. Circulation figures for the various papers are not known, though Franko is reputed to have said, at a time when *Narod* (The People) had 251 subscribers, that "for such a heretical newspaper, it was even too many."[94] The more mainstream Old Ruthenian and Ukrainophile newspapers had significantly larger circulations.

Newspapers were most frequently delivered to rural regions by mail, since Austria had inexpensive rates for newspaper service. *Batkivshchyna* had several accounts of postmasters being unwilling to pass on copies to subscribers because either they had not yet finished reading the paper or they considered the contents subversive. It is clear, nonetheless, from reports by or about reading clubs, and from other fragmentary evidence, that newspapers were received in the Southern Podillian villages. The evidence is perhaps clearest in the case of the populist *Batkivshchyna*, with its regular reports on village activities contributed by village people themselves, but there is no reason to think that the Old Ruthenian *Russkaia rada* did not also have significant circulation. Most of the evidence that is available concerns reading hall subscriptions, and only occasionally are individual subscribers identified. Lev Iasinchuk's father in Bilobozhnytsia, a "progressive farmer," was an atypical Ukrainian villager. At one time or another he subscribed to *Batkivshchyna*, *Russkoe slovo* (The Ruthenian Word), *Prosveshchenie* (Enlightenment), *Sion* (Zion), *Nauka*, *Hospodar i promyshlennyk*, *Svoboda*, *Dilo*, *Poslannyk* (Messenger), and *Dobri rady* (Good Advice).[95] The short-lived paper for children, *Priiatel ditei* (The Children's Friend), with its morally uplifting content, included among its initial subscribers the Greek Catholic priests of Nivra, Ozeriany, and Sapohiv (Borshchiv county), Darakhiv (Terebovlia), and Uhrynkivtsi (Zalishchyky).[96] The Borshchiv county school council bought a one-year subscription to *Hospodar i promyshlennyk* for the Sapohiv elementary school; this may not have been an isolated example of subscriptions for schools. A villager from Zhezhava wanted to receive the radical *Hromadskyi holos* (Community Voice), because it was the best and "it bothers the priest."[98]

Reading halls normally received two or more papers. In 1884 Kolodribka's subscribed to *Batkivshchyna*, *Russkaia rada*, and *Hospodar i promyshlennyk*.[99] In early 1887 the reading club in Strusiv subscribed to both Ukrainian and Polish periodicals.[100] In 1889 the reading club in Krovinka (Terebovlia county), took *Batkivshchyna* and *Zoria*; it decided not to take *Russkaia rada* because it was too much like *Batkivshchyna* and because some of its language was difficult to understand.[101] The reading club in Ustia Iepyskopske received *Batkivshchyna* and *Russkoe slovo* in 1890.[102] In 1891 the reading club in Hermakivka (Borshchiv county), subscribed to *Batkivshchyna*, *Dilo*, and *Narodnyi chasopys* (People's Chronicle), a semi-official account of parliamentary proceedings in Lviv and Vienna, with some texts of laws.[103] Mykhailivka's reading club in 1894 had *Batkivshchyna*, *Chytalnia*, and *Poslannyk*.[104] *Poslannyk*, a clerical paper, was also taken in 1894 by the reading club in Budzaniv, along with *Dilo* and *Narodnyi chasopys*.[105] Also in 1894, the reading clubs in Kudryntsi (Borshchiv county) and Bychkivtsi (Chortkiv county) took *Narodnyi chasopys*, *Batkivshchyna*, *Chytalnia*, and *Poslannyk*.[106] The Skala reading club in 1897 subscribed to *Svoboda* and other papers.[107]

It is difficult to gauge how much effect polemical articles about political issues, which appeared most salient to urban intellectuals and politicians, had among the village populations of Southern Podillia.[108] They were certainly interested in the news from the villages that was so assiduously reported in *Batkivshchyna*, and to a lesser extent by its competitors and its successor, *Svoboda*. The fact that village news was deemed sufficiently important to appear in weekly newspapers published in the Land capital, Lviv, probably helped to raise the self-image of the rural communities. The fact that peasants had village accomplishments to report, whether openings of new schools and reading halls or cultural events such as choir and dramatic performances,[109] both indicated that life in the rural areas was not static and served as an example to other villagers who had not yet become active.

At election times, newspaper columns would be devoted to the issues and to exhortations to vote.[110] The wider world, too, was regularly brought to the villages by the newspapers, which reported on Galician, Austrian, and international affairs. The mental horizons of the rural population were being broadened. Their involvement in the political process and the newspapers' explanations of this process and the issues involved had an educative effect. So did their participation in village affairs and newspaper reports of this. Important steps in the political socialization process were being taken, almost unnoticed, and that was enhanced by the popular press.

Newspapers gave advice on the censuses and on many other things that may be subsumed under the name "civic education." At times the articles were explicitly didactic. *Batkivshchyna* sometimes gave practical advice, but the more specialized agricultural journals, *Hospodar i promyshlennyk* in particular, gave extensive advice on practical matters. *Hospodar i promyshlennyk* provided a veritable education for peasants, often complete with diagrams, on such topics as the planting and cultivation of crops, drainage, the need for fertilizers, the care of animals, horticulture, and beekeeping. It also carried the market prices of grains, thereby ensuring that this information was widely known.[111] There were other specialist journals too, such as *Uchytel* (The Teacher) for educators, *Chasopys pravnycha* (The Legal Gazette) for those interested in legal matters, *Dzvinok* (The Bell) for children, *Lvivsko-arkhiieparkhiialni vidomosty* (The Lviv Archeparchial News) for those interested in ecclesiastical matters, and *Misionar* (The Missionary) for those interested in more general religious matters. For Ukrainian literary and scholarly circles there were *Zapysky naukovoho tovarystva Shevchenka* (Proceedings of the Shevchenko Scientific Society), *Besida* (Discourse), and *Literaturno-naukovyi vistnyk* (Literary-Scientific Herald). While there is no direct evidence of their circulation in Southern Podillia, no doubt they informed the intelligentsia of the region.

Polish publications also circulated in Southern Podillia. The Strusiv reading club subscribed to both the Ukrainian and Polish press. This reading club was unusual in that in the 1870s and 1880s it was a mixed-language club, but it may not have been the only one. Moreover, *Batkivshchyna*, on at least one occasion, advertised new Polish titles that were beginning publication.[112] Polish populist publications had objectives that, in some respects, were not dissimilar from the Ukrainian press. They, too, wished to enlighten the peasantry and some Ukrainians did read them: "When I read your newspaper [*Przyjaciel ludu* (The Friend of the People)] my heart was stirred at how educational a paper it was for villagers, farmers, poor people."[113] Publications from the nearby Russian Empire also entered the region (though not in the Ukrainian language, whose use in newspapers and journals was forbidden there), but it is not known whether any did so from the United States (*Ameryka*, *Ruske Slovo* (Ruthenian Word), *Novyi Svit* (The New World), and *Svoboda*). There can, however, be no doubt that the Galician Ukrainian press circulated widely and reached large numbers of people. Besides those who personally subscribed, there were others who availed themselves of the opportunity to read newspapers at the priest's or teacher's house[114] or at the reading clubs which sprang up during the years 1880-1900 all over Southern Podillia. They also reached the "ersatz-literacy" group,[115] comprised of those who had newspapers and other publications read to them in the various reading clubs.

The press in a region that is modernizing has been described as:

> a liberating force which breaks the bonds of distance and isolation. By bringing what is distant near, and making what is strange understandable, the media can bridge the transition between traditional and modern society.[116]

Given all these opportunities for the printed word to spread and the explicitly informative, not to say didactic, content of many publications, the press was a liberating force in Southern Podillia, which was educational and modernizing in function. It certainly extended the breadth and depth of that society's knowledge.

Reading Clubs

The Austrian Fundamental Laws of 1867 gave greater freedom of association at much the same time as the younger, secular intelligentsia, which drew inspiration from the Ukrainian populists in tsarist Russia (especially Taras Shevchenko and his works), formed student study circles (*Hromady*) in some county towns of Eastern Galicia. However, these were still elitist and self-serving, not directed at assisting the spread of education among the peasantry.[117] In the 1870s, however, formation of the reading clubs of the two enlightenment societies began, mostly on the initiative of the clergy. Many Greek Catholic priests who founded Kachkovsky Society reading clubs subscribed to the Old Ruthenian press established by their colleague, Fr. Naumovych— *Slovo*, *Russkaia rada*, and *Nauka*—which constituted the bulk of the popular press until 1879-80. They initiated reading clubs which "preserved for the later reading clubs that portion of the literate Ukrainian villagers and townspeople who, having something to read, didn't forget how to read as others had done."[118]

The reading club, in its simplest form, was a gathering of people for the purpose of conveying knowledge by having literate people read aloud to others who could not read. Meetings of this kind had their precedent in the meetings of church brotherhoods which, in the late nineteenth century, still played an educational role in the community, but in a religious sense.[119] There also were models for reading clubs among other peoples of the Austro-Hungarian monarchy, for example, the Czechs, Serbs, and Austrian Germans.[120] While the reading clubs of the last decades of the nineteenth century resembled earlier institutions, they had a new dimension, for they had access to the periodical press, with its news from other villages, regions, and countries. Whereas the "ancestors" of the reading club had emphasized knowledge of a more static kind—religious stories, morality lessons drawn from the Bible—these clubs were fueled by a dramatically larger and different type of publication, which offered new information and insights to its participants.

There were two types of reading clubs. Independent reading clubs were not affiliated with a formal voluntary enlightenment association but might be loosely connected with the village church brotherhood or sobriety brotherhood. Affiliated reading clubs were members of the two major enlightenment societies of Eastern Galicia. The Prosvita reading clubs, like all the organizations founded by Ukrainophile or populist activists, carried mostly Ukrainophile periodicals, and held programs appropriate to the Ukrainophile cause; Kachkovsky Society reading clubs followed the tenets of the Old Ruthenian group. Whether a reading club was independent or affiliated, it served as a "multiplier" of knowledge.

Prior to 1880 there were only a few reading clubs in Southern Podillia. Reading clubs have been positively identified at Ivanivka (1870) and Strusiv (1872) (Terebovlia county), Ivankivtsi (1874) (Borshchiv county), Kolodribka (1874) (Zalishchyky county), and in the town of Husiatyn (in or before 1875). It is very probable that the local priests played leading roles in their establishment.[121] In the early 1880s, only two further reading clubs appear to have been founded, in the towns of Kopychyntsi and Terebovlia (1882).[122] Thereafter, the reading-club movement spread rapidly (see Appendix V). As reported in *Batkivshchyna* alone, thirty-five reading clubs were formed in Borshchiv, Husiatyn, and Terebovlia counties between 1884 and 1890. Another big push to establish reading clubs took place in the 1890s, especially in Zalishchyky county, which had lagged behind, where ten were established in 1897. The forty-eight Ukrainian reading clubs in Southern Podillia in 1890 had grown to ninety-five by the end of 1898.

Some reading clubs that might have started as independents became members of one or both of the major enlightenment societies. By the middle of 1897 Prosvita claimed sixty-seven reading clubs in Southern Podillia, of which twenty-three were in Borshchiv county, which made that county third among Galician counties with Prosvita reading clubs.[123] By 1907, counting only reading clubs that belonged to Prosvita, there were 58 in Borshchiv, 45 in Chortkiv, 54 in Husiatyn, 30 in Terebovlia, and 49 in Zalishchyky.[124] Some of the first reading clubs in the five counties initially were associated with the Kachkovsky Society and then became Prosvita affiliates in the 1880s and 1890s.[125]

Organizers of the earliest reading clubs thought of them as places for the young, but later organizers stressed their adult education function. Compulsory education provided more sustained reading experience for youth, but adults were also increasingly eager to learn of the greater world through readings at the club. The initiation and operation of a reading club was a reflection of this change in character. Interested individuals normally approached the intelligentsia of the village about collecting, buying, borrowing, and reading books and periodicals, as these became more accessible in the countryside.[126] While the right to meet and form associations was recognized in principle by the authorities, the initiators of a club had to apply to the governor's office for an official charter, which could be refused if the purposes of a club seemed threatening to the state. Once such a charter was obtained, a founding meeting could be held. At this meeting, officers were elected who were then responsible for the management of the club.[127] Some officials hindered the establishment of clubs in the five counties,[128] but many local officials were sympathetic and helpful.[129]

The prime activity of the club was reading aloud, followed by discussion of the reading, but there was informal conversation about news and information, too, and literate persons might read by themselves. In the later years of the century, other activities began to be centred in the reading club, such as choral singing, amateur drama circles, and bands. There were certain advantages to affiliation with one of the enlightenment societies. The society (sometimes reading clubs belonged to both) would usually send free books to start the library; later, the membership publications would be sent to the club, usually every month. Some functions were prescribed by the society's charter. For instance, Prosvita member clubs were supposed to hold commemorative evenings for Taras Shevchenko, in addition to other activities which were determined by the membership, such as general evenings of verse and song, a lecture, or hosting a travelling theatrical group.[130]

Reading clubs were the hub of activity in Southern Podillian villages, for both adults and children, in the 1880s and 1890s. Most clubs were founded by clergymen, for example Fr. Hudyk in Trybukhivtsi (Husiatyn county),[131] Fr. Savchynsky in Hermakivka (Borshchiv county),[132] and Fr. Balytsky in Kolodribka (Borshchiv county).[133] Sometimes other village intelligentsia were responsible, as in Volkivtsi (Borshchiv county), which was formed through the efforts of I. Kovalchak and M. Savchak. Kovalchak also donated his house for the use of the reading club.[134] Occasionally villagers themselves formed a reading club, for instance, the clubs in Ozeriany and Tovstenke.[135]

Opening or founding meetings were special occasions in the life of the village, and were reported in some detail in the press. They usually began with a mass. In Kryvenke, in 1885, when the reading club began, Fr. Kotliarchuk held a mass at which the church was "filled to overflowing."[136] At the founding of the club in Hermakivka, Fr. Savchynsky concelebrated mass with a guest priest from Zalissia.[137] The village of Ozeriany made the occasion even more solemn by having a three-day mission prior to the founding meeting. The choir from Skala sang at the mission services, and Prince Leo Sapieha not only attended the mission, but also assisted the club with a donation of 100 g. Two of the missionaries stayed for the meeting and held a special service for the club at the request of the villagers.[138]

After the religious festivities were over, club members went en masse to the reading club—usually somebody's house in the 1880s but in the 1890s more frequently a separate building constructed by the reading-club members for this purpose. Decoration of the meeting room was not uncommon, with greenery and portraits of the emperor and empress, the saints, Shevchenko, and other "heroes" of the reading club.[139] The founding meetings were quite straightforward, with speeches of welcome and inspiration by the principal founder, followed by the signing up of new members and the election of officers. Women could and did become members of reading clubs, which was something of a novelty in village life.[140] Dues and donations were collected and acknowledged; decisions were made about subscriptions; and donations of books from enlightenment societies and private donors were announced.[141]

Special guests might attend the founding and anniversary meetings of a club. They could be people from neighbouring villages, intelligentsia from the county town, clergy, local government officials or administrative personnel. At the celebration meeting of the Kolodribka club, not only were the former priest and his wife in attendance but they were made honorary members.[142] Count Baworowski, the local squire, was made an honorary member of the reading club at Strusiv (Terebovlia county).[143] In Ozeriany the reeve, who was also a member of the County Council, was honored in this manner.[144] People at times came considerable distances to these events. The Volkivtsi reading club hosted people from the villages of Pylypche, Ustia Iepyskopske, Horoshova, Ivanie Puste, and Zalissia. When a club was founded in Ustia Iepyskopske a few months later there were guests from Bilche, Kolodribka, Hermakivka, Zalissia, Ivanie Puste, and Volkivtsi. Rosokhach (Chortkiv county) had guests from Uhryn and Iaholnytsia Stara; Hermakivka hosted the teacher from Zalissia, Hrushkevych. There were people from Ilavche and Khorostkiv to celebrate the Hleshchava founding.[145]

Particularly festive was the opening of a new building for the reading club in the town of Kopychyntsi. The new lawyer in Chortkiv, A. Horbachevsky, and other people from Chortkiv attended.[146] Budzaniv entertained the "local intelligentsia, the priest and their families, Judge Iosyf Kulchytsky and people from Verbivtsi, Kobylovoloky, Romanivka and Mohylnytsia." Tsyhany in Borshchiv had as its guests Dr. M. Dorundiak (one of the few Ukrainian lawyers in Southern Podillia) and Dr. R. Iarosevych (one of the few Ukrainian medical doctors there, and a Reichsrat deputy). Sometimes the eminent visitors gave a speech about the aims of reading clubs; Iarosevych spoke about human progress. These speeches would usually emphasize the need for education, as well as for village co-operatives, shops, and loan societies.[147] After the formal part of the meeting was completed, a festive communal meal was shared, followed by singing, dancing, and entertainment. The choirs of the Uhryn and Bile reading clubs, for example, performed at the founding meeting of the Rosokhach reading club.[148]

Not all villagers welcomed the founding of reading clubs. Some people resented them and some officials in villages charged illegal taxes on them. A letter from Shchytivtsi (Zalishchyky county) complained that while the former priest, Fr. Bodnarchuk, had been active in the enlightenment of the villagers, the new priests were "buddies of the local squire" and, like him, did not welcome the reading club.[149] The reeve of Ustia Iepyskopske, Ivan Fochak, opposed the founding of that village's reading club,[150] but reading clubs as a rule had the full support of organizations and the press. Narodna Rada, the political organization of the populists, wrote a petition to the state on behalf of reading clubs, which claimed they were being forced to pay income tax although they were clearly non-profit associations.[151] *Batkivshchyna* advised actual or potential reading club members:

> We will not only respond immediately to your questions regarding community affairs, but we ask you to turn to us without hesitation for advice and explanation in all instances of something being unclear, or when you are helpless in some way regarding your reading club.

The newspaper then explained how to apply for a charter for the club and how to conduct the founding meeting.[152] The enlightenment societies provided speakers for the founding and other meetings on special topics such as agriculture, science, economics and history. Once a club was launched its members met at intervals for their reading activities. Bychkivtsi reported that its club met seventeen times through the year, mostly on Saturday and Sunday evenings. Other clubs met on Sunday afternoons or holidays, but the most intense period was in the winter, when there was less farm work to be done (Kudryntsi's met three times per week in winter).[153] Activities such as rehearsals by choirs, bands, and drama groups came to be regular events in the reading club's hall. In the Terebovlia town reading club, Fr. Savula established a choir in 1887 that "sang from notes." He was assisted by a Roman Catholic, Ferdynand Szczepański, who was apparently attached "heart and soul" to the Ukrainian activities.[154] The reading club in Hleshchava was said to have the first Galician village brass band, founded in 1900.[155] Choirs were reported in Kobylovoloky, Bile, Uhryn, Skala, Bilobozhnytsia, and Terebovlia.

The year's program of a reading club was punctuated by the holding of evenings (*vechernytsi*), with programs displaying the talents of local and, sometimes, visiting people. There would be speakers on special themes, verse declamations (especially if these evenings were in honour of Shevchenko), solo or choral singing, and, in some places, a common meal and then dancing until late into the night. Annual meetings were celebrated in this fashion as well, and these were frequently described in the press:

> In the village of Verbivtsi near Budzaniv our reading club held *vechernytsi* initiated by the wife of the parish priest, Mrs. Tanchakivska, to which many people and local intelligentsia came, as well as people from neighbouring villages. The painter, Mr. Kovalsky, welcomed the audience with a fine speech; then the teacher from Skomorokhy gave a clear and understandable lecture on the theme of the history of

> printing, to which all listened attentively. The local teacher, Mr. Domansky, then spoke about child rearing; Mr. Kovalsky spoke again, and then one member of the reading club commented on the need for education. Interspersed between the speeches and lectures were verse recitations and singing by young men and women. Everyone then sat down together, intelligentsia and villagers, to a modest dinner during which Fr. Tanchakivsky led the singing of "Many Years" for the emperor and the church hierarchy. He spoke movingly about the material needs of our people, and our need for enlightenment.... Later there was a dance which went on until 4 a.m. This event was enjoyed by all; some people hadn't been enthusiastic about it initially, and had been reluctant to give 20 kr in advance, but they regretted this attitude later. Signed—A Farmer.[156]

Another evening, held in the Terebovlia reading club in May 1890, was similar:

> The evening was held in the Magistrate's Hall in the town of Terebovlia. The stage was decorated with the bust of Shevchenko. Our priest, Father Zalutsky, opened the evening. The mixed choir from Kobylovoloky directed by Mr. Semyrozum performed some numbers. Then a girl from town recited a verse. This is the first time for this to happen here. The teacher from Strusiv also declaimed some of Shevchenko's verse. In attendance were the County Officer and many intelligentsia and townspeople.[157]

During the 1880s and 1890s reading clubs spread widely throughout Southern Podillia. Villages without reading clubs were increasingly impressed by the benefits accruing to villages with clubs and sought to emulate them.[158] The successes of individual clubs and the extent of their activities varied considerably. Perhaps few were as committed to furthering general education as the reading club in Kolodribka:

> The reading club is a big help for the school, a strong and constant base for enlightenment and the education of youth. Also, the farmers, enthused by this, send their children to school sooner and more consistently; there are even some older people in the village who have taught themselves to read and to write a little, mostly from their children.[159]

Clearly, formal and popular education interacted with one another, to the benefit of both, and new cultural events, including theatre, were introduced.[160] Other reading clubs stressed other aspects of their activities. In 1897 the one in Skala reported that it possessed a stone building valued at several thousand gulden, with two rooms for reading, a hall for meetings, concerts, and theatrical performances, plus basement space; 320 books that were borrowed and "read diligently" by its 270 members; a grain-storage facility with space for sixteen *korets* of grain; and a savings and loan society with an annual turnover of 40,000 g.[161]

In size, the Skala reading club may have been atypical; in other respects it was not. The reading clubs of Southern Podillia thus provided not only general educational opportunities for the Ukrainian population of the region but also enabled them to band together to promote their economic well-being. The inter-linked activities of the enlightenment societies, the press, and the reading clubs thus provided for the dissemination of education and knowledge among adults, promoted the development of political consciousness among Southern Podillian villagers, and assisted in the development of their economic life.

Notes

1. M. Hrushevsky, *A History of Ukraine*, 148.
2. Brief descriptive passages about the brotherhoods, mostly in sixteenth-century Lviv and Kiev, can be found in I. Tyktor, ed., *Velyka istoriia Ukrainy*, 440-1, 449-50, 659; D. Doroshenko, *A Survey of Ukrainian History*, 148-51, 154, 181, 525-9, 535-6, 567, 803; Hrushevsky, *History of Ukraine*, 147-9, 184, 200-5, 212, 239, 266, 354, 486-7, 493-4; and Metropolitan Ilarion, *Ukrainska tserkva za chas ruiny (1657-1687)*, 53, 54, 72, *passim*. See also S. Persky, *Populiarna istoriia tovarystva "Prosvity,"* 5; and M. Pavlyk, "Pro rusko-ukrainski chytalni," 380.
3. Pavlyk, "Pro rusko-ukrainski chytalni," 464, 773.
4. In the first half of the 1870s, 200 Eastern Galician brotherhoods subscribed to *Nauka* (Pavlyk, "Pro rusko-ukrainski chytalni," 464).
5. Ibid., 524; IMZCh, 504-5.
6. I have consulted membership lists published in the agricultural paper *Hospodar i promyshlennyk* (which Narodna Torhivlia sponsored for a time).
7. J.-P. Himka, "Priests and Peasants: The Greek Catholic Pastor and the Ukrainian National Movement in Austria, 1867-1900," 6-7. For brotherhoods and sobriety campaigns in Southern Podillia see IMZCh, 504-5, 589, 604, 614, *passim*; on alcohol usage see also below, ch. VIII.
8. J. Kozik, *The Ukrainian National Movement in Galicia 1815-1849*, 53-6; Persky, *Populiarna istoriia*, 7-8.
9. Persky, *Populiarna istoriia*, 7-8; Hrushevsky, *A History of Ukraine*, 473.
10. Hrushevsky, *A History of Ukraine*, 490; Doroshenko, *A Survey of Ukrainian History*, 557; Tyktor, *Velyka istoriia Ukrainy*, 681-3; Pavlyk, "Pro rusko-ukrainski chytalni," 443. On the Ukrainian national awakening and the Supreme Ruthenian Council, see Rudnytsky, "The Ukrainians in Galicia," 26-35; Tyktor, *Velyka istoriia Ukrainy*, 668-74.
11. Tyktor, *Velyka istoriia Ukrainy*, 682; Pavlyk, "Pro rusko-ukrainski chytalni," 442-3.

The Matytsia did succeed in publishing, in 1850, the reader for children written by Markiian Shashkevych in 1834.

12. Tyktor, *Velyka istoriia Ukrainy*, 681-3, 715-20; Hrushevsky, *A History of Ukraine*, 490-3, 497-8; Doroshenko, *A Survey of Ukrainian History*, 556-559; Pavlyk, "Pro rusko-ukrainski chytalni," 453; Kubijovyč, *Ukraine*, 2: 534-5.
13. Pavlyk, "Pro rusko-ukrainski chytalni," 471, 489.
14. Tyktor, *Velyka istoriia Ukrainy*, 720; Kubijovyč, *Ukraine*, 2: 335; Doroshenko, *A Survey of Ukrainian History*, 559-60 and 578-9; Pavlyk, "Pro rusko-ukrainski chytalni," 473.
15. Pavlyk, "Pro rusko-ukrainski chytalni," 417.
16. "A vernacular-based language began to appear in publications during the 1830s. The most important of these was the first book of secular literature, *Rusalka Dnistrovaia*, published in 1837 by a group of writers, Markiian Shashkevych, Iakiv Holovatsky, and Ivan Vahylevych, known as the Ruthenian Triad" (P.R. Magocsi, "The Language Question as a Factor in the National Movement," 233). *Rusalka Dnistrovaia*, because of censorship and other opposition, had to be printed in Hungary. See also Rudnytsky, "The Ukrainians in Galicia," 27-8; and P. Brock, "Ivan Vahylevych (1811-1866) and the Ukrainian National Identity," 117-21, 125-7.
17. See Magocsi, "The Language Question," esp. 230-4; and Brock, "Ivan Vahylevych," 124-6, 130-3.
18. Magocsi, "The Language Question," 233-8; *idem*, "Old Ruthenianism and Russophilism: A New Conceptual Framework for Analyzing National Ideologies in Late 19th Century Eastern Galicia," 313-9; see also Rudnytsky, "The Ukrainians in Galicia," 42-8; Doroshenko, *A Survey of Ukrainian History*, 559; and, for one account of the coming of Shevchenko's ideas to Eastern Galicia, Pavlyk, "Pro rusko-ukrainski chytalni," 477.
19. On the Old Ruthenians and the Russophiles, I have followed the categorizations proposed by Magocsi ("Old Ruthenianism and Russophilism," 305-24). See also Rudnytsky, "The Ukrainians in Galicia," 43-4.
20. J.-P. Himka, *Socialism in Galicia*, 42-5; Rudnytsky, "The Ukrainians in Galicia," 46-8; Magocsi, "The Language Question," 225-38.
21. For the best brief account of the development of the radical intellectuals see Rudnytsky, "The Ukrainians in Galicia," 49-50. See also Doroshenko, *A Survey of Ukrainian History*, 580-1.
22. Himka, *Socialism in Galicia*, 40.
23. Ibid., 40-2; Rudnytsky, "The Ukrainians in Galicia," 43-6; Magocsi, "Old Ruthenianism and Russophilism," esp. 309-10, 317-20. For a related phenomenon, "naive tsarism," see J.-P. Himka, "Hope in the Tsar: Displaced Naive Monarchism Among Ukrainian Peasants in the Habsburg Empire," esp. 126-34.
24. Magocsi, "Old Ruthenianism and Russophilism," 318.
25. *Entsyklopediia ukrainoznavstva*, 6: 2365. See also Himka, "Polish and Ukrainian Socialism," 122; and Tyktor, *Velyka istoriia Ukrainy*, 681.
26. These figures are Prosvita's own, and refer only to those individuals and clubs which paid dues directly to the central "maternal" society in Lviv (Persky, *Populiarna istoriia tovarystva*, 140). Other authorities have cited different totals, ([V. Kubijowycz], *Ukrainskyj statystycznyj ricznyk*, 284). *Entsyklopediia*

ukrainoznavstva (6: 2366) gave membership totals as 1,500 in 1880, 4,800 in 1890, and 13,400 in 1900. Himka ("Polish and Ukrainian Socialism," 140) states that "by 1908, 23,163 members had joined Prosvita in the 40 years of its existence." P. Melnyk, "Das ukrainische landwirtschaftliche Genossenschaftswesen in Galizien," 11), attempted to arrive at a total for all those who not only joined the Lviv Prosvita but also those who were associated with it indirectly as dues-paying members of affiliates or reading clubs that were members of Prosvita. His figures were 1,700 in 1880, 31,800 in 1890, and 89,400 in 1900.

27. Persky, *Populiarna istoriia tovarystva*, 24.
28. Melnyk, "Das ukrainische Genossenschaftswesen," 11. *Entsyklopediia ukrainoznavstva* (6: 2366) gives the totals as four in both 1880 and 1890 and twenty-two in 1900.
29. Persky, *Populiarna istoriia tovarystva*, 124.
30. Ibid., 129.
31. Melnyk, "Das ukrainische Genossenschaftswesen," 11.
32. M. Borovsky, *Materialy do bibliohrafii hospodarskoi literatury vydanoi v Halychyni, na Volyni, Zakarpatti i Bukovyni*, 7.
33. Ibid., 8.
34. O. Oleskiv, *Pro vilni zemli*. On Oleskiv, see also M. Marunchak's edition of *Pro vilni zemli*, vi-ix; and Kaye, *Early Ukrainian Settlements in Canada, passim.*
35. *Svoboda*, 1 Apr. 1897.
36. Ibid., 4 Nov. 1897.
37. Borovsky, *Materialy do bibliohrafii*, 7.
38. Persky, *Populiarna istoriia tovarystva*, 121-3.
39. Ibid., 129-36.
40. Ibid., 34, 35, 41, 56, 142-6. Franko's "Twelve Commandments" are in *Batkivshchyna* (17 May 1889). See also "Report of the Central Branch of Prosvita Society for 1888" (*Batkivshchyna*, 2 Aug. 1889).
41. Members of Prosvita also established the Shevchenko Scientific Society in 1873 and the Ruthenian Pedagogical Association in 1881 ("Pro zasnovannia NTSh," *Zapysky Naukovoho tovarystva im. Shevchenka*, 1: 209; Iasinchuk, *50 lit Ridnoi Shkoly*, 14).
42. Contemporary radicals, and later scholars who have focussed on them, attempted to minimize the significance of Prosvita's work, to highlight its alleged shortcomings (as perceived by Mykhailo Drahomanov, who had very little first-hand knowledge of what was going on in Eastern Galicia), and to claim that the whole Ukrainophile populist movement was unduly under the influence of the Greek Catholic clergy. See, for example, Pavlyk, "Pro rusko-ukrainski chytalni," 535-9; Doroshenko, *A Survey of Ukrainian History*, 578-9; I. Vytanovych, "Sotsiialno-ekonomichni idei v zmahanniakh halytskykh ukraintsiv na perelomi XIX-XX v.," 17; Himka, *Socialism in Galicia*, esp. 49-50, 174-5. The clergy certainly played a role in Ukrainian populism, and, with certain exceptions, were active in village enlightenment in all its forms. There is very little evidence from Southern Podillia of radical activity there in the 1890s, but a great deal of evidence of the activities of the Prosvita and Kachkovsky societies and of the involvement of the clergy in enlightenment work, both in the 1880s and 1890s.
43. Persky, *Populiarna istoriia tovarystva*, 127. For an instance of a supporter selling

Prosvita publications in the villages, see ibid., 154-5.
44. Pavlyk, "Pro rusko-ukrainski chytalni," 533.
45. Ibid., 535.
46. Persky, *Populiarna istoriia tovarystva*, 127.
47. Pavlyk, "Pro rusko-ukrainski chytalni," 534.
48. M. Vozniak, "Korotkyi pohliad na doteperishniu diialnist 'Prosvity'," 10.
49. For accounts of the reactions of Old Ruthenians to the founding of Prosvita, see Persky, *Populiarna istoriia tovarystva*, 19, 24; Pavlyk, "Pro rusko-ukrainski chytalni," 487, 532; Tyktor, *Velyka istoriia*, 721.
50. While there is quite an extensive literature on Prosvita and its activities, the Kachkovsky Society has been ignored. The Kachkovsky Society has been of little interest to Ukrainian nationalist historians because of its Old Ruthenian, and allegedly Russophile, orientation or to Soviet scholars because of its conservative and clerical connections. It is possible that its contribution to Ukrainian enlightenment in Eastern Galicia has been seriously underestimated. The Kachkovsky Society was founded in Kolomyia, but transferred itself to Lviv in 1876.
51. *Entsiklopedicheskii slovar*, 15A: 814-5; *Entsyklopediia ukrainoznavstva*, 5: 1807; Pavlyk, "Pro rusko-ukrainski chytalni," 496-7; *Russkaia rada*, 8 Mar. 1880.
52. *Hospodar i promyshlennyk*, nos. 14 and 16, 1880.
53. O. Oleskiv, *O emigratsii*.
54. *Batkivshchyna*, 18 Sept. 1885.
55. For the Russkaia chytalnia series, see Pavlyk, "Pro rusko-ukrainski chytalni," 488-9. Naumovych had published other educational and practical literature before the founding of the Kachkovsky Society; one pre-1874 publication was *The Calendar of Beekeeping* (1866) (Borovsky, *Materialy do bibliohrafii*, 7).
56. Pavlyk, "Pro rusko-ukrainski chytalni," 489. For one of Naumovych's exhortations to establish reading halls, to write for model charters, and to join the Kachkovsky Society, see his article in *Viche*, 11 Feb. 1881.
57. See *Nauka*, 15 Sept. 1891, for an obituary notice of Fr. Naumovych. See also *Entsyklopediia ukrainoznavstva*, 5: 1716-7.
58. Borovsky, *Materialy do bibliohrafii*, 7.
59. *Hospodar i promyshlennyk*, no. 12, 1880.
60. *Entsiklopedicheskii slovar*, 15A: 814-5.
61. Ibid.
62. *Entsyklopediia ukrainoznavstva*, 5: 1807.
63. Persky, *Populiarna istoriia tovarystva*, 25-6.
64. Pavlyk, "Pro rusko-ukrainski chytalni," 496-7, 546-7.
65. Himka, "Polish and Ukrainian Socialism," 146.
66. *Svoboda*, 8 July and 9 Sept. 1897.
67. See *Hospodar i promyshlennyk*, no. 4, 1885; *Batkivshchyna*, 1 Mar., 14 June, 28 Sept. 1889; *Halychanyn*, 6 Jan. 1894; *Batkivshchyna*, 18 Sept. 1885; Pavlyk, "Pro rusko-ukrainski chytalni," 547. For other co-operation see K. Levytsky, *Istoriia politychnoi*, 2: 187.
68. *Otchet russko-narodnoho instytuta "Narodnyi Dim" vo Lvovi za 1881 hod*, 7. However, such collaboration was later not possible with the Russophiles. It was

attempted at the jubilee celebrations of Emperor Franz Josef in 1898, but ultimately the Russophiles celebrated the centenary of Pushkin while the Ukrainophiles honoured the twenty-fifth anniversary of the founding of the Shevchenko Society and of Ivan Franko's literary activities (*Literaturno-naukovyi vistnyk*, 2, no. 5 [Lviv 1899], 107).

69. "Pro zasnovannia NTSh," *Zapysky naukovoho tovarystva im. Shevchenka*, 1892, 1: 209; Iasinchuk, *50 lit Ridnoi Shkoly*, 14.
70. On Narodnyi Dim, see *Entsyklopediia ukrainoznavstva*, 5: 1687.
71. Ibid., 1688. See also the annual reports in *Batkivshchyna*, *Chytalnia*, and *Svoboda*.
72. On the Galician Agricultural Associations and Agricultural Circles see below, Ch. VI, "Agricultural Education." The circles are mentioned with some admiration in the Ukrainian press (*Batkivshchyna*, 17 July 1885 and 16 Apr. 1886) and their presence in Southern Podillia is noted infrequently in memoirs, usually as places for Polish people (IMZCh, 341, 376, *passim*).
73. See the report from Hermakivka (Borshchiv county), in *Batkivshchyna*, 20 June 1890, and Stefanyk, *The Stone Cross*, 67-9.
74. *Batkivshchyna*, 27 June 1884.
75. IMZCh, 584, 601, 631, *passim*.
76. *Nauka*, 15 Jan. 1886.
77. *Batkivshchyna*, 27 May 1887.
78. Ibid., 6 June 1884 and 10 July 1885.
79. *Chytalnia*, 6 Aug. 1894; *Svoboda*, 19 Dec. 1898.
80. *Batkivshchyna*, 5 Apr., 24 May, 12 Oct., 1889, and 14 Mar. 1890.
81. *Dilo*, 16 Jan. 1890.
82. *Svoboda*, 10 Nov. 1898.
83. *Batkivshchyna*, 28 Mar. 1890, *Chytalnia*, 6 July 1894, 6 Apr. 1895, 21 July 1895.
84. *Chytalnia*, 6 July 1894.
85. For the list of names of the representatives in the Southern Podillian counties, see *Chytalnia*, 20 Apr., 8 May, 20 May, 6 July 1894.
86. *Chytalnia*, 5 Jan. 1894.
87. *Svoboda*, 30 Dec. 1897.
88. *Chytalnia*, 6 Aug. 1895.
89. *Entsyklopediia ukrainoznavstva*, 6: 2366.
90. *Chytalnia*, 21 Aug. 1896. By the end of 1896, Korol had visited 102 communes, primarily in Eastern Galicia (*Svoboda*, 27 Mar. 1897).
91. The data on Ukrainian-language periodicals in Galicia and Austria-Hungary are taken from V. Ihnatiienko, *Bibliohrafiia ukrainskoi presy 1816-1916*, 19, 20, 23. The totals do not always agree with those in the volumes of *Oesterreichisches statistisches Handbuch*. On the press during this period see also A. Zhyvotko, "Istoriia ukrainskoi presy," 11-12. (I am grateful to Dr. M. Marunchak for making this work available to me.)
92. Some claim that *Slovo* received subsidies from the Russian government (Zhyvotko, "Istoriia ukrainskoi presy," 54-5; Himka, "Polish and Ukrainian Socialism," 115). However, according to Magocsi this occurred only in 1876 ("Old Ruthenianism and Russophilism," 316). On the other hand, Ukrainophile publications (*Pravda*, *Batkivshchyna*, *Hromadskyi druh*) received funds from the Kievan *hromada* in the

last quarter of the century (Zhyvotko, "Istoriia ukrainskoi presy," 65, 67 and 82; and Doroshenko, *A Survey of Ukrainian History*, 560).

93. Pavlyk, "Pro rusko-ukrainski chytalni," 489.
94. Zhyvotko, "Istoriia ukrainskoi presy," 89. J.-P. Himka, *Galician Villagers and the Ukrainian National Movement in the Nineteenth Century* (Edmonton: Canadian Institute of Ukrainian Studies, 1988), appeared too late to be used by me. Some details of press runs of Galician Ukrainian newspapers are given there (68, 70, 79).
95. IMZCh, 207-8.
96. *Priiatel ditei*, 1 Jan. 1881.
97. *Hospodar i promyshlennyk*, no. 7, 1884.
98. *Hromadskyi holos*, 15 Aug. 1900. This is one of the few references I have found to Southern Podillian interest in the radical press. A "letter from Podillia" in the 5 June 1891 issue of *Batkivshchyna* called a new radical paper, *Khliborob*, "argumentative" and firmly stated "there is nothing in it for the people."
99. *Batkivshchyna*, 27 June 1884.
100. Pavlyk, "Pro rusko-ukrainski chytalni," 518.
101. *Batkivshchyna*, 8 Mar. 1889.
102. Ibid., 6 June 1890.
103. Ibid., 10 Apr. 1891.
104. *Chytalnia*, 6 July 1894.
105. Ibid., 6 May. 1894.
106. Ibid., 6 Aug. 1894, and 6 Apr. 1895.
107. *Svoboda*, 13 May 1897.
108. For some examples of newspaper polemics see *Narod*, nos. 10-12, 1891; *Batkivshchyna*, 6 Feb. 1885, and 17 Apr., 5 June, 14 and 28 Aug. 1891; *Nauka*, 30 Sept. 1888; and *Prosveshchenie*, 25 Aug. 1893. They could also quote each other with approval, reprint each other's articles, and advertise events sponsored by other Ukrainian groups; see, for example, *Hospodar i promyshlennyk*, no. 4, 1885; *Batkivshchyna*, 1 Mar., 14 June, and 28 Sept 1889; *Halychanyn*, 6 Jan. 1894.
109. For entertainments see *Batkivshchyna*, 2 Apr. 1886, 2 Mar. 1888, and 4 July 1890; and *Svoboda*, 16 Sept. and 16 Dec. 1897.
110. For example, *Batkivshchyna*, 12 Apr. and 17 May 1889.
111. For the role of the newspapers in agricultural education see 126-30 and 139-41 below; on health education see Chapter VIII below.
112. *Batkivshchyna*, 12 Apr. 1889.
113. *Przyjaciel ludu*, 19 Nov. 1891, as cited in K. Dunin-Wąsowicz, *Czasopiśmiennictwo ludowe w Galicji*, 150.
114. L. Lototsky, "Na robotu," 53.
115. The term is J.-P. Himka's; see "Polish and Ukrainian Socialism," 385.
116. Cited in E.L. Sommerlad, *The Press in Developing Countries*, 59.
117. The Ukrainophile group and its activities prior to 1868 are described in Himka, *Socialism in Galicia*, 42-5.
118. Pavlyk, "Pro rusko-ukrainski chytalni," 480.
119. See pp. 86-7.
120. Tyktor, *Velyka istoria*, 680; Persky, *Populiarna istoriia tovarystva*, 10.
121. Pavlyk, "Pro rusko-ukrainski chytalni," 480, 503, 514, 518, 533.

122. *Russkaia rada*, 2 Apr. 1882. *Batkivshchyna* noted plaintively (15 Feb. 1884) that "at the moment, nobody knows how many Ruthenian reading clubs there are, where they are located, and how they are doing." There was a Jewish reading hall in Tovste, Zalishchyky county (*Batkivshchyna*, 11 Sept. 1885).
123. *Svoboda*, 15 July 1897.
124. M. Lozynsky, *Sorok lit diialnosty 'Prosvity,'* 46-7.
125. IMZCh, 226, 506, 510, 584, *passim.*
126. For one such instance see ibid., 210.
127. A. Lowell, *Government and Parties in Continental Europe*, 80. *Batkivshchyna* (27 July 1888) described the procedure to follow to establish a reading club.
128. *Batkivshchyna*, 13 Feb., 21 Mar., 15 Aug. 1890.
129. Ibid., 15 Mar. and 5 Apr. 1889; *Svoboda*, 16 Sept. 1897.
130. For the normally prescribed activities of Prosvita reading clubs see Persky, *Populiarna istoriia tovarystva*, 161-2; for supplies of books see ibid., 123ff. See also numerous reports in *Batkivshchyna*. For the founding of a reading club see also IMZCh, 210.
131. *Batkivshchyna*, 12 June 1885.
132. Ibid., 10 Apr. 1891.
133. Ibid., 27 June 1884; however, according to Pavlyk, "Pro rusko-ukrainski chytalni," the Kolodribka reading club was founded in 1874.
134. Ibid., 11 Apr. 1890.
135. Ibid., 15 Aug. 1884; *Svoboda*, 27 May 1897.
136. *Batkivshchyna*, 24 Apr. 1885.
137. Ibid., 10 Apr. 1891.
138. Ibid., 15 Aug. 1884.
139. *Chytalnia*, 6 May 1894; *Svoboda*, 7 Oct. 1897; *Batkivshchyna*, 27 June 1884.
140. See Stefanyk (*The Stone Cross*, 46) for a story of a man's opposition to his wife's attendance at the village reading club. See also *Batkivshchyna*, 15 Aug. 1884; *Chytalnia*, 20 July 1893.
141. *Batkivshchyna*, 10 Aug. 1888 and 24 Apr. 1885.
142. Ibid., 27 June 1884.
143. Vynnytsky, *Terebovelska zemlia*, 295.
144. *Batkivshchyna*, 15 Aug. 1884.
145. Ibid., 11 Apr., 6 June, and 27 July 1890; and 10 Apr. and 4 Oct. 1891.
146. *Chytalnia*, 20 July 1893.
147. Ibid., 6 May and 6 July 1894.
148. *Batkivshchyna*, 15 Aug. 1890.
149. *Hromadskyi holos*, 15 Mar. 1899; *Batkivshchyna*, 21 March 1890.
150. *Batkivshchyna*, 6 June 1890.
151. Ibid., 31 Aug. 1886.
152. Ibid., 27 July 1888.
153. *Chytalnia*, 6 Apr. 1895 and 20 July 1893.
154. Vynnytsky, *Terebovelska zemlia*, 632; *Batkivshchyna*, 4 Feb. 1887.
155. Vynnytsky, *Terebovelska zemlia*, 566.
156. *Batkivshchyna*, 2 Apr. 1886.
157. Ibid., 4 July 1890.

158. See, for example, *Svoboda*, 10 Feb. 1898.
159. *Batkivshchyna*, 27 June 1884.
160. In 1894 the Ukrainian theatre group from Lviv visited Borshchiv town. Their scheduled one-month engagement had to be extended to two because people from the town and from neighbouring villages and towns filled the hall consistently (IMZCh, 487-8). The press also reported on choir and drama productions at various village reading club halls.
161. *Svoboda*, 13 May 1897.

Chapter VI

Agriculture: (i) Background, Landholding, and Agricultural Education

In no area of development was progress so widespread and significant—and so ignored by the majority of scholars—as in agriculture. The preoccupation of contemporary experts was with the backwardness of Galician agriculture, compared with countries such as Germany, Denmark, and Britain, and with the fate of the large estates, with which the well-being of Galician agriculture and the future of the Polish nation were assumed to be closely linked. Peasant ownership of land, and especially of parcelled lands that had formerly belonged to great estates, deprived the gentry landowning class of agricultural labour. Insofar as peasant agriculture itself was concerned, there was a general assumption that successful production depended on the maintenance of "large peasant holdings" or "middle holdings." Such holdings of 10-50 ha were considered the essential prerequisite for successful agriculture; subdivision of peasant lands led to the progressive impoverishment of the peasant population.[1] The experts, who tended to take a macro view of Galician agriculture, made assumptions about the viability of smallholding agriculture, rather than examining what was actually going on. Further, with the exception of F. Bujak and L.W. Biegeleisen, they were generally oblivious to improvements in peasant agricultural productivity. Smaller holdings were uncritically equated with greater impoverishment.[2]

One French historian has estimated that in France the minimum area planted with subsistence crops required to sustain a family of five declined from about five ha in 1815 to two ha in 1892.[3] Others have reached similar conclusions about increases in agricultural productivity in that country in the nineteenth century.[4] Was there in Southern Podillia a similar increase in peasant productivity that would have offset such decline in the size of peasant landholdings as did occur?

Background

At the time Galicia was incorporated into the Habsburg lands in 1772, its predominantly peasant population were serfs, who held land in return for compulsory labour service on the large manorial estates. In Eastern Galicia this meant that Ukrainian-speaking peasants worked for and belonged to Polish or Polonized masters, who possessed almost absolute authority over them. Various

Austrian laws of the next fifteen years prohibited estate owners from taking traditional peasant land away from the peasants, restricted the peasants' ability to subdivide the land they held, abolished the personal bondage of the peasants to the landowners, and placed limitations on the extent of compulsory labour.

All Galician agricultural land was divided into two legal categories—"dominical" land, that is, land which was farmed or managed directly by the manor, and "rustical" land which, although in law the property of the manorial estate, was deemed to "belong" to the peasants. All land in use by the peasants on 1 September 1786 was reserved for their hereditary use.[5] Dominical land in Galicia was registered in special Registry Books (*tabula krajowa*) in Lviv (later in some other major towns). It thus acquired the name "tabular" as well. Tabular land could be owned or purchased only by the magnates or gentry, or by religious orders, corporate entities or the state itself. Rustical land transactions were not recorded in any special official registers, but a record of transactions was supposed to be maintained by the lord of each manor. (The absence of adequate records of peasant land was a source of problems in later years). Rustical land could "belong" only to the peasant class, that is, to those engaged exclusively in agriculture. The incorporation of rustical with tabular land or the exchange of one type for the other was forbidden, and rustical land could not be sold by the manor lord separately from the estate.[6]

A survey, the Josephinian Metryka (or "Cataster") was undertaken of all landholdings in Galicia between 1785 and 1788. Land was categorized by type of use—ploughland, gardens, hay-meadows, woodland, rough pasturage—and taxed at varying rates. Attempts were made in the nineteenth century to update the Josephinian survey, notably in 1819 (the Franciscan Metryka),[7] and in the land tax assessment revisions of 1882 and 1896.[8] While these revisions might have been adequate for contemporary tax purposes, they did not take the place of detailed records of peasant landholding patterns.

Joseph II hoped to prevent both the consolidation of individual peasant holdings, whether by inheritance or purchase, and their subdivision. Various regulations of the years 1787-90 sought to ensure these goals. The main heir to a peasant holding was always to be the eldest son, who was to inherit all the land registered in the manor land book and the house. If he already held land, he was obliged to choose between what he already had and the inheritance. However, the principle of equality of inheritance between heirs was also enunciated. The capital worth of an inheritance had to be divided equally among all the heirs, in cash or in kind, and if necessary in installments. A peasant who left a valid will (which few did) could bequeath his property in a different fashion, for example choosing a main heir other than the eldest son.[9] Further laws and regulations between 1804 and 1857 reaffirmed these inheritance laws and the restrictions on incorporating rustical and tabular lands.[10] They thus formally governed much of Galicia's agrarian land-holding relationships until in 1868 the Galician Sejm passed a law abolishing the hindrances to subdivision of land and restrictions on categories of ownership.[11] The legal distinction between tabular and rustical lands remained, and gave tabular owners some exemptions from local taxes, but otherwise came to have a political rather than an economic meaning.[12]

The Josephinian laws provided peasants with some protection against the manorial lords, although these laws were often ignored or circumvented. The legal status of peasant land was fundamentally changed by the political events of 1848. An imperial decree of 17 April 1848 put an end to compulsory labour and other duties to the manor lord throughout Galicia, effective 15 May 1848. A Patent of 7 September 1848 gave peasants actual ownership of the rustical land which they had used. The estate owners were indemnified for their loss of land and labour services out of state and Crownland funds, which were to be recovered over decades by a special tax on all taxpayers. The disposition of the "servitudes," as the right to use meadows, pastures, and woodlands held in common by peasants and manors was called, was left unsettled. Estate owners and peasants were initially expected to determine their respective rights amicably among themselves.[13]

In 1848 the majority of Galician peasants thus became instant owners of the land which they had worked. They lost much of the "free" access to woodlands and pastures which they had come to regard as their own, and for whose use they now frequently had to pay money or labour rents. There was much vociferous protest at the takeover by estates of land previously used jointly by peasants and manors. Villagers in the Chortkiv and Zalishchyky areas were among the most vocal protesters.[14] Typical was the village of Koshylivtsi, where peasants complained that pastures "from which our fathers and grandfathers derived benefit" were being wrongly taken away from them.[15] In 1858, special courts had to be established to settle disputes.[16]

The Josephinian laws promoting hereditary individual peasant holdings were in conflict with peasant practices in Southern Podillia. "Since time immemorial," they practised a "transitional system of agriculture," in which they were part pastoralists and part grain growers.[17] The landholding system associated with this "pastoral/grain-growing" economy was centred on the village commune (*hromada*).[18] There was a connection between this type of economy and the communally organized village society: as the economy changed into a full-scale grain-growing economy, the institution of the village commune tended to be weakened and some of its features disappeared altogether. Characteristic of the pastoral/grain-growing economy and the associated village commune system was the fact that members of the commune held the rustical land not individually but communally. The village commune's land thus comprised all the constituent peasant allotments. Those allotments varied in size according to the number of labour days per week performed by the peasant for the manor, and according to the number of draught animals the peasant provided. The commune's land was subject to periodic repartition and changes in use from pasturage (*toloka*) to tillage and grain growing (*tsaryna*). The only property not subject to repartition and changes in use was the commune members' houses and attached gardens. Village elders in consultation with commune members determined the time intervals of the use "rotation" and the location of members' holdings, and manor owners or agents usually played little part in this process, though there are indications that there was more interference after about 1830.[19]

Participation in the village commune proper, and in the conduct of its affairs, was limited to those peasants (*muzhyky*) who held land and were thus subject to compulsory labour. There were already larger and small peasant holdings, depending on the amount of labour service performed by these peasants. Two types of villagers who were not full members of the village commune were the landless peasants or cottagers (*khalupnyky*) who possessed their houses and gardens but held no manor-allocated land and the *komornyky*, who had neither houses nor gardens of their own. The latter were sometimes landless labourers or craftsmen, and sometimes contracted farm servants on the manor estates, for whom the lord provided accommodation and small portions of land on the tabular estate.[20] Landlessness was thus a fact of life for some Eastern Galician villagers throughout the late eighteenth and nineteenth centuries, and not an exclusively late nineteenth-century phenomenon, as some Soviet and Polish authors have maintained.

The communal landholding system survived in many parts of Southern Podillia until at least 1848. Even when the Viennese authorities instructed the villagers to break up their communal systems, with their periodic redistributions, they refused to comply. Peasants had other grievances too, and there were uprisings involving at least thirty-nine villages in Southern Podillia in 1838.[21] Pressure from the authorities no doubt contributed to the disintegration of the communal landholding system. The main reason for its decline, however, was the continuous displacement of the pastoral/grain-growing economy by one focussing on grain-growing only. A rise in the demand for grain, with its attendant increase in grain prices and an increased demand for grain for distilling, led the manors to seek to acquire control over more grain-growing land and generally to stimulate the production of grain.[22] To get more land, they began arbitrarily and illegally to annex rustical to tabular land. The extensive *toloka* land of the Southern Podillian village communes was especially vulnerable. Manor lords often succeeded in absorbing portions of these into their tabular land by claiming that the village commune land was actually dominical, and that the portions absorbed were being "regulated" in the interests of better farming.[23] A particular opportunity presented itself to them when Podillia was briefly under Russian rule between 1809 and 1815, and most of the land then arbitrarily acquired remained lost to the peasants.[24] Only occasionally were peasants able to win redress for these and other illegal seizures of land.[25]

The survival into modern times of the village commune system, and the attachment of Southern Podillian villagers to it, were probably assets when communes were established as the lowest level of local political authority after 1848. A tradition of village governance already existed, as did customary forms of village co-operation. Paradoxically, the drive for individual ownership of land and the acquisition of more land, so manifest among Ukrainian peasants in Eastern Galicia in the second half of the nineteenth century, may have been strengthened by the prolonged absence of permanent individual landholdings in those areas where the village commune system and periodic redistribution of land had survived longest. Also, the system of agriculture associated with the pastoral/grain-growing economy was an "extensive" rather than an "intensive" one and there was little incentive for individual peasants to undertake improvements if land was subject to periodic redistribution. There was also little opportunity to dispose of any surplus production, and thus no great incentive to produce more.[26] Prior to mid-century, and probably until as late as 1870 (when railways reached points relatively close to the region), most Southern Podillian peasants practised a form of subsistence agriculture of a relatively low intensity of cultivation, because there was little need or incentive to do otherwise.

It is noteworthy that population density per square kilometre was significantly lower in Eastern Galicia than in Western Galicia in the early nineteenth century. In 1815 Western Galicia had 59 persons per square kilometre and Eastern Galicia, 41.[27] The latter, particularly including Southern Podillia, had an absorptive capacity for later population increases and had, on average, larger peasant holdings than did the more densely populated Western Galicia. In addition, the differentiation or stratification of village society had begun prior to the modern period. Some peasants had more land, depending on the amount of labour service they performed. Some villagers had no land at all and, unless they were artisans or craftsmen, were landless labourers, working for others. The pre-1848 stratification of the village was carried forward into the modern era because the size of individual peasant landholdings, of which they became owners, was determined by the amount they had held before 1848.

Peasants were frequently able to ignore or circumvent restrictions on subdivision or consolidation of landholdings. Many de facto changes went unrecorded in land books; others were made during the years 1848-50, when peasants first obtained individual legal title to their holdings and the authorities were in disarray. Also, the law was circumvented by a legal device—long leases of peasant lands of up to 100 years—to get around the provisions prohibiting sale of rustical plots.[28] The Galician law of 1868 that removed restrictions on the alienation and subdivision of land, whether tabular or rustical, thus only legitimized what had long been a fact of life.

Size of Peasant Landholdings

The issue of the size of peasant landholdings has traditionally been regarded as crucially important to considerations of the Galician economy and agriculture in the late nineteenth century. Some contemporaries started with the assumption that the peasants had been quite unprepared for the freedom they were granted in 1848 and were not capable of managing their own affairs effectively.[29] Some said that Galicia was simply not able to produce enough grain for its own needs owing to the backwardness of its agriculture.[30] The subdivision of peasant land, legalized in 1868 and itself the result mainly of inheritance laws and dowry customs, was described as a prime reason for the alleged continuing deterioration of Galician agriculture, for it prevented the maintenance of the so-called viable productive holdings of ten hectares and more, and even fifty hectares and more, of which the experts thoroughly approved. There was agitation for the revision of the 1868 legislation.[31] Moreover, the peasants' possession of land was often regarded as inimical to the interests of the great landowners, who needed cheap labour. The Polish conservative deputy Abrahamowicz, in a speech in the Sejm in 1883, complained that "as soon as the peasant, with the help of subdivision of land, becomes owner of one morg of land, he regards himself as a landlord, and work as a hired hand is beneath his station."[32]

Notwithstanding such underlying assumptions, the issue of the size of peasant landholdings is of some importance, although many contemporaries took little account of land use and seemed obsessed by sheer size.[33] Unfortunately, the issue bristles with more problems and questions than answers, which has not prevented some authors from making very definite statements about size of peasant landholdings in Galicia. In fact there were no accurate central records of Galician peasant or rustical landholdings after the middle of the century. Many of the county tax-assessment records might be used to ascertain the number of peasant farms and the average size of peasant holdings only with the greatest care and the utmost difficulty. The Austrian system of recording peasant landholdings for tax-assessment purposes, especially in its Galician variant, might almost have been deliberately designed to create confusion if the tax-assessment data were used for any other purpose. Finance ministry regulations required two types of information sheets to be maintained by local officials. One was supposed to be a consolidated record of all the different pieces of land held by each owner. The other was to contain data on each individual surveyed parcel of land. The first type of information sheet sometimes did not contain a fully consolidated record, and records of peasant landholdings in different communes were difficult to collate. Perhaps more significantly, totals from the second type of information sheet on the total number of parcels were sometimes taken to denote the total number of landowners.[34] However, because of the absence of accurate data on the number of peasant landholdings, contemporary scholars were reduced to attempting to extrapolate data about landholdings from the tax-assessment data and sometimes from the average amount of tax paid.[35] Thus Z. Daszyńska-Golińska's conclusion that the number of agricultural land titles in Galicia rose by 168.7 per cent between 1857 and 1897, while the area of each decreased by 62.7 per cent, relied on the number of agricultural land titles derived from land tax-assessment data, without taking sufficient account of the difference between the two types of information sheets.[36]

Pilat was aware of some of the difficulties of working with the land tax-assessment data, but often did so nonetheless.[37] He noted significant increases in the number of payers of land tax in the five counties of Southern Podillia between 1882 and 1892,[38] but his data for his 1882 base year do not correspond exactly to the Austrian data (see Table 1 above). He concluded that in Podillia (which included the five counties of Southern Podillia) the average size of a peasant landholding, about 9 morgs (5.17 ha) around 1850, was 4.3 morgs (2.47 ha) in 1882 and 3.6 morgs (2.07 ha) in 1892.[39] The work of Pilat and others was later criticized by Bujak on the grounds that, because the tax data contained no information on the leasing of land, their computations ignored this dimension; that it included owners of land that consisted only of a house and garden and was therefore not a smallholding or even a "dwarfholding"; and that the intrinsic difficulty of working with the tax-assessment data was too great for the results to be acceptable.[40] It is interesting nonetheless to compare Pilat's conclusions to Daszyńska-Golińska's also flawed data on changes in the average size of landholdings in the Southern Podillian counties. According to her, between 1883 and 1897, the average size of peasant landholdings in Borshchiv county increased from 1.52 ha to 1.78 ha, in Chortkiv county from 1.97 ha to 2.18 ha, and in Zalishchyky county from 1.65 to 1.74 ha; and declined in Husiatyn county from 2.53 ha to 1.97 ha, and in Terebovlia county from 2.39 to 2.12 ha.[41] The trend for all the Podillian counties stressed by Pilat was not confirmed by Daszyńska-Golińska for Southern Podillia.

It is clear that it would be foolhardly to take at face value the estimates of contemporary experts, for they were based on sources compiled for a different purpose which were themselves replete with errors and extraordinarily difficult to use. Nevertheless, their conclusions have been cited repeatedly, and apparently in accordance with individual preferences, by later scholars. There is one further very important reason why the computations based on tax-assessment data should not be equated with the number and average size of peasant "agricultural enterprises" or farming operations in Galicia. The tax-assessment data naturally deal with the legal ownership of land; each owner was thus a separate entity. This legal situation often did not correspond to the practical one. In Galicia, largely because of dowry practices, peasant families normally had two holdings, the husband's and the wife's.[42] City-based statisticians generally were not conscious of this very important feature of Galician rural life. The peasant family, as an agricultural enterprise or productive unit, thus usually had more land than has generally been credited. This is of very great significance for peasant agriculture everywhere in Galicia.

Perhaps the best verdict on nineteenth-century endeavours to resolve issues of Galician peasant landholding was delivered by F. Bujak in 1908:

> Until recently we had no accurate concept of landholding conditions and no official general enquiries into this matter. Some authors made conjectures on this theme on the basis of the number of parcels of land or the number of taxpayers paying land tax. As a result, they depicted the situation in far darker tones than it was in reality, although it is easy to ascertain that the land book entries or the tax authority entities were inconsistent with the number of agricultural enterprises.[43]

Bujak wrote a year after the publication of the results of the special Austrian "agricultural census" of 1902, an attempt by the Viennese authorities to gain a more accurate idea of agricultural conditions throughout Austria. He believed that it did not produce perfect statistical compilations; nevertheless, the 1902 data were a great deal more reliable than any that had hitherto been available.[44]

The information published in tabular form in *Oesterreichische Statistik* (volume LXXXIII) detailed the number of "agricultural operations," categorized by size of total area, productive area, ploughland and meadows, woodlands, and so on. Correlations were made between size of landholdings and ownership of animals. The size of "productive area" (area exclusive of buildings and other unproductive land) is clearly the most significant; it is of course smaller than the total area of a holding.[45] (Land categorized as garden was not included in the 1902 survey.) The use of the term "agricultural operation" was an attempt to overcome the problem of counting individual parcels of land separately or failing to note that husband and wife, or perhaps father, mother, and eldest son, although separately identified for land-tax purposes, were engaged in one peasant family enterprise. As the number of "agricultural operations" in 1902 was significantly lower than the total number of land-taxpayers in 1882 (compare Table 10 and Table 1), it may be assumed that this objective was largely achieved.

Table 10
Number and Percentage of Agricultural Operations in Southern Podillia, by Size in Hectares, in 1902: Productive Area

	Under 0.5	0.5-1	1-2	2-5	5-10	10-20	20-50	50-100	over 100	Total Agricultural Operations in County
Borshchiv	751	3,078	5,296	5,079	874	201	74	27	80	15,460
per cent 100	4.9	19.9	34.3	32.9	5.7	1.3	0.5	0.2	0.5	
Chortkiv	527	1,396	2,732	3,621	965	215	60	23	58	9,597
per cent 100	5.5	14.5	28.5	37.7	10.1	2.2	0.6	0.2	0.6	
Husiatyn	797	2,279	3,678	4,396	1,103	240	79	23	75	12,660
per cent 100	6.3	18.0	29.0	34.7	8.7	1.9	0.5	0.2	0.6	
Terebovlia	697	1,821	3,190	4,051	1,286	316	68	20	63	11,512
per cent 100	6.1	15.8	27.7	35.2	11.2	2.7	0.6	0.2	0.5	
Zalishchyky	1,012	2,322	3,820	3,673	702	85	34	18	77	1,1753
per cent 100	8.6	19.8	32.9	31.6	6.0	0.7	0.3	0.2	0.7	

Source: Raw data in *Oesterreichische Statistik*, vol. LXXXIII, no. 5, table IIb.

Many of the peasant holdings, excluding the garden, were very small indeed. In each county the largest number of peasant agricultural operations fell into the 1-2 and 2-5 ha categories. There were also many in the 0.5-1 ha category and a significant number in the 5-10 ha category. The process of subdivision had advanced furthest in Zalishchyky county.[46]

Not all land used by peasants in Southern Podillia at the turn of the century was their own property. More than 10 per cent of peasant landowners in Borshchiv county and about 15 per cent of those in Terebovlia county also leased land, but fewer in the other three counties did so. In addition, there were about 400 persons whose farming operations were conducted only on leased land.[47] The peasants' leasing of land, which had been ignored by many experts, was clearly important. The area of land leased was most frequently in the 1-5 ha range.

The communes also owned land, and sometimes such land was leased to individuals. However, in many other instances communal use of common land, especially for pasturage, continued. Use of common land would then augment the peasants' own "agricultural operations." The question asked in the Austrian survey of 1902 was whether the landowner had rights of use on the undivided pasture and woodlands of a commune or a corporation. The resultant data do not, of course, make clear what constituted these "servitude rights" by the late nineteenth century. What they do show is that almost 40 per cent of the agricultural operations in Terebovlia county, 34-35 per cent of those in Borshchiv and Zalishchyky counties, 31.5 per cent of those in Chortkiv county, and under 9 per cent of those in Husiatyn county possessed grazing rights on land that did not belong to them. Between two-thirds and three-quarters of those enjoying these rights themselves had holdings of 1-5 ha, while most of the remainder had less. For these peasant operations, such rights were of considerable importance. The woodlands use rights were not so extensive (non-existent in Husiatyn and negligible in Chortkiv counties), but they too were important to those who held them.[48]

The issue of landholdings is indeed very complex. The trend throughout Galicia to subdivide holdings obviously prevailed in Southern Podillia, too. It is clear from the representative data given in Appendix I that the area of rustical land attached to each village varied greatly. Leasing of land played a role in peasant agricultural operations; whether the leased land was rustical or tabular cannot be determined. It is clear, too, that by the end of the nineteenth century most of the family holdings were below the 10 morgs or 5.75 ha that contemporary experts regarded as necessary to sustain a family.[49] What was truly important, however, was the use made of the land, and not its mere area.[50] It is also clear that Ukrainian peasants cherished their smallholdings and did not like to work on other people's land, although many did so. There were of course landless villagers and persons who held land but also worked for others—the so-called "village proletariat."[51] However, it is doubtful whether villagers thought of themselves as anything other than smallholders. As Dr. Oleskiv, who knew Eastern Galician villages well, confidently told the 1896 annual meeting of Narodna Rada, "we are used to seeing the villager not as a worker, but as a householder."[52]

Pride in ownership and in not having to work for others was also evident in interviews with children of migrants from Southern Podillia to Canada: "We were not poor. My father owned his own eight or ten morgs of land...and didn't have to work for others"; "father had four morgs of ploughland and two horses, and worked for himself, not for the *pan*"; "My mother had land given to her by her father who was reeve in Strilkivtsi and owned a little store besides. They didn't have to work anywhere else for earnings"; and "My father said he had six morgs of field. My uncle and my father worked only on their own land, and even had to hire others to work for them."[53] There was also pride in having good farm buildings: "We had sixteen morgs and the finest agricultural buildings, but our house was already very old."[54]

Agricultural Education

The chief Galician Crownland statistician, Tadeusz Pilat, referred scathingly in 1893 to the "lack of intelligence, industry, and relevant knowledge" of the peasants of Southern Podillia.[55] He decried subdivision of peasant holdings as the doom of Galician peasant agriculture. A few years later he acknowledged that there had been important improvements in all sectors of Galician agriculture.[56] This development could not have come about without new knowledge and information, often from elementary schools, enlightenment societies, and reading clubs. In addition, several Ukrainian publications, including *Nauka*, *Prosveshchenie*, *Viche*, *Novost*, and *Chytalnia*, kept their readers informed about agricultural innovations, especially new crops. The newspapers *Dilo* and *Batkivshchyna* ran frequent agricultural columns. After *Dilo* became a daily, its agricultural news was continued as an occasional feature, but *Batkivshchyna* continued to publish its agricultural columns until its demise in 1896. From its beginning in 1897, *Svoboda* carried a great number of agricultural items.

By far the fullest information, during the years 1879-87, was in *Hospodar i promyshlennyk*. It not only announced new strains of traditional grains and new crops, but also expanded on their characteristics. For example, there would frequently be an illustration of the plant, its botanical name, use, best type of soil for the plant, seedbed preparation, time and rate of seeding, place in crop rotation, disease and weed control, time for harvest, methods of harvesting, storing and marketing tips, as well as the economics of production, including figures on the profit to be made from its production. Articles like "Does weight of seed have any influence on the yield?" commented specifically on the relationship between good-quality seed and yields.[57] There were also advertisements, announcements, and testimonials on new seed varieties. Often included were the names and addresses of persons, usually parish priests, who were selling seed privately. For example, there was an advertisement for "Hybrydo-Shampanske" Rye and "Kolosalnyi Hybryd" Wheat sold by Fr. Voliansky in Bile (Chortkiv county), which stated that seeds for these varieties could be purchased from him "cheaply (12 g per 100 kg)," and that "these seeds are twice as expensive to buy on the open market";[58] for "white American pearl rye" and "Banatka" wheat which could be purchased from Rev. Hryhorii Hrytsai in Demianiv; for a new type of potato, "Witterische Dauerkartoffel"; and for fifty different varieties of grapes.[59]

Other newspapers also had advertisements for new strains of traditional crops. Fr. Naumovych announced a new variety of barley, "Triumph," a Hungarian strain that was being tested in the Podillian area. The supplier, from Erfurt, Germany, also advertised seed potatoes named "Early Sunrise" and "Scottish Queen."[60] Soybean seeds were advertised at 60 kr per litre in 1881.[61] Mr. Temnytsky from Shydlivtsi (Husiatyn county) offered in 1893 to sell seed from his harvest of a new strain of rye called "Imperial Giant Rye." He claimed that he had been using it for three years and was very happy with it.[62] One especially interesting instance was a letter from a priest in Drohobych county who wrote that eight years earlier he had purchased 14 litres of barley seed called "Scottish," 10 litres of oats called "Urbita," and 100 kg of "Shampion" potatoes from another priest in Zalissia in Podillia. He wanted people to know that he had had good yields from his investment. The editor, who published the item under the heading "Does it pay to upgrade seeds?" added a note encouraging other readers to emulate this example.[63] The Ukrainian press also advertised new strains of fruit in 1884, for example, new varieties of apples—"Sara Alma" (a Crimean type) and "Babka"—and a new type of grape in 1885.[64] The Section for Horticulture and Beekeeping of the Galician Agricultural Association encouraged more productive fruit growing. For example, at a branch meeting in Strusiv (Terebovlia county) in 1886, fifty fruit-tree grafts and fifty lots of apple and gooseberry seeds were distributed to the twenty-six members present.[65] Even earlier, the same section sent to several county school councils (including those of Husiatyn and Chortkiv) 1,000 of "the finest grafts" for distribution among the schools.[66]

Hospodar i promyshlennyk published articles on such topics as the "Benefits from planting maize" and the advantages of crop rotation.[67] The benefits achieved by sound crop-rotation practices in Southern Podillia were noted by a Sejm enquiry commission as early as 1881.[68] That same year, an article "from Podillia" in *Viche* noted that many new types of grain were being grown there, including one named "Kostromskaia," and that they were doing well.[69] *Batkivshchyna* was pleased to note in 1885 that Ukrainian peasants in Eastern

по живвахъ зъ р. 1885. Вже такій станъ рѣчи не може намъ давати пôдставы до надѣи на лучшій часы и на тревале пôдвысшенье цѣнъ збôжа. Надѣя така мала-бы тымъ меншу пôдставу, коли зважимо що обшаръ землѣ, занятои пôдъ управою пшеницѣ, не то що въ Америцѣ, Индіяхъ та Австраліи але навѣть въ самôй Европѣ зббльшаєся. Всѣ державы западнй силуются черезъ положенье мыта на чужестороній збôжа заспокоити свои потребы своєю домашною продукцією а сей моментъ ôтбирає также надѣю на тревале пôдвысшенье цѣнъ збôжа (въ першôй линіи пшеницѣ) въ будучности.

Якй зъ того стану рѣчей повиннй вытягнути внесеня нашй практичнй господарѣ, особливо такй, що продукуютъ пшеницю на продажь — про се иншимъ разомъ.

Цѣна товару и иншихъ продуктôвъ у Вѣдни.

Волы (д. 19. с. м.) На торзѣ було зъ Галичины 1184, зъ Угорщины 673 а зъ нѣмецкихъ провинцій 816 штукъ волôвъ и коровъ. За галицкй волы плачено по 54—60 зр. за коровы и бугаѣ 45—53 зр.; за волы зъ пашѣ 52—55 зр. за 100 к. мертвои ваги.

Телята (д. 15 с. м.) На торзѣ було 3212 телятъ. За живй плачено по 34—36 кр.; за найлучшй по 40—46—50 кр.; за зарѣзанй по 36—46 кр. за 1 кильограмъ ваги.

Свинѣ (д. 13. с. м.) Всѣхъ свиней було до 6.444 штукъ. Зъ Галичины привезено 2.979 штукъ. Плачено за пазимки по 35—41 кр.; за тяжкй штуки 38—39½ кр., за середнй 36—37½ кр., а за плохй по 33—34½ кр. за 1 кгр. живои ваги.

Яйця и масло. Ôтъ 12—19 с. м. довезено 532.000 штукъ яєць; по 44—47 штукъ за 1 зр., а 21.400 кильо масла по 70—110 зр. за 100 кильогр.

Мѣдъ (д. 20 липня). За мѣдъ бѣлый зъ Банату 30—32 зр., за угорскій жовтый 28—30 зр. за 100 кгр.

Смалець 56—64 кр. за 1 кильо.

Ленъ и конопль. Конопль галицкй нетертй 30—32, конопл. повѣсма 112—117; ленъ нетертый галицкій 32—40, спускане повѣсмо лняне 142—178 зр. за 100 кильо.

Вовна. Зъ овець краєвыхъ однострижа 95—100 зр. двострижа 80—90 зр. вовна лѣтна 85—90 зр.; вовна зъ овечихъ шкôръ 50—130 зр. зъ ягнятъ 70—80 зр.

Курсъ збôжа зъ дня 21. липня.

100 кильо безъ мѣшка на мѣсци	Вѣдень ôтъ	до	Львôвъ ôтъ	до	Тернопôль ôтъ	до	Пôдволочиск ôтъ	до	Ярославъ ôтъ	до	Черновцѣ ôтъ	до
	зр.		зр.		зр		зр.		зр		зр.	
Пшениця бѣла, червона (банатка)	7 87	7 92	7.50	8 10	7 25	8	7.—	7.75	[illegible]			
Жито	6.45	6.50	5 50	6 25	6 —	—.—	5.65	5 75	6.—	6 50	5.30	[illegible]
Ячмѣнь броварный . .	—.—	—.—	5.90	6.20	5 50	6 75	—.—	—.—	5 50	7 —	—.—	—.—
„ на пашу . .	—.—	—.—	—.—	—.—	—.—	—.—	5.—	5.50	—.—	—.—	5 50	5 70
Овесъ	6.33	6 38	5 80	6.20	6 20	—.—	6.—	—.—	6.35	—.—	5 —	5 40
Горохъ до варки . .	—.—	—.—	6.—	9.—	6 —	8.—	5 50	7.—	6.—	9 —	5 90	8.50
„ на пашу . .	—.—	—.—	—.—	—.—	—.—	—.—	—.—	—.—	—.—	—.—	—.—	—.—
Вика	—.—	—.—	—.—	—.—	—.—	—.—	—.—	—.—	—.—	—.—	—.—	—.—
Бобъ	—.—	—.—	—.—	—.—	—.—	—.—	—.—	—.—	—.—	—.—	—.—	—.—
Фасоля	—.—	—.—	—.—	—.—	—.—	—.—	—.—	—.—	—.—	—.—	—.—	—.—
Просо	—.—	—.—	6 25	7 —	—.—	—.—	—.—	—.—	—.—	—.—	—.—	—.—
Гречка	—.—	—.—	8 25	8.75	—.—	—.—	—.—	—.—	—.—	—.—	—.—	—.—
Кукурудза	5.40	5 50	7 25	7.75	—.—	—.	—.—	—.—	—.—	—.—	4.95	5 20
„ чинкантино .	—.—	—.—	—.—	—.—	—.—	—.—	—.—	—.—	—.—	—.—	5 40	5.60
Рѣпакъ	10 15	10 20	8.75	8.80	8 35	8.55	8 25	8 85	8.75	9.—	8 50	9
Лнянка	—.—	—.—	—.—	—.—	—.—	—.—	—.—	—.—	—.—	—.—	—.—	—.—
Конопляне сѣмя . .	—.—	—.—	—.—	—.—	—.—	—.—	—.—	—.—	—.—	—.—	—.—	—.—
Лняне сѣмя . . .	—.—	—.—	—.—	—.—	—.—	—.—	—.	—.—	—.—	—.—	—.	—.
Конюшина червона . .	—.—	—.—	25.—	35.—	25.—	30 —	25 —	30 —	25 —	30.—	25 —	30.—
„ бѣла . .	—.—	—.—	25.—	30.—	25 —	30.—	25.—	30.—	25 —	30.—	25.—	30.
„ шведска . .	—.—	—.—	25 —	30 —	25.—	30. —	25.—	30 —	25.—	30.—	25.—	30.—
Тимотка	—.—	—.—	—.—	—.—	—.—	—.—	—.—	—.—	—.—	—.—	—.—	—.—
Хмѣль новый за 56 кильо	—.—	—.—	50.—	55.—	—.—	—.—	—.—	—.—	—.—	—.—	—.—	—.—

Оковита 10 000 литр проц. у Львовѣ 25 50 до 25 75.

Зъ друкарнѣ Товариства им. Шевченка, пôдъ зарядомъ К. Беднарского.

A page from *Hospodar i promyshlennyk* (16 July 1886) advertising rye to be bought from Fr. Voliansky

Выходитъ два разы въ мѣсяць, 1. и 16 р

Редакція и администрація въ каменици руской Бурсы при улици Середной нръ. 13.

Издатель и отвѣчательный редакторъ **Аполлонъ Ничай**.

Одно число 10 кр.

Предплата цѣлор., 2 зр., пôвр. 1 зр. 15 кр. — для селянъ членôвъ Станиславôвскои филіи Общества им. М. Качковского за весь годъ 1 зр

Ч. 13. Станиславôвъ, дня 1. мая 1880. Г. I.

Справозданіе.

О господарскôмъ промыслѣ и о спôлкахъ. II. — Расы курей. (Продовженье.) — Розхôдъ насѣня изъ рускои крамницѣ въ Станиславовѣ. — Правила до користнои худôвлѣ свиней. — Користи изъ управы кукурудзы I Говодыского. — Дрôбніи вѣсти. — Вѣсти общественніи. — Переписка со Всѣми. — Цѣны збôжа. — Отозва — Инсераты.

О господарскôмъ промыслѣ и о спôлкахъ.

II.

Кôлька лѣтъ тому, коли то по разъ першій зайшла до насъ вѣсть за бульбу американьску; собравъ въ однôмъ селѣ одинъ господарь кôлькохъ иншихъ, и намовивъ ихъ, щобы собѣ вразъ записали тои бульбы по гарнцеви, а гарнецъ стоявъ тогды съ приставою 2 зр. Зложилося бôсьмохъ на тое, не грôшми, но словомъ, и овый першій господарь записавъ 8 гарнцевъ; грошѝ мали всѣ донести, коли прійде бульба. И не чекали довго, бо за границею люди рухливѝ, высылаютъ сейчасъ, скоро ся що замовитъ, щобы не робити никому заводу. Принесли бульбу зъ почты и собралися всѣ замовившѝ газды, щобы зобачити насѣнье, дороге; дѣялося то въ хатѣ ового господаря, котрый другихъ до того намовивъ. Розпечатали, розпаковали, и нуже одинъ за другимъ заглядати до мѣшка; заглянувъ одинъ, скрутився, такъ само другій, третій, шестый, щось межи собою пошипотѣли, стискали раменами, тай мало помалу одинъ за другимъ вынесли ся зъ хаты. Та отъ що за причина: тымъ семомъ газдикамъ здавалося, що

Front page of *Hospodar i promyshlennyk*, 1 May 1880

Galicia were switching to the cultivation of hops, flax, and orchards. A letter to the same paper in the following year exhorted peasants to reduce the amount of land under grain and to cultivate more peas, beans, fodder crops, and fruit.[70] In 1890 *Batkivshchyna* included advice to peasants about manure and other fertilizers, animals, bees, cattle disease, gardening, and fruits. Its quasi-successor, *Svoboda*, instituted a regular question-and-answer column for peasants conducted by the well-known agronomist Vasyl Korol, who answered questions on such topics as fertilizers, crop rotation, ploughs, the feeding of potatoes and beets to pigs, and cattle. "Don't worry how well you write—it's the content of your letters that counts," was the paper's exhortation to its readers.[71]

There is a myth that Eastern Galician Ukrainian peasants continued to use primitive ploughs into the twentieth century.[72] Contemporaries knew that most did not. Fr. Naumovych wrote: "Our ploughs are better than our fathers'; they are lighter and break up the soil better."[73] There were frequent advertisements for ploughs, including the new steel ploughs, in the press of the 1880s and 1890s. Testimonials, too, were published for good ploughs; those made by the factory of the brothers Shulakevych "are light, don't torture the cattle, and do a good job" and were available in all Narodna Torhivlia stores including the one in Ternopil.[74] There were free courses on ploughing for peasants at the Dubliany Agricultural College[75] and probably also at Iaholnytsia.[76] Before the end of the century even Pilat recognized that "small landowners have indeed abandoned the primitive implements, that is, the *radlo*, and the peasant plough. Constant and significant progress in the use of improved implements cannot be denied."[77]

Southern Podillian blacksmiths and craftsmen were also involved in making the newer and more effective ploughs. Fr. Velyhorsky of Ivanie Puste (Borshchiv county), for example, trumpeted abroad the skills of a man in his parish who made ploughs on the German Sakk model, the most expensive version of which, all of iron, sold for 24 g (he had already made some 70 ploughs).[78] The use of seed drills was also urged. By the end of the nineteenth century many holdings had straw cutters. Shop-bought scythes and sickles were also available.[79] The Galician Agricultural Association and its offshoots, such as the Agricultural Circles and the Sections for Horticulture and Beekeeping, also actively promoted agricultural improvements. They, as well as Prosvita and the Kachkovsky Society, exhorted their members in their publications and at various meetings to use better seed, which they supplemented with free samples or discount-priced seeds.[80] How many peasants in Southern Podillia actually bought the new or improved varieties of seed cannot be determined, but the example set by the parish clergy and large landowners helped to point them in that direction. The use of improved strains of crops by the latter had a far-ranging spinoff effect upon the peasants because of the still widespread custom of making payments in kind to day labourers. The latter might be local landless villagers or itinerant workers from West Galicia or the Carpathian mountain areas, but many of them were local smallholders (see Appendix IX). A good day's work on a large landholding could provide the peasant with about ten sheaves of grain that might be better than his own, some of which could be used as the peasant's own seed the following year.[81]

The Galician or Lviv Agricultural Association, originally funded out of members' dues, received state and Land subsidies during the last part of the century. It had had a great preoccupation with the affairs of the large landowners, but after 1880 it played an increasing role in the promotion of agricultural education for the peasantry. As a quasi-government agency it collected information for the Viennese and Lviv authorities. After the appointment of the Galician Pole, Count Alfred Potocki, as Austrian Minister of Agriculture in 1867 and subsequently as Minister "for Galicia," it also became a vehicle for dispensing subsidies.[82] It organized "sections" that dealt specifically with forestry (established 1852), horticulture (1853), silk (1854), beekeeping (1857), and cattle and horse breeding (1858). Sometimes local sections might combine, as at Strusiv (Terebovlia county); there was also a section in Chortkiv.[83] The Association sponsored agricultural exhibitions and had responsibility for Galicia's first higher agricultural school at Dubliany, and later for seven lower agricultural schools (including one at Iaholnytsia), which offered the three-year course in agriculture as well as summer courses. The Association issued publications, such as *Rolnik* (Farmer), after 1867, and had itinerant teachers who provided general instruction or specific information on a great variety of agricultural topics, including the growing of hops and tobacco and the construction of buildings.[84] On a visit to Zalishchyky county in 1894 the itinerant teacher gave lectures and visited a number of holdings to tender specific advice.[85]

Although the association was often regarded as a particularly Polish organization, its services were available to all. The short courses it provided, for example on horseshoeing, elementary veterinary knowledge, and ploughing were advertised or described in the Ukrainian press, as were its other activities, such as provision of seeds and fruit tree grafts.[86] At the Association's annual meeting in 1894, Ukrainians expressed their satisfaction with its activities.[87] As the years went by, and particularly in the 1890s, the Galician Agricultural Association received increasing subsidies from the Sejm.[88] After 1881 it also assumed increasing responsibility for the "Agricultural Circles" (*Kółka rolnicze*) which had been formed by Polish peasants in some localities, though not in Southern Podillia. In structure, these circles somewhat resembled the Ukrainian enlightenment societies' reading clubs. Each had a library and reading hall; they had Sunday afternoon meetings with discussion of common agricultural problems and reading aloud of the press. A circle might be formed by any group of at least six "non-Jewish farmers." The general goal of the circles was to enhance the agricultural knowledge of its members.[89]

Sixteen agricultural circles were formed in Southern Podillian towns and villages in the years 1883-5. Their locations and membership in 1885 were: Borshchiv (17); Iaholnytsia (23), Sosulivka (27), Zalissia (12), and Zvyniach (42) (all in Chortkiv county); Husiatyn (75), Lychkivtsi (15), and Zhabyntsi (26) (Husiatyn county); Ianiv (38), Lozhniv (79), Mohylnytsia (8), Pidhaichyky (81), Strusiv (31), and Tiutkiv (18) (Terebovlia county); Myshkiv (8) and Tluste (21) (Zalishchyky county).[90] By 1892 the number of agricultural circles in Southern Podillia had risen to twenty-five.[91] The agricultural circles' central committee in Lviv published *Przewodnik kółek rolniczych* (Guide for Agricultural Circles), which also had a Ukrainian edition, *Providnyk rilnychykh kruzhkiv*.[92] The central committee sent out speakers on agricultural topics such as ploughing and preparing the soil, improving the quantity and quality of fertilizers, what grain seeds to use, and animal husbandry. These speakers would be noted by the Ukrainian press and *Batkivshchyna* urged Ukrainian peasants to request their attendance, too.[93] Members also were able to order seed, fertilizer, fruit-tree grafts, and farm implements through the central committee at discounted prices. Later, the central committee helped found village shops. Ukrainians were members of some of the agricultural circles and of the central committee in Lviv.[94]

The extensive network of Ukrainian reading clubs in Southern Podillia also played a major role in spreading agricultural knowledge and education throughout the region. Because of their greater number, their work in this sphere must be accounted more significant than that of the Agricultural Association and the agricultural circles. Prosvita, too, sponsored visits to villages by itinerant teachers of agriculture. In 1896 it hired agronomist Vasyl Korol to assist villagers with their agricultural problems. He went to Borshchiv county in the same year to give agricultural advice and to visit peasant holdings for individual consultation. He visited twenty-one communes and held lectures that 944 people attended.[95]

While there was so much agricultural education activity going on in Eastern Galicia and Southern Podillia during the last two decades of the nineteenth century, "improvements in crop production follow upon demonstrated improvements by a few enterprising farmers. Mere urging of farmers to change their methods isn't enough."[96] Pilat believed that peasant agriculture was improving because of the example of the large landowners.[97] However, since many large landowners were experiencing great difficulties, it is unlikely that his explanation is sufficient or correct. More likely, as a Galician agronomist stated in 1886, "it is the example of the priest which is best accepted and copied by the peasants."[98] Greek Catholic clergymen were required, as seminarians, to attend agronomy classes, and as village priests they generally displayed a "service" mentality which led them to set examples to their flock by their own agricultural practices.[99] Quite a large number of examples can be found in the recollections of persons from Southern Podillia of enterprising farmer-priests who led by example as well as by exhortation. Fr. M. Krushelnytsky, the long-term priest of Iaholnytsia Stara (Chortkiv county), was remembered fondly because "he cultivated new varieties of grain and enjoyed gardening and raising thoroughbred livestock."[100] Other priests mentioned for their exemplary agronomic practices included Fr. Kysilevsky of Krehulets (Husiatyn); Fr. Uhrynkivsky of Shchytivtsi (Zalishchyky); Fr. Hankevych of Ustia Iepyskopske and Frs. Hlibovetsky and Kaznovsky of Hlubichok (Borshchiv). Kaznovsky "even gave his parishioners information about various branches of agriculture from the pulpit."[101] Fr. Velyhorsky of Ivanie Puste took such great interest in his parishioners' ploughs that he publicized them.[102] Fr. Zvarychevsky had a "model farm" in Zalissia (Borshchiv county); Fr. O. Kniahynytsky of Zalishchyky "developed near the rectory one of the first large-scale apricot orchards in the area."[103] Many Greek Catholic village priests indeed played their role as agricultural educators in Southern Podillia.

Teachers also played a part, though a lesser one, as agricultural educators and exemplars. Since the Galician Agricultural Association offered agricultural courses at Galician Teachers' Colleges,[104] many teachers received some training in agriculture. Several teachers were remembered by memoir writers for their fine agricultural practices, including S. Hnitsky of Ustia Iepyskopske (Borshchiv county) and V. Khraplyvy of Lysivtsi (Zalishchyky county).[105]

Over the years much information about and instruction in the latest agricultural techniques, and access to improved varieties of field and other crops, thus became available to Southern Podillian villagers. That their own customary leaders acted as role models for the improvement of agriculture was of considerable significance, as was the fact that in so many villages there were reading clubs where Ukrainian peasants could discuss agricultural issues. In light of all this activity, it is scarcely surprising that productivity increased.

Notes

1. See Hryniuk, "Peasant Agriculture," 228-9; B.P. Murdzek, *Emigration in Polish Social-Political Thought, 1870-1914*, 83-6; A. Suligowski, "Pierwszy zjazd prawników i ekonomistów polskich."
2. See, especially, Z. Daszyńska-Golińska, *Własność rolna w Galicyi*; and Z. Ludkiewicz, *Kwestia rolna w Galicji*. For differing views see F. Bujak, *Galicya*; and L.W. Biegeleisen, *Rozwój gospodarczy nowoczesnej*.
3. Ernest Labrousse, "The Evolution of Peasant Society in France from the Eighteenth Century to the Present," 58.
4. See P. McPhee, "A Reconsideration of the 'Peasantry' of Nineteenth-Century France," 14-15.
5. Austrian laws and regulations on land tenure in Galicia are conveniently

summarized by H. von Schullern-Schrattenhofen in *Geschichte der österreichischen Land- und Forstwirtschaft und Ihrer Industrien*, I, pt. ii: 338-40. For the principles underlying these measures see Blanning, *Joseph II and Enlightened Despotism*, 10-11, 53; and K. Sojka-Zielińska, *Prawne problemy podziału gruntów chłopskich w Galicji na tle Austriackiego ustawodawstwa agrarnego*, 9-11. For other details of the Austrian laws see Inglot, *Historia chłopów polskich*, 184-5.

6. T. Pilat, "Landtäflicher Grundbesitz," 288-90, and the sources cited above.
7. P. Zakharchyshyn, ed., *Iosyfinska i Frantsyskanska Metryky, pershi pozemelni kadastry Halychyny, pokazhchyk naselenykh punktiv*.
8. The later land-tax assessment revisions are sometimes referred to as those of 1883 and 1897.
9. Sojka-Zielińska, *Prawne problemy*, 20-2; *Geschichte der österreichischen Land- und Forstwirtschaft*, I, pt. ii: 338. Other arrangements were permitted only in exceptional cases, e.g., if local officials deemed the consolidation of small rustical plots into one larger holding to be in the interests of better agricultural practice.
10. *Geschichte der österreichischen Land- und Forstwirtschaft*, I, ii, 339; Sojka-Zielińska, *Prawne problemy*, 27, 54.
11. Sojka-Zielińska, *Prawne problemy*, 68.
12. M. Marasse, "O wolności parcelowania gruntów ze względu na stosunki galicyjskie," 100.
13. For these measures in Galicia see K. Grzybowski, *Galicja 1848-1914*, 24ff., 122ff.
14. *Istoriia selianstva Ukrainskoi RSR*, 1: 429; M.P. Herasymenko, *Ahrarni vidnosyny v periodi kryzy panshchynnoho hospodarstva*, 291.
15. Herasymenko, *Ahrarni vidnosyny*, 292.
16. S. Kieniewicz, *The Emancipation of the Polish Peasantry*, 137-8.
17. Rozdolski, *Wspólnota gminna w b. Galicji wschodniej i jej zanik*, 6.
18. In many of their features the village communes resembled the Russian *obshchina* system, to which they had historic links. See ibid., 63-78, for comparisons with other regions.
19. For a full description of the working of this system in Eastern Galicia see ibid., *passim*. In some exceptional cases even houses were exchanged by peasants when the land-usage cycle changed, ibid., 82. W. Stys was of the view that labor dues were for a long time lighter in Eastern than in Western Galicia (*Rozdrąbnienie gruntów chłopskich w byłym zaborze austrjackim od roku 1787 do 1931*).
20. Rozdolski, *Wspólnota gminna*, *passim*; Inglot, *Historia chłopów Polskich*, 254.
21. These uprisings are described in *Radianska entsyklopediia istorii Ukrainy*, 4: 502.
22. W. Pruski, *Hodowla zwierząt gospodarskich*, 28-31; Inglot, *Historia chłopów Polskich*, 176.
23. Rozdolski, *Wspólnota gminna*, 41-6.
24. The five Southern Podillian counties of the late nineteenth century were then part of the Ternopil and Chortkiv districts (*Kreise*). In these two districts approximately 55,600 hectares of rustical land were annexed to tabular land during the six years of Russian rule (Rozdolski, *Wspólnota gminna*, 48-9).
25. Villagers in Zalishchyky succeeded in 1848 in recovering some pasture land illegally annexed to the manor earlier in the century (Grzybowski, *Galicja 1848-1918*, 30).

26. See, for example, E. Weber, *Peasants into Frenchmen*, 126; R. Pipes, *Russia under the Old Regime*, 166. However, even in the early nineteenth century Galician villagers travelled to places as far afield as Hungary and Vienna to sell their handicraft products and agricultural produce (Inglot, *Historia chłopów Polskich*, 205-7).
27. Stys, *Rozdrąbnienie gruntów*, 107-8.
28. Schullern-Schrattenhofen in *Geschichte der österreichischen Land- und Forstwirtschaft*, I, ii, 339; Sojka-Zielińska, *Prawne problemy*, 37.
29. T. Pilat, "Die Auswanderung," 82.
30. Szczepanowski, *Nędza Galicyi*, 20-2.
31. T. Pilat, "Die Auswanderung," 85-6; B.P. Murdzek, *Emigration in Polish-Political Thought 1870-1914*, 83-6.
32. Quoted in Murdzek, *Emigration*, 84.
33. Pilat, though aware of the importance of what was produced, still focussed on size ("Die Auswanderung").
34. Pilat, "Der landtäflicher Grundbesitz," 288-9; Bujak, *Galicya*, 1: 253; Inglot, *Historia chłopów Polskich*, 201; *Batkivshchyna*, 2 July and 8 Oct. 1886, 19 Jan. 1889, 21 Aug. 1891, 28 Mar. and 13 Apr. 1896; *Nauka*, 28 Feb. 1889.
35. Subsequent studies of Galician landholding patterns all rely to a greater or lesser extent on the 1868 study by M. Marasse. He acknowledged that some areas were excluded from his calculations and that he did not trust some of the land-tax assessment data he had used. He concluded that the average Galician peasant holding had declined from 5.4 hectares in 1819 to 5.1 in the 1850s (Marasse, "O wolności parcelowania," 90, 93, 94, 97, 100). I. Franko used Marasse's work and data from the land-tax assessment revision of 1882-3 to conclude that between 1819 and 1883 the average size of Galician rustical landholdings had declined in the ratio of 100:37, while the number of such holdings had increased in the ratio of 100:275 (Franko, "Zemelna vlastnist u Halychyni," 285-6). V. Budzynovsky, whose work contains transpositional and computational errors, arrived at the conclusion that while the average size of the Galician peasant holding in 1897 was 2.35 ha, 46.4 per cent of the peasantry had on average only 1.1 ha each (Budzynovsky, *Khlopska posilist*, 8-11, 53; for an instance of inconsistency, compare pages 14 and 45; for other errors, see, for example, pages 3 and 10). In the above, I have recalculated morgs into hectares. In view of a later finding that the subdivision of land in Galicia was greatest near large towns (*Geschichte der österreichischen Land- und Forstwirtschaft*, I, pt. ii: 340), it is unlikely that any of the above computations would throw much light on the situation in a region as far removed from large towns as was Southern Podillia.
36. Daszyńska-Golińska, *Własność rolna w Galicyi*, 2. See also the criticism of her methodology in Bujak, *Galicya*, 1: 240.
37. Pilat, "Die Auswanderung," 75.
38. Ibid.
39. Ibid., 76.
40. Bujak, *Galicya*, 1: 240, 420-3. Stys (*Rozdrąbnienie gruntów*, 54-5) was also very critical of the use of tax-assessment data and surveys by earlier authors. In his view, the number of catastral parcels should have been divided by four or five to

arrive at the real number of landholdings.

41. Daszyńska-Golińska, *Własność rolna w Galicyi*, 19.
42. F. Bujak, "Wieś zachodnio-galicyjska u schyłku XIX wieku," 287.
43. Bujak, *Galicya*, 1: 240.
44. Ibid., 241-2. For instance, the data did not differentiate between households for which the use of land was a primary or a secondary source of income.
45. For details see S. Hryniuk, "A Peasant Society in Transition," tables 31, 32.
46. By way of comparison it may be noted that 44 per cent of all "agricultural operations" in Galicia had fewer than 2 ha, as did 45.6 per cent of those in Bohemia and 51.1 per cent of those in Moravia (*Oesterreichische Statistik*, vol. LXXXIII, no. 1, table IIb). The process of land division in Zalishchyky county presents a problem. There may have been some consolidation of peasant holdings there between 1848 and 1877 (Kleczyński, "Ekonomiczne stosunki Galicyi," 7). The average holding there may have increased between 1883 and 1897 (see flawed data in Daszyńska-Golińska, *Własność rolna w Galicyi*). Possibly peasant landholdings there were already smaller than the norm at emancipation.
47. *Oesterreichische Statistik*, LXXXVI, no. 5, table XI.
48. Servitude rights in Southern Podillia were held by smaller proportions of the agricultural operations than in many other Galician counties (ibid., no. 5, tables XXIII and XXIV). The way in which the 1902 questionnaire was phrased leaves open the possibility that some peasants retained some rights to pasturage and woodland use on tabular properties.
49. See Inglot, *Historia chłopów Polskich*, 262.
50. This is also recognized by Marxist scholars, with their interest in social stratification (T. Kolossa, "The Social Structure of the Peasant Class in Austria-Hungary: Statistical Sources and Methods of Research," 421).
51. Statistical data about smallholders who also worked for hire are in *Oesterreichische Statistik*, vol. LXXXIII, no. 5, and in Appendix IX below.
52. *Batkivshchyna*, 13 Feb. 1896.
53. Interviews with Mr. Horobec, Stuartburn, 29 June 1979; Mrs. Seniuk, Ethelbert, June 1979; Mrs. Sokolyk, Dominion City, 19 July 1979; and Mrs. Rekunyk, Stuartburn, 12 July 1979. It is quite possible that other immigrant families had different experiences in "the old country," but the persons I interviewed were selected solely on the basis of their Southern Podillian origin.
54. Havrysh, *Moia Kanada i ia*, 18.
55. Pilat, "Die Auswanderung," 78.
56. T. Pilat, "Landwirtschaft und Viehzucht," 797-819.
57. *Hospodar i promyshlennyk*, no.1, 1884.
58. Ibid., no. 1, 1886.
59. Ibid., no. 19, 1880; no. 7, 1884; no. 2, 1885.
60. *Nauka*, 15 Feb. 1886. The titles were in English in the original.
61. *Russkaia rada*, 20 Mar. 1881.
62. *Chytalnia*, 5 Aug. 1893.
63. *Batkivshchyna*, 28 Mar. 1896.
64. *Hospodar i promyshlennyk*, no. 1, 1884; no. 2, 1885.
65. *Batkivshchyna*, 21 May 1886.

66. *Dilo*, 17 Apr. 1880.
67. *Hospodar i promyshlennyk*, no. 13, 1880; no. 2, 1886.
68. Pruski, *Hodowla zwierząt gospodarskich*, 1: 587.
69. *Viche*, 15 July 1881. This newspaper also gave occasional advice on what to plant (ibid., 8 April 1881).
70. *Batkivshchyna*, 17 July 1885; 7 May 1886.
71. *Svoboda*, 21 Jan., 4 and 11 Feb., and 18 Mar. 1897.
72. See, for example, W. Najdus, *Szkice z historii Galicji*, 1: 113; and S. Kieniewicz, *Galicya w dobie autonomicznej 1850-1914, wybór tekstów*, 197-209, 224-7 and 234-42, who does not differentiate sufficiently between East and West Galicia. See also Rudnytsky, "The Ukrainians in Galicia under Austrian Rule," 52.
73. *Nauka*, 15 June 1886. Even earlier, on the basis of responses to the 1877 survey of peasant agriculture, Kleczyński had noted the widespread use of improved ploughs and other implements in Eastern Galicia, a development which he ascribed to the influence of the affiliates of the Agricultural Association; the attention paid by the Ukrainian press to the spreading of useful information among the people; and the influence in the villages of the priest and the elementary school teacher (Kleczyński, "Ekonomiczne stosunki Galicyi," 25-6).
74. *Batkivshchyna*, 17 May and 21 June 1889.
75. Ibid., 5 Aug. 1887.
76. See 73-4 above.
77. Pilat, "Landwirtschaft und Viehzucht," 810. Much the same opinion was enunciated by a near contemporary Ukrainian author, who wrote that "the primitive wooden plough, without metal mounting, has been retained only in places, in the Polissye [*sic*] region and the Carpathian country" (Rudnitsky, *Ukraine*, 258).
78. *Svoboda*, 10 June 1897. The use of "German" ploughs in Podillia was noted as early as 1881, but they were deemed inferior to the "Czech model" (*Viche*, 29 July 1881).
79. *Batkivshchyna*, 17 May 1889; *Oesterreichische Statistik*, LXXXIII, no. 5; interview with Mr. W. Michalchyshyn, Winnipeg, 6 Oct. 1983.
80. See, for example, *Viche* (8 Mar. 1880); *Dilo* (17 Apr. 1880); *Russkaia rada* (6 June 1881); *Batkivshchyna* (25 Jan. 1884; 2 Jan., 20 Mar., 3 Apr., 17 July 1885; 2 Apr. 1886; 29 Mar. 1889; 20 and 27 Feb. 1891); *Chytalnia* (23 Apr. 1893). See also A. Gurnicz, *Kółka rolnicze w Galicji*, 204-6.
81. Only L.W. Biegeleisen (*Rozwój gospodarczy nowoczesnej wsi Polskiej*, 1: 290ff) appears to have made the connection between payments in kind and better seed grain.
82. See above, 95. The work of the Agricultural Associations in Galicia is extensively treated in Rutkowski, *Historia gospodarcza Polski*, 1: 58-63, 2: 280, *passim*; and Pruski, *Hodowla zwierząt gospodarskich*, 1: 90-6, 305-6, 310-32, *passim*.
83. *Batkivshchyna*, 21 May 1886 and 27 Feb. 1891.
84. *Batkivshchyna*, 3 Apr. 1885, 5 Aug. 1887, 2 Mar. and 20 July 1888.
85. *Chytalnia*, 8 July 1894.
86. *Batkivshchyna*, 7 Jan. and 5 Aug. 1887; *Chytalnia*, 20 July 1893, and 21 June 1894; *Svoboda*, 5 May 1898.
87. *Chytalnia*, 6 Oct. 1894.
88. For details see E. Wytanowicz, "Polityka agrarna sejmu Galicyjskiego w cyfrach

budżetów krajowych," esp. 274.

89. See J. Dawidowa, *Kółka rolnicze w Galicyi*; Gurnicz, *Kółka rolnicze w Galicji*.
90. *Statistische Monatschrift* XII (1886): 368-74.
91. By 1912 there were fifty agricultural circles in Southern Podillia (Gurnicz, *Kółka rolnicze w Galicji*, 82-3).
92. *Entsyklopediia ukrainoznavstva*, 8: 2835.
93. Gurnicz, *Kółka rolnicze w Galicji*, 121, *passim*; *Batkivshchyna*, 17 July 1885. In 1893 there were 851 agricultural circles in Galicia, half of them in Eastern Galicia; Ukrainians were among the total membership of 40,061 (*Khliborob*, 15 April 1893).
94. *Batkivshchyna*, 2 and 16 Apr. 1886.
95. Persky, *Populiarna istoriia tovarystva*, 162-70; *Batkivshchyna*, 2 Mar. and 20 July 1888, and 16 June 1896; *Chytalnia*, 21 Aug. 1896.
96. J. Martin and W. Leonard, *Principles of Field Crop Production*, 5.
97. Pilat, "Landwirtschaft und Viehzucht," 806.
98. *Hospodar i promyshlennyk*, no. 2, 1886.
99. J.-P. Himka, "The Greek Catholic Church and Nationbuilding in Galicia," 432, *passim*.
100. IMZCh, 249.
101. Ibid., 361, 608, 628 651, 788.
102. *Svoboda*, 19 June 1897. There was a lively Greek Catholic village priest network, for a later issue of *Svoboda* (10 Feb. 1898) contained a letter from a priest in a different county thanking Fr. Velyhorsky for making available the name of the plough maker.
103. IMZCh, 674, 714.
104. Inglot, *Historia chłopów Polskich*, 276. In 1890, the Ministry of Education permitted the addition of a whole year to the program of men's teachers' colleges in Eastern Galicia to better prepare graduates to teach agricultural subjects in the schools (*Uchytel*, no. 22, 27 Nov. 1890).
105. IMZCh, 651, 822.

Chapter VII

Agriculture: (ii) Land Use, Field Crops, and Animal Husbandry

Productivity of agriculture in Galicia lagged behind that of most agricultural regions of Western Europe in the late nineteenth century. Many contemporary authors seem almost to have enjoyed making these comparisons,[1] but by themselves they tell little about the progress made by Galician agriculture. Two recent Polish authorities have acknowledged that improvements were under way by 1880.[2]

Most of the available data on crop production do not distinguish between what was produced on "tabular" land or on the land of large landowners and what was produced on "rustical" or peasant lands.[3] Data in Table 11 do not differentiate between tabular and rustical land; they are compiled on the basis of the legal categorization of land subject to land tax in Southern Podillia.

Table 11
Land Use in Southern Podillia,
by Legal Category, 1900, in Hectares

	Area subject to land tax	Plough-land	Meadows	Gardens	Pasturage	Woodland
Area	382,315	293,877	8,705	12,287	14,544	52,902
Percentage	100	76.9	2.3	3.2	3.8	13.8

Source: *Gemeindelexicon*, 1900.

Most of the garden land was owned by villagers; Pilat in 1893 estimated that in the southern portion of Borshchiv county gardens constituted about 9.5 per cent of the total rustical land.[4] The area devoted to gardens was not included in the category "productive land" as used in the 1902 agricultural census, although produce from their gardens was of great importance to peasant smallholders and other villagers. Almost all of the woodland in the Southern Podillian counties—generally 95 per cent—was owned by the tabular landowners. Woodland ownership played little direct part in the peasant economy (other than through its absence and some lumbering work). More than one-half of Southern Podillian meadowland was the property of tabular owners;[5] "meadows" and "pasturage" formed only a small proportion of the productive land of Southern Podillia. More than three-quarters of the taxable land area consisted of "ploughland." In each county, between 34 per cent of the ploughland (Terebovlia county) and 42 per cent (Zalishchyky county) was owned by tabular owners in 1902. The proportions had not varied greatly over the previous twenty or so years,[6] for the parcellation of landed estates had proceeded more slowly in Southern Podillia than in Galicia as a whole.

Changes in Cultivation Patterns

Throughout the nineteenth century, four grain crops predominated among the crops grown on Eastern Galician ploughland, including Southern Podillia:[7] wheat, rye, barley, and oats. Maize was also widely cultivated in Borshchiv, Chortkiv, Husiatyn, and Zalishchyky counties. What crops were actually planted in any one year depended in part on prevailing weather conditions and market prices. Peasants were just as likely as the large landowners to make changes in what they cultivated, though there was a constant requirement to grow as much as possible of what was needed to sustain their own families. Large landowners devoted a greater proportion of their arable land to the cultivation of wheat and oats than did peasants.[8]

The total area devoted to the five main grain crops in Southern Podillia declined by about 9 per cent in the years 1884-99. Although there were fluctuations during that period, the trend was toward a reduction in the hectarage devoted to rye and barley and an increase in wheat. The increased hectarage under wheat perhaps denoted some growth in wheat consumption in the villages, in part replacing the traditional rye bread.[9] However, the two major reasons for the increase in wheat were recovery in the last half of the 1890s of wheat prices throughout Europe[10] and several years of poor weather, which convinced some grain growers that wheat tolerated the local climatic conditions better than rye and some other grains.[11] This explains, too, the decline in the area under rye. There was a decrease in the area under barley, but a considerable increase in yield per hectare for this crop.

The areas under buckwheat and millet also decreased, which modern experts would have welcomed as a sign of modernization, for these crops are regarded as having low nutritional value.[12] The cultivation of millet certainly declined; the decline in the hectarage under buckwheat might have been due to a change in the diet of Southern Podillian villagers, for imported rice was increasingly used.[13] However, this decline was probably more apparent than real. The statistics maintained by the Austrian Agriculture Ministry, with one exception, recorded only the area devoted to, and the yields of, first or main crops. The decrease in the recorded areas under buckwheat was due mainly to another manifestation of modernization, as peasants increasingly heeded advice given by agronomists that buckwheat could be effectively grown as a second crop. It required only a short growing season and could often be planted as soon as fall-sown rye was harvested in the first week of July; it was also a good crop to plant if others failed.[14] Certainly buckwheat continued to be used in the villagers' diet and for certain ceremonial dishes. There was a temporary increase in the area under maize in the years 1889-92 that some who supposed it was a main food item thought was due to the population increase.[15] In fact, it was only one of many foods in the Southern Podillian diet,[16] and it appears more likely that much of the maize crop was used as feed for the growing number of farm animals, especially pigs. Maize also provided an opportunity for the peasants to grow more of the valuable "intercrops," the unrecorded crops such as pumpkins, beans, beets, hemp, and sunflowers that were grown between the rows of maize.[17]

In all, the amount of ploughland devoted to the growing of the seven traditional grain crops fell by about 7 per cent between 1884 and 1899, and the area represented a smaller percentage than in Austria as a whole.[18] In part, this was due to the 2-3 per cent increase in the area used for the cultivation of potatoes, which has often been regarded as an indication of increasing impoverishment of a society.[19] The decline in the proportion of ploughland devoted to the growing of grain was also due to other factors, all of which denote departures from traditional practices. Some of the crops grown on larger areas were not new, but the attention given to them in literature reaching the villages in the 1880s and 1890s and the apparent response of the peasantry were significant. Peas had been noted by the Lviv market authorities as early as 1814.[20] Clover was introduced into Eastern Galicia by German colonists in the late eighteenth century; it and fodder root crops thereafter were promoted by large landowners in Podillia such as Prince Adam Czartoryski.[21] By 1870 beans, lentils, rapeseed, flax, caraway seed, aniseed, linseed, and hops were all being bought and sold at Lviv.[22]

Commercial Crops and Fodder Crops

The hectarage devoted to legumes in Southern Podillia fluctuated, but was about the same at the end of the century as it had been in the early 1880s.[23] It is noteworthy that in any year in the 1880s and 1890s 4-8 per cent (usually 5-7 per cent) of the land was planted with legumes, especially peas. As commercial crops, legumes were of growing importance on European markets in the last quarter of the nineteenth century. The podded crops added variety and nutrients, especially protein, to the local diet, and also nitrified the soil. As *Batkivshchyna* pointed out, each type of legume also contributed to the overall improvement of agriculture by providing fodder for animals from leaves and stalks, and some beans and most vetches were grown specifically as fodder crops.[24] While the areas devoted to some commercial crops such as flax and rape varied over the years, hemp hectarage declined in the 1890s, as railways penetrated the region and factory-manufactured rope displaced the homemade variety on large estates and the larger smallholdings. Field-grown cabbage represented only a portion of the total crop, for cabbages were also grown in gardens. Hops and caraway seed were grown in small quantities, and both were quite profitable if sold commercially. Hops were grown principally by large landowners, but they grew very few of the other specialty cash crops; one hectare of caraway could produce 7-15 metric centner of seed, worth 20-40 g per metric centner.[25]

Tobacco growing was very profitable. It was state-regulated and had earlier been the preserve of the large landowners, but because of its labour-intensive nature, it came to be concentrated in peasant hands. The number of individual peasant households involved in tobacco cultivation in Galicia grew from 25,000 in 300 communes in 13 counties in 1890 to 37,150 in 456 communes in 14 counties by 1905. Because of the climatic conditions it required, Galician tobacco cultivation was centred in Southern Podillia (largely excluding Terebovlia county, though yields there could be very high) and neighbouring Pokuttia. Between 1884 and 1898 the hectarage under tobacco rose 233 per cent in Southern Podillia, and the profit on the crop grown on a quarter-hectare plot could amount to as much as 200-300 crowns (100-150 g) in 1906. Some specialty tobaccos were grown in villages in Husiatyn county.[26] Tobacco was also grown illegally, hidden among the maize, for the villagers' own consumption.[27]

Aniseed, fennel seed, poppy seed, and other commercial crops were also grown on small plots, though the total area of land devoted to their cultivation was small. The spread of these crops was facilitated by a growing marketing network organized by Narodna Torhivlia. As early as 1885 *Hospodar i promyshlennyk* asserted that "a buyer can always be found for these crops," and one hectare of poppy seed could bring in a return of 200-400 g.[28] The production of even small amounts of such crops could thus be a substantial supplement to the peasants' income. The hectarage devoted to the production of fodder beets remained small throughout the period, and that recorded as used for the growing of mixed fodder of various types (green maize or a mixture of oats and vetches) declined in South Podillia in the 1890s. However, more than one crop might be grown on a given area of land, and a mixture of oats, vetches, and clover was recommended as a good crop for late sowing;[29] some fodder crops and the land devoted to them might thus not have shown up in the official statistics.

If there was a decrease in the area of land under mixed fodder, the increase in the growing of clover was very striking. The area devoted to clover more than doubled between the early 1880s and the late 1890s, and by the last decade of the century peasants were cultivating just under one-half of all the Southern Podillian land under clover.[30] Clover was emphasized by *Hospodar i promyshlennyk* in its recommended crop rotations.[31] It often required only a short growing season, which meant that either a second clover crop could be obtained (whose yield would be unrecorded except for the valuable clover seed), or another crop of a different type might be grown with it or after it.[32]

Fallow

In Southern Podillia the amount of land apparently left fallow each year varied between 10-18 per cent of the total ploughland, except in 1890 and 1892 when, following poor harvests the previous years, it was a little lower; in Terebovlia county it was consistently higher throughout the period.[33] "Ploughland" was a legal category dating back to Josephinian times in Galicia. Once made, land-use categorization for tax purposes was very difficult to change. Ploughland was, at times, grassland, and in the late nineteenth century, especially when crops such as alfalfa and clover were used more and the number of animals rose, it was increasingly used as animal pasture land.[34] Technically, it continued to be described as "fallow," though recognition of reality caused the Ministry of Agriculture to change the designation from "fallow" to "unspecified crops and fallow" in the mid-1890s.

An increasing proportion of truly fallow land belonged to the great estates rather than to peasant smallholders. The former were principally affected by the depressed world prices for grain until the late 1890s and by the "high" cost of hired labour. The peasant family farm or smallholding operation generally did not have to take the latter factor into consideration. By the 1890s it strove to make productive use, consistent with good agricultural practices, of all available land. Whereas large landowners might deliberately take land out of production because returns on its use were not sufficient, peasants were being taught by professional agronomists and parish priests that fallow need play little part in crop rotation, for it could be replaced by beans, root crops (including potatoes), and pasturage grasses.[35] While they did not abandon altogether the practice of leaving land fallow, their agriculture was very intensive. "In the cultivation of their respective locations, not even the width necessary for the furrow of a plough is wasted... crops may be seen at any stage of growth."[36]

That may have been a result of the peasants' land hunger, but it was more likely an outcome of constant advice given to Ukrainian peasants on how to increase productivity:

> It is most important that no portion of the land should be empty, not a single week, ever; when you take off one crop there should immediately be something growing in its place; plant between the other plants; plant earlier ones among later ones.[37]

Second Crops, Intercrops, Gardens, and Orchards: The Unrecorded Economy

With one exception, the statistics of the Austrian Ministry of Agriculture did not take note of "second crops." The exception was clover seed, for which yield but not hectarage was recorded (see Appendix VII). Mainly red clover seed was produced in Southern Podillia. Although much was exported at good prices, domestic market prices were quite high also; for example 52-60 g per 100 kg at Lviv and 48-59 g per 100 kg at Ternopil in February 1889.[38] Otherwise, second crops as well as intercrops were part of an unrecorded economy of unknown but significant dimensions.[39]

Intercrops, planted between rows of maize, cabbage or potatoes, were important to agricultural labourers and peasant smallholders alike. Large landowners condoned the practice of day labourers growing peas, beans, pumpkins, hemp, and root crops between rows on estate lands.[40] As early as 1880, peasants were being urged to grow intercrops on their own lands, for beans and pumpkins grown between rows of maize could increase the value of a plot's produce by 50 per cent.[41] Agronomists writing for various Ukrainian papers taught the peasants what best to grow as an intercrop.[42] Buckwheat was recommended as a good second crop because of its short growing season; it might also serve as a replacement crop if the original crop failed.[43] Advice was regularly given in *Batkivshchyna* on what compensatory action to take if fall-sown crops were destroyed by rodents or severely damaged by inclement weather conditions such as insufficient snow cover. The noted agronomist A. Hlodzynsky advised peasants, early in 1890, to compensate for the shortage of fodder that year by planting oats mixed with vetches and clover. Around St. John's Day (7 July), the oats and vetches could be harvested, while the clover would continue to grow until the fall and produce three wagonloads of good clover fodder per morg (1.74 morgs = 1 hectare approx.)[44] *Chytalnia* also ran a regular column of agricultural advice.

Like the volume of second crops and intercrops, the amount of produce from peasants' gardens was not recorded in any official statistics. Gardens comprised an unusually high percentage of the total tax-assessed land in Southern Podillia. They were usually tended by the women of the household,[45] and a great variety of vegetables, fruits, spices, medicinal and aromatic plants, and flowers were grown in them, including potatoes and cabbages, which were also field crops.[46] Garden produce clearly accounted for a considerable portion of the peasantry's plant-based diet, and although no quantitative record of this produce is available, it cannot be ignored as a factor in Southern Podillia's overall productivity.

Fruit growing was widespread in the Southern Podillian villages, especially in the two southern counties of Borshchiv and Zalishchyky; one S. Pistrakevych from Zalishchyky won a first-class medal for his apples and pears at a fruit exhibition in Vienna in September 1888.[47] The peasants grew fruit for their own use and for sale. The principal orchard fruits were apples, pears, plums, cherries, and apricots. An Austrian traveller through Zalishchyky county marvelled that "this place is distinguished by its beautiful orchards and vineyards.... All types of fruits and vegetables grow splendidly here."[48] The reference to vineyards is of special interest, for officially there were none in Galicia.[49] However, it is known that in the village of Letiache (Borshchiv county), about twenty morgs (11.5 ha) were used for the growing of grapes, some of which were dried after picking, and that there was some wine-making activity in Borshchiv.[50]

Some changes occurred in cultivation patterns in the 1880s and 1890s. There was a decline in the cultivation—at least as a first or main crop—of cereal grain and hemp, and an increase in the amount of land devoted to growing potatoes. There was a very considerable increase in the amount of land on which clover was grown. These changes affected large landowners and peasants alike. In a region which had relatively little officially designated meadow and pasturage land, more of the ploughland was de facto used for pasturage. The new or expanded cultivation of specialty cash crops was principally a peasant activity. Quantitative data to support this statement are generally lacking, except in the case of tobacco, which was a very significant cash crop in Southern Podillia for thousands of peasants. In the case of other cash crops, the evidence that peasants were growing these is of a more fragmentary and descriptive nature, but is reasonably firm.

Yield of Field Crops

Data on the yield of field crops were assiduously collected by the Galician Agricultural Association and published by the Austrian Ministry of Agriculture. They were derived from information supplied by local landowners, commune officials, and "village intelligentsia." The Podillian data were thus based on estimates made by local experts. The contemporary expert F. Bujak believed that crop yields in Galicia were underestimated by those who supplied the data.[51]

Crop yield was affected by the prevailing weather conditions as well as by the activities of pests like field mice.[52] Podillia did not escape the hail and thunderstorms, with their attendant crop damage, which affected Eastern Galicia. It was, however, sometimes spared natural disasters, particularly the flood damage to which many other regions in Galicia were prone. In 1893 a summer drought, which "amounted to a calamity" in other parts of Galicia, had relatively little effect in Southern Podillia. In 1896 and 1897 Podillia was spared the excessive summer rainfall which caused much crop damage in other regions of Galicia; in 1900 it was untouched by widespread flood damage experienced elsewhere.[53] However, Southern Podillia was greatly affected by the general drought of the disaster year, 1889, with low yields of grain, potatoes, and clover, and by the adverse growing conditions of 1891 and, to some extent, of 1895.[54]

Conditions which were adverse for most crops could nevertheless be advantageous for some. The most extreme example of this was in 1889, when the tobacco crop was favoured by the dry heat that seared other plants.

In general, with the exception of excessive summer heat in some years that had adverse effects on the rye crop, conditions for grain growing and for most other types of crop production were exceptionally good in Southern Podillia in the years 1884-8, and yields were, for the region, correspondingly high. The 1890s were very different. Planting conditions for fall sown wheat and rye were often difficult: winter snow cover was deficient in two of the years; there were some late frosts as well as plagues of field mice; and there were years of excessive or inadequate spring or summer rainfall.[55] At best, the growing conditions of the 1890s in Southern Podillia may be characterized as "mediocre."

The changing weather patterns were reflected in the annual data of crop yields. In many instances there was not the increase in yields that one might have expected to see in view of improvements in agricultural techniques such as better implements and seeds, as well as more effective crop rotation, manure, and artificial fertilizer. Contrary to some suppositions, Ukrainian peasants used manure,[56] and agricultural education alerted them to the advantages of its use, and the increased number of farm animals provided more natural manure. The latter phenomenon was also connected with the increased growing of clover: "Since clover has spread, we feed cattle more in barns" and peasants used the resulting greater amounts of manure on their fields.[57] The use of artificial fertilizers was also being urged upon the peasants by agricultural circles and others and there are indications that this advice was being heeded.[58]

Given the prevailing weather conditions of the 1890s, maintaining the yield levels of the 1880s would have been a victory in itself. (Details of the yield of field crops in the region are given in Appendix VII.) With the exception of the yield of rye during the early nineties, productivity per hectare in general either held its own (wheat and maize), or rose somewhat (potatoes), or showed dramatic increases (barley and oats). In fact, there was a general trend toward improved yields of wheat, rye, and maize, which was masked by the bumper crops of the exceptionally favourable years 1884 and 1885 and poor or indifferent harvests in some years in the 1890s. This becomes very clear when the data on average yields for these crops for the period 1896-1905 are considered (see Table 12).

Table 12
Average Yields per Hectare in Metric Centner, 1884-1905

	Wheat	Rye	Barley	Oats	Maize	Potatoes	
S. Podillia	9.6	8.2	6.5	5.7	9.1	102.0	1884-1890
	9.3	7.7	8.3	8.7	9.8	111.5	1891-1900
	11.2	9.7	n/a	n/a	11.1	n/a	1896-1905
N. Podillia	9.2	8.5	6.3	4.8	9.9	106.4	1884-1890
	9.5	8.0	7.9	7.8	9.9	109.3	1891-1900
	11.3	9.4	n/a	n/a	11.0	n/a	1896-1905

Sources: *Podręcznik statystyki Galicyi*, VII, part 1: 160, VIII, part 1: 169.
Note: The data for "S. Podillia" refer to Borshchiv, Chortkiv, Husiatyn and Zalishchyky, as well as the neighbouring county of Buchach; "N. Podillia" comprised Terebovlia and four other northern Podillian counties. They thus do not apply specifically to the region under study here, but they are highly indicative.

Productivity per hectare, with the exception of maize, was increasing in Galicia as a whole during the last two decades of the nineteenth century. Yields tended to be higher, and in some instances significantly higher, in Southern Podillia than in Eastern Galicia or Galicia as a whole. The increased yield of barley and oats in Southern Podillia is very notable. The region had yields of these two important crops that were below the Eastern Galician average in the 1880s, but well above that average in the 1890s. Whether this was due to the use of improved strains of these grains or better cultivation methods or some combination of these factors cannot be determined, but a 52 per cent increase in the yield of oats and a 27 per cent increase in that of barley in South Podillia in the 1890s were significant developments.

Straw was of great importance to the Southern Podillian rural economy. Apart from its agricultural uses, it was also used for thatching and fuel. The annual amounts of straw produced fluctuated with the prevailing growing conditions for grain. Long-stemmed grain was prized on account of the length of straw that it gave. V. Korol's description of the grain he saw on his tour of Borshchiv county in 1896, "long, heavy, and with good yields," would have gladdened all peasant hearts.[59]

There was an assumption that yields of the main grain crops were greater on the large estates than on small landholdings, which was in fact justified. However, the gap in productivity was not always very large, and was narrowing in the 1890s.[60] Peasants contributed to and shared in the general increase in productivity of grain and other field produce. Because peasants were the principal producers of specialty cash crops, other than hops and the very small quantities of sugar beet grown in Southern Podillia, they benefited from their increased cultivation and production in ways not open to large landowners. All the data, except those on production of clover seed, refer only to main crops. The unrecorded yield of second crops and intercrops provided for the peasants a further and quite significant supply of foodstuffs, animal fodder, and cash income.

Animal Husbandry

In 1886 Fr. Naumovych exhorted readers of *Nauka*: "My dear farmers, plant clover, alfalfa, esparcet, timothy; fodder is the main element of your operation—it multiplies the livestock, the livestock gives manure, and manure produces grain and money."[61] Naumovych was on the right track, even though he tended to view livestock mainly as a means to improve grain production. Twenty years later, Bujak put the matter into a more accurate perspective: "In Galicia, as in many other European countries, income from domestic animals, especially from cattle, is higher than income from crop production."[62] Nevertheless, the topic of animal husbandry was neglected, by both contemporary and later writers: "nothing was discussed and less was written about peasant husbandry until the 1880s besides vague complaints about its pathetic state."[63]

Prior to 1848 peasants had kept oxen and horses for their draught power, which they had to supply to the manor as part of their compulsory labour service, and cows, sheep, pigs, and poultry for their various products such as milk, cheese, meat, wool, and eggs. Some large landowners fattened cattle on potato mash, a by-product of their distilleries.[64] In the late eighteenth century both the imperial authorities and some prominent individuals tried to effect improvements in livestock. Joseph II had fine wool merino sheep introduced into Eastern Galicia in the 1770s, and Southern Podillia boasted some of the best sheep farms in Galicia. New breeds of cattle were also introduced, including Dutch, Swiss, and Tyrolean types, by some of the large estate owners, as were Arabian and English horses.[65] After the 1848 liberation, peasants adjusted better than did large landowners to the changed situation. The latter had generally to train new people to handle their livestock, while the peasants brought into the new era their animals and their expertise, however limited.[66] A fresh phase began with the appointment of Count Alfred Potocki as Austrian Minister of Agriculture, for thereafter more extensive state subsidies were provided to support improvement of Galician agriculture, the greater portion of which went toward upgrading livestock used for breeding purposes. A share of these subsidies created benefits for the peasantry:

> Since 1868, when a Ministry of Agriculture was again established

> under the knowledgeable and enterprising Count Potocki, even the peasantry, through prizes for breeding bulls, were inspired to practise real breeding, which had previously been done only by a few large landowners.[67]

Three factors initially hindered efforts toward real improvement in Eastern Galician and Southern Podillian animal husbandry. One was the shortage of winter feed. This was gradually overcome, in part, through the cultivation and production of more fodder crops, and grasses, including clover, maize, vetches, beans, alfalfa, esparcet, timothy, and seradella.[68] Also important was the better care given to meadowland, and the steady increase in the proportion of meadows that was mown for hay throughout the 1880s and 1890s.[69] Southern Podillian meadowland, while relatively very small in total area, was of excellent quality, capable of yielding two or three crops of hay each year for a total yield of up to 35 metric centner per hectare rather than the lower official total yield. Its pasture land was also "mostly very good."[70] Indeed, as a modern Polish authority has noted, "The more animal fodder there was, the more animals one could keep through the winter."[71]

The initial shortage of a sufficient amount of good quality animal fodder, together with the lateness of the arrival of the railways in Southern Podillia, also imposed another impediment to effective animal husbandry. Relatively few cattle and pigs could be fattened effectively in the region, and that largely on the mash that was a by-product of distillery operations. In any case, livestock that were walked long distances to market or to the nearest railhead lost condition and weight, and continued to deteriorate during the rail journey to major population centres such as Vienna and Prague. Galician livestock was therefore sometimes fattened elsewhere, and Galician pigs often completed their existence on Viennese tables as "Bohemian ham."[72] After 1880, and especially in the 1890s, the fattening of livestock was more frequently done locally, and the greater profits kept at home.[73]

The third impediment was the open border with the Russian Empire. Horses and oxen of good quality could be imported relatively inexpensively from Dnieper Ukraine and Bessarabia. The oxen would be used locally or fattened somewhat and then sold; the horses, after some local care, were frequently sold to meet Austrian cavalry requirements. Much local animal husbandry was therefore really livestock trading rather than livestock breeding and rearing. The steppe animals often brought diseases with them which devastated local herds and peasant animals. Regulations enacted in 1881 closed the frontier to Russian cattle and, to some extent, to Russian horses too. Although animal smuggling continued throughout the period, the incidence of cattle plague was immediately and drastically curbed. Veterinary measures thus forced Southern Podillians to pay more attention to the breeding of cattle and horses.[74]

The total number of farm animals kept in winter rose quite considerably, despite the significant decline in the number of sheep (except in Borshchiv and Zalishchyky counties, where the decrease in the number of sheep was modest). Declines and increases varied in different counties. The decline in the sheep population was most precipitous in Husiatyn county; the increase in the number of pigs was most marked in this county and in Terebovlia, cattle in Terebovlia, and horses in Zalishchyky county. Greater rates of increase in the number of horses, cattle, and pigs occurred in the 1890s than in the 1880s. The overall Southern Podillian rate of increase in the number of cattle and pigs exceeded that of Galicia by a quite significant margin, and was considerably greater than the rate of increase of the human population (see Table 13).

Table 13
Number of Farm Animals in Southern Podillia, 1880-1900
(on 31 December)

	1880	1890	1900
Horses	52,073	55,964	61,144
Cattle and Oxen	82,213	90,597	108,821
Pigs	40,079	45,615	84,630
Sheep	86,036	70,777	49,450

Sources: *Oesterreichische Statistik*, vols. II, no. 2; XXXIV, no. 2; LX, no. 3, pt. 1.

Peasant Ownership of Farm Animals

The peasantry owned very significant proportions of Southern Podillia's farm animals. By 1900, 76.2 per cent of the region's horses and 74.1 per cent of its cattle and oxen were on rustical lands (a little more in Terebovlia county and a little less in Borshchiv county). These data caused surprise, for peasant ownership of such animals was more extensive than had been anticipated.[75] In the two counties where sheep were still maintained in large numbers, they were overwhelmingly on rustical lands, as were almost 90 per cent of Southern Podillia's pigs. That animal husbandry was to a very considerable extent a peasant operation was confirmed by the findings of the special agricultural census of June 1902. Because the 1902 agricultural census was conducted at a very different time of the year from earlier farm animal censuses, which were on 31 December, their absolute numbers are not comparable. What is really significant about the 1902 data is that they show that ownership of animals was widespread and that even the holders of dwarf plots owned animals in quite unexpected numbers.

Smallholders, that is, those who owned and/or leased land with a total of up to five hectares of productive area, owned 61.5 per cent of the region's cattle (which includes draught oxen), almost 50 per cent of its farm horses, 63 per cent of its sheep, and 75 per cent of its pigs (see Table 14). Almost 50 per cent of the cattle, sheep, and pigs owned by this group of peasants, but only a little less than 25 per cent of its horses, were in fact owned by the category of peasants who held fewer than two hectares. The percentage of horses and sheep owned by the two major categories of peasant smallholders varied in the different counties. For sheep the data are skewed by a few large flocks maintained by some individual large landowners in Husiatyn and Terebovlia counties.

Table 14
Percentage of Farm Animals Held in Southern Podillia, by Size of Productive Area of Landholding, 1902

	<2 ha	**2-5 ha**	**5-20 ha**	**20-100 ha**	**>100 ha**
Cattle and Oxen	28.9	32.7	15.9	3.0	19.5
Horses	11.5	38.1	21.9	3.4	25.1
Sheep	30.2	32.8	17.9	1.7	17.3
Pigs	37.0	38.0	17.7	2.8	4.5

Source: Based on *Oesterrichische Statistik*, vol. LXXXIII, no. 5, table xv.

Thus Southern Podillian peasant smallholders, by the turn of the century, were very much involved in animal rearing. The number of farm animals maintained by the larger peasant proprietors (who held 5-20 hectares), was also considerable. The two categories of smallholders, of course, comprised the greatest number of all landowners.

Almost 96 per cent of the smallholders with between two and five hectares owned farm animals, and quite clearly many of them had two or three (and possibly even four) different kinds of animals. It is also clear (see Appendix IX) that they frequently owned more than one of a particular kind of animal. Sheep owners in this category in Borshchiv county owned on average six sheep; pig owners in Chortkiv an average of 1.7 pigs each; cattle owners in Husiatyn an average of 1.8 head; and horse owners in Terebovlia county an average of 1.6 horses. Not only did this category of smallholders thus generally keep more than one kind of animal, but they also, on average, owned more than one animal of one or more kinds. The ownership of animals was more widespread still among the 5-20 ha category of landowners.

About 80 per cent of smallholders with fewer than two hectares owned a farm animal. Further, of those in this category who owned an animal, most must have had more than one kind, for instance an ox and a pig. More than 50 per cent of this category of smallholder owned at least one cow or ox, and sometimes more than one. In Borshchiv and Zalishchyky counties, where the ownership of cattle among this category of peasants was not quite as widespread, they were more likely to own sheep. Very few of the under two hectare smallholdings in the other three counties possessed sheep. Between 30-46 per cent of this category of smallholders, depending on the county, owned pigs, but only 13-18.3 per cent of them had their own horses.

Pilat had asserted in 1893 that draught animals could not be maintained on holdings of fewer than two morgs (about 1 1/2 ha) in Podillia.[76] The data of a decade later showed that he had been wrong (see Appendix IX). In fact, of the group with less than 0.5 ha each, around 60 per cent owned a farm animal. Most commonly this was a cow or ox, but in Borshchiv and Zalishchyky counties, around 20 per cent owned sheep (an average of four sheep each). Very few owned horses, but somewhat more than 25 per cent kept pigs. Multiple ownership of animals other than sheep also occurred: for example, in Borshchiv county, cattle owners with less than 0.5 ha had, on average, almost 1.5 head each, and pig owners in Chortkiv had almost 1.4 pigs each.

Animal holdings were much more extensive among those with 0.5-1 ha. Almost 75 per cent of this group owned animals. About 50 per cent of them had cattle—considerably more in Chortkiv, Husiatyn, and Terebovlia counties, and significantly fewer in Zalishchyky. As with the under 0.5 ha category, sheep raising was important for this group in Borshchiv and Zalishchyky counties; indeed, they owned about 10 per cent of the total number of sheep in the two counties. The ownership of pigs was also quite widespread among this group, accounting for about 11 per cent of Southern Podillia's total pig population. Around 7 per cent of the 0.5-1 ha holders kept horses. Some of these smallholders maintained more than one kind of animal. Sheep owners generally had just over four sheep each; owners of other kinds of animals not infrequently had more than one, for example, cattle owners in Husiatyn county had, on average, 1.4 head each, and pig owners in Chortkiv 1.3 pigs (a slightly lower average than for the under 0.5 ha landholders).

Between 82 per cent (Zalishchyky) and 90 per cent (Chortkiv) of all smallholders with 1-2 hectares kept animals. About 75 per cent of them in Chortkiv, Husiatyn, and Terebovlia counties had cattle, but fewer in the two sheep-raising counties. In these, however, more than 25 per cent of this category of peasant smallholders kept sheep, and owned almost 25 per cent of all the sheep in Borshchiv and Zalishchyky counties. Between 20 per cent (Zalishchyky) and 28 per cent (Husiatyn) of peasants in this category possessed horses, and between 29.6 per cent (Terebovlia) and 49.6 per cent (Chortkiv) owned pigs. The statistical data clearly indicate both that peasants with 1-2 ha of land tended to keep more than one kind of farm animal, and that, on average, they maintained more than one animal of each kind (in Borshchiv county, a horse owner had, on average, 1.3 horses, a cattle owner 1.7 cows or oxen, a sheep owner 4.7 sheep, and a pig owner 1.7 pigs).

It is therefore clear that by the turn of the century ownership of the four main kinds of farm animals was widely diffused among the Southern Podillian peasantry. The number of these animals, except sheep, had increased significantly between 1880 and 1900. This increase was particularly significant for cattle and pigs. All strata of the peasantry were involved in animal husbandry, even the holders of less than half a hectare of land. The involvement of the 0.5-1 ha smallholdings in animal raising was quite extensive, and that of the next category, the 1-2 ha holdings, even more so. The 2-5 ha smallholdings owned about 33 per cent of all the region's cattle and a rather higher percentage of all its horses, as well as about 50 per cent of its pigs and, in Borshchiv and Zalishchyky counties, over 33 per cent of the sheep.

An article entitled "How to have more income" stressed the importance of keeping bees and raising poultry and rabbits.[77] Little is known about peasants keeping rabbits, although they were featured at the big Agricultural Exhibition in Lviv in 1894 and also at an exhibition in Iaroslav in 1896.[78] Many books and pamphlets advocated beekeeping, but, owing to the increased use of sugar and a decline in the demand for candles upon the coming of gas-lighting and electricity to the cities and the arrival of kerosene for lamps in rural areas, there was in fact a decline in the extent of beekeeping; the number of beehives recorded for the region fell from 42,708 in 1880 to 36,673 in 1890, and 23,168 in 1900.[79] (It should be noted that these data are for 31 December, so they may underestimate summer activity.) In 1890 there were 528 owners of beehives in Borshchiv county, 480 in Chortkiv, 442 in Husiatyn, 542 in Terebovlia, and 254 in Zalishchyky. Owners of 1-5 hives formed the largest single category in Borshchiv and Zalishchyky counties, with those owning 6-20 not far behind. In the other three counties, owners of 6-20 hives formed the largest single category, but in Terebovlia there were also many who owned 21-50 hives. Many priests and schoolteachers kept bees,[80] but for some peasants bees continued to be a useful source of income. Others were not afraid to abandon one possible source of income if a better one presented itself. Poultry undoubtedly provided that other source. The Ukrainian press gave advice on how to raise poultry, increase egg production, feed ducks and geese, make geese a good investment, feed poultry in winter, build chicken coops, recognize and treat eye disease in poultry, and so on.[81] There are, unfortunately, no data for poultry which could give statistics on numbers over a period of years, but data for 1900 show that there were extensive poultry holdings in Southern Podillia, for more than 650,000 head were counted in the depth of winter.[82]

It was the women of the peasant households who looked after the poultry and sold or bartered the fowl, eggs, and feathers. Poultry and poultry products do not seem to have been much used in peasant households themselves, except on special occasions. The local hens laid only 50-100 eggs per year, but they had the important quality of being able to tolerate the cold. The eggs were rather small, but as they were sold by the piece there was no incentive to produce large eggs. Small peasant holdings had on average 20-22 hens (larger holdings usually had fewer), which roamed the yards and pastures and were also fed on scraps. Geese were less numerous and required more care and the right type of pasturage. They gave good returns for their feathers, meat, and grease, especially in the vicinity of Jewish town populations. Peasants in the neighbourhood of the town of Husiatyn, with its quite large Jewish community, knew the dates of Jewish holidays and brought their geese and goose grease in for sale just prior to these occasions.[83]

Galicia exported large quantities of eggs, mainly to Germany, and smaller amounts of feathers and poultry. Zalishchyky was a principal source of marketed poultry.[84] Husiatyn had several depots to which eggs were brought from all over the county and tested, sorted, and packed in preparation for shipment. Egg and poultry production was clearly of significance for peasant smallholders in Southern Podillia, and more than compensated for the decline in beekeeping.[85]

Improvement in the Quality of Farm Animals

The fact that there were so many horses and that even some of the smallest landholdings kept horses may seem surprising. However, Galicia was one of the prime areas from which the Austrian army obtained its cavalry horses. The raising of such animals appears to have been done largely on the great estates, but peasants shared in an organized system of maintaining "reserve" horses on peasant land, which were used by the army in the event of mobilization.[86] There were also some famous stables, renowned for their thoroughbreds and other types of horses, in Southern Podillia, but they had little direct impact on peasant animal husbandry.[87] For the peasants, horses were important as draught animals for ploughing, harrowing, hauling harvests to granaries, and carting goods. They were also used in the building and repair of roads, bridges, and other structures, and for transporting goods to market or to the nearest railhead. Traders, of course, also required horses.

Within the Southern Podillian villages, the co-operative tradition of the pre-1848 village communes manifested itself into the twentieth century. Peasants with draught animals shared them with other villagers who had none or only one. The practice in the village of Bychkivtski (Chortkiv county) in the early twentieth century, was:

> In my village, some people owned two horses, quite a few owned one. There were a few oxen, maybe two pair in the whole village. There were usually five or six people to one horse as a result. We joined together regarding the use of these animals. If you wanted ploughing done, you exchanged some work, grain, or other goods for the use of somebody's animals or for your neighbour (who owned animals) doing it for you.[88]

This sensible village practice obviated the need for every smallholder to maintain draught animals; it also seems to have led to some modest degree of specialization, so some peasants with little land would keep horses and do hauling and delivery work for others, as well as cultivate their own smallholdings.[89]

The number of horses in Southern Podillia, as in some other parts of Eastern Galicia, increased following the closing of the Austrian frontier to Russian cattle in 1881, for this action deprived the inhabitants of a ready supply of cheap oxen. Horses thus came, to some extent, to replace oxen as draught animals: as *Hospodar i promyshlennyk* noted, "a horse can do the work of six oxen in a day."[90]

Quantitative considerations are important, but so is quality. The Eastern Galician peasant horse was an indigenous steppe horse, with admixtures of Mongolian, Arab, and English breeds. It was undoubtedly smaller in stature and musculature than Western horses, and was, for this and other reasons, criticized by Polish and other writers.[91] It was, however, hardy, even-tempered, with good stamina, and relatively inexpensive to maintain.[92]

Pruski, in his thorough study of Galician animal husbandry, concluded that "the numerous critics who accused the peasants regarding the poor quality of their horses had no rationale whatsoever." From the perspective of economic efficiency, peasant horses were well suited to the tasks they had to perform and bigger animals, whose upkeep would cost more, would not have been more effective.[93]

In fact, by the end of the nineteenth century, both the Austrian and the Galician governments had made some efforts to improve the quality of Galician horses. There were extensive subsidies for breeding operations, and two state stud farms in Eastern Galicia as well as 90-100 breeding stations. At the latter, local mares could be serviced at fees varying from 2-6 g, depending on the quality of the stud horse. There were also subsidies for peasants who owned good quality stallions. Selective crossbreeding with local horses did have a beneficial effect and by the 1890s had produced an improved admixture.[94]

From 1882 onward, the Galician Agricultural Association also owned stud horses that were placed in subsidized stud stations or rented to peasants and large landowners to service their mares.[95] It also organized horse shows, probably the largest of which was run in conjunction with the Galician Land Exhibition of 1894. Of the 600 horses on exhibit there, 200 belonged to peasants. From 1897 onward, the Association hired inspectors of horse-raising and also sponsored courses on veterinary matters.[96] Items about horses in the Ukrainian press also show that there was an interest in promoting better husbandry. The introduction into Eastern Galicia of new breeds such as the Belgian horse and the Scottish pony was noted. Articles discussed horses' teeth, the care of the mane, horse disease, and care of animals generally. There was also advice about pasturage, fodder crops, and the feeding of maize to horses, and descriptions of the sale of horses' hides and hair.[97]

References in the press to cattle and oxen were far more numerous, indicating a much greater degree of concern with this branch of animal husbandry. Such items ranged from the trivial—the best way to rouse a sleeping cow was to tickle her nose with a straw[98]—to more important advice. For example, there were announcements of and reports on large cattle markets and shows.[99] Courses, discussions, and papers on cattle raising were covered.[100] There was information on how to improve milk production, feed cattle, market dairy products, winter cattle, treat skin diseases, on women's roles in cattle rearing, how to recognize a healthy animal, care for and feed newborn calves, leech cattle, and give salt to cattle.[101] Advice from German journals on the care and feeding of cattle was translated.[102] Following the disastrous crop of 1889 there were many reports of starving cattle as well as advice from experts on how to save them. Particularly pertinent, because of an outbreak of hoof-and-mouth disease the previous year, *Batkivshchyna* ran a series of articles on cattle disease from 29 August to 26 November 1890.

The Podillian variety of grey steppe cattle (*Bos taurus primigenitus*) were large, fleshy animals noted for their strong and easy movement. They were good draught animals and, when fattened, produced good meat, but they were also slow to mature and to fatten, and were low in milk production—about 1,000-1,500 litres per annum.[103] Efforts to improve the local breed, to become more efficient producers of both meat and milk while maintaining its capacity as draught animals, were vigorously pursued in the late nineteenth century. The Galician authorities were inclined to push the virtues of another indigenous cow, usually known as Red Polish, which had higher milk yields, and in respect of which *Svoboda* deemed it necessary to inform its readers that it was not really "Polish" but "Galician."[104] However, most of the upgrading endeavours involved importation of foreign breeding stock: Bernese, Simmenthal, Tyrolean, Ayrshire, Frisian, and Oldenburg were all tried, but Simmenthal cattle appeared to thrive best and to produce the best stock when interbred with the local cattle.[105]

The Austrian Ministry of Agriculture provided subsidies for the importation into Galicia of foreign breeding stock. These ran at a particularly high level in

1882 and 1883, immediately after the frontier was closed to Russian cattle. These subsidies were also used to set up breeding stations across the Land; one of the earliest was established, with Simmenthal bulls, in Zalishchyky in 1882. The Sejm also provided funds for these purposes.[106] By 1886 in Galicia there were 240 subsidized breeding stations with imported and selected native bulls to service peasant cattle. A law of 1892 required that only licensed bulls be used in the subsidized stations; by 1895 there were 2,581 such licensed breeding bulls for peasant cattle, and by 1900, 5,785 plus several hundred belonging to the Galician Agricultural Association, also for peasant use.[107] By the same law, there were to be maintained for the peasantry in each commune, whether in private hands or in commune-owned breeding stations, a certain number of bulls per cow and heifer (1:100); and the Sejm allocated 50,000 g to enable county and commune authorities to purchase or lease more licensed breeding stock.[108]

Besides the advice on cattle raising given in the Ukrainian press and the agricultural education activities of the enlightenment societies, the Agricultural Association, its regional branches, and the Agricultural Circles were all engaged in supporting animal husbandry. The Association employed an animal inspector from 1882 onward. It searched out good local and foreign breeding stock, and sponsored animal shows.[109] At the 1894 Exhibition in Lviv:

> The most important portion of the exhibit is the peasant cattle section. Anyone who is a supporter of the improvement of animal husbandry in our Land could not but be pleased to see the quality of the peasant cattle from various counties.[110]

Very little is known about the breeding bull stations for peasant cattle "despite the huge amount of money given to them."[111] Nor is there much direct evidence on whether Southern Podillian peasants heeded the advice given by the press, animal husbandry experts, and enlightenment societies. It is known, however, that the ratio of bulls to cows and heifers was much more favourable in Borshchiv and Zalishchyky counties than in most parts of Galicia.[112] After the Sejm appropriated funds to appoint a Land dairying instructor, his first course was held in May and June 1892 at the lower agricultural school in Loshniv (Terebovlia county); three of the eight students were female.[113] A cream separator was installed in the same year at the lower agricultural school in Iaholnytsia (Chortkiv county), one of the first for instructional use in Galicia.[114] Southern Podillia participated in the general improvement in cattle raising in Galicia, and one traveller through the region expressly commented on its "fine-looking animals."[115]

Particularly in the 1890s, Galicia shared in a general Austrian process of "transition from the 'keeping of animals' to the 'breeding of animals'."[116] During this period the foundations were being laid for the emergence of a modern dairying industry in Eastern Galicia, including Southern Podillia, which a Ukrainian co-operative movement brought into prominence in the early years of the twentieth century.[117] The number of cattle increased significantly in Southern Podillia in the 1890s and fewer of them were draught animals. Galician cattle were being exported in large quantities to other parts of Austria, as well as to Germany and Russia:

> The export of cattle is quite significant. Stock cattle and milk cows are exported to Russia, Siberia, Moravia, and Bohemia; fattened cattle to Vienna, Prague, Olmutz, and Germany.... Most fattened cattle come from Podillia.[118]

One significant indicator of improvement in cattle rearing was the average weight of the animals when sold. The average weight of cattle sold at the Lviv market ranged between 184 and 196 kg in the years 1875-87; in the years 1893-6 it ranged between 246 and 263 kg.[119] Another notable product of Southern Podillia were milk-fed calves (*Milchkalben*), which Viennese and other European buyers of veal favoured.[120] The Southern Podillian cattle industry was assisted by the coming of the railway to Chortkiv and Husiatyn counties in 1885 and to the rest of the region in the 1890s, and by the increasing use of a new type of railway cattle car. The weight loss of cattle incurred by transporting them "on the hoof" or in older, primitive cattle cars was thus avoided.[121]

Southern Podillian cattle raisers owned not only more animals but also better quality animals, and some were probably among those Eastern Galician peasants who "became wealthy, eager, and intelligent cattle raisers of the best cattle in the Land."[122] Writing of Galician cattle in 1899, another authority stated that "the best cattle are to be found in the southeast corner between the Zbruch and the Dnister."[123]

Sheep rearing in Southern Podillia generally was on the decline in the period 1880-1900, though still of considerable significance to peasant agriculture in Borshchiv and Zalishchyky counties. Sheep—usually a native black wool breed—were usually pastured on the banks of rivers such as the Dnister, the Nichlava, and the Zbruch. In the village of Zalissia (Borshchiv county):

> The peasants collectively supported the shepherd who, with his assistants, grazed the sheep on the slopes of the Zbruch River. Women or older children would lead the sheep to the communal pasture outside the village in the morning and leave them in the care of the shepherd who brought them back at night. As the shepherd returned the flock home in the evening, at a special signal from him, the sheep would separate and enter the yards of their respective owners, announcing their

> return with their bleating. The shepherd and his assistants were given food by the owners of the sheep. Each day a different housewife would take the day's food supply out to the communal pasture for them.[124]

Sheep were kept principally for their wool and hides. Cheesemaking from ewes' milk was of secondary importance in this region, and there was little demand for mutton. Villagers made winter trousers (*kholoshni*), coats (*serdaky*), and other items of clothing from wool they wove. Sheepskins were used for winter coats and hats, and Galician demand continued for coarse wool for clothing and blankets.[125] Nevertheless, it is clear that the overall demand for wool declined in Southern Podillia, as elsewhere, as factory-made textiles made greater inroads into Galicia, and as export opportunities for Galician wool declined.[126]

Increasing interest was manifested in the Ukrainian press in pig raising, especially in the 1890s. Articles span a whole range of topics, from advice on good pig breeding to weaning piglets, and the feeding of potatoes and beets to sows.[127] Both the state and the Land gave subsidies to support improved pig rearing. With these funds and contributions from its members, the Galician Agricultural Association bought foreign breeding stock such as Yorkshire and Westphalian boars. As with cattle, boar-breeding yards and pig-breeding stations were set up to improve the native breed. The native Podillian pig was, however, considered to be a good animal, with a better type of meat than its formidable Hungarian competitor. Galician pigs were favoured in the important German market because of their firm, tasty, and lean meat.[128]

Ukrainian peasants too savored their pork, and in Borshchiv and Chortkiv counties they protested vigorously and successfully when the authorities tried to make them pay excise tax on the pigs they slaughtered for their own use.[129] They sold pork fat and preserved salt pork in barrels for their own use.[130] Over the years, as a result of breeding, Eastern Galician pigs became whiter and smoother, which had some adverse effect on a quite lively trade in bristles that was, however, offset by improvements in meat production. Selective breeding with Tamworth boars, advertised in the 1890s, probably resulted in bigger litters.[131] Ten thousand Eastern Galician pigs were sent to market each week, 4,000 of them to Vienna, by the late 1890s.[132] Clearly, pigs were becoming an important component in Galicia's agriculture. As Bujak confidently stated in 1908, the peasants "had a great predominance in pig raising over the estates not only in the quantity of animals raised but also in terms of their attentiveness to this speciality."[133]

The significance of pig raising and selling in Southern Podillia by the end of the nineteenth century is demonstrated by the fact that about 250 persons from 25 communes attended a meeting in Borshchiv in October 1898 to discuss the possibility of joining a pig-marketing co-operative that was being formed in Stanyslaviv (about 90 kilometres away), which would also have its own

Villagers from Krehulets, Husiatyn county, photographed at the Ternopil exhibition, 1892

Villager from Synkiv, Zalishchyky county, wearing a sheepskin coat, photographed at the Ternopil exhibition, 1892

breeding barn. Thirty-six persons immediately signed up for membership, at 10 g per person. About 100 people attended a similar meeting in Uhrynkivtsi (Zalishchyky county), but there the County Officer prohibited people from signing up for membership. *Svoboda* thereupon advised people to apply for membership in writing. A few weeks later the same newspaper printed instructions on how members might use the producers' co-operative, which was now operational.[134]

Veterinary Regulations

Various veterinary measures, not all of them popular, were taken by the authorities to foster animal husbandry and maintain its external markets. By the turn of the century, Galicia had a total of 230 veterinary doctors, of whom three were in Borshchiv county, two in Chortkiv, four in Husiatyn, two in Terebovlia, and two in Zalishchyky.[135] Each county had its veterinary officer, but they were not highly regarded by the peasantry, as they rarely attended to peasant needs. In addition, the state recognized certain lesser trained men with veterinary knowledge (*Kurschmiede*) and ran special courses for them. In most villages there were also local persons with a reputed healing touch for animals, who usually did have some special knowledge of animals and their sicknesses.[136]

Local lore, however, was no remedy against hoof-and-mouth disease, tuberculosis, and bronchial pneumonia in cattle, and swine fever. Vaccination against tuberculosis in cattle began in Galicia only in the late 1890s.[137] Cattle with pulmonary diseases were to be slaughtered, with the state recompensing the owners at 1 per cent of market value, but the owners could use all parts of the animals except the lungs.[138] Hoof-and-mouth disease and swine fever were met with quarantine and other restrictions, which the authorities attempted to enforce and the peasants to evade. 1889 was a year of bad harvests and hoof-and-mouth disease in Eastern Galicia, including Southern Podillia. A circular from the governor of Galicia urged county officers strictly to enforce the law on quarantine and the restricted movement of animals; trade was to be suspended altogether if necessary.[139] At various times in 1889 all the Southern Podillian counties were subject to quarantine restrictions as the authorities endeavoured to isolate and eradicate the disease. On occasion, the movement of hooved animals was forbidden; at other times markets were closed to them, although the movement of cattle might be allowed if they were being transported by rail direct to slaughterhouses. Sometimes railway stations were completely closed to animal traffic; at other times it was merely the export of animals from certain localities to places outside Galicia or Austria that was prohibited.[140] Clearly the authorities strove to maintain credibility with foreign buyers and to cause minimal local disruption.

In the long run the animal-quarantine and other health regulations in Galicia were successful. During the severe epidemic of swine fever which swept Eastern Europe in the second half of the 1890s, and which destroyed about 33 per cent of Hungary's pigs in a decade, only 1 per cent of Galicia's pigs were lost to the disease in 1895, and 0.7 per cent in 1896.[141] Inevitably, however, the strict regulations and their observance elicited protests from those whose interests were adversely affected. In 1889, for instance, there was a petition requesting the lifting of the prohibition of weekly markets in Khorostkiv, Kopychyntsi, and Probizhna (Husiatyn county), which had been imposed because of sporadic cattle plague.[142]

Marketing Mechanisms and Prices

With the exception of sheep, peasants had more farm animals, and, just as important, better quality farm animals, by 1900 than they had had in 1880. They also had large numbers of poultry. Furthermore, they were producing greater quantities of most field crops, including some specialty crops which brought high returns. Some of the increased production of crops and animals was consumed by the growing population of the five counties. The rest was sold or bartered.

Neither the peasants' marketing mechanisms nor the prices they received for their produce are readily ascertainable. (The annual average market prices of various commodities at the Lviv market are given in Appendix II.) The Lviv and Vienna prices of the main agricultural produce were reported fairly regularly in the Ukrainian press, but tell little about prices at the numerous local markets or what itinerant traders paid to villagers for their produce.[143] Grain prices at both large and local markets also fluctuated, generally being at their lowest in the

Table 15
Price of Four Cereal Grains, in Gulden per Hectolitre, at Selected Southern Podillian Markets, 1890

Market	Wheat	Rye	Barley	Oats	Total Value of Four Grains in Gulden
Borshchiv	7.43	5.24	3.83	2.75	867,000
Chortkiv	7.49	5.64	3.77	2.65	898,000
Husiatyn	7.36	5.95	3.52	2.85	858,000
Terebovlia	6.83	5.52	3.82	2.65	752,000
Tovste					362,000

Source: *Statistisches Jahrbuch des K.K. Ackerbau-Ministeriums*, 1891, table XIII (individual prices for Tovste are not reproduced here, for they are given in gulden per metric centner and thus are not comparable).

fall and early winter.[144] Thus, unless one knew precisely when the peasants sold their grain, any attempt to identify the prices they received would be misleading. The information presented on prices in this section must consequently be regarded as somewhat tentative, but certainly indicative. Data are available for the year 1890 only in respect of wheat, rye, barley, and oats sold at forty-eight Eastern Galician markets and those in Cracow and Chernivtsi (see Table 15).

What is particularly interesting about the data in Table 15 is that they pertain entirely to grain marketed by smallholders (*Kleingrundbesitz*). The large estates apparently marketed their grain directly or through brokers in Lviv, Cracow, and other places.[145] These data would thus appear to be an effective refutation of Bujak's contention that peasants did not produce grain for sale.[146] The total value of peasant grain sold at the five Southern Podillian markets is also noteworthy. There were, of course, many other markets in Southern Podillia at which grain was bought or sold. Moreover, the totals do not include maize and other produce such as specialty crops. The total value of peasants' crops brought to market was obviously much higher, and the total worth of the peasants' production of field crops, including the portions that were consumed and bartered, was much higher still. The 1890 data on which Table 15 is based also contained information on the proportion of each type of grain that was not of premium quality (*nicht marktfähig*). Between 15-16 per cent of each grain crop was deemed to be of poorer quality, and sold at discounts of 15-18 per cent (27 per cent for oats). Some asserted that grain that was peasant-produced was inferior to that produced by the large landowners, but the 1890 statistics do not show them to have had any significant difference in quality.[147]

A time series is available only for grain prices which prevailed at Borshchiv, Chortkiv, and Terebovlia markets for the years 1894-1900 (see Table 16).

Table 16
Price of Grain at Selected Markets, in Gulden per Metric Centner, 1894-1900

	Wheat	Rye	Barley	Oats	Maize
1894					
Borshchiv	8.56	7.00	7.23	10.60	6.01
Chortkiv	7.19	5.26	5.01	5.91	4.59
Terebovlia	6.47	4.58	4.41	4.76	5.26
1895					
Borshchiv	8.60	8.63	8.41	12.29	6.99
Chortkiv	6.85	5.70	5.10	5.26	5.55
Terebovlia	6.80	6.55	5.27	5.10	6.21

1896					
Borshchiv	9.23	8.60	7.72	11.57	5.78
Chortkiv	6.83	5.53	4.88	4.99	5.47
Terebovlia	6.85	5.40	4.07	4.84	4.88
1897					
Borshchiv	9.89	9.31	9.85	13.38	6.59
Chortkiv	10.21	7.11	5.92	6.28	5.55
Terebovlia	8.63	6.03	5.05	5.52	5.56
1898					
Borshchiv	12.19	9.86	9.32	13.19	7.21
Chortkiv	9.00	7.61	6.14	7.58	5.75
Terebovlia	9.71	7.25	6.32	6.30	5.94
1899					
Borshchiv	10.39	8.29	7.85	n/a	6.71
Chortkiv	7.93	6.74	5.10	5.62	5.14
Terebovlia			n/a		
1900					
Borshchiv	9.10	7.20	7.79	5.40	6.63
Chortkiv	7.47	5.72	5.58	5.70	5.30
Terebovlia	7.64	5.94	5.58	5.70	5.30

Source: *Oesterreichisches statistisches Handbuch*, vols. 13-19.
For 1899 and 1900, prices have been recalculated from crowns to gulden.

A large price differential, not present in 1890, prevailed in the mid- and late 1890s between Borshchiv, on the one hand, and Chortkiv and Terebovlia, on the other. Significantly, it persisted even after the railway reached Borshchiv in 1898, indicating that only relatively small quantities of grain were being brought to market there or that demand continued high, or both.[148]

By the second half of the 1890s, although there were fluctuations depending on the state of the current harvest, prices for grain were generally moving upward. This price movement was of benefit to the peasants, who were mostly sellers, rather than buyers, of grain.[149] The improvement in their yield of grain crops in the 1890s, together with the upward movement of prices, enabled peasants to earn more income from the production and sale of grain. Crops of specialty produce, such as clover seed, caraway and poppy seed, and tobacco, could give the peasants very considerable returns. Tobacco, in particular, was very significant as a source of peasant income in Southern Podillia.[150]

If there is a tentativeness in these conclusions about prices of field crops and the incomes peasants derived from them, it will be even more pronounced for income from animals and animal products. (Some prices at Lviv are given in Appendix II; however, these are not necessarily indicative of prices that peasants could obtain.) Most trade in animals and animal products, except in pigs, was in the hands of Jewish people; the pig traders were usually Polish.[151] Local dealers may have exploited the sellers' ignorance of international prices,[152] although the press available in the reading clubs, particularly *Batkivshchyna* and *Svoboda*, regularly reported on Vienna and Lviv prices for animals and their products. There were certainly complaints in the press about the real or alleged exploitation of peasants by traders, mostly Jewish traders.[153] The concept of the middleman's profit was still strange to Ukrainian villagers, and there were indeed situations in which they could be, and doubtless were, exploited. For example, a buyers' combine might be at work in local markets. The press tried to persuade peasants that it was not worthwhile taking cattle to market in order to receive only 25 g per head with all the costs incurred in taking them there, when an itinerant trader was willing to pay the same amount.[154] Some other local practices, such as a trader supplying a calf to the peasant for the latter to rear with a subsequent 50:50 split of the animal's sale price, led to later doubts about the equity of the arrangement.[155]

There are references to the sale price of particular animals, but without knowledge of the condition of those animals they are not very meaningful. Some of the prices mentioned are 25 g for a cow, 9 g from a trader or 10 g at market for a pig,[156] around 15 g for a small pig of 50 kg,[157] 100-150 g for a workhorse,[158] 2 g each for lambs, and 45 g each for two fattened pigs on a large peasant holding of about 10 ha.[159]

In general, the price of animals and animal products remained firm throughout the 1880s and increased somewhat in the 1890s. With more attention being given to fattened cattle and pigs in Southern Podillia, and with more, heavier, and better quality animals, the peasants were receiving a better income from animal rearing than ever before. It was certainly contemporary opinion that livestock raising was a far more profitable operation for peasants by the late 1890s than it had been earlier.[160] Moreover, animal production accounted for a much greater proportion of the peasants' increased income than at an earlier time: "Our peasants in 1894 made three times the income from the export of pigs than they did from the export of grain."[161] Probably not all peasants benefited equally from the various and undeniable improvements in crop production and animal husbandry that occurred in the 1880s and 1890s. However, for most peasants these improvements were much more significant than any decline in the average size of landholding, which had so greatly exercised contemporary experts:

> Our grandfathers had twenty or more morgs but didn't have as much from it as the grandsons now get from four or six morgs. From one morg of field they got two wagons of bad hay, today we get 10-15 wagons of clover. Our grandfathers did not have buildings for cattle, now the grandsons build "German-style" barns, whitewashed inside and out, with good doors, that have ladders.[162]

Thus much was accomplished in the 1880s and 1890s in peasant agriculture in Southern Podillia. While many intangibles remain, the fact of great improvement and progress is obvious.

Notes

1. See, for example, S. Szczepanowski, *Nędza Galicyi*, 3-19, *passim*; Z. Ludkiewicz, *Kwestia rolna w Galicji*, 26-8; Z. Daszyńska-Golińska, *Własność rolna w Galicyi*, 30; *Khliborob*, 25 Nov. 1893.
2. Pruski, *Hodowla zwierząt gospodarskich*, 2: 30; J. Buszko, "Zum Wandel der Gesellschaftsstruktur," 9.
3. By the late nineteenth century, "tabular estates" were not exactly synonymous with "large landholdings," though insofar as ownership was concerned they still largely tended to be so. By the turn of the century, "large landowner" (*Grossgrundbesitzer*) generally denoted a person who owned more than 200 ha, with an assessed value for tax purposes of more than 100 g (A. von Hohenbruck, "Die Verteilung der Gesammtfläche Oesterreichs zwischen Gross- und Kleingrundbesitz," 126).
4. T. Pilat, "Die Auswanderung," 72-3.
5. J. Bużek, "Własność tabularna w Galicyi według stanu z końcem roku 1902," 27, 33.
6. Ibid., 29.
7. See Appendix VI below.
8. K. Jasiński, "Obszary uprawione pod poszczególne płody rolnicze na własności tabularnej w 1896/7," 9.
9. Local preference as much as any other factor determines what grain is principally used for bread (N. Jasny, *Competition Among Grains*, 25-8).
10. S. Hoszowski, *Ceny we Lwowie w latach 1701-1914*, 100; Biegeleisen, *Rozwój gospodarczy*, 2: 51, 62.
11. T. Pilat, "Landwirtschaft und Viehzucht," 808. See also *Batkivshchyna*, 25 June 1886, for the effect of heat upon rye.
12. See N. Jasny, *The Socialized Agriculture of the USSR*, 536.
13. Pilat, "Landwirtschaft und Viehzucht," 808.
14. See, for example, *Hospodar i promyshlennyk*, no. 3, 1885.
15. Pilat, "Landwirtschaft und Viehzucht," 808; Daszyńska-Golińska, *Własność rolna w Galicyi*, 6.
16. See Chapter II above; J. Bużek, "Der Einfluss der Ernten, respective der Getreidepreise auf die Bevölkerungsbewegung in Galizien in den Jahren

1878-1918," 181; and F. Umlauft, *Die österreichische-ungarische Monarchie*, 641.

17. *Hospodar i promyshlennyk*, nos. 1 and 2, 1885; *Batkivshchyna*, 14 Mar. 1890; *Chytalnia*, 9 Sept. 1896; Jasiński, "Obszary uprawione pod poszczególne," 12; Pilat, "Die Auswanderung," 80; Bujak, *Galicya*, 1: 286.
18. Bujak, *Galicya*, 1: 287.
19. Szczepanowski, *Nędza Galicyi*, 48; Bujak, *Galicya*, 1: 302. For modern views on the nutritive value of the potato see Salamon, *The History of the Potato*, 121-5; and D.W. Kent-Jones and A.J. Amos, *Modern Cereal Chemistry*, 146-9.
20. S. Hoszowski, *Ceny we Lwowie w latach 1701-1914*, 21.
21. Pruski, *Hodowla zwierząt gospodarskich*, 1: 36, 69; F. Bujak, "Rozwój gospodarczy Galicji (1772-1914)," 132.
22. Hoszowski, *Ceny we Lwowie w latach 1701-1914*, 21-32.
23. See Appendix VI below for details.
24. *Batkivshchyna*, 7 May 1886. By the mid-1890s the agricultural statistics differentiated among types of beans, principally kidney and broad beans.
25. IMZCh, 834; *Hospodar i promyshlennyk*, no. 1, 1885; Jasiński, "Obszary uprawione pod poszczególne," 12. Caraway seed could be grown only on some types of local soil. For hemp and its local use see also Vynnytsky, *Terebovelska zemlia*, 364-5.
26. Pilat, "Landwirtschaft und Viehzucht," 809; Jasiński, "Obszary uprawione pod poszczególne," 18; Bujak, *Galicya*, 1: 309-10. For tobacco cultivation in Southern Podillia see also IMZCh, 440, 447, 846, 855, *passim*.
27. Interviews with Mr. W. Michalchyshyn, Winnipeg, 6 Oct. 1983; and Mr. J. Horobec, Stuartburn, 20 June 1979.
28. *Hospodar i promyshlennyk*, no. 2, 1885. For the production of aniseed and tobacco in the village of Shchytivtsi (Zalishchyky county) see IMZCh, 787.
29. *Batkivshchyna*, 13 Feb. 1890.
30. Extrapolated from data in Appendix VI below and in Jasiński, "Obszary uprawione pod poszczególne," 12. He stated that in 1896-7 10 per cent of Podillia's tabular ploughland was under clover.
31. *Hospodar i promyshlennyk*, no. 22, 1885. See also *Nauka*, 31 Jan. and 28 Feb. 1890.
32. *Batkivshchyna*, 13 Feb. 1890.
33. On the use of fallow in general see N.S.B. Cras, *A History of Agriculture in Europe and America*, 31, 36-41; and C. Warner, *Agrarian Conditions in Modern European History*, 1. Traditionally a reduction in the amount of land left fallow has been regarded as a sign of modernization. Paradoxically, the reduction of fallow came late in Eastern Galicia because the native fertility of the soil allowed peasants to grow enough for their own use on the lands they chose to cultivate (Pruski, *Hodowla zwierząt gospodarskich*, 2: 27). See also Rudnitsky, *Ukraine*, 257; Pilat, "Landwirtschaft und Viehzucht," 807. By 1913, only 5 per cent of Galician land was being left fallow (Pruski, 2: 27).
34. Pilat, "Die Auswanderung," 78.
35. *Hospodar i promyshlennyk*, no. 22, 1885; *Hospodar*, no. 1, 1900.
36. W.T.R. Preston, "Report of Inspector of Agencies in Europe," 12-19.
37. *Hospodar i promyshlennyk*, no. 2, 1884.

38. Pruski, *Hodowla zwierząt gospodarskich*, 1: 305, 2: 32-3; *Batkivshchyna*, 22 Feb. 1889.
39. Mr. E. Michaels, Portage la Prairie, interviewed 6 Oct. 1983, stated that his father, in Chortkiv county, as soon as the rye was harvested in the first week of July, regularly planted buckwheat on that land.
40. Pilat, "Die Auswanderung," 80; Bujak, *Galicya*, 1: 286.
41. *Hospodar i promyshlennyk*, no. 13, 1880. According to the example given there, one morg planted with maize would yield 10 korets of grain, to be sold at 4 g each (=40 gulden), plus stalks worth a total of 2.40 g, and intercrops of 2 korets of beans at 6 g (=12 gulden) and 10 wagonloads of pumpkins at 1 g each (=10 gulden); with good cultivation more could be obtained (1 korets = 3.62 bushels).
42. *Hospodar i promyshlennyk*, nos. 1 and 2, 1885; *Batkivshchyna*, 14 Mar. 1890; IMZCh, 495.
43. *Hospodar i promyshlennyk*, no. 3, 1885.
44. *Batkivshchyna*, 13 Feb. and 14 Mar. 1890.
45. There are a number of allusions to this "division of labour." See, for example, *Lastivka*, no. 10, 1880; and *Batkivshchyna*, 19 Jan. 1889.
46. In an interview 29 Dec. 1983, Mr. W. Michalchyshyn, Winnipeg, stated that the following were grown in his family's garden in Bychkivtsi, Chortkiv county: cabbages, cucumbers, small melons, various sorts of beans, peas, beets, parsnips, turnips, cauliflower, potatoes, maize, celery, onions, garlic, dill, parsley, raspberries, strawberries, gooseberries, currants, and loganberries. Although his mother did not plant tomatoes or spinach, he had heard of people growing them. He added that not many people had raspberries or strawberries because they took up too much space. People with large gardens sometimes grew hemp. His father grew wheat, rye, potatoes, maize, and tobacco on his ploughland.
47. Many memoirs by former villagers from Southern Podillia noted the orchards and fruits. See, for example, Vynnytsky, *Terebovelska zemlia*, 98; and IMZCh, 67, 180, 189, 206, 500, 587, 612, 627, 630, 666, 668, 671, 674, 701, 787. For the prize-winning fruit, see *Batkivshchyna*, 2 Nov. 1888.
48. *Oesterreichisch-ungarische Monarchie*, 19: 62.
49. Vineyards and their production were recorded in the annual Austrian agricultural statistics for many Austrian Crownlands, including Bukovyna, but not for Galicia.
50. IMZCh, 839; for wine-making see *Sefer Borszczow*, 108.
51. Bujak, *Galicya*, 1: 285ff. Selected data were also published by the Galician Statistical Bureau.
52. The Austrian state recognized these natural disasters and waived the payment of land tax in particular localities in any years when yields were unduly low on their account.
53. For weather information relevant to the crop-growing cycle see annual volumes of *Statistisches Jahrbuch des k.k. Ackerbau-Ministeriums*.
54. Ibid., *passim*.
55. Ibid.
56. See, for example, Stefanyk, *The Stone Cross*, 21. For an instance of a village "working bee" devoted to manuring the land see IMZCh, 643. See also *Hospodar*

i promyshlennyk (no. 1, 1886), which stated that "a farm without manure is like a man without a soul."

57. *Chytalnia*, 6 Aug. 1894. See also ibid., 23 Mar. 1893, 21 May 1984, 6 Nov. 1896; *Hospodar i promyshlennyk*, no. 1, 1884, no. 1, 1886, no. 6, 1887; *Batkivshchyna*, 11 June 1886.
58. It was reported at the 1885 annual meeting of Kółka Rolnicze that peasants "even use artificial fertilizer" (*Batkivshchyna*, 5 July 1885). See also ibid., 2 Apr. 1886; *Dilo*, 17 Jan. 1890), *Chytalnia*, 6 July and 6 Nov. 1894, 6 July 1895, 6 Mar. 1896; S.M. Trusevych, *Suspilno-politychnyi rukh u skhidnii Halychyni v 50-70-kh rokakh XIX st.*, 17.
59. *Chytalnia*, 26 Aug. 1896. On the importance of straw see also *Hospodar i promyshlennyk*, no. 1, 1886.
60. See the discussion in M. Kiniorski, "Większa i mniejsza własność ziemska wobec parcelacyi," 96-9. For the Kopychyntsi judicial district of Husiatyn county, which comprised about one-half of its area, available details are given below (in other parts of the region the productivity gap was at times somewhat greater):

Yield of main grain crops in hectolitres on large and small landholdings in Kopychyntsi District, 1894-7

	Large Landowners				**Small Landowners**			
	1894	**1895**	**1896**	**1897**	**1894**	**1895**	**1896**	**1897**
Wheat	10.6	12.0	12.0	7.8	9.3	11.2	11.8	7.8
Rye	8.8	7.9	8.2	9.7	8.2	7.5	8.2	9.7
Barley	11.1	17.4	8.1	10.0	9.3	14.3	7.8	8.6
Oats	10.4	14.0	8.8	11.3	9.4	12.3	7.0	10.8

Source: *Statistisches Jahrbuch des k.k. Ackerbau-Ministeriums*, 1894, 1895, 1896, and 1897.

61. *Nauka*, 15 Apr. 1886.
62. Bujak, *Galicya*, 1: 313. See also Inglot, *Historia chłopów Polskich*, 176; W. Kula, *Historia gospodarcza Polski w dobie popowstaniowej 1864-1918*, 68; Rutkowski, *Czasy porozbiorowe*, 303; R. Drazniowsky, "Galizien unter oesterreichischer und polnischer Herrschaft: Kulturpolitische und wirtschaftliche Entwicklung der Ukrainer," 128.
63. Pruski, *Hodowla zwierząt gospodarskich*, 1: 6.
64. For detailed information on pre-1880 animal husbandry in Galicia see ibid.; for the connection between potato growing, alcohol production, and cattle raising prior to 1848 see ibid., 36, 69-74. See also Inglot, *Historia chłopów Polskich*, 176; Rutkowski, *Czasy porozbiorowe*, 65.
65. Pruski, *Hodowla zwierząt gospodarskich*, 1: 46-58, 174-219, 251.
66. Ibid., 289.
67. K. Dinklage, "Die landwirtschaftliche Entwicklung," 1: 428.
68. See *Hospodar i promyshlennyk*, nos. 12 and 13, 1880, no. 7, 1884, and no. 1, 1886;

Nauka, no. 4, 1886; *Batkivshchyna*, 8 Mar. and 10 Aug. 1889, 13 Feb. and 14 Mar. 1890; *Chytalnia*, 21 July 1894.

69. From less than 60 per cent to more than 90 per cent between 1884 and 1896 (*Statistisches Jahrbuch des k.k. Ackerbau-Ministeriums*, annual volumes).
70. K.v.d. Marlsburg, "Die Rindviehzucht in Galizien," 650. Hay cost around 3 gulden per 100 kg in 1898 (*Svoboda*, 20 Oct. 1898).
71. Rutkowski, *Czasy porozbiorowe*, 66.
72. A. Lipp, *Verkehrs- und Handelsverhältnisse Galiziens*, 229.
73. Pruski, *Hodowla zwierząt gospodarskich*, 1: 379-6; 2: 53, 375ff.
74. Ibid., 1: 40-1, 79, 103, 107, 143; G.R.von Wiedersperg, "Die Entwicklung des Veterinärwesens in Oesterreich," 790.
75. The fact that such a large proportion of Galicia's cattle was in peasant hands was deemed worthy of special note in the general introduction to the 1900 animal census (*Oesterrichische Statistik*, LX, no. 3, pt. II: xxviii). For detailed information see Appendix VIII below.
76. Pilat, "Die Auswanderung," 76.
77. *Chytalnia*, 6 Mar. 1896.
78. Ibid., 21 Apr. 1894, 21 Mar. 1896.
79. *Rocznik statystyki*, 1: 155, 4: 241; *Podręcznik statystyki*, vol. 7, pt. 1: 172. For the decline in demand for honey and wax see *Nauka*, 1 Jan. 1884, 15 Dec. 1886.
80. The data in this paragraph are from *Oesterrichische Statistik*, XXXIV, no. 2. The number of pamphlets published on beekeeping, the frequency of newspaper articles on this topic (e.g., *Novost*, nos. 1, 5/6 and 7/8, 1883; *Batkivshchyna*, 21 Sept. 1888, 8 Mar. 1889; *Nauka*, 15 Jan. and 15 Mar. 1887; *Chytalnia*, 5 Mar. and 6 May 1893) and the attention devoted to this subject by the Beekeepers' and Gardeners' Section of the Agricultural Association (*Batkivshchyna*, 2 Jan. 1885 and 27 Feb. 1891) all suggest that beekeeping was practiced more extensively than data derived in winter would indicate. For beekeeping see also IMZCh, 383 (in "Austrian times," people mostly had 10-15 hives, though some had up to 125; 100 kg of honey sold for about 100 crowns), 420; and Vynnytsky, *Terebovelska zemlia*, 98. A price of 28-32 kr per kg for the cheapest Podillian honey was cited in *Batkivshchyna*, 21 Sept. 1888. See also Bujak, *Galicya*, 1: 351; Vovk, *Studii z ukrainskoi*, 45.
81. *Hospodar i promyshlennyk*, no. 14, 1880; *Russkaia rada*, 18 Jan. 1881; *Batkivshchyna*, 9 Nov. 1889; *Chytalnia*, 5 Feb. and 5 Mar. 1893, 21 July and 21 Oct. 1894, 6 and 21 Sept., and 6 Dec. 1895, 6 Mar., 21 Apr. and 6 May 1896. The Agricultural Association was not involved in promoting poultry until after the turn of the century.
82. v. Meinzingen, "Die häusliche Nutzthiere in Oesterreich nach dem Stande von 31 December 1900," 686-7.
83. *Hospodar i promyshlennyk*, no. 6, 1887; *Chytalnia*, 6 Dec. 1895; Bujak, *Galicya*, 1: 347-8; Biegeleisen, *Rozwój gospodarczy*, 2: 1-8; Pruski, *Hodowla zwierząt gospodarskich*, 1: 567, 574, 2: 445-60; Birnboim, *From My Father's House*, 25-31. See also IMZCh, 627, 643. According to Biegeleisen, poultry raising entailed too much work and trouble for the women on larger landholdings.
84. Pruski, *Hodowla zwierząt gospodarskich*, 2: 449. According to Bujak (*Galicya*, 2: 350), in 1903 Galicia exported 35 million crowns worth of eggs, plus feathers worth

3 million crowns, and poultry worth 1.5 millions. For trade in eggs, predominantly by Jews, see also IMZCh, 410, 502, 759; Birnboim, *From My Father's House*, 17.

85. Birnboim, *From My Father's House*, 14.
86. In the 1890s the Austrian army maintained 6,000-10,000 such reserve horses on contract in Galicia (Pruski, *Hodowla zwierząt gospodarskich*, 1: 505, 2: 291). While I have found no direct evidence of these in Southern Podillia, it seems likely, in view of the region's proximity to the Russian border and the presence of army garrisons, that there would have been some.
87. For some of the famous studs and stables of Southern Podillia see Pruski, *Hodowla zwierząt gospodarskich*, 1: 457, 469, 479-81, 493, 496, and 510.
88. Interview with Mr. E. Michaels, Portage la Prairie, 6 October 1983. See also IMZCh, 467.
89. Mr. M. Sokolyk, Dominion City, interviewed 19 July 1979, recalled that his uncle, Nykola Smuk of Synkiv (Zalishchyky county), had horses that he used to deliver grain and various goods for other people. He and his team would be hired for such hauling work from time to time. See also Koenig, "The Ukrainians of East Galicia," 130; Biegeleisen, *Rozwój gospodarczy*, 2: 2-3; Havrysh, *Moia Kanada i ia*, 14, 64.
90. *Hospodar i promyshlennyk*, no. 5, 1884. On the decline in the use of oxen, see Pruski, *Hodowla zwierząt gospodarskich*, 1: 356-7, 385, 2: 72, 259.
91. Pilat, "Landwirtschaft und Viehzucht," 818; Ludkiewicz, *Kwestia rolna w Galicji*, 31; Bujak, *Galicya*, 1: 317.
92. Pruski, *Hodowla zwierząt gospodarskich*, 1: 443-4.
93. Ibid., 2: 262-3.
94. Ibid., 263-5, 355; Bujak, *Galicya*, 1: 327. Many of the activities in support of better horse breeding were of assistance primarily to large landowners. Peasants benefited too, but the Central Executive of the Agricultural Circles found it necessary to issue a plea to increase the number of breeding stations and improve peasant access to them (Dawidowa, *Kółka rolnicze w Galicyi*, 15).
95. Pruski, *Hodowla zwierząt gospodarskich*, 2: 364.
96. Ibid., 367. See also ibid., 52; Ludkiewicz, *Kwestia rolna w Galicji*, 167.
97. See, for example, *Hospodar i promyshlennyk*, nos. 1, 2, and 5, 1884; *Batkivshchyna*, 25 Oct., 2 and 9 Nov., 14 Dec. 1889; *Chytalnia*, 5 Jan. 1894; *Hospodar*, Dec. 1900.
98. *Batkivshchyna*, 7 Jan. 1887.
99. *Hospodar i promyshlennyk*, no. 1, 1886; *Batkivshchyna*, 10 July 1891; *Chytalnia*, 5 June 1893.
100. *Batkivshchyna*, 7 Jan. 1887, 29 Mar. 1889.
101. *Hospodar i promyshlennyk*, nos. 1 and 2, 1886, and 6, 1887; *Batkivshchyna*, 26 Oct. 1888, 20 June 1890, 8 May, 3 July 1891. *Nauka* (15 Sept. 1886) advised peasants to slaughter and eat cattle rather than try to keep them if pasturage was inadequate.
102. *Batkivshchyna*, 2 Oct. 1891.
103. Pruski, *Hodowla zwierząt gospodarskich*, 1: 45; Bujak, *Galicya*, 1: 331; Pilat, "Landwirtschaft und Viehzucht," 813. According to Pruski (2: 68), contemporary Alpine cows gave over 1,500 litres of milk per annum, Oldenburgs 2,300, Simmenthal 2,200, Ayrshire 2,200, and Dutch upward of 3,500 litres.
104. *Svoboda*, 18 Mar. 1897. See also Pruski, *Hodowla zwierząt gospodarskich*, 1:

412-3, 2: 120ff.

105. *Oesterrichische Statistik*, vol. LX, no. 3, pt. 2: xxviii; Marlsburg, "Die Rindviehzucht," 651.
106. Pruski, *Hodowla zwierząt gospodarskich*, 1: 430, 2: 59, 218-29, 238-9; Drazniowsky, *Galizien*, 133-4; for the Simmenthal breeding station in Zalishchyky see Pruski, 2: 57.
107. *Hospodar i promyshlennyk*, no. 7, 1886; Pruski, *Hodowla zwierząt gospodarskich*, 2: 228; Bujak, *Galicya*, 1: 342.
108. Bujak, *Galicya*, 1: 341-2; Pruski, *Hodowla zwierząt gospodarskich*, 2: 238-9; *Svoboda*, 24 Mar. 1898.
109. Pruski, *Hodowla zwierząt gospodarskich*, 2: 230-2, 241-3, 248ff. Prosvita appointed its own dairying inspector-teacher in 1900 (*Hospodar*, Dec. 1900).
110. Cited in Pruski, *Hodowla zwierząt gospodarskich*, 2: 248. On the improved quality of peasant cattle see also Marlsburg, "Die Rindviehzucht," 651.
111. Pruski, *Hodowla zwierząt gospodarskich*, 2: 241.
112. *Oesterrichische Statistik*, XXXIV, no. 2: xxxiv.
113. Pruski, *Hodowla zwierząt gospodarskich*, 2: 96.
114. Ibid., 72.
115. *Oesterreichisch-ungarische Monarchie*, 19: 56.
116. Dinklage, "Die landwirtschaftliche Entwicklung," 427. The introduction of fodder crops and selective animal breeding are very important indicators of agricultural progress (René Dumont, "Agriculture as Man's Transformation of the Rural Environment," 141-9).
117. Pruski, *Hodowla zwierząt gospodarskich*, 2: 94ff.; I. Vytanovych, *Istoriia ukrainskoho kooperatyvnoho rukhu*, 151; Bujak, *Galicya*, 1: 356; Melnyk, "Das ukrainische Genossenschaftswesen," 24; Drazniowsky, "Galizien," 134.
118. *Oesterrichische Statistik*, LX, no. 3, pt. 2: xxviii.
119. Hoszowski, *Ceny we Lwowie*, 120.
120. Pruski, *Hodowla zwierząt gospodarskich*, 2: 77-8.
121. Ibid., 1: 372-4.
122. Ibid., 2: 202.
123. Marlsburg, "Die Rindviehzucht," 651.
124. IMZCh, 678. For other references to sheep rearing in Borshchiv and Zalishchyky counties see ibid., 624, 637, 641, 672; *Batkivshchyna*, 13 Jan. 1890 and 16 Oct. 1891. For sheep-rearing practices in general see Pruski, *Hodowla zwierząt gospodarskich*, 2: 417-43.
125. Pilat, "Die Landwirtschaft," 814; IMZCh, 637, 678, 780.
126. Exports of wool from Galicia declined to zero as a result of competition from Australia, New Zealand, and the Americas (J. Łukasiewicz, *Kryzys agrarny na ziemiach polskich w końcu XIX wieku*, 230; Bujak, *Galicya*, 1: 315, 319.
127. See, for example, *Hospodar i promyshlennyk*, no. 13, 1880 and no. 1, 1886; *Svoboda*, 11 Feb. and 3 June 1897, and 10 and 17 Feb. 1898.
128. Pruski, *Hodowla zwierząt gospodarskich*, 2: 382, 383ff.
129. *Batkivshchyna*, 9 July and 24 Aug. 1886. Pigs were usually slaughtered by peasants in anticipation of Christmas and Easter holidays and other festive occasions (Vovk, *Studii*, 79, and IMZCh, 467).

130. Pruski, *Hodowla zwierząt gospodarskich*, 1: 552; Stefanyk, *The Stone Cross*, 65; interview with Mr. E. Michaels, Portage la Prairie, 6 Oct. 1983.
131. Stefanyk, *The Stone Cross*, 54; *Chytalnia*, 21 Nov. 1894.
132. *Svoboda*, 17 Feb. 1898.
133. Bujak, *Galicya*, 1: 345. Podillian pigs were often left to fend for themselves in summer and fall on pasture and woodland.
134. *Svoboda*, 3 and 17 Nov., and 22 Dec. 1898.
135. Austria, k.k. Ackerbau-Ministerium, *Bericht über das oesterreichische Veterinarwesen für das Jahr 1902*.
136. Interview with Mr. E. Michaels, Portage la Prairie, 6 Oct. 1983; IMZCh, 512; Havrysh, *Moia Kanada i ia*, 65.
137. Pruski, *Hodowla zwierząt gospodarskich*, 2: 64-5.
138. *Chytalnia*, 6 Aug. 1894.
139. AGAD, Min. des Innern, file V6, "Viehtransport 1889," circular of the governor of Galicia to all county officers, 19 Feb. 1889.
140. There are numerous documents, principally proclamations, in AGAD, Min. des Innern, file V6, dealing with quarantine regulations and movement restrictions in 1889, including many relating to the individual counties of Southern Podillia. For press reports on animal disease, the closing of markets, and the slaughtering of animals see *Batkivshchyna*, 7 June, 6 and 28 Sept., and 14 Dec. 1889.
141. Dinklage, "Die landwirtschaftliche Entwicklung," 447.
142. Petition by Husiatyn county executive of 6 June 1889, AGAD, Handels-Ministerium, file HG 1, "Restrictions of the movement of cattle and meat, 1888-1896." No action appears to have been taken in response. For a complaint about the strictness of veterinary regulations see *Svoboda*, 3 June 1897.
143. For a lengthy discussion on why one cannot rely on prices in international markets when considering local prices see Biegeleisen, *Rozwój gospodarczy*, 2: 90-105. On peasant income see Chapter II above. On local markets in general see Gorski, "Das Marktwesen," 854-7. On grain at the great annual fair at Ulashkivtsi, see IMZCh, 245.
144. H. von Schullern-Schrattenhoffen, "Die Bewegung der Getreidepreise in Oesterreich," 219-40.
145. For the grain sale practices of large landowners in the late 1870s see Hempel, "Ekonomiczne stosunki Galicyi," 174-5.
146. Bujak, *Galicya*, 1: 303.
147. *Statistisches Jahrbuch des k.k. Ackerbau-Ministeriums*, 1891, table XIII. It may be extrapolated from data in this source that the following amounts of grain (both premium and second quality) were sold at Chortkiv market in 1890: wheat, 35,880 hectolitres; rye, 87,518 hl; barley, 19,926 hl; and oats, 27,965 hl.
148. I have not found explanations of the continued price differential between Borshchiv and other markets after 1898. Possibly there was a shortage of railway cars to transport grain in an isolated region of Galicia; possibly some cartel operation was at work to keep local selling prices up. Schullern-Schrattenhoffen ("Die Bewegung," 240) believed that poor communication routes accounted for the Borshchiv prices.

149. Bużek, "Der Einfluss," esp. 213, engaged in a lengthy discussion to show that Galician peasants were generally sellers and not buyers of grain.
150. According to *Chytalnia* (6 Sept. 1894), the total income of peasants from tobacco alone amounted to 6,000 g per commune in December of any year; much of this would be used to pay taxes.
151. There are frequent references to Jewish traders in the literature, but never in connection with the pig trade. For Polish (*Mazur*) pig traders see *Batkivshchyna*, 16 Jan. 1895; Stefanyk, *The Stone Cross*, 54.
152. Biegeleisen, *Rozwój gospodarczy*, 2: 89-90.
153. *Batkivshchyna*, 9 Mar. 1888, 5 Apr. 1889.
154. *Chytalnia*, 21 Apr. 1896.
155. Interview with Mr. E. Michaels, Winnipeg, 30 Dec. 1983; Pruski, *Hodowla zwierząt gospodarskich*, 1: 372-82.
156. *Chytalnia*, 21 Apr. 1896.
157. Extrapolated from *Svoboda*, 3 June 1897, in a lengthy article urging peasants not to go to market too frequently.
158. *Chytalnia*, 6 June 1894.
159. Bużek, "Der Einfluss," 215.
160. *Svoboda*, 22 Dec. 1898.
161. Ibid., 3 June 1897.
162. *Batkivshchyna*, 8 Mar. 1889.

Chapter VIII

Public Health

In the last two decades of the nineteenth century there were certain important improvements in the health of the people of Southern Podillia. After severe epidemics of cholera, smallpox, and typhus in the 1870s, the Austrian government turned its attention to implementing some preventive health measures. Major scourges like cholera and smallpox were contained better geographically and their outbreaks declined in length and severity. Public and private efforts were made to educate the population about health matters. Mortality rates and birth rates declined. Nevertheless, there were many indications of shortages of medical care personnel and facilities in Southern Podillia, and traditional folk medicine continued to exist alongside more modern medicine.

The Organization of Health Care

Public health services in Austria were the responsibility of the Ministry of the Interior. This office, through its laws and regulations, administered all health personnel, approved and supervised all health-care facilities, maintained statistics about health matters, and determined and directed the various measures to prevent, limit, and treat diseases, especially communicable diseases.[1] Each level of government had health matters to administer clearly delineated by the state Health Law of 30 April 1870.[2] Answering to the Minister of the Interior were Crownland Health Officers who were in charge of the district or county Health Officers in a given Land. Each county in Galicia had a Medical Officer of Health (hereinafter MOH), who was usually a doctor of medicine, but might be a veterinary physician. The MOH was most immediately responsible for public health, and was also answerable to the County Officer. On orders from the County Officer or on his own authority, the MOH had a number of duties which affected all health matters in the county, including supervision of health personnel and inspection of schools. Other doctors needed official permission from the MOH before they could open an office; apothecaries were controlled by number and location.[3]

One of the most important functions of the county MOH was the collection of statistical data on health matters in his area. Quarterly statistical records were compiled from official parish registers which were maintained by the clergy. The data noted: marriages, births, deaths (by age as well as by cause of death), infectious diseases, whether a certified midwife assisted at a delivery, and whether there was medical certification of death. A regulation of 1888 required each commune to report immediately to the county office any cases of infectious disease. Then the commune officials were to report regularly each week until the outbreak of the disease was over. The MOH was personally to check on cases of cholera, smallpox, typhus, and plague. Such a reporting system enabled the central authorities to make decisions on medical intervention, although this was sometimes a matter of "too little, too late." The MOH was also to meet with the certified midwives in his county on his regular tours and to scrutinize their register books. Midwives were to have annual conferences at which their registers and delivery instruments were inspected and, by the end of the century, they were to receive lectures on the revised official instructions for midwives.[4]

Other areas of the public health-care delivery system in Galicia were not as clearly designated, nor did they seem to operate as effectively as the state MOH systems. This was partly due to the fact that although the 1870 state law recognized the necessity of a network of medical services complete with expert personnel and facilities, the implementation of most of the health measures rested with the Sejm and the Land Executive. The state gave subsidies and put pressure on the Land Administration to provide services, but these were made available only if the Galician political authorities saw fit to budget for them. As a result, considerable gaps existed in these services, and the improvements which occurred were probably due mainly to state intervention and subsidies as well as to contributions to health care by private individuals and corporations. The Land, county, and commune government bodies undertook some health-improvement activities, but services were generally poor at the village level, where the majority of the population lived.[5]

The communes had a number of legal obligations. They were to provide, from communal budgets, free medical care and medication to the indigent; fund the "institutes for the poor"; and carry out any measures decreed by the state or the Land, especially in the event of outbreaks of infectious diseases. Often these responsibilities were simply too onerous for communes to take on, and most communes were without doctors or the means to stem illness, especially infectious diseases, as effectively as they might have done with more support from higher levels of government.[6] Thus, people in the villages were frequently thrown back on their own home-based resources for health care.

Infectious Diseases

There were notable improvements in health care of villagers in the 1880s and 1890s, especially for the most dreaded communicable diseases, smallpox and cholera. For cholera, regulations were issued on the setting up of quarantine stations with proper equipment, and the number of these rose through the 1880s and 1890s. Steam disinfection units (autoclaves) were installed in various areas.

Isolation stations were to be established along railway lines to accommodate people suffering from cholera. Courses were provided to train non-professionals to give service in case of an epidemic.[7] But the most far-reaching arrangements by the state were for prevention and containment of smallpox.

The great smallpox epidemic of 1873 caused the death of 64,849 persons in Austria (excluding Dalmatia).[8] An intensified preventive vaccination program was thereafter undertaken by the Austrian authorities. Vaccination was free and, in theory, compulsory; all costs of the vaccination program were borne by the state.[9] Gradually, the resistance of the population to vaccination was overcome and the quantity and quality of vaccine were improved.[10] The process in Galicia was the same as in other parts of Austria, and quite straightforward. Children were brought together on a certain day in one location for each village, or sometimes for a group of villages, where they were vaccinated by specially designated doctors. There was then a follow-up examination of these children to determine whether the vaccination had "taken." In 1885 there were 59 such vaccination stations in Borshchiv, 43 in Chortkiv, 51 in Husiatyn, 51 in Terebovlia, and 57 in Zalishchyky. Each year, thousands of children were vaccinated in Southern Podillia, at costs which varied in 1885 from 13 kreuzer per vaccination in Husiatyn to 21 kr in Zalishchyky.[11] In 1881, 13,937 individuals were vaccinated successfully in the five counties; in 1885, the total was 14,577; in 1890, 17,410; and in 1895, 21,934. Every year there were several hundred children with unsuccessful vaccinations who were supposed to return for the following year's vaccination. As well, there were several hundred who were not brought back for the follow-up examination. Their number was generally greater in Borshchiv and Zalishchyky counties, and deaths from smallpox were often greater in those two counties than elsewhere in the region.[12]

Although the disease was not eradicated, the vaccination campaign did have a positive result. Never again was there a smallpox epidemic of the proportions of 1873. The death rate in Galicia from smallpox per 1000 population was lowered from 4.82 in 1873 and 3.50 in 1874 (the average rate was 1.94 in the five counties in 1873-77) to average rates of 0.71 for 1877-82, 0.62 for 1883-8, and 0.54 for 1888-94.[13] In Southern Podillia an improving trend was obvious, especially after the 1881-3 outbreak (see Appendix X). Revaccinations of both school children and the wider population were also undertaken on a selective basis. There were occasional reminders of this in the Ukrainian press.[14] There were still some bad years in particular localities, such as in Zalishchyky county in 1889, when an outbreak of smallpox led to the closing of markets, shops, and some schools in the towns of Zalishchyky, Tovste, and Ustechko.[15] That year, 244 died from smallpox in that county. This was the last time until the end of the century that such a number were killed by this disease in any of the five counties. Smallpox, while not eradicated, was brought under control.

Cholera was another age-old problem that had appeared in the Austrian lands in epidemic proportions in 1855, 1866, 1872-3, 1886, and 1893-5.[16] In 1866,

165,292 persons had died from the disease, 34,857 of them in Galicia, and in 1873, 106,441 died, 90,802 in Galicia. Austrian authorities believed that some of the epidemics had been brought in through northern Galicia from Russia.[17] The Ukrainian press reiterated similar claims for a minor outbreak in 1889 and the epidemics of 1893 and 1894.[18] Austrian public-health measures and the agreements reached at the international health conferences in Venice in 1892 and Dresden in 1893 aimed at containing an outbreak once it began by placing restrictions on the movement of people and goods.[19] The small cholera outbreak of 1886 left Southern Podillia almost untouched, and in the years 1887-9 and 1890-1 the five counties were nearly free of the disease. A total of thirty-one deaths from cholera were reported from Southern Podillia in 1892, all in the two counties bordering on the Russian empire.[20] This outbreak was officially declared to be over at the end of January 1893, but in fact the press continued to report cholera in Borshchiv county, first specifically in Kudryntsi and later in a number of localities, as well as in neighbouring Bukovyna and Russian Podillia.[21] By 20 June 1893, it was reported that cholera was gone from Galicia, but further cases were later reported from a number of areas. Fifty-seven people died from cholera in Southern Podillia in 1893 out of a Galician total of 903 deaths from this disease.[22]

There were now three areas of infection—Russia, Galicia, and Hungary—and an epidemic could not be readily contained. This is probably not surprising, for international control efforts were designed not to interfere too greatly with the free flow of traffic. In 1893 it was Galician railway workers who were said to have brought the disease into Hungary. In April 1894 the renewed incidence of cholera in Borshchiv and Husiatyn counties manifested itself first at Skala and Sokyryntsi, which were legal crossing points from Russia; it was allegedly brought in by labourers from Russia.[23] However, the continued smuggling of animals and goods across the frontier also hindered attempts to control the disease. By the spring of 1894, there were probably a number of local Galician sources of cholera, and the disease spread widely across the Land. In 1894, 2,292 persons died of *cholera asiatica* in the five counties of Southern Podillia out of a Galician total of 8,236 and an Austrian total of 8,748. Galicia had a total of 459 deaths from cholera in 1895, indicating that the epidemic was finally being brought under control. There were six deaths from cholera in Southern Podillia in 1896, all in Terebovlia county, out of a total of eleven in Galicia for that year.[24] Thereafter Southern Podillia was free of cholera until after 1900.

In this period, while diseases like cholera often had to run their course, there were official actions which contributed to the containment of contagious diseases. Autoclave equipment and isolation stations along the railway lines helped. In June 1894 the Ministry of the Interior attempted to prevent fresh sources of infection from entering Austria by prohibiting the importation of articles of clothing from Russia, and by decreeing that all persons coming from Russia had to be quarantined for five days.[25] To prevent the further spread of cholera within the empire, and in conformity with the provisions of the 1893 Dresden Convention on Infectious Diseases, the Austrian authorities declared areas in which the incidence of cholera was high to be "centres of contagion," and restricted trade between such areas and other parts of Austria and Europe. An area comprised of Borshchiv, Chortkiv, Husiatyn, and Zalishchyky, along with three neighbouring counties, was identified as the original centre of the 1894 epidemic and declared a "closed area." Nevertheless, cholera spread westward and by September 1894 several other regions, including the city of Cracow, had to be declared centres of contagion.[26]

Eradication of the disease was slow. Zalishchyky was free of cholera by 16 December 1894, and it and fourteen other counties were removed from the list of areas of trade restrictions early in 1895.[27] In February 1895, with the eradication of the disease in Chortkiv county, restrictions on the county's trade with Hungary were ended. In March 1895, prohibitions on the trade between most of Galicia and Bukovyna on the one hand, and Hungary on the other, were lifted.[28] There was, however, one more limited outbreak of cholera in the fall of 1895, this time centred in Terebovlia and neighbouring Ternopil county. Prohibitions on exports from these two counties were immediately reimposed. In Terebovlia, the first case was reported on 25 September in Ianiv and in the next few weeks a total of thirty-eight cases were reported from ten communes with twenty-nine deaths. It was not until February 1896, after a few weeks without cases, that Terebovlia, with the whole of Galicia and Austria, could be declared free of cholera and all export prohibitions were lifted.[29]

County authorities took preventive measures in areas where cholera had broken out or where it was apprehended. Instructions were given that the immediate vicinity of wells was to be kept specially clean, and communes were to designate a building as an isolation station and train a person to disinfect actually and potentially infected materials. County offices sent supplies of carbolic acid to villages. Attempts were made to prevent the gathering of people: in 1893 a gendarme stopped the Greek Catholic parish priest of Nivra, Borshchiv county, from entering Zaluche to conduct a funeral service for cholera victims, and various meetings were forbidden or postponed in 1894. Attempts were also made to stop the spread of the disease by keeping victims isolated. Specially appointed "cholera doctors" were to examine cholera patients daily, but in fact very little could be done for those who contracted the disease other than to give them ample fluids.[30] The death rate from cholera in 1894 was high—of the 12,025 who contracted cholera in Austria that year, 8,748 died.[31] *Batkivshchyna* charged that "the authorities have not managed the epidemic well,"[32] but given the knowledge and resources of the times, the only other measure that could have been taken was the imposition of much stricter quarantine and travel regulations.

The diseases to which the authorities paid the most systematic attention were smallpox, cholera, and rabies.[33] These diseases were the most deadly and the most readily amenable to public health measures, although by the end of the century progress was also being made with inoculation against diphtheria.[34] Any differentiation in the mortality statistics on death caused by specific diseases other than these three is not fully reliable, partly because the statistics for a long time included three unspecific categories of cause of death: children under one year of age, old age, and "other." Another reason for the questionable reliability of the statistics on the particular cause of death is that county authorities generally left it up to the local priest to state it. Nevertheless, as the local clergy acquired experience as "coroners," the summary data in the official sources are of some validity.

Tuberculosis was fairly widespread, and was more prevalent in Borshchiv and Zalishchyky than in the other three counties. Childhood diseases such as measles, scarlet fever, diphtheria, and whooping cough also took their severe annual toll. In the 1887 semi-epidemic outbreak of scarlet fever, Chortkiv had the highest death rate from this disease in all of Austria.[35] Diseases identified as typhus and dysentery were endemic. One Viennese authority suggested that the incidence of dysentery in Galicia rose with the ripening of the fruit; he also attributed it to general climatic and local weather conditions.[36] Given the relative scarcity of doctors and health-care facilities it is hardly a surprise that mortality rates for many infectious diseases were higher in Galicia than in most other parts of Austria. This was not invariably the case, however, for the Bohemian mortality rate from typhus was higher than that of Galicia.[37]

The Decline in the Death Rate

There was an overall downward trend in the absolute number of deaths and in the death rate in Southern Podillia, as in Galicia as a whole. (For the total number of deaths in each of the five counties for the years 1880-1900 see Appendix X.) There were annual fluctuations because the figures were often affected by the high incidence of mortality from one or more diseases. Thus, for example, in 1881 Terebovlia had an unusually high number of deaths from measles, diphtheria, and croup, while Zalishchyky had a high mortality from these as well as from smallpox and typhus; in 1887 Chortkiv, Husiatyn, and Terebovlia, but not the other two counties, had many more deaths than usual from scarlet fever (Husiatyn and Terebovlia suffered from diphtheria and croup also); in 1891 Borshchiv had many more deaths from whooping cough than any of the other counties. In each of the years 1892-4, Borshchiv had an unusually high incidence of typhus-caused deaths; in 1892 all the counties except Zalishchyky had a higher than average number of deaths from scarlet fever. However, a very high number of deaths in one county was not necessarily replicated in a neighbouring one. Thus, Borshchiv recorded 405 deaths from smallpox in 1883, while neighbouring Chortkiv had only four. Similarly, while there were 367 deaths from measles in Terebovlia and 262 in Husiatyn in 1884, in nearby Chortkiv there were only 95. In 1888, Husiatyn had 186 deaths from scarlet fever, while Chortkiv had only 38 and Borshchiv 69. The same disease was the cause of death of 545 persons in Borshchiv in 1898, but only 26 in adjacent Husiatyn.[38]

The relative isolation of some of the counties might have accounted in some instances for the limited spread of a disease. This may help to explain the differences which existed between the mortality rates of Borshchiv and/or Zalishchyky on the one hand and the remaining three counties on the other. The example of scarlet fever in 1888 shows that this cannot be the only explanation, because the railway already connected Husiatyn and Chortkiv counties. Other differences, such as reporting practices or natural causes such as temporary immunity derived from previous outbreaks or a more progressive commune or county administration are likely partial reasons for the differences in the number of deaths in these counties from contagious diseases. Moreover, they were somehow spared from diseases affecting other parts of Galicia, as for example during 1894, when smallpox killed a total of 2,045 people in Galicia but only 7 in the five counties of Southern Podillia.

Even taking into account the annual fluctuations in mortality figures (including the effects of the 1894 cholera epidemic), the five-year mortality data show clearly that progress in fighting disease was being made (see Table 17).

Table 17
Quinquennial Annual Average of Number of Deaths in Southern Podillia, 1881-1900

Years	Number of Deaths
1881-1885	14,035
1886-1890	13,318
1891-1895	13,460
1896-1900	11,965

Source: Annual statistics in *Oesterreichische Statistik.*

These numbers are significant in their own right, but they become more so in the context of the large population increases. (Mortality statistics for any single year are of doubtful validity, which is why five-year averages are given in Table 17.) However, mortality rates for the single years which were also the census years—1880, 1890, 1900—are also presented here, because they show both exactly and plainly the significant declines in the death rate (see Table 18).

Table 18
Mortality Rate per Thousand of Population, Southern Podillia, 1880-1900

County	1880	1890	1900
Borshchiv	35.4	36.9	26.2
Chortkiv	39.2	35.4	26.4
Husiatyn	36.4	29.9	26.7
Terebovlia	32.5	32.9	29.7
Zalishchyky	45.6	34.1	26.4
Southern Podillia	37.6	33.9	27.0

Source: Annual statistics in *Oesterreichische Statistik.*

The containment and large-scale eradication of cholera before the end of the century was obviously one reason the death rate declined; the success of the vaccination campaign in preventing massive epidemics of smallpox was another. Improvements in hygiene and health education as a result of measures undertaken by the county MOHs, such as their inspection of school and industrial premises and wells, and the periodic prohibition of markets owing to the presence of disease, although largely undocumented, were probably a third.[39] In addition, there was a slight increase in health personnel and convents where the nuns dispensed some form of medical care. Improvements in the local diet, made possible by better and more varied crops and improved animal husbandry, were probably also significant in helping the population to resist certain diseases.

Changes in the Birth Rate

Taking the last two decades of the nineteenth century together, there was an overall decline in the rate of live births in the five counties of Southern Podillia. In fact, in the 1880s there was an increase in an already very high rate of births, a phenomenon probably related to the relatively bountiful harvests of much of this decade. In the year 1890 the birth rate suddenly plummeted, a consequence of the poor harvest of the previous year and the associated decline in the marriage rate of Southern Podillians.[40] That this was a short-term effect is made clear by the rise in the birth rate in 1891, although this did not attain previous heights. Thereafter the birth rate declined steadily, so that by 1900 there had been a drop of almost 20 per cent compared to the mid-1880s (see Table 19).

Ч. 10 и 11

Р. II.

ПРОСВѢЩЕНІЕ

Газета съ рисунками
для
РУССКОГО НАРОДА.

Редакторъ-издатель
ГРИГОРІЙ КУПЧАНКО.

Вѣдень, 25 жолтня 1894 г.

Газета „ПРОСВѢЩЕНІЕ" выходитъ каждого мѣсяца въ Вѣдни и стоитъ на весь годъ въ Австро-Угріи 4 короны (2 зол. рень.), въ Россіи 3 рубля, въ Америцѣ 2 доллары. Цѣна одного числа 40 геллерôвъ (20 кр.). — Редакція и управленіе находятся въ Вѣдни, III, Adamsgasse No. 32. Почтовû перекавы (Postanweisungen) адресуются такъ: **An die Administration der Zeitschrift „Просвѣщеніе" in Wien, I. Hauptpostlagernd.**

Русскій господарь и русска господиня изъ коцманского округа въ Буковинѣ.

Front page of *Prosveshchenie*, 25 October 1894

Рочникъ VIII. У Львовѣ дня 26. (14.) Марця 1886. Число 12.

БАТЬКÔВЩИНА.

Выходить у Львовѣ що тыждня, въ Пятницю о 5-ôй годинѣ вечеромъ.

Передплата (вôдъ 1-ого Сѣчня, Цвѣтня, Липня або Жовтня) выносить: въ австрійско-угорской монархіи за цѣлый рôкъ 4 зр., за пôвъ року 2 р., за чверть року 1 зр.; за границею за цѣлый рôкъ 5 рублѣвъ або 12 франкôвъ, за пôвъ року 2½ рубл. або 6 фр., за чверть року 1¼ рубля або 3 франки. — Рекламаціѣ въ отвертыхъ листахъ вôльнѣ вôдъ оплаты почтовои.

Выдавництво „Батькôвщины“ находить ся на улици Академичнôй нр. 8.

СПРАВЫ ПОТОЧНІ.

Читальнѣ и Народна Рада у Львовѣ. Доносять знову зъ кôлькохъ сторôнъ (якъ се росказуємо въ нынѣшнѣмъ числѣ Батькôвщины), що цѣсарскі власти, именно ц. к. староства, а навѣть ц. к. намѣстництво роблять всѣлякі перепоны и трудности читальнямъ. Мы о тôй справѣ писали вже давнѣйше и подавали такожь гдекоті рады. Нынѣ где-що найважнѣйшого повтаряємо.

1) Єсли где мае ся завязати читальня, нехай собѣ основателѣ спровадять зô Львова зъ Просвѣты (на улици Скарбкôвской ч. 2) потрѣбнѣ до того формулярѣ (за 20 кр.) и книжочку Костя Антоновича Законъ о товариствахъ (30 кр., всѣ разомъ зъ пересылкою 55 кр.); въ тôй книжочцѣ є розтолковано, якъ брати ся до завязаня товариства и въ загалѣ що приписує устава о стоваришеняхъ. 2) На статутахъ и поданю до намѣстництва досыть якъ пôдпише ся три-чотыри людей; найлѣпше щобы пôдписавъ бодай оденъ зъ интелигенціѣ (священикъ або учитель чи хто тамъ, зъ того самого села), а решта по можности письменнѣ люде и власноручно. (Однакожь и неписьменнѣ люде можуть бути основателями товариства.) 3) Єсли бы котрого зъ основателѣвъ кликано до протоколу до староства, нехай не боить ся нѣчого а вôдповѣдає все по правдѣ, и нехай не дає ся нѣчимъ анѣ вôдрадити анѣ вôдстрашити. 4) Нехай основателѣ и выдѣлъ читальнѣ держать ся вô всѣмъ докладно права (уставы о стоваришеняхъ) и своихъ статутôвъ.

Помимо того однакожь може неразъ зайти якась перепона вôдъ ц. к. властій. Єсли бы тогды котра читальня не знала собѣ дати рады, нехай удасть ся до товариства „Народна Рада у Львовѣ“, котре якъ въ сѣй такъ и вô всѣхъ инщихъ справахъ, где ходить о яке народне або политичне право, дає пораду и помôчь. Товариство Народна Рада знаходить ся на улици Скарбкôвской ч. 2 на 1-ôмъ поверсѣ (въ тôй самôй камяници, где Просвѣта и Руска Бесѣда). Тамъ можна що-день поговорити або зъ головою товариства, д-ромъ Александромъ Огоновскимъ, або зъ заступникомъ головы, п. Юліяномъ Романчукомъ, або зъ секретаремъ, д-ромъ Костемъ Левицкимъ.

Єзуиты въ Добромили. Звѣстный протоигуменъ оо. Василіянъ Климъ Сарницкій вразъ зъ протоконзультôромъ о. Яковомъ Загайскимъ оголошуе таке письмо: Противъ „обновленю Василіяньского закона“ черезъ Єзуитôвъ пôдносять ся безъосновнѣ протесты и неслушнѣ жалобы. Але жь о таке „обновлене“ постарались самъ „протоигуменъ зъ своими совѣтниками при согласію краєвыхъ найвысшихъ властей св. церкви“ у папы римского. Обновлене стало ся послѣдними часами конечнымъ, и высоко въ єрархіи поставленѣ мужѣ неразъ вôдзывались: кобы то Василіяне були подôбнѣ монахамъ латиньскимъ, хотьбы Єзуитамъ! Але Василіяне самѣ не могли обновленя перевести, бо въ 14 монастыряхъ було лишь 33 Василіянъ, зъ котрыхъ анѣ одного не можна було до такого дѣла покликати; тымъ менше могли се зробити свѣтскѣ священики або свѣтскѣ люде, бо нѣхто не може подати другому се, чого самъ не мае. Треба було отже до того выбрати латиньскихъ монахôвъ, и то такихъ, що знають по руски або бодай по польски, щобы могли зъ молодиками порозумѣвати ся. Въ инщихъ орденахъ галицкихъ не було вôдповѣднихъ до того людей, а Єзуиты суть найодвѣтнѣйшѣ, бо они вже въ 17-ôмъ столѣтю перепроваджали двократно зъ великимъ пожиткомъ обновлене Василіяньского закона“. Тай теперь за чотыри роки выховали вже звышь 50 кандидатôвъ, такъ що имъ вже за тѣснѣ муры Добромильского монастыря. Отже мы (т. є. оо. Сарницкій и Загайскій) протестуємо „противъ всякому мѣшаню ся непокликаныхъ, хотяйбы самыхъ краєвыхъ послôвъ, въ нашѣ домашнѣ законовѣ справы“, освѣдчаємо, що нашому законови не стала ся нѣяка кривда, бо маєтки якъ були власностію Василіяньского закона такъ и зôстануть, и „дякуємо сердечно Єзуитамъ, що они не уступають и не залишають свою працю“.

Мы на тое письмо, котре вызване зôстало очевидно выступленємъ рускихъ послôвъ въ соймѣ при нарадѣ надъ запомогою для Змартвыхвстанцѣвъ, скажемо коротко: 1) На прикликане Єзуитôвъ не годили ся самѣ оо. Василіяне; 2) инщого способу обновленя, безъ Єзуитôвъ, зовсѣмъ и не пробовано; 3) якъ можуть люде инщого обряду, ще до того дышучѣ найбôльшою ненавистію до тогожь обряду, чинъ того инщого обряду обновляти? 4) Єзуиты знадили до новиціяту Василіяньского звыжь 50 молодцѣвъ доброю стравою тай тымъ, що приймають и ученикôвъ зъ низшихъ клясъ гимназіяльныхъ, а такои штуки потрафили бы и Василіяне доказати; 5) мôй маєтокъ перестає бути моимъ, коли хтось чужій противъ моей волѣ завѣдуе нимъ такъ, якъ ему хоче ся. — Можна бы о тôй справѣ ще багато сказати, але на теперь чей и се выстане.

Front page of *Batkivshchyna*, 26 March 1886

Table 19
Representative Data on Birth Rates in Southern Podillia
(per thousand of population)

County	1881	1885	1887	1891	1894	1900
Borshchiv	46.61	48.33	50.13	48.34	46.25	41.34
Chortkiv	49.53	53.33	52.36	49.89	46.73	43.76
Husiatyn	49.74	52.15	50.13	44.33	43.08	42.87
Terebovlia	51.40	52.40	53.47	47.02	45.22	41.44
Zalishchyky	52.02	53.00	56.60	49.24	47.61	41.40

Source: *Oesterreichische Statistik*, vols. V, pt. 1; XIII, pt. 4; XXI, pt. 3; XXXVII, pt. 1; XLVI, pt. 2; LXVII, pt. 1.

Health Education

Very important also to the health of the population, though direct causal connections cannot be established, was the dissemination of preventive medical information in the Ukrainian press and other publications. Writers in this period launched a "consciousness-raising" campaign to alert their readers to the dangers of unsanitary living conditions as potential predisposing causes of disease or its spread, and to ways in which diseases could be contained, alleviated or cured. Sometimes this took the form of reporting on the unsatisfactory hygienic conditions of other groups, namely Poles, Jews or Russians.[41] Touring lecturers spoke in reading clubs and other halls about domestic hygiene, illness, infant care, and the benefits of moderate living.[42] In August 1889 *Nauka* carried a feature article, "Signs and Symptoms of Important Infectious Diseases," giving pragmatic advice, and at various times this newspaper stressed the need for fresh air, light calisthenics, and mother's milk, and chided those who refused to seek medical advice.[43]

Other articles dealt with specific topics such as bathing and cleanliness, good food, and moderate living, all in the context of the maintenance of good health;[44] with first-aid treatment of illnesses, burns, and heat-stroke; with the danger of treatment by unqualified people such as the local "sorcerers" (*vorozhky*) or of ingesting poisonous substances, especially poisonous mushrooms.[45] A lengthy series of feature articles, under the general heading "How to lead a healthy life" in *Chytalnia* in 1895 gave practical advice on the importance of sleep, personal cleanliness, clothing, and diet; the newspaper commented that "we eat too much cabbage, beets, and potatoes" and urged people to use more milk, eggs, wheat bread, and meat, including poultry.[46] *Prosveshchenie* carried a regular column on health called "The Domestic Doctor," in which safe domestic therapies were described and recommended by experts.

Circumstances in Southern Podillia would not, however, always permit people to follow all the advice. For example, in the case of diphtheria it was obviously sound counsel to isolate the patient, but calling a doctor or taking the patient to hospital was not readily feasible in most localities.[47] Prosvita published a ninety-six page booklet, written by Dr. Barshchysky, entitled "How to Look After Your Health," which retailed for 25 kr.[48] Cures being used in other countries or regions were at times reprinted in the press.[49] More straightforward was advice to use onions and honey as cures for coughs and colds; and to treat springtime childhood illnesses by making the patient drink plenty of fluids and encouraging sweating. *Hospodar* in 1900 advocated methods to aid convalescence from illness.[50]

The effect of all the health education disseminated by the schools, newspapers, Prosvita, certified midwives, itinerant lecturers, doctors, and others cannot be known precisely.[51] It would appear, however, that Southern Podillia shared a "wave of revulsion against environmental filth [which] swept through Western civilization. The quarter century 1890-1915, in particular, witnessed the beginning of a mass change in bathing, laundering, and domestic hygiene practice" in Europe and America.[52] The making and use of soap was being emphasized in Eastern Galicia.[53] There are references to bathing in ponds, springs, streams, and rivers in the memoirs of people from Southern Podillia, and to the washing of clothes.[54] From speeches at the 1908 Prosvita congress reiterating the importance of bathing, use of disinfectants, and other preventive measures,[55] one might perhaps infer that prior to 1900 the general cleanliness movement was still in its infancy. However, the testimony of a Canadian official on a tour of south-eastern Galicia, including Southern Podillia, shows that even by the turn of the century much had been accomplished.[56]

Professional Health Care

Southern Podillia continued to be poorly supplied with doctors and public health facilities, other than the annual vaccination stations, during the last quarter of the nineteenth century, although some improvement took place in the 1890s. By Austrian legislation of 1872, only doctors who had graduated from Faculties of Medicine were allowed to practice medicine. There was only one exception to this new regulation. Physicians and surgeons who had learned their profession through the old apprenticeship system, whose qualifications were recognized before 1872, were allowed to practice until they retired or died.[57] The short-term effect of that legislation was to reduce the total number of medical practitioners in Austria, as the number of apprentice-trained doctors (*Wundärtzte*) declined and there was no corresponding increase in the number of graduates from medical faculties.[58]

Southern Podillia followed the Austrian trend, but generally in a more exaggerated form. There were fewer doctors in Chortkiv and Zalishchyky counties through the 1880s and 1890s than there had been in 1873; only in 1900 did Chortkiv have more doctors than in 1873. Terebovlia county showed an increase in medical practitioners in the 1880s and early 1890s, only to register a drop in their number again by 1900. Husiatyn county maintained a stable number of doctors for most of the period, at slightly above the 1873 level, with a significant increase in their number in the late 1890s. Borshchiv county showed an increase in doctors in the 1880s and then a decline in the 1890s. The prolonged decline in the number of medical practitioners in Southern Podillia was clearly due to the progressive decrease in the number of apprentice-trained doctors. As the population increased, the doctor/patient ratio became worse in Borshchiv, Chortkiv, and Zalishchyky counties. Some doctors were salaried employees of the state, Land, commune or an agency or corporation, but few Southern Podillian communes or combinations of communes ("health districts") could afford the 750 g per annum salary (among the very highest in Austria), which was the average for Galician government-paid doctors by the end of the century.[59] In general, Southern Podillia experienced the difficulties commonly found in rural regions of not offering sufficient earning potential and cultural amenities to qualified doctors. In 1900 Southern Podillia had 48 doctors for a civilian population of about 425,000.[60]

Although the number of medical graduates was small and grew only slowly in the late nineteenth century, they were better qualified than the apprentice-trained doctors. This was evident even by the early and mid-1880s, for some of them possessed specialist diplomas; of the four in each of Chortkiv and Zalishchyky counties in 1882, one in each county was qualified as a surgeon and one as an obstetrician; while of Husiatyn's three, one was likewise a surgeon and another an obstetrician. In Borshchiv county in 1885, of four graduates, three were surgeons (one of whom was also an obstetrician) and one was an eye specialist.[61]

Many of the doctors in Southern Podillia, and perhaps especially in Borshchiv county, were Jewish.[62] The arrival in the region of a Ukrainian doctor was apt to be specially noted.[63] By 1900 there were medical practitioners in most Southern Podillian market towns (Borshchiv county: Borshchiv 3, Korolivka 1, Melnytsia 2, Ozeriany 1, and Skala 1; Chortkiv county: Bilobozhnytsia 1, Chortkiv 7, Iaholnytsia 2; Husiatyn county: Husiatyn 6, Khorostkiv 2, Kopychyntsi 4, and Probizhna 2; Terebovlia county: Budzaniv 1, Strusiv 2, Terebovlia 4, and Ianiv 1; Zalishchyky county: Tovste 2, Ustechko 1, and Zalishchyky 5).[64] The doctor/patient ratio remained, of course, very unfavourable, but by 1900 only the southern part of Borshchiv county and the south-eastern and westernmost portions of Zalishchyky county were without reasonable access to medical practitioners. Southern Borshchiv county was especially disadvantaged.[65] However, the extent to which villagers normally availed themselves of the services of doctors must remain an open question.

Until late in the 1890s, civilian hospitals were very scarce in the region. One of these, in the town of Husiatyn, was a commune hospital of ten beds, which treated only a few patients annually. The Sisters of Mercy operated small hospitals at Budzaniv (Terebovlia county) and at Nyrkiv (Zalishchyky county), with 16 and 10 (later 14) beds respectively. There was no regular charge to patients. The average length of hospitalization there was 11-15 days in the 1880s. In 1882 these hospitals treated 314 and 265 patients respectively, for such illnesses as undulating fever, typhus, rheumatism, ulcers, scabies, anemia, and lung disease. A high proportion of patients was reported to have been "discharged, cured." Basically these convent hospitals appear to have cared for local patients with chronic diseases, but they admitted some acute cases.

For a long time, the only public general hospital in the region was in the town of Zalishchyky. It had forty beds and treated more than 400 patients each year. Local people were charged 30 kreuzer per day, others 50 kr. It had a patient profile which differed from that of the convent hospitals, because it was more of an acute care facility. In the 1880s almost half the patients were being treated for venereal diseases, especially syphilis. Other principal reasons for admission were typhus, diphtheria, bronchial problems, and accidental injuries. Again, a high proportion of the patients was described as "cured."[66] By 1900 the Zalishchyky general hospital was a fifty-two-bed institution which treated 1,232 patients that year at a charge of 51 kr per day. The average length of hospitalization was twenty-two days. Venereal diseases still accounted for a large number of cases (251); other principal causes for admission were tuberculosis, eye disease, respiratory ailments, diseases of the digestive system, accidental injuries, and scabies and other skin diseases.[67] In 1898 an important new facility was opened, the sixty-bed Emperor Franz Josef Hospital in Husiatyn town. Thus the small commune hospital was replaced with a large public general hospital. It had a Ukrainian hospital director and the daily charge to patients was 60 kr. In 1900 this hospital treated 884 patients whose average length of hospitalization was twenty-seven days.[68] The only other new hospital in the region was the twenty-bed Jewish hospital in Zalishchyky town, opened in 1890.[69] By the end of the nineteenth century these new facilities, together with the Zalishchyky general hospital and the convent hospitals in Budzaniv and Nyrkiv, constituted Southern Podillia's hospital facilities.[70] For a civilian population of around 425,000 these hospital facilities, though improved in number, clearly remained inadequate. Particularly striking is the fact that there was no hospital in Borshchiv county, which by 1900 had a population well in excess of 100,000.[71]

In each county there were a few public apothecaries, each operated by a licensed apothecary who had earned a diploma as "Magister der Pharmazie."[72] It is likely that they dispensed not only pharmaceutical compounds and patent remedies but also some medical advice. The number of public apothecaries changed only slightly over the years. In 1900 they were located in Borshchiv county: Borshchiv, Korolivka, Melnytsia, Ozeriany, and Skala; Chortkiv county: Chortkiv and Iaholnytsia; Husiatyn county: Husiatyn, Khorostkiv, Kopychyntsi, and Probizhna; Terebovlia county: Budzaniv, Strusiv, and Terebovlia; and Zalishchyky county: Tovste and Zalishchyky.[73]

Midwives were another category of medical personnel who played an important role in the health delivery system, particularly in the absence of qualified doctors and proper care facilities. They were trained at midwifery schools and given a certificate which allowed them to assist at childbirth independent of doctors. Their numbers remained fairly stable during the last three decades of the century, except in Husiatyn and Terebovlia, which had large increases between 1873 and 1881 (Terebovlia also had increases in the late 1890s, and Zalishchyky had a notable increase in the 1880s). While the population rose, the birth rate declined in the 1890s, hence the relative stability or rise in the number of midwives could be seen as an improvement, or at least as not a worsening of the situation in this area of health care. Midwives could be employed by any level of government, from the communal to the imperial. The majority in the five counties were in private practice.[74]

By 1900 some of the larger towns had quite a number of licensed midwives: Zalishchyky had eight and Terebovlia had seven. Size of town, however, was not necessarily an indicator of the number of officially recognized midwives who practised in the vicinity. Kopychyntsi, for example, had only two midwives and Husiatyn four, while Probizhna had five and Tovste had six. The geographical distribution of midwives across Southern Podillia was quite good, especially so in Terebovlia county, where in 1900 there were thirty-one licensed midwives in nineteen communes. However, there were no midwives in western Zalishchyky county, except for one at Ustechko, and very few in southern Borshchiv county.[75] In 1900 licensed midwives or medical practitioners (probably mainly the former) attended about 50 per cent of all the births in Terebovlia county; they attended 28.1 per cent of the births in Husiatyn, 26.4 per cent in Chortkiv, 24.3 per cent in Zalishchyky, and only 15.8 per cent in Borshchiv.[76]

The statistical evidence suggests that either the services of the Southern Podillian certified midwives (augmented no doubt by those of the local "wise women") were very good or the women of the region had exceptionally healthy reproductive systems. The proportion of stillbirths to live births in Galicia during the period 1886-98 was 2.52 per 100. This rate was lower than in most Austrian Crownlands; it was in fact much lower in Eastern than in Western Galicia. Terebovlia with 1.58:100 and Husiatyn with 1.65:100 had respectively the second and the fourth lowest rate of stillbirths in all the Galician counties. Borshchiv with 1.92:100, Chortkiv with 2.06, and Zalishchyky with 2.37 were all also below the Galician average.[77] More and better-trained midwives, improved general and health education, and more neonatal advice all clearly had an effect.[78]

Another public health facility in Southern Podillia was care homes for invalids and the aged. Only four were recorded in the 1900 *Gemeindelexicon*: at Chortkiv and Sydoriv (Husiatyn county), both obviously run by nuns, and at Chortkiv Staryi and Kopychyntsi, presumably commune institutions. The practice of families caring for their own old and invalids was thus obviously being continued in Southern Podillia. By 1900, there were also orphanages at Chortkiv, Budzaniv, Chervonohorod, and Zalishchyky, and a number of infant/child care facilities, run by nuns, in three of the five counties. Six of these were in Borshchiv county, seven in Husiatyn, and two in Zalishchyky.[79]

Folk Medicine

A rural society long accustomed to being without official medical practitioners had its own network of informal therapeutic services, especially in those places which were most isolated and not well served by the formal health profession.[80] Indeed, "folk cures" and those who practice them tend to survive even in advanced societies with a profusion of modern medical services.[81] It is scarcely surprising, then, that they should also have endured in Southern Podillia. Nuns who provided informal health services did not necessarily rely on traditional rural remedies. They gave first aid and other medical services even outside the setting of convent hospitals.[82] Some large landowners also visited the sick and provided treatment to them, or arranged to have such treatment provided.[83] Local priests and their wives also gave medical advice and treatment; the wife of the Greek Catholic priest in Chornokintsi Velyki (Husiatyn county), for example, had a "handy apothecary" chest, and visited the sick.[84]

The priests and others who also "practised" folk medicine relied especially on the use of various locally occurring plants in a variety of forms such as potions, salves, and infusions.[85] The use of herbs and other plants for medicinal purposes was denigrated by some writers, yet it made good sense to the villagers of Southern Podillia, especially given the shortage of qualified personnel and adequate facilities, to resort to time-tested remedies to provide palliative care and probably, from time to time, cures. Accordingly, herbs, grasses, leaves, and flowers with known therapeutic value were cultivated or picked and used when needed. Some of these were salvia, St. John's weed, absinth, tansy, melissa, mint, rue, poppy and the ubiquitous garlic.[86] The extent to which herb therapies were valued by local people was indicated by *Batkivshchyna*'s characterization of a woman whose home was well-stocked with such ingredients as "A Happy Woman." She would also have grown such plants as camomile, centaury, caraway, and dill, some of these on the roof of her house.[87]

Besides herbal and other plant "cures," there were medicinal waters, such as Ulashkivtsi's miracle-working waters for eye disease, and those of Kozachchyna

(Borshchiv county), whose ceremonial use was preceded by a religious procession.[88] Local "barbers" gave "treatment" with leeches and suction cups. They and village "sorcerers" and "sorceresses" also at times performed illegal abortions. Village "wise women" acted as unauthorized, though by no means unskillful, midwives. It was herbal and other plant treatment, traditional but with some real medicinal effect, and often accompanied by incantations that may have had a positive psychological effect, which constituted the bulk of local folk medicine. Generally it was the women of the household who knew how to use the medicinal properties of the local plants.[89] The popular "cures" of the period and the belief in their effectiveness indicate a highly developed self-sufficiency among peasants for treating common, curable ailments such as childhood fevers, diseases of the upper respiratory and gastrointestinal systems, and illness caused by overindulgence in food or drink.[90] More complex problems and terminal illness led people at times to resort to various forms of so-called magic, witchcraft or sorcery. In this, Southern Podillia did not differ from other societies of the late nineteenth or the twentieth century.

Alcoholism

The literature on Eastern Galicia in the late nineteenth century frequently refers to alcohol abuse and drunkenness as causes of physical disability, family quarrels, and economic backwardness. Volodymyr Navrotsky asserted in 1882 that "people in Eastern Galicia are given over to drunkenness."[91] Specifically, he claimed, on the basis of calculations that cannot inspire confidence, that in 1876 the per capita consumption of spirits was 26 litres of 50 proof alcohol.[92] Regrettably, Navrotsky's statement has been accepted at face value by some modern historians and generalized to embrace the late nineteenth century as a whole.[93] However, Navrotsky had simplistically equated production with consumption, despite exports of Galician alcohol to other parts of Europe and industrial use within Austria. Whatever may have been true of 1876, there are indications that the drinking of spirits and alcohol abuse were on the decline in the 1880s and 1890s, and that the number of taverns decreased. There were in fact fewer taverns per capita in Galicia than in Austria as a whole.[94]

It is possible to calculate, on the basis of data presented by the Austrian statistician F.C. Presl, that in 1893—a peak year for the production of spirits in Galicia—the per capita consumption would have been at most six litres of 100 proof alcohol.[95] A contemporary Polish authority estimated that the average annual consumption of spirits per adult was in the 5-20 litre range.[96] The same authority concluded that there had been a definite reduction in the drinking of vodka. He ascribed this to the combined effects of a law against drunkenness, the activities of the church brotherhoods, and the higher price of vodka.[97] The sobriety movement of the 1870s and later years must certainly have had a significant effect. Temperance activities, which brought many villagers together in a common cause, have been positively identified in twenty-five villages of Southern Podillia,[98] and may have taken place in many more. Often it was the Greek Catholic clergy who took the lead.[99] Vows to abstain from alcohol, or sometimes specifically from spirits, were generally made in church; in one village it was the priest's daughter who was the first to take the pledge.[100]

It is very likely that some persons became permanent abstainers. Cybulski thought that in some areas, including Terebovlia county, one-third or even one-half of the people did not drink vodka at all.[101] In many other instances, the sobriety societies contributed to the development of sensible drinking habits rather than ongoing abstention. Some persons interpreted their abstinence vows rather narrowly, avoiding spirits but drinking beer, home-produced fruit wine and cider or rum (in tea) instead.[102] In Hovyliv (Husiatyn county), the people vowed specifically that they would not drink vodka, and, except for some young people, drank only beer, with its three or four per cent alcohol content.[103] In Zalissia (Borshchiv county), where the sobriety movement was particularly successful, the village tavern was locked up.[104] At times, particular individuals took matters into their own hands to save their fellows from drink, as at Ivankiv (Borshchiv county), where the reeve, a burly man "terribly opposed to the tavern keeper," physically dragged people from the tavern.[105]

Available evidence suggests that the picture of drunkenness in the villages was overdrawn. People did drink—to celebrate important life-cycle events, to "cure" illnesses, and to drown their sorrows. Alcohol use was associated with festivities: more was drunk on holy days and at celebrations such as weddings than on working days. It was estimated that at a "wealthy" wedding in the village of Hovyliv, 400-500 litres of beer and 2-3 litres of vodka would be consumed.[106] Villagers did make their own alcoholic drinks. In Chortkiv, Husiatyn, and Terebovlia counties peasants made apple cider, fruit wines, and "sweet waters" (liqueurs).[107] Alcohol was certainly a fact of life for many Ukrainian villagers in Southern Podillia, but there is nothing in the literature to suggest that in the 1880s and 1890s they had a particularly great problem with alcohol.[108]

In 1887 the Archduke Rudolph attended a special exhibit in Ternopil arranged in honour of his visit to Galicia. There he chatted with some Podillian peasants and inspected the typical Podillian house erected on the exhibit site. Later, in his quarters, he was said to have remarked to one of his aides, "But this East Galicia isn't so wild nor its people so uncivilized as they have been said to be."[109] An English traveller noted the vigor and "natural capacity and manliness of character" of Eastern Galicia's Ukrainian peasants.[110] The general cleanliness of their habitations and of their drinking water, as well as their overall healthy appearance, clearly merited comment. Alcoholism was not noted by such travellers, and if it did represent a problem, it was not one of the dimensions that have usually been alleged.

Childhood diseases and tuberculosis still took an inordinate toll, and folk medicine and new medical knowledge existed side by side, but government action and the wider dissemination of health information were bringing about improvements in the field of public health. Except for the increase in the number of certified midwives, there was only a slight increase in the number of health professionals, and it was only toward the end of the period that the number of hospitals increased. However, the imperial government's measures drastically reduced the toll that smallpox had traditionally taken in Southern Podillia, and the cholera epidemic of the 1890s took far fewer lives than those of the 1850s, 1860s, and 1870s. Finally, it must be emphasized that the death rate in Southern Podillia declined very significantly. Although much in the field of health care remained to be accomplished, important progress had been made.

Notes

1. For an overview of public-health measures and organization in the Austrian part of the Habsburg Monarchy, see K. v. Dubrav, "Die Organisation des Sanitätsdienstes in Oesterreich," 1ff; F. C. Presl, "Die öffentliche Gesundheitspflege in Oesterreich seit dem Jahre 1848," 369-437.
2. Dubrav, "Die Organisation," 2-3. There were other laws and regulations applicable to health services in Galicia. For example, a Land Law was passed on 2 Feb. 1887 regarding county health personnel (Grzybowski, *Galicja 1848-1914*, 274). In 1891 a Land Law brought into existence a Chamber of Physicians (Grzybowski, 180).
3. Dubrav, "Die Organisation," 4-6.
4. Ibid., 10. The 1897 "Service Rules for Midwives," published by the Austrian Ministry of the Interior, cost 30 kr and contained sections on the midwives' general responsibilities, pregnancy and delivery, infant and child care, and midwives' legal obligations. All midwives had to own this book (*Svoboda*, 21 Apr. 1898).
5. Inglot, *Historia chłopów Polskich*, 657.
6. Great Britain, Royal Commission on Labour, *Foreign Reports:* vol. XI, *Austria-Hungary and the Balkan States*, 130-1. An Austrian Law of Domicile was passed in 1863 which provided that indigent persons were entitled to assistance from their commune upon application to the chief communal authority. They could receive food, lodging, medical care, and maintenance in a commune-operated public institution. This was to prevent begging in the streets and vagrancy. Travellers without work or subsistence could utilize these temporarily as well. Various religious orders, corporations, and private individuals also supported health-care institutions. Some health-care institutions were founded in Southern Podillia by the Sapieha family. (S. Kieniewicz, *Adam Sapieha, 1823-1903*, 352; IMZCh, 579, 602, 606).
7. Dubrav, "Die Organisation," 11.
8. *Oesterreichische Statistik*, VIII, no. 3, xxix.
9. Vaccination had been carried out in Austria since the early nineteenth century (Dubrav, "Die Organisation," 10, 13). A number of Austrian articles discussed the

more concerted effort after 1873 by the Austrian state to provide protection against smallpox (E. Bratassević, "Vergleichende Statistik der wichtigsten Todesursachen während der Jahre 1873-1890 in den im Reichsrat vertretenen Ländern," 389-90; idem, "Die Infektionskrankheiten in Oesterreich während des letzten Decenniums 1890-1899," 384-7; F.C. Presl, "Die Gesundheitspflege," 386-9.

10. Presl, "Die Gesundheitspflege," 387.
11. *Oesterreichische Statistik*, XVIII, no. 4.
12. *Oesterreichische Statistik*, V, no. 2; XVIII, no. 4; XLIX, no. 4; LXVIII, no. 2. In 1894 there were no vaccinations in Husiatyn, only about 600 in Borshchiv, and less than half the normal number in Zalishchyky because of the cholera epidemic. The next year's vaccination data show a corresponding increase over normal levels of vaccination in these counties (*Oesterreichische Statistik*, XLIX, no. 4; LXVIII, no. 3).
13. Presl, "Die Gesundheitspflege," 388.
14. *Batkivshchyna*, 15 Jan. 1886 and 9 Dec. 1887; *Oesterreichische Statistik*, LIX, no. 1 and LX, no. 1.
15. *Batkivshchyna*, 1 Mar. 1889.
16. Borshchiv appears to have been free of cholera in 1873. There were 58 deaths in Chortkiv, 39 in Husiatyn, 39 in Terebovlia, and 268 in Zalishchyky in that year (mortality tables in A. Killiches, *Statistik des Sanitätswesens.... nach den für das Jahr 1873 vorgelegten Berichten*).
17. Presl, "Die öffentliche Gesundheitspflege," 392.
18. *Batkivshchyna*, 6 Dec. 1889; *Chytalnia*, 21 Apr. 1894.
19. Presl, "Die öffentliche Gesundheitspflege," 393-4.
20. E. Bratassević, "Die Sterblichkeit in den grösseren Städten Oesterreichs im Jahre 1893," 98. The total number of deaths from cholera in Galicia in 1892 was 119 (Presl, "Die öffentliche Gesundheitspflege," 392).
21. *Halychanyn*, 25 Jan. 1893; *Chytalnia*, 23 Jan., 8 Feb., 20 Apr., and 5 May 1893.
22. *Chytalnia*, 20 June 1893; *Halychanyn*, 9 Aug. and 31 Oct. 1893; *Prosveshchenie*, 25 Aug. 1893; Presl, "Die öffentliche Gesundheitspflege," 392.
23. Presl, "Die öffentliche Gesundheitspflege," 394; *Halychanyn*, 9 Aug. 1893; *Chytalnia*, 21 Apr. 1894.
24. For information on cholera in the 1890s see Presl, "Die öffentliche Gesundheitspflege," 392-4; F. Prinzing, "Die Todesursachen in den Europaischen Staaten 1891-1900," 767-807; Bratassević, "Die Sterblichkeit in den grösseren Städten," 98; Bratassević, "Die Sterblichkeit im Jahre 1894," 127; Bratassević, "Die Infektionskrankheiten," 401-2; S. Rosenfeld, "Die internationale Nomenklatur der Todesursachen," 132. Data for the cause of death in the individual counties in 1895 were not published, apparently because the Austrian health administration undertook a recategorization of causes that year.
25. *Chytalnia*, 21 July 1894. For references in the press to cholera in Southern Podillia in 1894 see ibid., 21 Apr. and *Prosveshchenie*, 15 Mar., 20 May, 25 June, 25 and Oct. 1894; see also IMZCh, 632 ("people died like flies").
26. AGAD, Handels-Ministerium, file HG 1, "Eischränkungen des Vieh- und Fleisch Transport, 1888-1896," Ministry of the Interior to Foreign Ministry, 19 Sept., 3 and 9 Oct., and 5 Nov. 1894.

27. Ibid., Ministry of Interior to Foreign Ministry, 10 Jan. 1895. However, the counties of Ternopil and Skalat, bordering on Southern Podillia, were then declared centres of contagion.
28. Ibid., Hungarian Ministry of Commerce to Austrian Ministry of Commerce, 16 Feb. and 20 Mar. 1895.
29. Ibid., Ministry of the Interior to Foreign Ministry, 24 Oct. 1895 and 25 Feb. 1896.
30. *Halychanyn*, 25 Jan. 1893; *Chytalnia*, 20 June 1893 and 21 July 1894; Dubrav, "Die Organisation," 11. Makovei (*Zalisia*, 58-66) sought to use the county instructions to a commune to show how backward villagers were. In his novel the commune authorities chose an abandoned shack as their isolation station and appointed the village idiot as the orderly in charge. Although only one instance has been identified from the Southern Podillian counties of gendarmes being involved in quarantine activities, it is likely that they played a considerable role (F. Neubauer, *Die Gendarmerie in Österreich 1849-1924*, 77). Neubauer also reprinted (405-7) a lengthy account of the heroism of the Kolomyia detachment of the gendarmerie during the 1893 cholera outbreak there.
31. Bratassević, "Infektionskrankheiten," 401.
32. *Batkivshchyna*, 28 Jan. 1895.
33. Deaths from rabies were in fact very few in number, but this disease exercised a fascination upon contemporaries (Presl, "Die öffentliche Gesundheitspflege," 396).
34. Bratassević, "Infektionskrankheiten," 390-2.
35. *Oesterreichische Statistik*, XXII, no. 3, xxx. For various diseases in Southern Podillia and/or Eastern Galicia, including typhus in Chortkiv county in 1885, see *Batkivshchyna*, 10 April 1885; *Chytalnia*, 21 Jan. and 6 Mar. 1894 (tuberculosis) and 6 Dec. 1896 (scarlet fever). The county authorities tried to prevent gatherings of people during outbreaks of "adult" diseases. See *Svoboda* (25 Feb. 1897) for an account of two gendarmes dispersing a meeting of 300 peasants at Ivanie Puste (Borshchiv county), on account of a local outbreak of typhus.
36. Bratassević, "Die Infektionskrankheiten," 396.
37. Ibid., 393.
38. Annual statistics in *Oesterreichische Statistik*.
39. Prime Minister Taaffe issued a circular in 1891 to all local officials in Galicia exhorting them to pay more attention to the sewage systems, the provision of clean drinking water, and general health care (*Batkivshchyna*, 20 Mar. 1891). Preston noted some years later that community wells were invariably suitably placed and protected against surface drainage (Canada, *Sessional Papers*, "Report of Inspector of Agencies in Europe," vol. 10, 1900, 7).
40. *Oesterreichische Statistik*, XXXI, no. 1.
41. See, for example, *Batkivshchyna*, 9 Jan. 1885, for a complaint that a large landowner had brought in "Mazurs" (Polish peasants), who were presumed to have lower standards of hygiene than nearby Ukrainians—unlike other, old-established Mazurs in the region whose "houses are clean" and who "speak Ukrainian now." See also a report on an outbreak of typhus in the town of Sniatyn, where hundreds were ill, especially Jews: "It is no wonder that typhus has broken out there, because there is no more filthy a town than Sniatyn" (ibid., 6 December 1889).
42. Vynnytsky, *Terebovelska zemlia*, 403.

43. *Nauka*, 31 Aug. 1889 (the importance of prayer was also stressed), 15 Sept. 1886, and 15 Oct. and 15 Dec. 1887.
44. *Nauka*, 1 July 1884, 15 June 1886, 15 Oct. 1887, 30 and Apr. 1889; *Batkivshchyna*, 28 Sept. 1889; *Chytalnia*, 21 July 1895; *Hospodar*, January 1900.
45. *Hospodar i promyshlennyk*, no. 2, 1885; *Batkivshchyna*, 27 July 1888, and 16 Aug. 1889; *Nauka*, 15 Apr. 1887, 31 Aug. 1889, and 30 June, 31 July, and 31 Aug. 1890. Deaths resulting from eating poisonous mushrooms were reported on occasion (*Batkivshchyna*, 28 Sept. and 12 Oct. 1889).
46. *Chytalnia*, 21 May to 21 Sept. 1895, inclusive; *Chytalnia* was a bi-weekly paper. By way of contrast, it may be noted that between 8 Nov. 1892 and 1 Aug. 1893, *Narod* ran, in irregular instalments, a series "About Mortality in Galicia and Its Causes" by V. Okhrymovych, a budding Galician Ukrainian ethnographer and political writer, who seemed intent on showing that a "miraculous harmony" of facts and figures, which he had compiled, demonstrated that landholding arrangements were the root cause of high mortality rates in East Galicia. The study is not without interest, but its simplistic theoretical base and selective quotation of sources renders it invalid as a serious scholarly explanation of the problem. (Okhrymovych was a lawyer in Zalishchyky after 1903 [IMZCh, 708-9].)
47. *Prosveshchenie*, 25 May 1895, 15 Dec. 1894 and *passim*.
48. *Chytalnia*, 20 June 1893.
49. *Hospodar* (March 1900) described a "cure" for influenza offered by a Viennese doctor. *Nauka*, in the mid- to late 1880s, advocated hydrotherapy.
50. *Chytalnia*, 6 Jan. 1896; *Svoboda*, 25 Feb. 1897; *Hospodar*, Jan. and May 1900. On occasion, the Ukrainian press also warned of the possibility of certain diseases appearing because of a poor crop year such as 1889-90 (*Batkivshchyna*, 24 Jan. 1890) or of disease in a nearby centre of contagion such as Russia (*Batkivschyna*, 9 Jan. 1885, 14 Dec. 1889). Special opportunities were also noted. For example, Dr. M. Boryshkevych, a famous eye specialist and professor at the University of Innsbruck, was coming to visit his father in Zarvanytsia (Pidhaitsi county) and would treat people during his stay there (*Batkivshchyna*, 20 July 1888).
51. As might be expected in view of their general position in Eastern Galician society, Greek Catholic priests played a role in health education, too. There are, however, only a few references (Makovei, *Zalisia*, 66; IMZCh, 453 (a priest's wife); Vynnytsky, *Terebovelska zemlia*, 469). For health education in the schools see 73 above.
52. V. M. Greene, "Soap leads march toward longer life, scientist says."
53. *Batkivshchyna*, 28 Sept. 1889, for example, carried a recipe for making laundry soap.
54. For bathing, see, for example, IMZCh, 202, 383, 574, 827; for the washing of clothes, ibid., 203, 383, 466-7, 574, 827; clothes were washed by hand and beaten with flat boards in a partially dammed pool (interview with Mr. E. Michaels, Portage la Prairie, 25 July 1984).
55. I. Bryk and M. Kotsiuba, eds., *Pershyi Ukrainskyi prosvitno- ekonomichnyi konhres v 40-littia T-va "Prosvity,"* especially the papers of E. Ozarkevych, I. Rakovsky, T. Hvozdetsky, and V. Kobrynsky.
56. See 21 above.

57. E. Bratassević, "Die Bewegung im Stande der Sänitatspersonen in den letzten 40 Jahren," 810.
58. The number of medical practitioners in Austria declined from 7,608 in 1875 to 7,071 in 1888; by 1892 it had increased to 8,085, and by 1896 to 9,102. In 1875 there had been 3,282 apprentice-trained doctors; there were still 1,200 in 1896 (Presl, "Die öffentliche Gesundheitspflege," 408). The total number of medical practitioners actually rose in Galicia in the 1870s and 1880s, from 748 in 1870 to 846 in 1880, and 860 in 1890 (Bratassević, "Die Bewegung," 810).
59. Dubrav, "Die Organisation," 16.
60. By contrast, Lviv in 1900 had 276 medical practitioners for a civilian population of just under 140,000 (*Gemeindelexicon*, 1900, 2-3). Information on the number of health personnel in each county was published annually in *Oesterreichische Statistik*.
61. *Oesterreichische Statistik*, vols. VIII, no. 3 and XVIII, no. 4.
62. See IMZCh, 511, where the memoirist stated that all of Borshchiv's doctors were Jewish. This was not, in fact, the case, for Dr. Iarosevych, a Ukrainian, was a doctor in Borshchiv and also a Reichsrat deputy (ibid., 486; *Svoboda*, 15 July 1897).
63. For example, Dr. Korolyk, who became the doctor of the general hospital in Husiatyn, "is a good man" who helped people (*Svoboda*, 10 Feb. 1898; IMZCh, 413). Khorostkiv had a Ukrainian surgeon who was also its reeve and a member of the Husiatyn county council (*Batkivshchyna*, 30 Jan. 1885).
64. *Gemeindelexicon*, 1900 (this source does not differentiate between medical graduates and apprentice-trained doctors). There were still five apprentice-trained doctors in Husiatyn county, two each in Chortkiv and Terebovlia counties, and one in Zalishchyky county in 1900 (*Oesterreichische Statistik*, LXVIII, no. 2).
65. The only complaints about poor medical services voiced by former residents of the region came from the Melnytsia area of Borshchiv county, where in 1900 two doctors were attempting to provide medical services to more than 35,000 people, and from Letiache in the far west of Zalishchyky county (IMZCh, 512, 842).
66. *Oesterreichische Statistik*, III, no. 2 and VIII, no. 3. The Zalishchyky general hospital was later expanded. The primary symptoms of syphilis usually disappear after two or three weeks, which is presumably the reason for the reported "cures."
67. *Oesterreichische Statistik*, LXVIII, no. 2.
68. Ibid., LXVII, no. 2; *Svoboda*, 10 Feb. 1898; IMZCh, 413.
69. *Oesterreichische Statistik*, XXXVII, no. 2.
70. Ibid., LXVIII, no. 2. This source also lists, for 1898-1900, a twelve-bed Revenue Officers' Hospital at Skala (Borshchiv county), but in 1900 it treated only five patients, so it may have been phased out. This hospital is not shown in *Gemeindelexicon*, 1900. There were also military hospitals at Chortkiv, Terebovlia, and Zalishchyky.
71. The provision of public general hospitals was the responsibility of the Land. It is strange that neither of the region's two largest urban areas, Terebovlia and Chortkiv-Vyhnanka, had a civilian hospital. Perhaps the military hospitals there also served some civilian role, at least in emergencies. The absence of public hospitals in Chortkiv and Terebovlia is all the more curious as these two towns (as well as Husiatyn) by 1900 each had an office of the Austrian public health-insurance scheme (*Krankenkasse*, *Kasa Khvorykh*). This was a modernizing development, but

only urban workers qualified to participate.

72. Bratassević, "Die Bewegung," 826.
73. *Gemeindelexicon*, 1900. Most of the apothecaries in Borshchiv county were Jewish (IMZCh, 512).
74. *Oesterreichische Statistik*, various volumes.
75. *Gemeindelexicon*, 1900. The proportion of certified midwives to total population was best in Terebovlia county and worst in Borshchiv county. Overall, Southern Podillia had one midwife per 4,126 people. The rate in Galicia was 1:3,674; in Austria it was 1:1,395 in 1900 (Bratassević, "Die Bewegung," 821).
76. *Oesterreichische Statistik*, LXVII, no. 1.
77. S. Rosenfeld, "Die Totgeburten in Österreich während der Jahre 1886-1898," esp. 313, 332-9. Among Galician counties with very high stillbirth rates were Żywiec (4.83:100), Nowy Targ (4.12:100) and Myślenice (4.07:100).
78. For midwives in Southern Podillia see also IMZCh, 282, 365,511-12, 811; Dubrav, "Die Organisation," 4-6; *Svoboda*, 21 Apr. 1898.
79. *Gemeindelexicon*, 1900; *Oesterreichische Statistik*, vol. LXVIII, no. 1 (which lists only six infant/child-care facilities in Husiatyn county). Where such infant/child-care facilities were run by Roman Catholic nuns, they often aroused fears that Ukrainian children might become Polonized (*Prolom*, 11 Dec. 1881; *Batkivshchyna*, 18 Oct. 1888). See also IMZCh, 579, 606, 609, 719. On the early child-care activities of the Greek Catholic rite order of the Sisters Servants of Mary Immaculate, see Sr. C.H. Popowich, *To Serve is to Love*, 13-17.
80. Doctors were more expensive than local providers of treatment in the villages (IMZCh, 512, 842; P. Humeniuk, *Hardships and Progress of Ukrainian Pioneers*, 78-79).
81. "Prof. finds folk cures alive, well," *Winnipeg Free Press*, 11 May 1984.
82. IMZCh, 579, 606, 615. Convents increased in number in three of the Southern Podillian counties in the last two decades of the nineteenth century, owing in part to the founding of the Greek Catholic order Sisters Servants of Mary Immaculate (Popowich, *To Serve is to Love*, 5-13; Kubijovyč, ed., *Ukraine*, 2: 188). By 1900 there were seven convent houses (RC and GC) in Borshchiv county, ten in Husiatyn, and eight in Zalishchyky, but only one each in Chortkiv and Terebovlia counties (*Gemeindelexicon*, 1900). The Sisters Servants set out to provide elementary home nursing care for the sick, although initially few had any nursing training (Popowich, *To Serve is to Love*, 14-15).
83. IMZCh, 351, 419.
84. Ibid., 453; Vynnytsky, *Terebovelska zemlia*, 468-9.
85. Inglot, *Historia chłopów Polskich*, 175, 658-68; Vynnytsky, *Terebovelska zemlia*, 468. For an exhortation to give up "the old ways," see Ozarkevych in I. Bryk and M. Kotsiuba, *Pershyi Ukrainskyi prosvitno-ekonomichnyi Konhres v 40-littia T-va "Prosvity"*, 256.
86. The medicinal properties of these and other plants are described in J. Volak and J. Stodola, *Plantes Medicinales*. See also M.E. Brownlow, *Herbs and the Fragrant Garden*. For criticism of folk medicine see Bryk and Kotsiuba, *Pershyi Ukrainskyi*, 253.
87. *Batkivshchyna*, 29 May 1891.

88. IMZCh, 241, 604. Chortkiv had medicinal waters, too (*Gemeindelexicon*, 1900, 132). Okopy (Borshchiv county), had "fruit cures" (*kuracja owocowa*) (M. Orłowicz, *Co zwiedzać w Galicji*, 22).
89. IMZCh, 365, 512, 812; Vynnytsky, *Terebovelska zemlia*, 468; *Batkivshchyna*, 29 May 1891; Inglot, *Historia chłopów Polskich*, 658-68; Havrysh, *Moia Kanada i ia*, 17.
90. Emigrants from Podillia and other parts of Eastern Galicia and Bukovyna brought their belief in the efficacy of herbal and other natural plant treatments with them to Canada (Martynovych, "Village Radicals and Peasant Immigrants," 88-92, *passim*).
91. [Volodymyr Navrotsky], "Piianstvo i propinatsiia na Halychyni," 56.
92. Ibid., 50.
93. See, for example, Kubijovyč, *Ukraine*, 1: 47; O.T. Martynowych, *The Ukrainian Bloc Settlement of East-Central Alberta, 1890-1930: A History*, 19.
94. F.C. Presl, "Produktion, Ausschank alkoholhältiger Getränke und die Trunkenheitsgesetzgebung," 590-92; W. Najdus, *Szkice z historii Galicji*, 131.
95. S.M. Hryniuk, "The Peasant and Alcohol in Eastern Galicia in the Late Nineteenth Century: A Note," 77.
96. N. Cybulski, *Próba badań nad żywieniem się ludu wiejskiego w Galicyi*, 145.
97. Ibid., 143.
98. *Lastivka*, no. 5, 1878; Vynnytsky, *Terebovelska zemlia*, 269; Pavlyk, "Pro rusko-ukrainski chytalni," 518, 524; IMZCh, 231, 322, 360-1, 369, 390-1, 444, 445-7, 452, 468, 604, 607, 625, 628, 642.
99. IMZCh, 231, 322, 361, 390, 444, 452, 628.
100. IMZCh, 322.
101. Cybulski, *Próba badań nad żywieniem*, 143.
102. Ibid., 143-5.
103. IMZCh, 390.
104. See 20 above.
105. IMZCh, 589.
106. Ibid., 391; Cybulski, *Próba badań nad żywieniem*, 147-8.
107. Cybulski, *Próba badań nad żywieniem*, 144. I have found no specific reference to "home brew" vodka or whiskey in Southern Podillia, but in view of the illegal distillation of spirits by Ukrainians in Canada (for example, M. Paximadis, *Look Who's Coming: The Wachna Story*, 88-90), it is unlikely that this "art" was not practiced in the old homeland, too.
108. For a fuller exposition of the argument see Hryniuk, "The Peasant and Alcohol," 75-85.
109. *Batkivshchyna*, 22 July 1887.
110. F.H.E. Palmer, *Austro-Hungarian Life in Town and Country*, 79. The author also claimed that "The Ukrainians... are usually as strong and vigorous as the Polish peasantry now generally are the reverse" (ibid.).

Chapter IX

Changes in Attitudes

"Peasants remain notable for their blend of traditional and modern values."[1] Southern Podillian peasants in the last quarter of the nineteenth century experienced a period during which they adapted to change while also maintaining old values.

At the turn of the century, Southern Podillia was still an overwhelmingly agricultural region. Most of its people continued to derive their principal livelihood from the land.[2] Yet railways and improved roads were changing marketing opportunities for agriculture. The annual cycle of the seasons continued to dictate the routine of the peasant's work. Nevertheless, new types of crops and the increased cultivation of second crops called for different work schedules, and increased animal husbandry provided more income and more work for an increased population. Some new small-scale secondary industries—egg-packing plants, jam-making factories, sawmills—came on the scene, alongside the old established distilleries and quarries.[3] The literacy rate was increasing, and through the intermediary of the reading halls even the illiterates had the opportunity to become better informed about the wider world.

The basic attachment of Ukrainian villagers to the Greek Catholic Church remained.[4] Despite increasing contact with the external, secular world and the occasional radical atheist, a deep-rooted attachment to religion remained. There is no indication of a decline in church attendance, and church ceremonial and ritual were faithfully observed. In the decades 1880-1900 there was much construction of churches, both completely new ones and new structures to replace the old. There were nine new Greek Catholic churches built in Borshchiv county alone between 1880 and 1900, and several were renovated or expanded.[5] Although a wealthy local landowner would sometimes give money for the construction of a new church,[6] there is every indication that villagers provided, and provided gladly, the necessary labour and funds. Costs were often quite great: the new stone church at Hleshchava (Terebovlia county), for instance, cost 13,000 g in 1897. People there were proud that they had prayer books along with their new church,[7] an indicator of the growth of literacy. Village co-operation toward the attainment of common objectives was traditional. When expressed in the building of a new church, the goal, too, was a customary one, but the traditional means were also used to further new ends. The prime example of this was the construction of those purveyers of new ideas, schools

"Big Stone Church" at Kopychyntsi, Husiatyn county, built 1890. V. Nahirnyi, architect.

Interior of Skala church, Borshchiv county, built 1882. Photographed by the author, May 1990

Interior of Ilavche church, Terebovlia county, built 1862. Photographed by the author, May 1990 (above)

Cross of freedom, Davydkivtsi, Chortkiv county. Photographed by the author, May 1990 (right)

and reading halls. Without rejecting innovation, people remained true to their tradition of sturdy self-reliance, and were proud of doing so.[8]

The ready acceptance in the 1890s of the principle of fire insurance is an example of the willingness to try new things. A Galician Ukrainian insurance company, Dnister, was founded in 1892; by 1893 it had a network of agents in Southern Podillia, including prominent local residents like the vice-reeve of Borshchiv. It no doubt benefited from having a considerable number of local priests among its "delegates" (persons who attended its annual meetings). In some villages the majority of householders took out policies.[9] Commune loan associations, credit unions, post office savings banks, and even private savings banks were also much in evidence by the end of the century, and provided new sources of credit for villagers and the people of the small towns.[10] Similarly, communal grain-storage facilities and the spread into the region of marketing and distributing co-operatives, although not without links to the old tradition of village co-operation, were essentially new manifestations.[11]

J.-P. Himka has asserted that priests brought the secular world to the countryside and then were pushed aside from their leadership role by the very forces they had created.[12] Here again, however, at least in Southern Podillia, the old and the new co-existed. Certainly by the end of the nineteenth century there were persons other than priests who were taking the lead in the educational and political fields—mainly teachers, lawyers, and doctors, but also reeves and occasionally a cantor or a postmaster. The leading role of the Greek Catholic clergy continued, despite the fact that they did not always have a good press. "You should not believe all you hear about bad priests" was a concluding comment in the newspaper report on the opening of the new church at Hleshchava.[13] No doubt there were indifferent as well as "good" priests, but the latter easily predominated in Southern Podillia. They provided their parishioners with the regular rituals and ceremonials of the church; they gave them moral precepts and initiated anti-drunkenness campaigns; and they provided spiritual guidance and pastoral care. Priests were one of the principal driving forces behind the founding of reading clubs. They were also the earliest exponents of improved agricultural practice, and among the main providers of agricultural education. They contributed greatly to bringing the outside world, with its new ideas and techniques, into the rural areas.

There was little that was outside the sphere of the local Greek Catholic priests. In Kopychyntsi, Ukrainian "cultural, educational, and even political life developed under the leadership of unusually active priests."[14] In Lanivtsi (Borshchiv county), a family dynasty of priests was responsible for founding the local reading club, credit union, and child-care facilities.[15] In Terebovlia town, Fr. Savula was the driving force behind the establishment of a reading club and a choir.[16] Another Terebovlia priest, Fr. Zalusky, was described as a "patriot" who took part in many Ukrainian cultural activities and ultimately left his sizeable estate for the furtherance of Ukrainian causes, principally education.[17]

Sometimes the priests' activities were overtly political, at other times they straddled a fine line between cultural-political or socio-economic activity on the one hand and outright politics on the other. Fr. M. Sichynsky of Kopychyntsi was elected to the Sejm in 1883. He was defeated by the Polish candidate Count Borkowski in a by-election for the Reichsrat in 1889, which brought allegations of bribery, denials from village electors who claimed that Sichynsky had sided against them in a dispute about pasturage rights, and a stern injunction from the editor of *Batkivshchyna* that they should have voted for the Ukrainian candidate rather than thinking of their personal interests.[18]

The same activities were continued in the 1890s. The attendance of priests at public meetings, especially those of a political or quasi-political nature, was important, and was recorded in newspaper accounts: twelve priests attended a *viche* in Borshchiv, while "only three priests" came to a meeting in Zalishchyky county a few weeks later.[19] Fr. Halushchynsky of Zvyniach (Chortkiv county) ran unsuccessfully in the 1897 Reichsrat election.[20] The names of Frs. Tsehelsky of Strusiv, Levytsky of Skala, and Velyhorsky of Ivanie Puste, for example, appeared time and again in the press in connection with political, socio-economic, and cultural activities such as the opening of reading clubs, the formation of choirs, lectures, the spread of information, and political meetings. In 1897 Velyhorsky initiated and spoke at a *viche* in Zvyniachka (Borshchiv county); was a guest at the opening of reading clubs at Ivanie Zolote and Zalishchyky Stari, and attended a meeting of the club at Dobrovliany (all in Zalishchyky county); informed all Eastern Galicia of the excellence of Ivanie Puste's ploughmaker; and spoke at a *viche* in Zalishchyky. In February 1898 he was chairing a *viche* in Shchytivtsi (Borshchiv county) when it was suspended by order of the County Officer.[21] Clearly he was a prominent force in many Ukrainian activities in the southern part of the region.

The Ukrainian parish clergy thus remained fully involved in various educational and "consciousness-raising" activities.[22] They were joined by others, such as the medical practitioners Dr. Hlady of Khorostkiv, who was the town's reeve in the 1880s, and Dr. Roman Iarosevych of Borshchiv, who was elected to the Reichsrat in 1891. Iarosevych occasionally attended commune reading club openings; at Tsyhany in 1895 he lectured his audience on human progress in the nineteenth century.[23] Some of these new influences at work in Southern Podillian cultural and political enlightenment activities were perhaps best epitomized in the careers of two lawyers. One of them, Antin Horbachevsky, formerly an editor of *Dilo*, became Chortkiv's first Ukrainian lawyer in 1893. It has been written about him—with some exaggeration, for there was already a handful of Ukrainian reading clubs in the county before his arrival—that "All Ukrainian organizations in Chortkiv and its county were founded in the office of Dr. A. Horbachevsky." Among the organizations in which Horbachevsky was actively involved or helped to found were the Prosvita reading club, the Nadiia

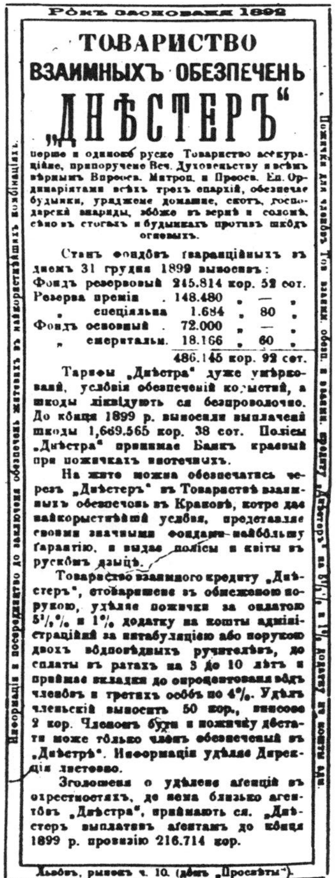

Рôкъ заснованя 1892

ТОВАРИСТВО
ВЗАИМНЫХЪ ОБЕЗПЕЧЕНЬ
„ДНѢСТЕРЪ"

перше и одинокоє руске Товариство асекураційне, припоручене Вел. Духовеньству и всѣмъ вѣрнымъ Впреосв. Митроп. и Преосв. Еп. Ординаріятами всѣхъ трехъ епархій, обезпечає будынки, урядженє домашнє, скотъ, господарскі знаряды, збôже въ зернѣ и соломѣ, сѣно въ стогахъ и будынкахъ противъ шкôдъ огневыхъ.

Станъ фондôвъ ґаранцiйныхъ въ днемъ 31 грудня 1899 выносивъ:

Фондъ резервовый	245.814	кор.	52 сот.
Резерва премій	148.480	„	— „
„ специяльна	1.684	„	80 „
Фондъ основный	72.000	„	— „
„ смертальн.	18.166	„	60 „
	486.145	кор.	92 сот.

Тарифы „Днѣстра" дуже умѣркованй, условія обезпеченій корыстнй, а шкоды лiквiдують ся безпроволочно. До кôнця 1899 р. выносили выплаченй шкоды 1,669.565 кор. 38 сот. Полiсы „Днѣстра" принимає Банкъ краєвый при пожичкахъ ипотечныхъ.

На жите можна обезпечатись через „Днѣстеръ" въ Товариствѣ взаимныхъ обезпеченъ въ Краковѣ, котре дає найкорыстнѣйшй условія, представляє своими значными фондами найбôльшу ґарантію, и выдає полiсы и квiты въ рускôмъ языцѣ.

Товариство взаимного кредиту „Днѣстеръ", стоваришене зъ обмеженою порукою, удѣляє пожички за сплатою 5½% и 1% додатку на кошты адмiнiстрацiйнй за интабуляцiєю або порукою двохъ вôдповѣдныхъ ручителѣвъ, до сплаты въ ратахъ на 3 до 10 лѣтъ и приймає вкладки до опроцентованя вôдъ членôвъ и третихъ особъ по 4%. Удѣлъ членьскій выносить 50 кор., вписове 2 кор. Членомъ бути и пожичку дôстати може тôлько членъ обезпеченый въ „Днѣстрѣ". Информацiя удѣляє Дирекцiя листовно.

Зголошеня о удѣленє аґенцiй въ округахъ, де нема близько аґентôвъ „Днѣстра", приймають ся. „Днѣстеръ" выплативъ аґентамъ до кôнця 1899 р. провизiю 216.714 кор.

Львôвъ, рынокъ ч. 10. (домъ „Просвѣты").

Информацiя и посередництво до заключеня обезпеченъ житевыхъ въ найкорыстнѣйшихъ комбiнацiяхъ.

Пожички для членôвъ Тов. взаимн. обезп. и взаимн. кредиту „Днѣстеръ" на 5½% и 1% додатку на кошты адм.

Advertisement for Dnister Insurance Company from *Svoboda*, 31 May 1900 (left)

Antin Horbachevsky, first Ukrainian lawyer in Chortkiv (right)

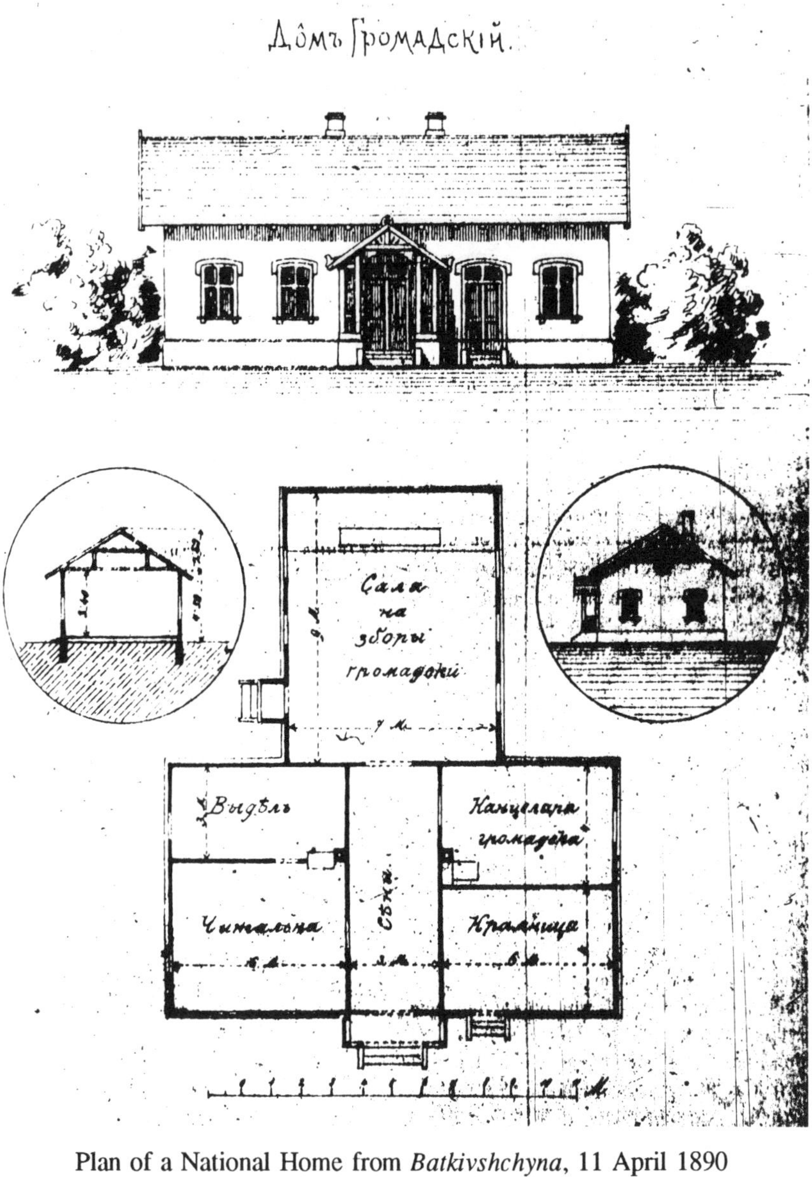

Plan of a National Home from *Batkivshchyna*, 11 April 1890

credit union, and the Chortkiv branches of Narodnyi Dim (National Home) and the theatrical group Ukrainska Besida (literally Ukrainian Discourse); he also attended, as a special guest, openings of reading clubs.[24]

The career of Mykhailo Dorundiak was similarly bound up with the ongoing socio-economic, cultural, and political awakening of Borshchiv county. He set up his office in Borshchiv town in 1892, and he ran it almost strictly in Ukrainian. He worked continuously at founding organizations or revitalizing those that already existed. He founded the Borshchiv town reading club in 1895, and expanded it to include a library of 1,500 volumes and a drama club. He successfully initiated and conducted a campaign to build a Narodnyi Dim branch for various cultural and political activities in the county; set up Ukrainian shops in a number of villages and supervised their operation; encouraged and assisted bright but needy children to attend higher schools; and in 1897 established a branch of the co-operative Narodna Torhivlia and later a county-wide credit association. Dorundiak contributed to *Batkivshchyna* on legal issues, and was willing to take up clients' grievances against public authorities, often free of charge. On Sundays and holy days he would visit nearby reading clubs, giving talks to encourage people to further educational and political work. He also ran, unsuccessfully, for the Sejm in 1895 and the Reichsrat in 1897, and was a member of the Borshchiv town and county councils.[25] Dorundiak and Fr. Velyhorsky were without doubt the most active individuals in the political socialization process in Borshchiv county in the 1890s, and at times they appeared on the same platform.

New knowledge spread through newspapers and reading clubs. Also, the efforts of clerical and lay intelligentsia activists brought about a growing awareness of the ability to influence events. Care must be taken, however, not to overestimate either the pace or the extent of this development or to misunderstand its character. Old habits died hard, and in the 1880s peasants only slowly weaned themselves from voting for the candidate favoured by the local landowner for the fourth curia of Reichsrat and Sejm elections. In the 1889 election to the Sejm, all the counties of Southern Podillia responded to the call of the Central Ruthenian Committee in Lviv and formed Ukrainian pre-election committees. Voters were urged not to vote for large landowners or their candidates, but in fact, of the recommended candidates, only one, a Pole, was elected.[26] Reports then filled the Ukrainian press on the corrupt practices of Polish political and administrative personnel, all intended to prevent the election of peasants and populists, whether Ukrainian or not.[27] These practices took various forms. Free food and drink were available for the electors. In Chortkiv county in 1889, voters were beaten, enumeration cards were destroyed, and electors were arrested to prevent them from taking part in the next stage of the election. Some electors were also arrested in Borshchiv and Zalishchyky counties. Intimidation was used elsewhere in Southern Podillia and in other parts of Eastern Galicia. Corrupt reeves often co-operated with large landowners by not posting the list of voters or failing to publicize the date or time of voting, as required by law.[28]

The 1891 Reichsrat elections proceeded in a somewhat freer atmosphere, which prevailed for three years. This was the period of the "New Era," when some Ukrainian politicians co-operated with Poles in the Vienna parliament. This attempted reconciliation lasted only a short time.[29] By 1897 the repressive apparatus was again extensively used. Some scheduled election meetings were banned. Gendarmes dispersed a meeting in Ivanie Puste and broke up its continuation in a local field. At Turylche (Borshchiv county), where the first stage of the election was held on the local landowner's estate, voters from the village were beaten up by manor servants as they approached the voting place. At Nyzhbirok (Husiatyn county), the reeve was said to be running the elections with the help of the gendarmes and dragoons. In a number of localities in Eastern Galicia the announced results of the voting differed from how the electors claimed they had voted, but complaints were ignored or complainers were threatened with violence or arrest.[30] Intimidation was also practiced in local elections; at Rizdviany (Terebovlia county), a county commissioner and gendarmes were present at the voting for the commune council in 1898.[31]

Ukrainians in Southern Podillia were at times able to organize themselves effectively for elections, and even at the village level by the 1890s they were beginning to fight back against the intimidating tactics of the traditional power brokers. In the county council elections in Husiatyn in 1890, all eleven Ukrainian candidates were elected.[32] Dr. Iarosevych's Reichsrat election victory in 1891 was an occasion for great rejoicing; he was driven in style from village to village and to the railway station at Chortkiv.[33] Some of his election meetings were proscribed as he became more radical in his pronouncements, but he was again elected to the Reichsrat in 1897, this time in the newly established fifth curia.[34] It was also in the 1897 election that Ukrainian villagers in Husiatyn county beat up the local landowner's men, who were trying to prevent them from voting.[35]

Commune councils, and especially reeves (who after 1884 were elected for six-year terms by the councils), were much more significant than other elected bodies or individuals to the lives of the villagers.[36] Newspaper reports and memoirists tended to judge reeves as good or bad largely on the basis of whether they favoured reading clubs and schools. Rizdviany gained a good reeve in 1898, unlike his predecessor, who had been opposed to the reading hall.[37] Krovinka had a corrupt reeve who had the local teacher jailed for three days; moreover, the reeve helped the County Officer in elections.[38] The "bad" reeve at Tovstenke (Husiatyn county), together with the Jews, manipulated the commune council; "bad" reeves at Ustia Iepyskopske and at Chortkiv were opposed to reading clubs.[39] A reeve at Bilobozhnytsia was a drunkard; another at Zalishchyky Stari appeared to have embezzled funds and drowned himself, but "now we have a good one."[40] Zazdrist had a bad reeve who falsified the electors' list.[41] Good or progressive reeves supported the reading club and the school, and participated in other socio-cultural developments. Tudoriv had a "good Ukrainian reeve" who helped to "enlighten the village." Dr. Hlady at Khorostkiv was a "good" reeve (Khorostkiv was a town where Poles and Ukrainians took it in turn to be reeve).[42] Laskivtsi had a good reeve who helped to direct the building of the school and started the reading hall; Kolodribka had a good reeve, as did Rosokhy and Borshchiv.[43] Two reeves were suspended by the County Officer in Husiatyn county in 1897 for showing too much independence; three years later the reeve of Babyntsi (Borshchiv county) was arrested for siding with his villagers during a work stoppage on the local estate.[44]

Reeves were important to the lives of the villagers for what they could do and for what they could leave undone. Some were apathetic, others were activists; some were subservient to the local landowner or to the County Officer, others stood up for the rights of the villagers. Many were Ukrainians and peasants.[45] What went on in the communes as a result of decisions made by the reeves and the commune councils was central to the people. Few local towns had the resources of Khorostkiv, where progressive councils developed the town, constructed a new magistrates' building, paved the streets, and planted trees. However, memoirists have taken pride in noting that their village streets were macadamized and their communes neat, tidy, and prosperous.[46] One recalled that people in his commune were little interested in "politics" (by which he meant Reichsrat and Sejm elections); they were much more interested in commune elections.[47] By the mid-1890s assemblies (*viche*, plural *vicha*) in Southern Podillia were discussing means of improving commune business, and demands were expressed that reeves should be elected by the whole commune and not by the commune council, and that commune councils should have the authority to suspend "bad" reeves.[48]

Most of the available evidence on peasant attitudes comes from those who were not themselves peasants. It is possible, indeed probable, that this evidence presents the peasants primarily as they reacted to others' actions. Certainly the newspapers, in their editorials, exhortations, and reports—unless they were directly from the villages—depicted political aspects of the rural scene through an urban filter. The objectives of national political movements were, in fact, not as important in the countryside as in Lviv and other major towns. Ukrainophiles and Old Ruthenians could collaborate in many parts of Southern Podillia, as could Ukrainophiles and Russophiles in Dzhuryn,[49] though a change is apparent in the mid-1890s, when a number of reading clubs switched allegiance from the Kachkovsky Society to Prosvita. Poles and Ukrainians might dispute bitterly in Lviv or Vienna, but no necessary echo of this was found in the villages of Southern Podillia.[50]

What went on in the commune and, as communications improved, in the county, was more immediate to the lives of the people than affairs in the capitals. This simple truth was not readily appreciated by the urban intelligentsia, which tended sometimes not to differentiate between various levels of elections and simply rejoiced that Ukrainians were becoming more effective at all elections.[51] The enlightenment societies and the newspapers did the villagers a service by informing them how commune council elections should be conducted and about their rights.[52] There was often a condescending note in such advice and in other comments that were meant to encourage village political activities:

> Your fathers and mothers were illiterate. They knew only how to plough and their knowledge ended at the edge of the village. You read books and newspapers. You enquire about commune, county, and Land matters. You know what is happening among other peoples in the world.[53]

This newspaper comment recognized that the transition from the old to the new involved a generational change. "Young people were much more interested than their fathers" in the leadership of the commune, in reading clubs, and in *vicha*.[54] The fact that the peasants might have interests that were not necessarily synonymous with those of the urban intellectuals was glossed over, even in *Batkivshchyna*, the newspaper that was generally so well attuned to the rural scene. It had been the same in 1889, when this paper had reproached Podillian peasants for voting in accordance with their own perception of their self-interest rather than "Ukrainian" interests.[55]

It was the affairs of the commune that gave villagers their main "grounding in political life."[56] It was a perception of peasant interests rather than "national" ones that led them to further participation. A change in the degree of participation, including large attendances at meetings, occurred in Southern Podillia in the mid-1890s. Urban intellectuals were again capable of misjudging this trend, as this patronizing editorial in *Svoboda* shows:

> The soul sings when...one reads about political meetings and assemblies of our peasants in various parts of the Land. It is evident that this political menu suits our peasants, and at these gatherings, as they listen to the speeches of our patriots, they rub their eyes and awaken to new realities about themselves.... Again our patriots spare no efforts to educate the peasants, and they can be sure that their words will fall on fertile ground.[57]

Large numbers of people did indeed attend meetings in Southern Podillia in

1897, 1898, and subsequently (about 350 in Chortkiv, 400 in Zalishchyky, and 700 at a *viche* in Borshchiv).[58] Some of these meetings as well as others[59] were essentially political, but one, in late 1898, was held to discuss joining a pig-marketing co-operative, and others increasingly took up the peasants' socio-economic concerns. The 700-person *viche* at Borshchiv in early 1898, for instance, began with a discussion, led by Dorundiak, of the political situation, but turned to the formation of an agricultural co-operative, whose membership was to consist only of peasants, and which was to be responsible to the imperial authorities in Vienna and not those of the Land in Lviv.[60]

Large public assemblies were no longer novel events in Eastern Galicia. The first *viche* held in Lviv in 1880 gave the Ukrainian people confidence. Subsequently, such meetings were held in other major towns, and then in rural areas.[61] Whether and in what number persons from Southern Podillia attended *vicha* held in other parts of the country is generally not known. It is recorded, however, that some people from Borshchiv county attended a *viche* at Stanyslaviv in late 1886. This incurred the displeasure of the local Poles: "They knew that a peasant who had been to a *viche* knows and thinks differently about his rights." At least one of them was subsequently harassed by the local gendarme.[62] *Vicha* in such large numbers in Southern Podillia were a new phenomenon in the mid- and late-1890s. This development coincided roughly with the rising self-awareness and self-confidence of the Ukrainian peasantry of Southern Podillia.

The peasantry was, of course, not an homogeneous entity, and what occurred in Southern Podillia probably affected only a portion of it. Societal leadership in the villages and small market towns of Southern Podillia until the mid-1890s had come largely from the priests and other local intelligentsia. Even in this period, however, some initiatives at the village level were undertaken by peasants, and by reeves, commune, and local school district councillors who were peasants elected to these offices. As early as 1885 in Mykulyntsi, a small market town just north of the boundary between Terebovlia and Ternopil counties, three peasants gave addresses at the meeting of the local reading club on the basis of their own reading of articles in newspapers and books.[63] In the mid- to late-1890s the local intelligentsia continued to play important roles in the affairs of the villagers. Nevertheless, there is some direct evidence that peasants themselves were becoming more self-confident, that issues of concern to them were coming to the fore in public discussion in Southern Podillia, and that they realized that, if organized, peasants were capable of working to achieve their own goals. The peasants might still need the organizational skills of priests, teachers, and lawyers—it was Fr. Velyhorsky who convened a *viche* to deal with the problem of landlords taking advantage of villagers at harvest time[64]—but peasants were themselves taking increased organizational initiatives. A peasant writing from Terebovlia county in 1897 stated:

> In our deaf corner till recently, few of our peasants knew their rights. The poor peasant knew only that he had to pay taxes, even if there was no money, and to do road work. And he was told that he was too immature to get any sort of rights.... Our people have come to their senses and now know "which path leads to the peas."[65]

There were many reasons for this rising consciousness of their qualities and abilities. The cumulative effect of being told by speakers at *vicha*, by the newspapers, and by politicians that they had rights and were not stupid ultimately achieved its purpose.[66] Perhaps more important than exhortation was the careful exposition of laws and rights of individuals, including peasants, in newspapers and at *vicha* and reading club meetings (especially the clubs' annual meetings, when special guest speakers were usually present). Increased confidence likely also developed among peasants through contact with one another at *vicha*. The enlightenment societies also contributed to the peasant's increasing awareness of himself and his rights and abilities directly through their various publications and sponsorship of reading clubs, and more indirectly through the activities which the clubs conducted as well as through the opportunities for interaction which they provided. Increased educational opportunities through provision of more schools and the rising literacy rate are also important. Peasants were aware that they knew more than their forefathers.

There were other factors, too. The economic difficulties of the large landowners who had dominated the peasants' lives in the past, though somewhat less evident in Southern Podillia than in most other parts of Galicia, were not concealed from the peasants. Certainly the newspapers reminded them of it: "It is time for weak-souled Ruthenians to stop fearing those who are today bankrupt and tomorrow will be paupers."[67] The fact that there was a law which did not always work against the peasant was of some importance, too. Landowners and county authorities might use intimidation at election time, but at a trial in Husiatyn county in 1897 Ukrainian villagers who had stood up to "local bullies" during the election campaign earlier that year were exonerated.[68] Finally and most significantly, there was the greater well-being of the peasantry as a result of the changes and improvements in agricultural practice. Greater self-confidence came in Southern Podillia as an effect of greater affluence, however modest, and not as an outcome of increased misery. The knowledge that they were capable of their own thoughts and actions seems at times to have come as something of a surprise to the peasants themselves. As one peasant wrote: "When the peasants spoke, one couldn't be more surprised, thinking to oneself: well, we are not so stupid, we Ruthenian peasants, as they always tell us."[69]

With increased knowledge and self-awareness came also a realization that the interests of peasants were often not being addressed adequately by other organizations. Peasants began to want their own organizations.[70] Increasingly, matters of direct concern to peasants were featured on the agendas of *vicha* held in Southern Podillia in the late-1890s. At a *viche* in Husiatyn in November 1897 the topics discussed were: enlightenment, affiliation to Prosvita, establishment of more reading clubs, elections to commune councils (including changes in the way in which reeves were elected), improving peasant welfare, and local politics. Two large landowners were not permitted to speak by the audience, a clear indication of the new sense of confidence. At a *viche* in Zalishchyky the following month, the seven issues raised were: the political position of the Ukrainians, the division of Galicia, elections to commune councils, elections to county councils, elementary schools, peasant unions, and the purchase of land.[71] Both the Husiatyn and the Zalishchyky *vicha* forwarded resolutions to the annual meeting of the Ukrainophile political organization Narodna Rada in Lviv, but at that meeting political issues were discussed first and there was no time to tackle economic questions of interest to the peasants. No wonder they demanded a separate meeting to discuss economic issues.[72]

Perhaps the most interesting development in Southern Podillia, and a real indicator of the changes that had taken place, was the founding in Strusiv (Terebovlia county) of Khlopska Rada (Peasants' Council) in late 1896. It was to be an economic-political organization for all Galicia; the membership fee was 25 kr, and five of its seven founders were peasants from four different villages of Terebovlia county. Although they did not reject the participation of the intelligentsia, peasants were to help themselves.[73] This Khlopska Rada is symptomatic rather than particularly important in itself. It did not achieve great things, though by the time of its second annual meeting, in January 1898, it claimed 476 members in 66 communes. It championed peasant rights and urged involvement in commune council elections. It appealed for funds to help in the reconstruction of Hleshchava after that village had been much damaged by fire. It took part in the 1897 election campaign, organizing meetings in Khorostkiv and Terebovlia. Fr. Tsehelsky, the parish priest of Strusiv, played a role in its affairs. It sought to extend its influence throughout Galicia, advising "the people of Lemkivshchyna," for example, to organize in similar manner: "We'll send you our charter." It was anti-radical, but was nevertheless a thorn in the side of the authorities, and early in 1898 the County Officer suspended its operations.[74]

The suspension of this council, like the banning of meetings, whether political or economic, by county authorities, was a reflection of fear. Such repressive actions were a recognition of the peasants' increasing consciousness of their own interests and ways to further them. Their activities continued, as was shown by the attempted founding of a peasants' organization in Borshchiv,[75] and by later economic *vicha*. Such peasant movements, facilitated by improved communications, were a manifestation of a new spirit in Southern Podillia.

Inherent in this new spirit was recognition that conditions for the peasantry had improved and that further improvements were desirable: "It's better for us than for our fathers. If only it could be better for our children."[76] Peasant activism in fact displayed a belief that more improvements were possible, and could be attained by hard work and self-help.[77] The old world had clearly been left behind; economic progress and political awareness was there for all to see.

Among the new ideas that were finding acceptance during this modernization process was the idea of emigration. Most authors on emigration from Eastern Galicia have seen this as a move of desperation by suffering and economically deprived people. The leading Soviet Ukrainian specialist on emigration wrote:

> But together, these socioeconomic and political circumstances gave rise to moods of desperation among the bereaved Galician peasants—the most deprived stratum of the population—and caused their firm determination to force their way out of the vice of misery and hunger, come what may.[78]

In one way or another, similar views appear in writings in the "host" country about the migrants: "They were men and women who were driven by poverty, oppression, and hopelessness."[79]

Although the circumstances of individual migrants varied, evidence presented in this study points to different conclusions, particularly about emigration to Canada in the second half of the 1890s. Among the new attitudes that were developing in Southern Podillia in the 1880s and 1890s was an inclination toward greater risk-taking and adventurousness than anything this peasant society had experienced before. Literacy and the awareness of the outside world this brought in its train were probably important, and it is likely that the younger generation was more disposed to move than its elders.[80]

There is no evidence of any large scale out-migration for purposes of settlement prior to the 1890s.[81] Migration to seek seasonal work did, however, take place even in the 1870s, when locals sought work in Russian Podillia. Later they also sought short-term work in Bukovyna, Bessarabia and Hungary, while Hutsul and Lemko people from the Carpathian foothills and Poles from elsewhere in Galicia came to work on a seasonal basis in Southern Podillia. Seasonal workers tended to be single men or women, but sometimes were heads of households, especially when the wife and older children could manage the smallholding in the absence of the male.[82]

There were three different emigrations from Southern Podillia in the 1890s. The first best conforms to the traditional image of the emigrant. In 1892, several thousand Podillians, including many from Husiatyn and Borshchiv counties, packed up or sold off their belongings and set off for the Russian Empire, lured by false rumors that the tsar was about to distribute lands left vacant by deaths

Villagers from Loshniv, Terebovlia county, photographed at the Ternopil exhibition, 1892

Advertisement for the F. Missler shipping firm offering Galician emigrants passage from Bremen to New York

in the recent famine. Pilat's investigations, based in part on responses by county authorities to his enquiries, led him to the conclusion that the overwhelming majority of these migrants were estate servants with little or no land of their own, or cottagers and day labourers who likewise were lured by the vision of becoming smallholders. Most of the emigrants returned disillusioned to their home villages.[83] The second emigration was to Brazil, beginning around 1890. Although this clearly involved the use of railways and transatlantic shipping, usually from Italian ports, the cost of the ocean voyage was covered by the Brazilian government, which was anxious to clear virgin lands. A rumor that the Archduke Rudolph was alive, living in Brazil, and would welcome Ukrainian settlers there, probably made the prospect of travel to a far-off land more attractive to some people. Either 202 or 316 emigrated to Brazil from nine communes of Terebovlia between June and November 1895; during the next few months a further 700 left Terebovlia county for Brazil despite obstacles placed in their way by the County Officer, but markedly fewer went from the other four counties combined.[84]

The mass emigration to Canada from the mid-1890s onward differed from the earlier migrations. There was the great attraction of 160 acres of land (68.8 ha) that could be acquired for 10 dollars (about 50 g), but emigrants to Canada were required to pay their own fares, which represented a considerable investment. In this situation, however, there was systematic information about Canada available to prospective settlers that had not been available for earlier emigrations, most notably the booklets by Dr. Oleskiv published by Prosvita and the Kachkovsky Society.[85] It was principally the smallholding peasants, the 2-5 ha holders, who left Southern Podillia for Canada in the late 1890s.[86]

An overseas move, whether to Brazil or Canada, in family groups involved risk-taking. In the Canadian case it appears that those who bade their sad farewells to their home villages did so not because of increasing poverty, but because they sought even better opportunities in another country. This migration, which required an outlay of capital, thus was principally motivated by rising expectations, which for one reason or another the migrant did not expect to be adequately met in the homeland.[87]

Such findings, though preliminary, are consistent with other modern views on migration. As Donald Treadgold has written in the context of the Russian Empire, "[It] appears less as a flight from grinding misery than as one facet of an overall adjustment in Russian agriculture."[88] There was adjustment to new conditions in Southern Podillia, particularly adjustments in agriculture to the better communications which, together with agricultural and general education and more advanced techniques, improved commodity production and animal husbandry. That independent small and medium producers were better able to make this adjustment than large landowners is also consistent with the findings of recent scholarship on other peasant societies.[89] To make this adjustment successfully required changes in attitudes. These changes in Southern Podillia were initiated by educational activities of both a general and practical nature. The utility of adjustment was made plain when new marketing opportunities became available. The response of the peasantry to such new opportunities was both to increase and to diversify production. In this process experimentation was encouraged, experience proved the value of new ways, and the strength of tradition was largely eroded. New attitudes developed and these in turn sought political expression. It was in this way that Ukrainian peasants in Southern Podillia, in the relatively brief span of twenty years or so, made the transition from a traditional to a more modern society.

Notes

1. P. Stearns, *European Society in Upheaval: Social History since 1750*, 332.
2. The 1900 data show very little change from 1880 in the percentage of the population (including dependents) whose primary occupation was in agriculture: Borshchiv 84 per cent (an increase of 6 per cent), Chortkiv 81 per cent, Husiatyn 80.6 per cent, Terebovlia 81.9 per cent, and Zalishchyky 75.9 per cent (*Oesterreichische Statistik*, LXVI, pt. 11).
3. By 1902 two sawmills in Husiatyn county employed ninety men. The tobacco factory at Iaholnytsia, with 575 workers, was among the largest industrial enterprises in Eastern Galicia, and there was a second state tobacco factory in the region, at Ozeriany, with almost 200 employees (*Oesterreichische Statistik*, LXXV, pt. 11).
4. F. Umlauft, *Die österreichisch-ungarische Monarchie*, 643; Havrysh, *Moia Kanada i ia*, 20-3; IMZCh, 202-3, 504, *passim*. The importance of religion was shown, too, by the determination of emigrants from Eastern Galicia (many of whom came from Southern Podillia) to rebuild their religious life in Western Canada (S. Hryniuk and R. Yereniuk, "The Ukrainian Experience"). Nothing said here is intended to indicate that Southern Podillia's Polish peasantry differed greatly in religiosity from the Ukrainian.
5. Cf. *Special-Orts-Repertorien*, 1880 and *Gemeindelexicon*, 1900. See also IMZCh, 582, 584, 596, 608, 610, 614, 630, 674, 689.
6. E.g., IMZCh, 621; O. Makovei, *Zalisia*, 284-5.
7. *Svoboda*, 30 Dec. 1897.
8. K. Grzybowski, *Galicja 1848-1914*; W.J. Klabouch, "Die Lokalverwaltung"; Kubijovyč, *Ukraine*; T. Pilat, "Der landtäflicher Grundbesitz"; W. Ogris, "Die Rechtsentwicklung in Cisleithanien"; E.C. Hellbling, "Die Landesverwaltung"; IMZCh, 196, 377, 643, 665; *Batkivshchyna*, 7 Mar. 1890 and 12 Jan. 1896.
9. *Batkivshchyna*, 14 Dec. 1891; *Chytalnia*, 20 Apr., 8 and 20 May, and 8 July 1893; *Svoboda*, 13 Jan. and 30 Dec. 1897; IMZCh, 231. See also 56 above. In 1900 Dnister had 84,765 policies in force in 3,168 Galician communes, as well as some in Bukovyna (*Podręcznik statystyki*, VIII, pt. 2: 258). The insurance company also established a credit union in 1896 (*Svoboda*, 7 Jan. 1897).
10. In 1900 there were 57 commune loan associations in Borshchiv county, 45 in Chortkiv, 53 in Husiatyn, 30 in Terebovlia, and 36 in Zalishchyky (*Podręcznik*

statystyki, VII, pt. 2: 228-9). These were organized by commune councils, but there were complaints that their interest charges of 10-12 per cent were too high (F. Schmid, "Die Gemeinde- und Bezirksdarlehenscassen in Galizien," 712-4). In addition, there were the post office savings banks (see 56 above), the many credit unions associated with reading clubs, and independent savings and loan associations. For the establishment and early progress of a savings and loan association at Nahiriany (Chortkiv county), founded by 200 householders, see *Svoboda*, 5 May 1898. Terebovlia town had a savings and loan association as early as 1883. In 1886 its office was open six days per week and it was paying 5 per cent interest, making mortgage loans at 6.5 per cent, and other loans at 7 per cent (*Oesterreichische Statistik*, XVIII, pt. 3). A new savings and loan association opened in Zalishchyky in 1897: see H. Ehrenberger, "Oesterreichs Sparcassen im Jahre 1897," 209). The problem of usury requires further investigation, but it is likely that its dimensions, and particularly the rates of interest after the 1870s have been much exaggerated (L. Caro, *Auswanderung und Auswanderungspolitik in Oesterreich*, 153-67).

11. On co-operatives see I. Vytanovych, *Istoriia ukrainskoho kooperatyvnoho rukhu*, 79-92, 133-53. For grain-storage facilities see *Chytalnia*, 6 Mar. and 6 Apr. 1895; *Svoboda*, 21 May and 26 Sept. 1897.
12. J.-P. Himka, "Priests and Peasants," 9.
13. *Svoboda*, 30 Dec. 1897. The radical newspaper *Khliborob*, in its October 1893 issue, wrote that the priest of Lysivtsi (Zalishchyky county) wanted to make his cantor reeve of the village and denied a blessing to those who voted against him.
14. IMZCh, 283.
15. Ibid., 605.
16. *Batkivshchyna*, 4 Feb. 1887.
17. Ibid., 8 Mar. 1889, and 4 July 1890; I. Vynnytsky, ed., *Terebovelska zemlia*, 407.
18. IMZCh, 283; *Batkivshchyna*, 19 and 26 Jan., 15 Feb., 1 and 8 Mar. 1889.
19. *Svoboda*, 3 and 24 Mar. 1898. The turnout of twelve priests at the Borshchiv *viche* was regarded as unduly low.
20. IMZCh, 187.
21. *Svoboda*, 21 Jan., 13 and 27 May 13, 10 June, and 16 Sept. 1897, and 13 Jan. and 24 Feb. 1898; *Hromadskyi holos*, 1 Mar. 1898. For the ploughmaker see above, 127 and 130; for Fr. O. Levytsky see also IMZCh, 584-6; for Fr. Tsehelsky see *Svoboda*, 29 Apr. 1897.
22. See for example, *Batkivshchyna*, 27 June 1884 and 12 Mar. 12 1886; *Dilo*, 1 July 1890; *Chytalnia*, 6 and 21 July 1895; IMZCh, 231, *passim*. The sources make only scattered references to the role of priests' wives. In Shyshkivtsi the priest's wife gave talks, taught embroidery, and was the life and soul of cultural education (IMZCh, 628). See also Vynnytsky, *Terebovelska zemlia*, 469; N. Kobrynska, "Ruske zhinotstvo v Halychyni v nashykh chasakh," 100.
23. On Hlady, see IMZCh, 377. On Iarosevych see ibid., 487; *Chytalnia*, 6 July 1895.
24. In 1913 Horbachevsky was elected to the Sejm as deputy for Chortkiv (IMZCh, 68-71; *Chytalnia*, 8 July 1893 and 6 Aug. 1896; *Svoboda*, 28 Apr. 1898; A. Zhyvotko, *Istoriia ukrainskoi presy*, 68).
25. For Dorundiak's activities see the illustrated Prosvita publication *Dlia vsikh* (Lviv

1908), 90-4; IMZCh, 488, 510; Zhyvotko, *Istoriia ukrainskoi presy*, 67; *Narod*, 1 May 1895; *Chytalnia*, 6 July 1895, and 6 Aug. 1896; *Batkivshchyna*, 28 June 1896; *Svoboda*, 21 Jan., 13 and 25 Feb., and 4 Mar. 1897.

26. The Pole was Dr. Olpiński of Terebovlia, who was described in *Batkivshchyna* (14 Dec. 1889) as a good deputy who co-operated well with Ukrainians.
27. For the battles of the Polish peasant movement with the large landowners see S. Kowalczyk et al., eds., *Zarys historii polskiego ruchu ludowego 1864-1918, passim.*
28. See, for example, *Batkivshchyna*, 21 and 29 June 1889; for some allegations of similar practices see also ibid., 4 Feb. 1887. There was a report of a later election when the local landowner dismissed a number of employees who voted "the wrong way" (Havrysh, *Moia Kanada i ia*, 25-6).
29. For a detailed account of the disintegration of the New Era compromise see [N.V.], *Ruska sprava v rokakh 1891-1894*.
30. *Svoboda*, 18 and 25 Feb., 18 and 25 Mar. 1897; *Ukrainsko-polska sprava v Avstriiskim parliamenti*, 10-11; V. Dudykevych, *Iak prokhodyly vybory v zakhidnii Ukraini za chasiv Austrii ta panskoi Polshchi*, 8-9.
31. *Svoboda*, 12 May 1898.
32. *Batkivshchyna*, 1 Aug. and 12 Sept. 1890. On the role priests were to play that year in the Borshchiv county council elections see *Dilo*, 9 June 1890.
33. IMZCh, 487.
34. *Svoboda*, 15 July and 16 Sept. 1897. A fifth curia, in which all adult males "not in domestic service" could vote, was instituted in 1896. In 1897 Iarosevych was defeated in the fourth curia but elected in the fifth.
35. *Svoboda*, 14 Oct. 1897, 25 Mar. 1897.
36. *Batkivshchyna*, 7 Aug. 1891, *Svoboda*, 24 June 1897. For the powers of the communes see 9 above.
37. *Svoboda*, 12 May 1898.
38. *Batkivshchyna*, 3 Aug. 1888. Later the commune got a good reeve who co-operated with the priest in opening a large store (ibid., 9 Oct. 1891).
39. Ibid., 13 Feb., 21 Mar., and 4 Apr. 1890.
40. IMZCh, 204; *Svoboda*, 15 July and 16 Sept. 1897.
41. *Hromadskyi holos*, 29 Nov. and 6 Dec. 1900.
42. IMZCh, 345, 377. In Khorostkiv the thirty-six seats on the commune council were equally apportioned between Ukrainians, Poles, and Jews, but reeves were chosen only from Ukrainians and Poles (ibid., 377).
43. *Batkivshchyna*, 31 Jan., 7 Mar., and 4 July 1890; *Chytalnia*, 21 Apr. 1895.
44. *Svoboda*, 9 Sept. 1897; *Hromadskyi holos*, 1 Apr. 1900. There was a history of bad relations between the village and the local landowner in Babyntsi—in 1897 the latter had ploughed up the roads leading to the villagers' lands (*Svoboda*, 22 July 1897).
45. For other Ukrainian reeves in Southern Podillia see *Batkivshchyna*, 5 Apr. 1889; *Chytalnia*, 8 July 1893; IMZCh, 330, 462, 584, *passim*; for Ukrainian commune scribes see IMZCh, 489.
46. IMZCh, 377, 462, *passim.*
47. Vynnytsky, *Terebovelska zemlia*, 403-4.
48. *Svoboda*, 25 Nov., 2 and 23 Dec. 1897.
49. IMZCh, 196. On the other hand, the village of Ivanie Puste, the home of Fr.

Velyhorsky, was "nationally conscious" (ibid., 665).

50. For examples of good relations see ibid., 644, 677, 683.
51. *Batkivshchyna*, 15 Jan. 1886.
52. Ibid., 7 Aug. 1891; *Svoboda*, 24 June 1897 and 13 and 20 Oct. 1898.
53. *Batkivshchyna*, 13 Mar. 1891.
54. IMZCh, 211.
55. *Batkivshchyna*, 19 and 26 Jan., 15 Feb., 1 and 8 Mar. 1889.
56. W.F. Reddaway et al., *The Cambridge History of Poland*, II: 458.
57. *Svoboda*, 21 Jan. 1897. The best survey of the major Ukrainian political factions in Galicia is by K. Levytsky, *Istoriia politychnoi dumky halytskykh ukraintsiv 1848-1914*; see also "Observator," "Lysty z-nad Poltvy," *Literaturno-naukovyi zbirnyk* 2, V (1899): 107-20 for a contemporary view. For a provocative view of Ukrainian populism, published by the Kachkovsky Society, see F. I. Svystun, *Shcho to est-Ukrainofilstvo? Eho istoriia i tepereshniaia kharakterystyka*. For a Polish view see W. Feldman, *Stronnictwa i programy polityczne w Galicyi, 1846-1906*, 2: 324-7.
58. *Svoboda*, 3 and 24 Mar. and 28 Apr. 1898.
59. *Svoboda*, 21 Jan., 25 Nov., and 23 Dec. 1897, and 10 and 24 Feb., 27 Nov. and 23 Dec. 1898; *Chytalnia*, 6 July 1894.
60. *Svoboda*, 3 Mar. 1898; for the pig-marketing co-operative see Chapter VII above.
61. For the first *viche* see *Viche* I, 1 and *Prolom*, 9 Jan. 1882; for later ones see *Batkivshchyna*, 11 Jan., 18 Apr., 9 May, and 29 Aug. 1884, 16 Jan. and 2 Oct. 1885, 24 Sept., 1 Oct., and 10 Dec. 1886, 5, 12, and 19 Oct. 1888, 7 June 1889.
62. *Batkivshchyna*, 10 Dec. 1886, 7 Jan. and 4 Mar. 1887.
63. Ibid., 13 Feb. 1885.
64. *Hromadskyi holos*, 1 Mar. 1898.
65. *Svoboda*, 29 Apr. 1897. The phrase "deaf corner" also describes the state which peasants were leaving: "We are glad that our deaf corner of Zalishchyky is moving more and more" (ibid., 23 Dec. 1897).
66. See, for example, *Batkivshchyna*, 16 Aug. 1889.
67. Ibid., 2 July 1886; see also the article "Protectors, who needs protection?" (*Svoboda*, 22 Apr. 1897).
68. *Svoboda*, 14 Oct. 1897.
69. Ibid., 16 Dec. 1897.
70. A "Podillian Council" (*Podilska Rada*) was formed in Ternopil in 1890 to give voice to local concerns (*Dilo*, 5 June 1890).
71. *Svoboda*, 18 and 25 Nov., 2 and 23 Dec. 1897, and 13 Jan. 1898.
72. *Svoboda*, 30 Dec. 1897.
73. *Batkivshchyna*, 28 Nov. and 13 Dec. 1896; *Svoboda*, 21 Jan. 1897. The establishment of this Council had been approved by the Governor of Galicia on 18 Oct. 1896. The home villages of two of the founders have not been identified. One of the founders was Peter Skorenky of the village of Rizdviany, who was later described as "poor but with a love of hard work" (*Svoboda*, 29 Apr. 1897).
74. *Svoboda*, 21 Jan., 4 Feb., 8 and 29 Apr., 27 May, and 16 Dec. 1897, 13 and 27 Jan., and 17 Feb. 1898.
75. Ibid., 3 Mar. 1898.

76. *Batkivshchyna*, 26 Jan. 1889.
77. The agrarian strike of 1902 falls outside the period of this study. It affected Southern Podillia as well as other regions of Eastern Galicia. Marxist writers have seen it as a real working-class manifestation; Ukrainian radicals claimed it developed as a result of their efforts and the increasing radicalization of the countryside. It deserves fresh scrutiny. A major impetus may have been the villagers' belief, not inconsistent with their growing awareness of the outside world and of international grain prices, that a fair day's work deserved a fair day's pay. The strikers' demands represented a mélange of the old and new worlds of the village: higher day cash wages or increased payments in kind (Z. Daszyńska-Golińska, "Neuere Literatur über galizisches Agrarwesen," 729).
78. A.M. Shlepakov, *The Emigration of Ukrainians to Canada: Reasons and Circumstances*, 11. The same sentiment is expressed in his *Ukrainska trudova emihratsiia v SSha i Kanadi (kinets XIX-pochatok XX st.)*. For other, briefer Soviet-Ukrainian views on emigration to Canada and elsewhere at the turn of the century see Osechynsky, *Halychyna pid hnitom Avstro-Uhorshchyny*, 38-9; *Istoriia selianstva*, 1: 438, *passim*; I.E. Shcherbatiuk, *Sotsialno-ekonomicheskie prichiny emigratsii trudiashchikhsia mass iz Galitsii, ee formy i posledstviia.*
79. Z. Keywan and M. Coles, *Greater than Kings: Ukrainian Pioneer Settlement in Canada*, preface. Similar, but more subtly stated assessments are in Himka, "The Background to Emigration" and M. Marunchak, *The Ukrainian Canadians: A History*, 17, 20-2. For differing views, see V.J. Kaye, *Early Ukrainian Settlements in Canada, 1895-1900*, xiii, xiv; B.P. Murdzek, *Emigration in Polish Social-Political Thought 1870-1914*, xvi; L. Wynar, "Iuliian Bachynsky, vydatnyi doslidnyk ukrainskoi emihratsii," 5, citing Iu. Bachynsky's *Ukraina irredenta.*
80. For Stefanyk's perception of this, see "The Stone Cross," 25-6.
81. Some aspects of pre-1900 general Galician emigration have been dealt with by scholars writing in Polish, Ukrainian, German, and English. Some contemporary examples are G. Pacher, *Die Arbeiterwanderungen zwischen Österreich-Ungarn und Nord Amerika*; K. von Englisch, "Die oesterreichische Auswanderungsstatistik"; L. Caro, *Auswanderung und Auswanderungspolitik in Oesterreich*; F. Probst, "Die überseeische österreichische Auswanderung, inbesondere 1889 und 1890," "...im Jahre 1891," "...in den Jahren 1892 bis 1895," "...in den Jahren 1896 bis 1898," "... in den Jahren 1899-1901"; J. Bużek, "Das Auswanderungsproblem und die Regelung des Auswanderungswesens in Oesterreich"; Ivan Franko, "Emihratsiia halytskykh selian" and "Emihratsiini ahenty v Halychyni," 311-24. Examples of more recent works are Murdzek, *Emigration in Polish Thought*; K. Groniowski, *Polska emigracya zarobkowa w Brazylii 1871-1914* and "Emihratsiia z Halychyny"; W. Serczyk, "The Participation of Ethnic Minorities in Emigration from Poland, with Particular Attention to the Ukrainians." A particularly useful work is H. Chmelar, "The Austrian Emigration, 1900-1914," (a lengthy article based on the author's Ph.D. thesis, University of Vienna, 1972, entitled "Die Auswanderung aus den im Reichsrat vertretenen Königreichen und Ländern in den Jahren 1905-1914").
82. For migrant labour from Galicia in general, see C. Bobinska and A. Pilch, "Employment-Seeking Emigrations of the Poles World-Wide XIX and XX C"; M. Myska, "Fossores ex Galicia: udział emigrantów z Galicji w formowaniu się klasy

robotniczej w górnictwie węglowym Morawskiej Ostrawy w drugiej połowie XIX wieku."

83. Pilat, "Die Auswanderung"; *Halychanyn*, 17 Feb. 1893; *Chytalnia*, 8 Mar. 1893; *Khliborob*, 15 Oct. and 25 Nov. 1892.
84. Groniowski, *Polska emigracya*, 80-2. See also K. Głuchowski, *Wśród pionerów polskich na Antypodach: materiały do problemy osadnictwa Polskiego w Brazylii.* The Ukrainian press carried frequent reports, letters, editorials, and items of general advice on emigration to Brazil throughout the period 1891-1900. See *Batkivshchyna*, 15 May, 5, 19, and 26 June, and 9 Oct. 1891, 28 Jan. 1895, and 13 Jan., 28 Feb., 28 Mar., 28 May, 28 June, 28 Aug., and 13 Sept. 1896; *Chytalnia*, 21 Apr. and 6 July 1895 (almost every issue for 1896 contained news on emigration to both Brazil and Canada). *Prosveshchenie* carried several editorials and items directly discouraging emigration, for example, 25 Aug. and 10 Nov. 1893, 10 Feb. 1894, 25 Apr., and 25 May 1895, 15 Apr. and 20 Aug. 1896. *Narod* also featured some articles on emigration.
85. Kaye, *Early Ukrainian Settlements*, 4-44, describes the visit of Dr. Oleskiv to Canada.
86. Immigrants in Canada wrote to the newspapers in Galicia describing their settlements and suggesting that only people with considerable cash reserves should set out; for example, a letter to *Svoboda* (6 May 1897) from Vasyl Ksionzyk, a former resident of Terebovlia county, stated that people should not come to Canada with fewer than 500 g; after his travels in Canada, Father Nestor Dmytriv wrote from Buffalo, N.Y., and claimed that 700 g was a minimum for a Galician settler in Canada. *Svoboda* had several items about emigration to both Brazil and Canada in its 1897 and 1898 issues. For example, the 11 Nov. 1897 issue described the deliberations of the All-Ukrainian National *Viche* in Lviv on that question, as well as its resolutions about the setting up of a State Emigration Bureau to organize migrant labour and to regulate and assist settlement immigration, such as that to Canada. See also ibid., 28 Apr., 5 May, 22 Sept., and 1 Dec. 1898 for items dealing with emigration. *Hromadskyi holos* contains informative material on emigration, especially letters from radicals in Canada such as Ivan Bodrug, Kyrylo Genyk and Yurii Syrotiuk (no. 20, 1899, and nos. 3, 4, 6, 14, 15, and 32, 1900). Even the radical press admitted that people who emigrated were moderately wealthy, free of debt, possessed land, and had 500-800 g when they emigrated. Their motive for emigrating was "for the good of the children" (V. Stefanyk, *Hromadskyi holos*, 9 [1899]).
87. This sentiment was expressed by persons who came from Southern Podillia or whose families came from there: Mrs. K. Chubaty, interviewed 9 July 1979; Mr. J. Storoschuk, interviewed 20 June 1979; Mr. J. Horobec, interviewed 20 June 1979; Mr. M. Sokolyk, interviewed 19 July 1979; Mrs. L. Salamandyk, interviewed 19 June 1979.
88. D. Treadgold, *The Great Siberian Migration*, 62.
89. See H. S. Nelli, *From Immigrants to Ethnics: The Italian Americans*; P. McPhee, "A Reconsideration of the 'Peasantry' of Nineteenth-Century France," 14-15.

Chapter X

Conclusion

It is worth asking why Eastern Galicia has been so often represented as a backward, stagnant, and impoverished society, whose predominantly Ukrainian peasantry lived in social, political, and economic oppression, since the evidence for Southern Podillia points in a very different direction. It is not here asserted that the Ukrainian peasantry of Southern Podillia in the late nineteenth century was representative of the Ukrainian peasantry of Eastern Galicia. It was probably not atypical in many features of its cultural and socio-economic development. In the development of the reading-club movement, village credit unions, and co-operatives, this region initially lagged behind many other areas of the Land, but Southern Podillia's exceptionally rich soil and relatively favourable climate may have given it advantages that other regions did not possess. Certainly there are some indications that crop yields there by the end of the century were among the highest in Galicia, and that once the railways had reached the region, the rate of agricultural progress—especially in the much ignored realm of animal husbandry—was faster than in many other regions. However, comparative rates of progress of various regions of Eastern Galicia can be determined only through further scholarly research that compares what they were to what they were becoming and not to contemporary societies at very different stages of development. Clearly, further area studies are needed before a new, credible picture of the Ukrainians of Eastern Galicia in the late nineteenth century can emerge.

Ukrainian writers themselves have played a large part in establishing and continuing the "gloom and doom" interpretation of late nineteenth-century Eastern Galician history. Some contemporaries thought of Eastern Galicia as a base for their project of establishing a linguistic and historical foundation for a distinct Ukrainian nation. Accordingly, they wrote programmatic statements, promoted Ukrainian literary and artistic development, discussed Polish-Ukrainian relations, and published polemical tracts on Galician Ukrainian political issues. Some believed that the Ukrainian peasant bore the burden of national and political oppression. These polemicists were generally urban-based, so changing socio-economic conditions in the rural regions were beyond their purview. Contemporary authors such as Franko, Pavlyk, and Budzynovsky were themselves much influenced by the ideas of Mykhailo Drahomanov and other socialist thinkers.[1] They had particular causes to promote and were outraged by the very evident inequalities that prevailed in their society. In their eagerness to highlight the need for radical reform they emphasized the poor performance of Eastern Galician agriculture compared to that of selected West European countries, and stressed the region's poverty and underdevelopment in general. With the exception of Pavlyk's early work on reading clubs, they appeared not to note the positive changes and improvements taking place around them.

These contemporaries made selective use of Austrian and Galician statistical data as bases for their critical analyses. One of them, Budzynovsky, was also led astray by his own mathematical and other errors. They also drew on Polish authors who were obsessed by Galicia's real and supposed backwardness, and whose work did not differentiate between western and eastern Galicia, though conditions were often quite different. These writers, especially the very influential Pilat, were primarily concerned with the fate of the large landowners and the agriculture which they practised. With seemingly fixed ideas, derived from much earlier in the century, about the size of individual landholding that allowed a viable agricultural operation, they decried the small area of the peasants' plots and did not consider the use to which the peasants put their land. The very small number of contemporary writers, such as Bujak, Kiniorsky, and Biegeleisen, who provided a more balanced treatment of Galician conditions at the turn of the century, were scarcely heeded; indeed, the *social* history of the Galician peasantry has been generally neglected.[2]

Twentieth-century Ukrainian writers have generally continued and elaborated on the interpretations of their predecessors. In part they may have done so because of the convenience of these interpretations. Economic stagnation could be blamed on the inequitable distribution of wealth, the sluggishness and anti-Ukrainian orientation of the Polish-dominated governing bodies of Galicia, and the Austrian authorities' indifference to an outlying province. Economic stagnation at a time of considerable population increase seemed to provide a ready-made answer to the question of why so many Ukrainian peasants emigrated from Eastern Galicia to the Americas in the 1890s and thereafter. Analyses which stressed stagnation and poverty in Eastern Galicia have remained attractive to some later Ukrainian scholars precisely because they were made by radical intellectuals. Often these later writers were concerned with intellectual, not social, history, and had little occasion to question previous interpretations. Moreover, the "gloom and doom" interpretation has its attractions for nationalist historians too. It provides a convenient explanation of the harm done to one's own nation by alien oppressors, which was the hallmark of much nationalist ideology among the stateless peoples of East-Central Europe. Stagnation and poverty became part of the national myth, but myths do need to be examined. Probably the reality of Ukrainian progress in late nineteenth-century Galicia, achieved in the face of many difficulties, can provide at least as satisfying an ingredient in the nation-building process—and one that is in accord with historical reality—as the "stagnation and poverty" interpretation.

Post-World War II Soviet and Polish writers have also espoused the "gloom and doom" concept. In their view, peasant agriculture in the late nineteenth century was hopelessly inefficient, and peasant society was mired in exploitation, poverty, ignorance, and backwardness. Not surprisingly, Soviet authors have stressed the continuing feudal nature of Galicia after 1848, the exploitation of the peasantry by Polish landowners and Jewish lessees and traders, the lack of progress in industry, low standards in agriculture and education, and the "revolutionary" nature of the peasantry and the working class.[3] What is at first sight surprising is that Western historians, unfettered by officially imposed ideologies, have been content to reiterate old positions without re-examining the evidence.

* * *

The historian of past agrarian societies is often confronted by deficiencies in source materials. Sometimes there are only fragments and sketchy or non-continuous information. Nevertheless, examination of available source materials—contemporary newspapers and statistical data, descriptive accounts and memoirs—which have never before been systematically analyzed has revealed a picture of Southern Podillia in the late nineteenth century which is very different from that presented in the generally accepted accounts and interpretations of Eastern Galician society as a whole. Southern Podillia in the late nineteenth century was not a stagnant society. The peasants built churches and schools; founded reading clubs, savings and loan societies, and communal granaries; kept their farm buildings in good repair and their houses whitewashed; participated in or attended drama and choir performances; established political organizations; sold fat animals; practised intensive agriculture; and drank less than has been generally supposed. Women were playing a greater public role, for instance as teachers and in reading clubs. Thus these peasants were not the impoverished and backward people of mythology, burdened by excessive taxes, political (let alone religious) oppression, general lack of opportunity, and the dead hand of the past.

The picture of a peasantry without any effective control over its destiny is consistent with a traditional or pre-modern peasantry. That picture, so frequently drawn in so many books about Eastern Galicia in the late nineteenth century, is not an accurate portrayal of Southern Podillia or, one suspects, of many other regions of the eastern portion of the Land. Political or administrative repression certainly existed, but even in this sphere, Southern Podillia's Ukrainian peasants were liberating themselves from an old psychological bondage and becoming more aware of their civil rights as Austrian citizens and their distinctive

Ukrainian culture. Reading-club activities and the growth of Ukrainian performing and other arts helped to give this peasantry a pride in its distinctiveness that had scarcely been felt before. City-bound contemporary commentators and later historians, some perhaps influenced by Marx's famous comment about the "idiocy of rural life," failed to see what the evidence makes so plain. They looked at the dimensions of the peasants' plots and not at what the peasants did with them. Peasants worked their own land, and if this did not provide a sufficient income they leased additional land, worked for someone else, supplemented their income with domestic industry, or migrated where earnings were greater. In this respect, what was important for the peasant's social status and self-image was that he owned land and wanted to own more. The peasant's land hunger was itself wrongly taken to be an indicator of impoverishment, whereas it actually manifested an aspiration to expand operations: "the small-holding peasant wants no socialism, but land, his own land, as much of it as possible."[4] This was more often an expression of increased expectations than a consequence of past decline.

The change from adherence to timeless tradition to courageous innovation, from a peasant economy geared to local markets to one which was integrated by railways into the European economy, from the throwing off of old fears of authority to the exercise of political rights, as well as expansion of knowledge of the wider world which literacy and education brought with them and the acceptance of new ideas and techniques, all were part of the process of modernization. Some of these elements were already present, in a minor way, in 1880. In the two decades that followed they developed in ways which meant that, despite the continued agrarian character of Southern Podillia, the region was very different in 1900. It was a tremendous leap.

Notes

1. See also the interesting discussion in J.-P. Himka, *Socialism in Galicia*, 106-21.
2. For a recent contribution to this subject, see J.-P. Himka, *Galician Villagers and the Ukrainian National Movement in the Nineteenth Century* (Edmonton, 1988).
3. See also P.R. Magocsi, *Galicia*, 140-1.
4. Cited in Himka, "Polish and Ukrainian Socialism," 500.

APPENDICES

Appendix I

Populations and Areas of Selected Towns, Villages, and Estates

a) Selected Market Towns

b) Selected Large Villages

c) Selected Smaller Villages

d) Selected Tabular Estates

Sources: *Special-Orts-Repertorien der im oesterreichischen Reichsrathe vertretenen Königreiche und Länder*, for 1880 and 1890; *Gemeindelexikon der im Reichsrate vertretenen Königreiche und Länder*, for 1900.

Notes:

1. The status of town or market was a privilege conferred or confirmed by Austrian, and later by county authorities.

2. The data on religious affiliation are from raw census data for 31 December of the given year. The data on language are derived from statistics for normally resident population. In most instances, there is no difference in the total number counted. Percentages do not necessarily add up to 100 because of rounding and omission of the category "other."

3. The number of houses and the area in hectares noted for each town, village or estate are for 1900.

(a) *Population of Selected Market Towns: 1880, 1890, 1900*

		Total Population	Religious Affiliation (%) RC	GC	Jewish	Language of Usage (%) Polish	Ukrainian	German
Borshchiv	1880	3,988	34.9	32.4	32.8	35.4	64.6	0.0
1,442 ha	1890	4,331	29.6	28.6	41.7	60.3	39.7	0.0
759 houses	1900	4,590	35.9	34.9	29.2	65.3	34.7	0.0
Melnytsia	1880	3,595	14.7	45.8	39.6	54.2	45.8	0.0
1,490 ha	1890	3,712	4.9	55.1	29.8	51.9	47.8	0.2
590 houses	1900	3,589	14.7	51.9	33.4	49.3	50.6	0.1
Skala	1880	6,154	10.1	33.8	56.0	61.1	37.9	0.0
1,287 ha	1890	6,163	12.3	35.3	52.4	30.5	65.5	4.0
667 houses	1900	5,638	13.0	42.8	44.2	53.0	46.9	0.1
Ustia	1880	2,444	29.8	33.3	34.7	53.8	43.5	2.7
Iepyskopske	1890	2,491	4.4	61.7	34.0	38.4	61.6	0.0
1,140 ha	1900	2,405	6.2	59.2	34.6	42.8	57.2	0.0
492 houses								
Chortkiv	1880	3,524	12.0	25.1	62.8	12.4	24.7	62.4
3,173 ha***	1890	4,531	18.0	11.6	68.5	78.3	12.5	9.2
536 houses	1900	5,099	25.5	11.8	59.7	83.9	13.2	2.6*

		Total Population	Religious Affiliation (%) RC	GC	Jewish	Language of Usage (%) Polish	Ukrainian	German
Iaholnytsia	1880	3,143	27.8	12.0	60.2	27.8	12.0	60.3
760 ha	1890	3,201	31.6	13.4	55.0	30.5	15.4	54.1
506 houses	1900	3,083	33.9	21.8	44.3	64.3	21.9	13.8
Ulashkivtsi	1880	2,270	6.7	61.2	32.1	35.2	59.1	4.9
1,325 ha	1890	2,260	9.4	61.4	29.2	10.9	61.0	28.1
406 houses	1900	2,280	6.7	71.8	21.4	19.8	70.8	9.4
Khorostkiv	1880	5,623	25.5	31.6	37.9	31.6	43.2	24.3
2,804 ha	1890	6,261	29.8	37.0	33.1	65.4	34.6	0.0
969 houses	1900	6,498	29.6	41.6	28.8	58.7	41.2	0.1
Husiatyn	1880	5,214	14.1	13.4	72.5	51.1	13.2	35.7
647 ha	1890	6,060	16.1	14.5	69.3	84.1	15.7	0.1
699 houses	1900	5,736	19.1	17.2	63.6	84.6	15.0	0.4
Kopychyntsi	1880	6,221	24.5	39.3	36.2	13.7	9.9	36.2
2,318 ha	1890	6,967	25.2	39.4	35.4	61.3	38.6	0.0
1,032 houses	1900	7,190	26.2	43.2	30.6	53.9	45.3	0.8
Budzaniv	1880	5,124	29.4	34.6	35.9	65.5	34.5	0.0
1,698 ha	1890	5,363	29.7	37.4	32.9	65.1	34.6	0.3
903 houses	1900	5,436	29.8	39.0	31.2	55.5	38.2	6.4

		Total Population	Religious Affiliation (%) RC	GC	Jewish	Language of Usage (%) Polish	Ukrainian	German
Ianiv	1880	2,483	40.0	19.8	40.2	83.9	16.1	0.0
992 ha	1890	2,563	44.1	22.1	33.7	78.3	21.7	0.0
403 houses	1900	2,667	45.4	26.4	28.1	74.5	25.4	0.1
Tovste	1880	3,199	10.8	21.7	67.4	73.7	21.8	4.5
804 ha	1890	3,579	10.5	23.2	66.3	43.4	25.9	30.2
432 houses	1900	3,671	11.5	29.3	59.2	70.7	29.3	0.0
Ustechko	1880	2,585	6.2	56.2	37.5	7.3	56.0	36.7
981 ha	1890	2,550	6.8	59.2	34.0	15.7	84.2	0.1
414 houses	1900	2,607	6.3	70.8	22.8	31.3	68.7	0.0
Zalishchyky	1880	5,588	12.4	7.4	79.2	92.5	3.9	3.6
80 ha	1890	5,751	12.4	8.7	78.5	92.8	5.3	1.9
580 houses	1900	5,916	23.6	11.2	63.9	93.9	5.2	0.8**

Notes: * Most of the German speakers were from the military garrison.
** All the German speakers were from the military garrison.
*** Includes area of Vyhnanka (see Appendix I, b).

(b) *Population of Selected Large Villages: 1880, 1890, 1900*

		Total Population	Religious Affiliation (%)			Language of Usage (%)		
			RC	GC	Jewish	Polish	Ukrainian	German
Borshchiv County								
Hermakivka	1880	2,190	13.1	83.9	2.4	16.9	83.1	0.0
1,578 ha	1890	2,562	16.8	78.7	4.3	16.0	83.5	0.5
503 houses	1900	2,532	15.1	82.2	2.6	17.7	82.3	0.0
Ivankiv	1880	2,002	0.5	98.5	1.0	0.9	99.1	0.0
1,755 ha	1890	2,178	1.2	98.2	0.6	0.4	99.3	0.3
455 houses	1900	2,392	1.6	97.1	1.2	2.2	97.4	0.4
Lanivtsi	1880	1,896	22.6	75.3	2.5	0.0	100.0	0.0
1,479 ha	1890	2,048	22.0	73.9	4.1	21.5	78.5	0.0
439 houses	1900	2,179	22.6	72.7	4.7	24.8	75.2	0.0
Vilkhovets	1880	2,113	3.1	92.9	4.0	7.2	92.8	0.0
1,632 ha	1890	2,293	2.7	92.1	4.9	0.5	94.6	4.9
521 houses	1900	2,319	3.4	93.2	3.3	6.9	93.1	0.0
Chortkiv County								
Bile	1880	3,287	7.3	90.5	2.2	7.3	90.5	2.2
3,168 ha	1890	3,628	9.5	88.0	2.5	3.2	96.6	0.2
647 houses	1900	4,083	9.7	88.2	2.1	10.8	89.2	0.0

		Total Population	Religious Affiliation (%)			Language of Usage (%)		
			RC	GC	Jewish	Polish	Ukrainian	German
Vyhnanka	1880	3,181	43.7	54.4	1.9	44.6	51.8	3.5
*	1890	3,628	9.5	88.0	2.5	3.2	96.6	0.2
831 houses	1900	5,212	48.9	43.3	7.1	57.4	41.9	0.6
Zalissia	1880	1,619	24.6	74.5	0.9	24.6	74.5	0.9
1,340 ha	1890	1,871	29.1	69.1	1.8	9.8	90.2	0.0
362 houses	1900	2,011	28.6	69.7	1.7	31.4	68.6	0.0
Husiatyn County								
Horodnytsia	1880	2,423	32.7	61.9	5.4	14.5	79.5	6.0
1,867 ha	1890	2,887	31.8	61.9	6.3	39.2	59.8	0.9
505 houses	1900	3,047	33.6	61.9	4.5	48.5	51.5	0.0
Vasylkivtsi	1880	1,967	22.8	67.7	9.5	4.9	86.4	8.7
943 ha	1890	2,397	25.4	65.8	8.7	15.0	82.6	2.4
487 houses	1900	2,618	24.5	68.4	7.1	24.8	75.0	0.0
Iabluniv	1880	2,007	15.4	82.5	2.1	12.2	87.7	0.1
1,339 ha	1890	2,271	14.3	84.7	1.1	10.7	89.3	0.0
432 houses	1900	2,529	13.6	84.6	1.6	12.7	87.3	0.0
Terebovlia County								
Kobylovoloky	1880	2,666	24.3	74.5	1.7	11.6	88.3	0.0
1,902 ha	1890	2,996	28.1	69.8	2.3	19.3	79.1	1.6
531 houses	1900	3,160	28.5	69.9	1.6	24.3	75.2	0.5

		Total Population	Religious Affiliation (%) RC	GC	Jewish	Language of Usage (%) Polish	Ukrainian	German
Laskivtsi	1880	2,210	13.7	79.7	6.7	14.5	85.1	0.4
1,682 ha	1890	2,745	14.6	79.0	6.4	6.7	93.3	0.0
506 houses	1900	2,945	14.1	80.9	5.1	15.9	83.7	0.8
Loshniv	1880	2,858	72.9	24.0	3.1	59.6	39.3	1.0
1,779 ha	1890	2,927	75.6	22.4	2.0	82.8	17.2	0.0
564 houses	1900	3,098	76.8	20.9	2.3	84.9	15.1	0.0
Zalishchyky County								
Kolodribka	1880	1,694	2.8	93.0	4.2	7.9	92.1	0.0
1,312 ha	1890	1,968	1.5	93.2	5.2	1.0	98.9	0.1
437 houses	1900	2,027	1.9	94.0	4.0	6.2	93.8	0.0
Synkiv	1880	2,003	1.0	96.4	2.5	4.0	96.0	0.0
1,300 ha	1890	2,246	1.0	96.5	2.4	3.7	96.3	0.0
507 houses	1900	2,247	2.3	95.3	2.4	4.4	95.6	0.0
Torske	1880	1,573	10.3	86.5	3.2	9.8	89.5	0.7
1,009 ha	1890	1,771	14.1	83.7	2.3	16.1	83.9	0.0
349 houses	1900	1,887	11.1	87.6	1.2	12.2	87.8	0.0

Note: * Included in area of Chortkiv (see p. 220).

(c) *Populations of Selected Smaller Villages: 1880, 1890, 1900*

		Total Population	Religious Affiliation (%)			Language of Usage (%)		
			RC	GC	Jewish	Polish	Ukrainian	German
Borshchiv County								
Hushtyn	1880	651	16.6	80.3	3.1	4.1	95.9	0.0
404 ha	1890	714	22.9	71.7	5.6	2.2	92.2	5.6
115 houses	1900	726	27.0	69.1	3.9	34.3	65.7	0.0
Mushkativka	1880	1,021	31.0	67.0	2.0	7.7	92.3	0.0
914 ha	1890	1,172	42.0	55.5	2.5	10.7	89.3	0.0
235 houses	1900	1,244	39.9	58.5	1.6	42.3	57.7	0.0
Mykhalkiv	1880	535	1.5	94.0	4.5	1.3	98.7	0.0
356 ha	1890	594	5.4	90.6	4.0	7.7	92.3	0.0
119 houses	1900	564	3.7	94.3	2.0	5.9	94.1	0.0
Zavallia	1880	219	2.7	93.6	3.7	11.0	89.0	0.0
57 ha	1890	216	0.9	96.8	2.3	0.0	100.0	0.0
45 houses	1900	231	3.5	92.6	2.6	5.6	94.4	0.0
Chortkiv County								
Kryvoluka	1880	562	4.4	91.5	4.1	4.4	91.5	4.1
474 ha	1890	652	3.7	91.6	4.8	1.8	97.2	0.9
122 houses	1900	739	1.8	95.5	2.7	4.7	95.3	0.0

		Total Population	Religious Affiliation (%) RC	GC	Jewish	Language of Usage (%) Polish	Ukrainian	German
Skorodyntsi	1880	947	28.1	67.1	4.9	28.1	67.1	4.9
960 ha	1890	1,095	33.7	63.7	2.6	37.9	60.9	1.2
189 houses	1900	1,271	30.6	65.9	3.5	38.7	60.7	0.6
Zabolotivka	1880	894	26.7	72.4	0.9	26.7	72.4	0.9
706 ha	1890	963	24.5	73.6	1.9	24.2	73.9	1.9
138 houses	1900	1,007	29.5	69.9	0.6	39.6	60.4	0.0
Husiatyn County								
Maidan	1880	596	70.1	25.2	4.7	4.0	96.0	0.0
273 ha	1890	718	69.8	25.8	4.5	4.5	95.5	0.0
138 houses	1900	794	68.0	27.7	4.3	73.0	27.0	0.0
Verkhivtsi	1880	590	33.4	62.0	4.6	36.3	63.7	0.0
463 ha	1890	619	34.2	63.0	2.7	43.5	56.6	0.0
125 houses	1900	634	33.3	64.0	2.9	34.7	65.3	0.0
Zelena	1880	546	1.8	97.4	0.7	1.1	98.9	0.0
166 ha	1890	655	3.1	69.9	0.0	0	100.0	0.0
114 houses	1900	669	0.9	97.3	1.8	2.3	97.9	0.0

		Total	Religious Affiliation (%)			Language of Usage (%)		
		Population	RC	GC	Jewish	Polish	Ukrainian	German
Terebovlia County								
Bernadivka	1880	525	44.7	53.5	1.7	18.3	81.7	0.0
404 ha	1890	591	42.5	55.3	2.2	76.8	23.2	0.0
90 houses	1900	598	46.2	53.2	0.7	55.9	44.1	0.0
Dovhe	1880	952	13.7	85.6	0.7	11.1	88.9	0.0
778 ha	1890	991	24.3	71.4	4.2	28.6	71.4	0.0
194 houses	1900	1,037	16.8	82.0	1.3	9.4	90.6	0.0
Skomorokhy	1880	379	26.4	72.6	1.1	37.5	62.5	0.0
289 ha	1890	464	47.8	48.1	4.1	47.0	53.0	0.0
82 houses	1900	538	28.6	69.5	1.9	28.3	69.9	1.9
Zalishchyky County								
Holihrady	1880	621	1.1	95.0	3.9	4.3	95.6	0.0
405 ha	1890	633	0.8	96.7	2.5	0.8	97.0	2.2
152 houses	1900	676	0.0	96.6	3.4	3.4	96.6	0.0
Rozhanivka	1880	596	30.9	67.1	2.0	31.7	68.3	0.0
322 ha	1890	726	32.4	67.6	0.0	36.5	63.5	0.0
139 houses	1900	827	23.8	76.2	0.0	24.7	75.3	0.0

		Total	Religious Affiliation (%)			Language of Usage (%)		
		Population	RC	GC	Jewish	Polish	Ukrainian	German
Zhezhava	1880	776	1.8	98.2	0.0	4.9	95.1	0.0
582 ha	1890	841	2.4	96.2	1.3	0.0	99.8	0.2
166 houses	1900	890	2.8	96.7	0.4	3.5	96.5	0.0

(d) *Size and Population of Selected Tabular Estates: 1880, 1890, 1900*

			Religious Affiliation (%)			Language of Usage (%)		
		Total Population	RC	GC	Jewish	Polish	Ukrainian	German
Borshchiv County								
Bilche/Monastyrok	1880	234	40.6	48.3	11.1	63.1	36.9	0.0
1,698 ha	1890	292	49.6	45.3	7.2	56.8	43.2	0.0
39 houses	1900	296	54.7	39.9	4.1	74.4	25.6	0.0
Hushtyn	1880	51	43.1	9.8	47.1	88.2	11.8	0.0
460 ha	1890	20	75.0	25.0	0.0	78.9	21.1	0.0
5 houses	1900	29	51.7	34.5	13.8	62.1	37.9	0.0
Lanivtsi	1880	147	19.7	37.4	42.9	55.1	44.9	0.0
1,126 ha	1890	184	32.1	46.2	21.7	44.0	56.0	0.0
25 houses	1900	238	42.0	50.4	7.6	36.1	63.9	0.0
Melnytsia	1880	383	40.5	55.9	3.7	44.2	55.8	0.0
1,587 ha	1890	388	38.1	57.7	4.1	83.3	16.7	0.0
63 houses	1900	332	37.7	56.6	5.4	98.8	1.2	0.0
Mykhalkiv	1880	43	18.6	16.3	65.1	44.2	55.8	0.0
293 ha	1890	29	69.0	24.1	6.9	55.1	24.1	0.0
9 houses	1900	65	27.7	29.2	43.1	67.7	32.3	0.0

		Total	Religious Affiliation (%)			Language of Usage (%)		
		Population	RC	GC	Jewish	Polish	Ukrainian	German
Zavallia	1880	36	33.3	27.8	38.9	78.8	21.2	0.0
380 ha	1890	53	32.1	43.4	24.5	30.2	69.8	0.0
5 houses	1900	18	0.0	22.2	77.7	77.7	22.2	0.0
Chortkiv County								
Bile	1880	146	30.8	42.5	26.0	31.5	42.5	26.0
1,807 ha	1890	216	28.7	40.3	30.6	37.6	57.7	4.7
25 houses	1900	237	32.9	36.7	30.4	67.5	32.5	0.0
Kolyndiany	1880	250	37.6	32.0	30.4	68.0	32.0	0.0
1,291 ha	1890	252	28.2	38.1	33.3	43.3	54.0	2.8
57 houses	1900	255	38.0	49.4	12.5	58.1	41.9	0.0
Skorodyntsi	1880	55	14.5	16.4	69.1	83.6	16.4	0.0
326 ha	1890	76	10.5	5.3	84.2	34.2	15.8	50.0
6 houses	1900	54	33.3	1.9	64.8	56.9	0.0	43.1
Ulashkivtsi	1880	188	50.5	44.7	3.7	52.5	42.5	5.0
792 ha	1890	177	46.9	49.7	3.4	61.0	39.0	0.0
22 houses	1900	178	50.0	42.1	7.9	50.0	50.0	0.0

		Total Population	Religious Affiliation (%) RC	GC	Jewish	Language of Usage (%) Polish	Ukrainian	German
Husiatyn County								
Khorostkiv	1880	224	82.1	16.5	0.0	99.1	0.0	0.9
1,424 ha	1890	194	89.7	7.2	3.1	96.4	1.5	2.1
35 houses	1900	291	69.1	22.7	7.2	86.1	13.2	0.7
Horodnytsia	1880	219	40.2	31.1	27.9	29.7	64.4	5.9
2,019 ha	1890	270	41.9	41.5	16.3	74.3	25.7	0.0
28 houses	1900	213	30.0	28.2	41.8	76.9	23.1	0.0
Hrynkivtsi	1880	51	27.5	21.6	51.0	70.6	29.4	0.0
222 ha	1890	22	27.3	0.0	72.7	100.0	0.0	0.0
3 houses	1900	14	0.0	0	100.0	100.0	0.0	0.0
Sukhostav*	1880	192	60.4	39.6	0.0	61.5	38.5	0.0
65 ha	1890					uninhabited		
0 houses	1900					uninhabited		
Iabluniv	1880	167	61.1	38.9	0.0	64.6	35.4	0.0
3,562 ha**	1890	485	50.7	49.3	0.0	91.2	8.8	0.0
40 houses	1900	507	42.2	55.6	0.0	49.2	50.8	0.0

		Total	Religious Affiliation (%)			Language of Usage (%)		
		Population	RC	GC	Jewish	Polish	Ukrainian	German
Terebovlia County								
Budzaniv	1880	93	58.1	28.0	14.0	72.0	28.0	0.0
1,880 ha	1890	134	41.8	46.3	11.2	59.2	40.8	0.0
23 houses	1900	165	27.9	40.0	32.1	64.2	30.9	4.8
Ianiv	1880	31	29.0	22.6	48.4	87.1	12.9	0.0
664 ha	1890	39	41.0	28.2	30.8	69.2	28.2	2.6
8 houses	1900	64	34.4	15.6	50.0	84.6	15.6	0.0
Laskivtsi	1880	36	38.9	61.1	0.0	58.3	41.7	0.0
1,370 ha	1890	197	43.7	54.3	2.0	32.5	67.5	0.0
30 houses	1900	321	26.5	57.6	16.2	48.3	49.2	2.5
Skomorokhy	1880	32	50.0	37.5	12.5	50.0	50.0	0.0
142 ha	1890	15	20.0	13.3	66.7	100.0	0.0	0.0
5 houses	1900	34	0.0	64.7	35.3	35.3	64.7	0.0
Strusiv	1880	150	49.3	16.0	34.0	49.7	8.7	40.3
2,406 ha	1890	207	45.4	27.5	27.1	67.6	32.4	0.0
33 houses	1900	165***	46.7	20.6	32.7	90.3	10.3	0.6

		Total Population	Religious Affiliation (%)			Language of Usage (%)		
			RC	GC	Jewish	Polish	Ukrainian	German
Zalishchyky County								
Kolodribka	1880	90	11.1	67.8	21.1	55.6	44.4	0.0
787 ha	1890	87	19.5	57.5	20.7	70.0	20.0	10.0
21 houses	1900	41	31.7	43.9	24.4	61.0	39.0	0.0
Synkiv	1880	80	36.3	62.5	0.0	46.3	53.7	0.0
781 ha	1890	73	37.0	32.9	28.8	71.2	28.8	0.0
18 houses	1900	68	22.1	44.1	33.8	47.1	52.9	0.0
Torske	1880	249	58.2	37.8	4.0	54.2	44.8	0.8
1,889 ha	1890	312	42.0	42.9	10.9	52.9	43.9	3.2
48 houses	1900	267	31.1	54.3	14.6	46.8	53.2	0.0
Tovste	1880	39	15.4	43.6	41.0	71.8	28.2	0.0
15 ha	1890	50	38.0	22.0	40.0	40.0	48.0	12.0
4 houses	1900	23	8.7	47.8	43.5	56.5	43.5	0.0
Zhezhava	1880	74	37.8	29.7	31.1	51.4	48.6	0.0
588 ha	1890	105	42.9	20.0	29.5	15.2	45.7	33.3
15 houses	1900	98	11.2	52.0	34.7	56.1	43.9	0.0

Notes:

* The tabular estate of Sukhostav had nine houses in 1880. In 1890 it was classified as "uninhabited, consisting of woodlands/meadows."

** In 1890, the Iabluniv estate had 4,901 hectares, with 38 houses.

*** Excluding the military personnel quartered on the estate.

Appendix II

Average Annual Prices at the Lviv Market, in Austrian Gulden and Kreuzer

	Wheat per hl.	Rye per hl.	Barley per hl.	Oats per hl.	Millet per hl.	Buckwheat per hl.	Peas per hl.	Potatoes per hl.	Cattle per 100 kg (deadweight)	Beef per kg	Bacon/ Side Pork per kg	Butter per kg	Milk per litre	Eggs per 5 dozen	Vodka per litre better quality	Vodka per litre 2nd class
1875	6.09	4.18	3.59	3.13	4.73	5.11	5.82	1.69	47.06	0.46?	0.78	1.13	0.13	1.44	0.36	0.28
1880	8.16	6.52	4.37	3.00	4.82	5.00	6.85	2.50	46.70	0.51	0.85	1.16	0.11	1.42	0.42	0.35
1881	7.78	5.95	3.87	2.76	4.86	4.95	6.17	2.01	46.05	0.50	0.85	1.09	0.11	1.44	0.41	0.34
1882	6.88	4.03	3.35	2.73	4.37	4.43	6.36	1.70	47.42	0.51	0.84	1.11	0.10	1.31	0.42	0.36
1883	6.48	4.42	3.37	2.84	4.93	4.88	6.78	2.21	48.91	0.54	0.80	1.21	0.10	1.49	0.41	0.36
1884	6.47	4.89	4.11	3.03	n/a	4.86	6.74	2.59	49.87	0.56	0.78	1.17	0.11	1.42	0.39	0.35
1885	5.39	3.99	3.48	2.77	n/a	4.69	6.15	2.16	49.72	0.55	0.72	1.03	0.10	1.35	0.36	0.29
1886	5.85	3.87	3.19	2.72	n/a	4.62	5.99	1.57	45.75	0.52	0.70	1.01	0.10	1.36	0.31	0.27
1887	5.66	3.40	2.65	1.99	3.94	3.87	5.07	1.22	44.26	0.52	0.67	0.99	0.09	1.32	0.33	0.27
1888	4.78	3.09	2.67	2.25	6.23	4.41	4.57	1.64	41.94	0.53	0.68	1.03	0.10	1.31	0.42	0.34
1889	5.49	4.20	3.46	2.99	4.63	4.59	5.37	1.51	41.28	0.52	0.68	1.05	0.10	1.31	0.44	0.35
1890	5.77	4.42	3.42	3.06	4.79	4.68	6.60	1.34	43.24	0.53	0.70	1.08	0.11	1.46	0.38	0.32
1891	7.32	5.23	3.71	3.14	5.34	5.11	6.19	2.15	52.39	0.56	0.69	1.11	0.10	1.42	0.41	0.34
1892	6.66	4.88	3.65	2.88	4.12	5.35	6.96	2.14	50.06	0.60	0.71	1.19	0.11	1.50	0.39	0.34
1893	5.77	4.13	3.03	2.95	4.45	4.38	6.40	2.17	49.46	0.65	0.67	1.26	0.11	1.62	0.43	0.37
1894	4.79	3.43	3.04	2.65	4.33	4.47	5.84	1.92	45.19	0.65	0.66	1.31	0.11	1.61	0.49	n/a
1895	5.43	4.19	3.10	2.83	4.29	4.84	5.76	1.75	46.04	0.63	0.70	1.18	0.09	1.56	0.48	n/a
1896	5.55	4.02	2.96	2.82	5.20	4.22	5.34	1.58	46.48	0.59	0.69	1.11	0.09	1.37	0.48	n/a

	Wheat per hl.	Rye per hl.	Barley per hl.	Oats per hl.	Millet per hl.	Buckwheat per hl.	Peas per hl.	Potatoes per hl.	Cattle per 100 kg (deadweight)	Beef per kg	Bacon/ Side Pork per kg	Butter per kg	Milk per litre	Eggs per 5 dozen	Vodka per litre better quality	Vodka per litre 2nd class
1897	6.41	4.31	3.18	3.11	n/a	4.66	5.61	1.29	50.13	0.60	0.68	1.15	0.10	1.37	0.48	n/a
1898	7.25	5.18	3.55	3.62	n/a	5.29	6.45	1.78	48.28	0.63	0.73	1.13	0.10	1.35	0.48	n/a
1899	6.30	4.14	3.27	2.93	n/a	4.63	5.95	1.13	47.19	0.61	0.67	1.08	0.10	1.75	0.47	n/a
1900	5.57	3.92	3.10	2.83	n/a	n/a	7.00	1.60	48.43	0.62	0.67	1.12	0.10	1.50	0.46	n/a

Source: S. Hoszowski, *Ceny we Lwowie w Latach 1701-1914*, tables 60, 61, 62, 66, 67, 68, and 69.

Appendix III
Religious Affiliations in Southern Podillia
(absolute totals and percentages)

	Roman Catholic		Greek Catholic		Jewish		Other	
a) 1880								
Borshchiv	16,876	(17.2)	65,577	(67.0)	15,362	(15.7)	120	(0.1)
Chortkiv	13,039	(22.8)	36,889	(64.4)	7,073	(12.4)	246	(0.4)
Husiatyn	19,293	(34.8)	46,182	(59.4)	12,286	(15.8)	30	
Terebovlia	22,747	(36.0)	32,856	(52.0)	7,286	(11.5)	346	(0.5)
Zalishchyky	8,540	(12.9)	47,616	(71.8)	10,101	(15.2)	100	(0.1)
Total (5 counties)	80,495	(22.2)	229,120	(63.2)	52,108	(14.4)	842	(0.2)
b) 1890								
Borshchiv	17,701	(16.6)	73,367	(68.7)	15,638	(14.6)	49	
Chortkiv	15,939	(24.6)	39,918	(61.7)	8,567	(13.2)	317	(0.5)
Husiatyn	22,521	(25.2)	53,469	(59.8)	13,368	(15.0)	19	
Terebovlia	25,633	(35.7)	38,130	(53.1)	7,963	(11.1)	97	(0.1)
Zalishchyky	9,356	(12.9)	5,2116	(71.8)	10,978	(15.1)	148	(0.2)
Total (5 counties)	91,150	(22.5)	257,000	(63.4)	56,514	(13.9)	639	(0.2)

	Roman Catholic		Greek Catholic		Jewish		Other	
c) 1900								
Borshchiv	19,550	(17.9)	75,324	(69.0)	14,306	(13.1)	40	
Chortkiv	18,010	(25.0)	45,495	(63.2)	8,202	(11.4)	274	(0.4)
Husiatyn	24,649	(26.3)	59,596	(60.3)	12,573	(13.4)	36	
Terebovlia	29,127	(37.7)	39,920	(51.7)	8,036	(10.4)	129	(0.2)
Zalishchyky	10,744	(13.8)	57,211	(73.7)	9,500	(12.2)	183	(0.2)
Total (5 counties)	102,080	(23.7)	277,546	(63.9)	52,617	(12.2)	622	(0.2)

Sources: *Special-Orts-Repertorien*, for 1880 and 1890; *Gemeindelexicon*, for 1900; based on the censuses in these years. In Chortkiv county a German colony of an evangelical denomination at Polivtsi Kolonia accounted for most of the "other"; in Terebovlia and Zalishchyky the "other" in 1900 consisted mainly of members of the military garrisons.

Appendix IV

Expenditures of Local School Districts
in Southern Podillia in 1890, by County, in Gulden

County	New Construction and Renovation	Maintenance and Repair of Buildings	Rental of School Buildings	Heating, Lighting, and Cleaning	Purchase of Equipment	Schoolbooks etc. for the Needy
Borshchiv	5,465	980	209	2,751	356	286
Chortkiv	996	356	104	2,697	225	226
Husiatyn	2,983	749	229	2,413	1,061	333
Terebovlia	1,242	894	360	3,281	326	265
Zalishchyky	1,212	547	1,003	2,318	317	175

County	Subsidies for Teacher Accommodation	Travel Expenses for Religious Instruction	Administrative and other Expenses	Total Expenses other than Teachers' Salaries	Remittances to County School Districts Toward Cost of Teachers' Salaries
Borshchiv	0	63	528	10,638	12,736
Chortkiv	100	0	704	5,408	9,676
Husiatyn	95	8	1,532	9,403	13,829
Terebovlia	235	125	836	7,564	11,239
Zalishchyky	348	242	859	7,021	10,420

Source: *Oesterreichische Statistik*, vol. XLII, no. 1, tables cvii and cviii.

Appendix V

Ukrainian Reading Clubs Established in Southern Podillia up to 1898, With Dates of Foundation

Borshchiv County

Bilche (1885), Borshchiv (? 1895), Boryshkivtsi (1886), Hermakivka (1891), Horoshova (1890), Ivanie Puste (1890), Ivankiv (1898), Kozachchyna (1884), Kudryntsi (1893), Lanivtsi (1884), Mushkativka (1898), Mykhailivka (1889), Nivra (1897), Ozeriany (1884), Panivtsi (1890), Pylypche (1890), Pyshchatyntsi (1895), Sapohiv (1884), Shyshkivtsi (1889), Skala (1884), Skoviatyn (1898), Slobidka Turyletska (1898), Ustia Iepyskopske (1890), Vilkhovets (1893), Volkivtsi n.D. (1890), Volkivtsi n.T. (1894), Zalissia (1890).

Chortkiv County

Bychkivtsi (1894), Chortkiv (?), Davydkivtsi (1895), Mukhavka (1894), Nahirianka (1897), Rosokhach (1890), Uhryn (1894), Ulashkivtsi (1895), Vyhnanka (1898).

Husiatyn County

Bosyry (1897), Chornokintsi Velyki (1898), Horodnytsia (1889), Hovyliv Velykyi (1884), Husiatyn (? 1875), Khlopivka (1884), Khorostkiv (1886), Kopychyntsi (1882), Kotsiubynchyki (1898), Kotsiubyntsi (1890), Kryvenke (1885), Peremyliv (1888), Probizhna (1898), Samolusky (1889), Sukhostav (1898), Tovstenke (1884), Trybukhivtsi (1884), Tseliiv (1884), Vasylkivtsi (1884).

Terebovlia County

Budzaniv (1894), Darakhiv (1885), Derenivka (1898), Hleshchava (1891), Humnyska (1898), Ilavche (1885), Ivanivka (1870), Krovynka (1889), Laskivtsi (1890), Mohylnytsia (1894), Ostrivchyk (1897), Rizdviany (1888), Romanivka (1893), Strusiv (1872), Terebovlia (1882), Verbivtsi (1884), Zazdrist (1889).

Zalishchyky County
Beremiany (1897), Burakivka (1897), Dobrovliany (1897), Dzvyniach (1898), Ivanie Zolote (1897), Kasperivtsi (1898), Kolodribka (1874), Koshylivtsi (1897), Pecharna (1897), Popivtsi (1891), Shchytivtsi (1897), Torske (1898), Tsapivtsi (1897), Ustechko (1897), Zalishchyky stari (1897).

Sources: *Batkivshchyna*; *Chytalnia*; *Hospodar i promyshlennyk*; *Prosveschenie*; *Russkaia rada*; *Svoboda*; and M. Pavlyk, "Pro rusko-ukrainski chytalni," 480, 503, 514, 518, 533.

Note: *Batkivshchyna*, the best source on the establishment of reading clubs, was not available to me for the years prior to 1884 or for 1887 and 1892. It is therefore probable that the above listing is incomplete.

Appendix VI

Proportions of Ploughland Devoted to Different Crops, 1884-99

The designation "Southern Podillia," as used by the Austrian Ministry of Agriculture, applied to the counties of Borshchiv, Chortkiv, Husiatyn, Zalishchyky, and Buchach. It is thus not exactly synonymous with "Southern Podillia" in this study. Terebovlia county was in what the ministry called "North Podillia," together with Skalat, Ternopil, and adjoining counties.

The data in Appendices VI and VII thus do not apply only to Southern Podillia, but they are presented here because they are highly indicative of cultivation patterns and crop yields in the five counties.

Source: *Statistisches Jahrbuch des k.k. Ackerbau-Ministeriums*, 1875-.

(a) *Proportions of Ploughland Devoted to Different Crops, "North Podillia", 1884-1899*

NORTH PODILLIA 1/1000 of "Ploughland"	Wheat	Rye	Barley	Oats	4 Main Grain Crops	Maize	Buckwheat	Millet	7 Main Grain Crops	Potatoes
1884	131	162	114	111	518	14	84	11	627	85
1885	148	133	110	105	496	23	55	15	589	97
1886	154	159	107	110	530	14	52	11	607	81
1887	141	145	118	109	513	13	53	10	589	112
1888	145	134	113	107	499	14	51	11	575	117
1889	97	124	129	115	465	23	58	13	559	105
1890	147	135	114	107	503	14	49	14	580	96
1891	153	148	104	106	511	14	46	8	579	95
1892	145	152	106	112	515	17	46	9	587	87
1893	149	147	113	111	520	16	37	7	580	88
1894	142	137	109	110	498	8	42	7	555	79
1895	143	124	111	125	503	9	55	7	574	76
1896	153	131	107	122	513	10	46	12	581	89
1897	154	131	101	129	515	10	34	4	563	97
1898	152	131	106	128	517	10	31	4	562	94
1899	151	132	103	123	509	5	34	7	555	81

	Cabbage	Flax	Hemp	Rapeseed	Peas/ Lentils	Vetches	Beans	Mixed Fodder	Fodder Beets	Clover	Fallow**
1884	2	1	4	2	----------	56	----------	22	2	47	
1885	5	1	10	3	----------	64	----------	42	3	47	
1886	5	1	7	1	----------	47	----------	37	2	47	164
1887	5	*	7	2	----------	53	----------	35	2	61	134
1888	4	1	7	3	----------	45	----------	37	3	65	142
1889	4	1	10	2	30	11	6	35	3	51	183
1890	6	1	9	4	34	15	7	41	5	57	144
1891	5	1	9	2	38	15	8	32	4	60	153
1892	4	1	8	3	42	19	9	31	4	66	142
1893	2	1	6	3	34	14	6	26	3	61	174
1894	1	2	4	3	41	10	6	17	4	53	223
1895	1	1	3	2	42	9	7	20	5	39	220
1896	3	2	4	4	41	12	10	28	6	55	163
1897	1	1	2	1	35	7	10	23	3	51	207
1898	1	1	3	*	35	7	10	19	3	55	207
1899	1	1	3	1	33	8	9	19	4	54	230

(b) Proportions of Ploughland devoted to different crops, "South Podillia", 1884-1899

SOUTH PODILLIA 1/1000 of "Ploughland"	Wheat	Rye	Barley	Oats	Maize	5 Main Grain Crops	Buck-wheat	Millet	7 Main Grain Crops	Potatoes	Cabbage	Flax	Hemp
1884	150	136	105	90	71	552	45	11	608	93	3	2	10
1885	149	152	118	68	83	570	40	11	621	84	3	2	11
1886	124	141	115	54	86	520	32	3	555	100	2	1	14
1887	130	142	99	63	89	523	30	3	556	103	2	1	14
1888	151	157	100	64	78	550	29	4	583	119	2	2	12
1889	126	140	109	67	102	544	35	4	583	113	4	2	12
1890	146	158	95	57	89	545	33	5	583	116	6	2	16
1891	132	177	92	53	105	559	29	3	591	113	6	1	13
1892	140	144	92	54	97	525	36	4	565	119	5	2	13
1893	132	127	97	62	88	506	33	3	542	120	7	1	13
1894	160	119	91	69	82	521	39	3	563	122	6	*	5
1895	143	96	95	70	82	486	36	3	525	122	5	1	6
1896	151	97	87	68	75	478	32	6	516	125	5	2	5
1897	166	103	89	88	77	523	17	1	541	127	3	2	4
1898	162	103	88	80	75	508	22	2	532	113	4	6	4
1899	157	118	87	69	82	513	24	3	540	119	3	1	5

	Rapeseed	Tobacco	Aniseed/ Fennel	Linseed/ Poppyseed	Other Commercial Crops and	Peas	Lentils	Vetches	Beans	Total Legumes Vegetables	Mixed Fodder	Fodder Beets	Clover	Fallow*
1884	5	3								58	48	5	31	n/a
1885	3	2								36	45	3	31	n/a
1886	3	2								52	46	2	41	179
1887	4	1								57	49	2	49	160
1888	3	2								64	63	2	38	102
1889	3	3				-----25------		23	11	59	52	4	34	128
1890	9	4				-----23------		32	16	71	42	6	49	92
1891	4	4				-----24------		20	11	55	44	6	50	112
1892	5	4				-----26------		18	27	71	50	5	67	88
1893	3	5				-----32------		24	19	75	42	7	65	120
1894	5	6			3	28	5	18	22	73	34	6	71	106
1895	4	6	1	2	3	26	7	14	24	71	37	5	66	144
1896	7	7	2	1	2	33	8	20	22	83	36	5	79	125
1897	2	7	1	2	5	32	2	4	11	49	20	3	63	175
1898	2	7	1	1	5	34	2	5	19	60	17	4	75	176
1899	3	4	1	**	2	24	3	6	14	51	22	5	74	172

Notes: * Beginning in 1893, the designation was changed to "unspecified crops and fallow".
** Less than 1/1000.

Appendix VII

(a) *Yields per Hectare, "North Podillia," 1884-99*

	Wheat	Rye	Barley	Oats	Maize	Buckwheat	Millet	Potatoes	Cabbage	Flax	Hemp	Rapeseed
1884	12.3	15.3	9.8	12.6	3.4	5.8	7.4	96		**3.7**	**7.1**	14.3
1885	14.0	18.1	14.0	16.0	8.8	11.1	14.3	100		**5.2**	**5.4**	19.4
1886	11.9	8.1	9.1	15.4	7.8	8.2	11.6	163		**1.7**	**5.8**	21.0
1887	16.4	16.2	14.8	17.7	2.1	7.2	9.2	154	**99**	**2.0**	**4.8**	26.1
1888	14.0	11.9	9.1	14.1	11.3	10.5	11.0	**117**	**179**	**4.0**	**4.6**	**16.5**
1889	10.6	8.5	7.0	10.6	8.3	8.2	8.4	**99**	**21**	**3.0**	**5.1**	**5.5**
1890	9.1	10.7	9.5	14.9	14.3	5.2	11.1	**142**	**78**	**2.8**	**7.5**	**14**
1891	9.3	7.1	10.6	15.6	12.7	11.4	4.6	**100**	**78**	**5.2**	**5.5**	**11.5**
1892	**10.8**	**9.3**	**9.0**	**8.0**	**12.1**	7.9	11.1	**123**	**127**	**5.0**	**7.8**	**17.3**
1893	**7.5**	**7.2**	**8.3**	8.1	**8.6**	5.7	11.9	**82**	**87**	**5.1**	**6.8**	**5.7**
1894	**10.4**	**9.5**	**9.4**	**8.5**	**5.5**	5.3	7.0	**117**	**108**	**5.4**	**5.9**	**12.8**
1895	**8.8**	**4.7**	**9.6**	**9.0**	**11.4**	11.1	10.4	**121**	**86**	**3.9**	**6.7**	**10.0**
1896	**10.1**	**8.9**	**7.5**	**6.7**	**11.1**	8.8	15.6	**100**	**148**	**3.5**	**7.4**	**15.0**
1897	**7.2**	**8.2**	**6.6**	**6.6**	**8.8**	10.3	11.0	**97**	**112**	**4.1**	**5.6**	**9.6**
1898	**12.0**	**9.4**	**8.2**	**9.4**	**11.7**	13.1	10.0					**11.0**
1899	**12.8**	**10.6**	**8.1**	**9.3**	**11.1**	13.2	13.0	**109**	**93**	**4.0**	**7.0**	**12.0**

	Tobacco	Linseed	Peas	Vetches	Beans	Mixed Fodder	Fodder Beet	Clover Hay	Clover Seed	Meadow Hay	Straw: Regional Total (000s of Metric Centners)
1884	**15.4**		11.0	9.1	11.5	**22.0**	**129**	34	4.0	**25.0**	**4,133**
1885	**9.1**		11.5	12.8	15.9	**28.0**	**136**	42	2.4	**27.0**	**5,679**
1886	**20.1**		12.5	12.9	15.2	**23.0**	**189**	33	1.9	**24.0**	**3,931**
1887	**19.5**		11.4	10.4	12.6	**23.0**	**154**	33	2.4	**24.0**	**4,220**
1888	**36.8**			-----------10.5-----------		**23.0**	**162**	31	**2.2**	**17.0**	**3,844**
1889	**30.1**		8.4	5.9	9.8	**9.0**	**102**	4	**0.2**	**11.0**	**1,961**
1890	**49.9**		10.4	9.8	11.8	**22.0**	**194**	35	**1.8**	**37.5**	**3,898**
1891	**27.3**		10.0	8.7	14.1	**30.5**	**139**	40	**1.7**	**31.0**	**3,659**
1892	**36.7**		12.6	11.8	13.2	**26.0**	**205**	26	**1.7**	**24.0**	**3,765**
1893	**22.9**		7.8	12.4	12.5	**31.0**	**209**	41	**1.7**	**19.0**	**4,246**
1894	**33.2**		13.3	14.2	14.7	**30.0**	**166**	35	**2.1**	**29.0**	**4,062**
1895	**24.0**	**7.0**	12.1	12.2	15.4	**31.0**	**214**	31	**2.2**	**25.0**	**3,076**
1896	**22.3**	**8.5**	13.5	14.4	12.4	**34.0**	**239**	42	**2.7**	**26.0**	**4,014**
1897	**24.9**		10.1	10.2	7.0	**43.0**	**133**	38	**3.2**	**32.0**	**3,717**
1898			14.3	11.4	10.6	**25.0**			**2.5**	**23.0**	**3,432**
1899	**14.7**	**11.0**	11.6	12.6	15.8	**27.0**	**202**	27	**2.7**	**22.0**	**4,020**

(b) *Yields per Hectare, "South Podillia," 1884-99*

	Wheat	Rye	Barley	Oats	Maize	Buckwheat	Millet	Potatoes	Cabbage	Flax	Hemp	Rapeseed	Tobacco
1884	14.2	12.8	9.7	14.7	14.4	7.5	8.8	91		**4.0**	**5.2**	13.7	**14.6**
1885	15.4	15.6	14.0	19.2	12.1	11.2	12.2	118		**3.0**	**4.7**	13.9	**13.3**
1886	13.2	11.2	12.0	20.7	17.6	9.2	10.8	144		**2.0**	**5.1**	22.4	**12.5**
1887	15.9	16.7	15.9	20.7	13.1	8.3	11.7	179	**62**	**2.5**	**5.0**	19.7	**17.8**
1888	14.6	11.7	9.8	11.5	10.3	9.2	10.8	**95**	**152**	**4.3**	**4.4**	**13.2**	**23.1**
1889	7.4	8.3	5.9	9.6	8.5	4.9	5.4	**78**	**13**	**2.0**	**3.0**	**2.4**	**22.2**
1890	11.2	12.9	8.3	15.1	16.8	8.2	12.7	**142**	**91**	**2.7**	**5.0**	**9.6**	**19.6**
1891	8.0	6.5	9.4	13.5	11.0	8.1	8.8	**89**	**87**	**3.4**	**4.8**	**8.2**	**17.1**
1892	**8.4**	**6.2**	**7.3**	**8.8**	**10.1**	7.9	9.7	**111**	**94**	**5.1**	**4.2**	**14.4**	**22.2**
1893	**8.5**	**7.9**	**8.1**	**7.6**	**9.3**	9.7	11.7	**99**	**87**	**4.3**	**4.9**	**5.5**	**15.7**
1894	**10.0**	**8.4**	**9.8**	**9.9**	**7.4**	6.5	6.6	**105**	**66**	**4.9**	**6.3**	**12.9**	**18.3**
1895	**7.7**	**6.0**	**12.6**	**12.0**	**12.3**	9.9	11.3	**136**	**213**	**3.9**	**8.5**	**10.0**	**17.7**
1896	**10.5**	**9.1**	**7.1**	**7.3**	**11.4**	5.0	11.7	**88**	**154**	**3.5**	**6.2**	**15.0**	15.8
1897	**7.0**	**7.7**	**7.6**	**9.2**	**11.1**	9.8	11.4	**101**	**95**	**4.1**	**6.2**	**10.1**	16.0
1898	**11.0**	**9.3**	**7.4**	**8.6**	**10.8**	10.5	10.2	**147**	**161**	**4.0**	**5.7**	**11.0**	**11.0**
1899	**12.0**	**12.0**	**10.0**	**11.1**	**10.8**	12.4	15.5	**124**	**163**	**3.0**	**6.0**	**11.0**	**8.5**

	Aniseed/ Fennel	Linseed	Poppyseed	Peas	Lentils	Vetches	Beans	Mixed Fodder	Fodder Beet	Clover Hay	Clover Seed	Meadow Hay	Straw: Regional Total (000s of Metric Centner)
1884				------12.2------		10.5	12.2	**26**	**141**	**43**	3.4	**30**	**4,137**
1885				------13.8------		15.1	7.8	**20**	**152**	**33**	2.6	**31**	**4,447**
1886				------11.7------		13.3	12.1	**25**	**170**	**38**	2.0	**25**	**4,447**
1887				------14.0------		10.5	13.3	**20**	**170**	**39**	2.6	**26**	**4,346**
1888				--------------11.0------------				**19**	**163**	**37**	**2.7**	**32**	**3,721**
1889				-------5.9------		4.7	7.9	**10**	**90**	**9**	**0.5**	**8**	**2,177**
1890				------11.0------		10.9	9.7	**20**	**136**	**34**	**1.5**	**32**	**4,604**
1891				------11.1------		6.3	14.6	**20**	**126**	**34**	**1.9**	**25**	**3,814**
1892				------10.8------		11.0	14.2	**20**	**160**	**26**	**1.9**	**22**	**3,839**
1893				------13.0------		11.8	14.3	**27**	**244**	**38**	**1.9**	**25**	**5,038**
1894				12.2	11.0	14.1	13.4	**28**	**195**	**42**	**2.1**	**27**	**4,757**
1895	**6.5**	**5.6**	**9.5**	10.4	8.4	13.0	15.7	**34**	**263**	**39**	**1.8**	**24**	**3,739**
1896	**7.8**	**8.5**	**6.0**	12.5	10.0	14.2	9.7	**36**	**175**	**40**	**2.6**	**19**	**3,653**
1897	**n/a**	**n/a**	**n/a**	10.7	9.5	9.6	7.6	**54**	**205**	**34**	**2.9**	**27**	**4,517**
1898	**5.0**	**13.0**	**6.0**	14.9	12.3	11.5	10.7	**33**	**173**	**37**	**2.7**	**20**	**3,832**
1899	**7.0**	**9.0**	**4.3**	12.3	9.4	14.7	15.3	**30**	**243**	**36**	**2.3**	**20**	**3,808**

Note: Bold print denotes metric centner; otherwise yields are expressed in hectoliters. Source: See prefatory note to Appendix VI.

Appendix VIII

Number and Percentage of Farm Animals on "Rustical" and "Tabular" Land on 31 Dec. 1900

	Horses		Cows and Oxen		Pigs		Sheep	
Borshchiv								
Rustical	7,738	(70.8)	17,160	(70.2)	17,597	(88.8)	20,883	(90.8)
Tabular	3,102	(29.2)	7,474	(29.8)	1,996	(10.2)	2,120	(9.2)
Total	10,840		24,634		19,593		23,003	
Chortkiv								
Rustical	8,965	(76.5)	13,704	(75.9)	13,121	(89.4)	5,757	(86.5)
Tabular	2,761	(23.5)	4,429	(24.3)	1,558	(10.6)	906	(13.5)
Total	11,726		18,133		14,679		6,663	
Husiatyn								
Rustical	10,740	(75.6)	18,445	(73.6)	19,173	(87.6)	2,292	(65.3)
Tabular	3,472	(24.4)	6,623	(26.4)	2,712	(12.4)	1,217	(24.7)
Total	14,212		25,068		21,885		3,509	
Terebovlia								
Rustical	10,295	(80.8)	17,346	(77.7)	14,697	(94.0)	1,173	(56.6)
Tabular	2,450	(19.2)	4,966	(22.3)	945	(6.0)	1,361	(43.4)
Total	12,745		22,312		15,642		2,534	

	Horses		Cows and Oxen		Pigs		Sheep	
Zalishchyky								
Rustical	8,781	(76.2)	13,532	(74.6)	11,528	(89.8)	11,192	(85.1)
Tabular	2,750	(23.8)	4,612	(25.4)	1,305	(10.2)	1,954	(14.9)
Total	11,531		18,144		12,833		13,146	

Source: *Gemeindelexicon der im Reichsrate vertrenen Königreiche und Länder*, for 1900, 44-55, 132-7, 216-33, 714-19, 756-65.

Appendix IX

Landholdings by size of Productive Area, with Type and Number of Farm Animals, Grazing and Woodland Rights, and Owners' other Occupations

The special Austrian agricultural census of 1902 compiled a wealth of data on agricultural operations, broken down by size of landholding. Each category had figures on the number and type of farm animals, grazing and woodland rights, and the smallholders' other occupations. Memoir evidence suggests that peasants understated their secondary involvement as craftsmen and artisans. Four categories of peasant landholders are represented in this appendix:

(a) landholdings up to 0.5 ha of productive area
(b) landholdings of 0.5-1.0 ha of productive area
(c) landholdings of 1-2 ha of productive area
(d) landholdings of 2-5 ha of productive area.

The designation "productive land" denoted all usable land, that is, total area of land minus the landholder's house, yard, farm buildings, and waste land. Source: *Oesterrichische Statistik*, LXXXIII (5).

(a) *Landholdings up to 0.5 hectares of "productive area," 1902*

	Borshchiv	Chortkiv	Husiatyn	Terebovlia	Zalishchyky
Number of agricultural operations	751	527	797	697	1,012
Percentage of total agricultural operations	4.8	5.5	6.3	6.1	8.6
Number with grazing rights	297	110	55	197	230
Percentage of agricultural operations in this category	39.5	20.9	6.9	28.3	22.7
Number with woodland rights	53	0	0	52	18
Percentage of agricultural operations in this category	7.1	-	-	7.5	1.8
Number of owners/lessees working as agricultural labourers	514	390	579	391	585
Percentage of owners/lessees in this category	68.4	74.0	72.6	56.1	57.8
Number also working as craftsmen or in industry	3	6	5	24	1
Number engaging in unspecified wage labour	142	28	15	87	42

	Borshchiv	Chortkiv	Husiatyn	Terebovlia	Zalishchyky
Percentage of owners/lessees in this category	18.9	5.3	1.9	12.5	4.2
Number also engaging in domestic industry	39	22	23	28	30
Number also engaging in an "industrial" business*					
Number also engaging in another agricultural business*					
Number owning farm animals	496	344	524	389	558
Percentage of owners/lessees in this category	66.0	65.3	65.7	55.8	55.1
Percentage of all animal owners in the county	3.7	4.0	4.2	3.9	5.8
Number owning horses	22	6	36	12	29
Percentage of owners/lessees in this category	2.9	1.1	3.5	1.7	2.9
Number of horses	31	9	36	13	33
Percentage of all horses in the county	0.3	0.1	0.2	0.1	0.4

	Borshchiv	Chortkiv	Husiatyn	Terebovlia	Zalishchyky
Number owning cattle	297	240	385	306	251
Percentage of owner/lessees in this category	39.5	45.5	48.3	43.9	34.8
Number of cattle	437	338	524	367	317
Percentage of all cattle in the county	1.7	2.0	2.2	1.8	2.2
Number owning sheep	143	20	13	7	208
Percentage of owners/lessees in this category	19.0	3.8	1.6	1.0	20.6
Number of sheep	594	71	41	52	804
Percentage of all sheep in the county	2.1	0.1	0.6	1.5	4.0
Number owning pigs	219	169	277	160	251
Percentage of owners/lessees in this category	29.2	32.1	34.8	23.0	24.8
Number of pigs	367	235	363	209	340
Percentage of all pigs in the county	2.5	2.5	3.4	3.4	4.6

(b) *Landholdings of 0.5-1.0 hectares of "productive area," 1902*

	Borshchiv	Chortkiv	Husiatyn	Terebovlia	Zalishchyky
Number of agricultural operations	3,078	1,396	2,279	1,821	2,322
Percentage of total agricultural operations	19.9	14.5	18.0	15.8	19.8
Number with grazing rights	769	366	205	603	696
Percentage of agricultural operations in this category	25.0	26.2	9.0	33.1	30.0
Number with woodland rights	339	4	0	129	46
Percentage of agricultural operations in this category	11.0	0.3	-	7.1	2.0
Number of owners/lessees working as agricultural labourers	2,103	1,084	1,663	1,020	1,515
Percentage of owners/lessees in this category	68.3	77.7	73.0	56.0	65.2
Number also working as craftsmen or in industry	14	19	10	37	0
Number engaging in unspecified wage labour	441	36	21	249	141

	Borshchiv	Chortkiv	Husiatyn	Terebovlia	Zalishchyky
Percentage of owners/lessees in this category	14.3	2.6	0.9	13.7	6.1
Number also engaging in domestic industry	162	49	76	93	55
Number also engaging in an "industrial" business*					
Number also engaging in another agricultural business*					
Number owning farm animals	2,357	1,085	1,769	1,290	1,560
Percentage of owners/lessees in this category	76.6	77.7	77.6	70.8	67.2
Percentage of all animal owners in the county	17.4	12.5	15.7	12.9	16.2
Number owning horses	223	97	178	128	143
Percentage of owners/lessees in this category	7.2	6.9	7.8	7.0	6.2
Number of horses	282	131	233	152	171
Percentage of all horses in the county	2.5	1.1	1.6	1.3	2.1

	Borshchiv	Chortkiv	Husiatyn	Terebovlia	Zalishchyky
Number owning cattle	1,419	839	1,448	1,093	860
Percentage of owner/lessees in this category	46.1	60.1	63.6	60.0	37.0
Number of cattle	2,171	1,037	2,026	1,412	1,079
Percentage of all cattle in the county	8.6	6.2	8.7	7.1	7.4
Number owning sheep	707	65	31	16	442
Percentage of owners/lessees in this category	23.0	4.7	1.4	0.9	19.0
Number of sheep	2,873	256	106	50	1,895
Percentage of all sheep in the county	10.3	3.3	1.5	1.5	9.4
Number owning pigs	1,076	611	895	492	726
Percentage of owners/lessees in this category	35.0	43.8	39.5	27.0	31.3
Number of pigs	1,678	802	1,210	646	976
Percentage of all pigs in the county	11.3	8.4	11.3	10.5	13.1

(c) *Landholdings of 1-2 hectares of "productive area," 1902*

	Borshchiv	Chortkiv	Husiatyn	Terebovlia	Zalishchyky
Number of agricultural operations	5,296	2,732	3,678	3,190	3,830
Percentage of total agricultural operations	34.3	28.5	29.1	27.7	32.6
Number with grazing rights	1,947	804	346	1,203	1,310
Percentage of agricultural operations in this category	36.8	29.4	9.4	37.7	34.2
Number with woodland rights	146	4	0	200	104
Percentage of agricultural operations in this category	2.8	0.1	-	6.3	2.7
Number of owners/lessees working as agricultural labourers	3,555	1,794	2,214	1,553	2,285
Percentage of owners/lessees in this category	67.1	65.7	60.2	48.7	59.7
Number also working as craftsmen or in industry	19	50	20	45	0
Number engaging in unspecified wage labour	533	147	27	364	255

	Borshchiv	Chortkiv	Husiatyn	Terebovlia	Zalishchyky
Percentage of owners/lessees in this category	10.1	5.4	0.7	11.4	6.7
Number also engaging in domestic industry	187	78	91	138	71
Number also engaging in an "industrial" business*	291	91	151	410	138
Number also engaging in another agricultural business*	45	16	33	39	5
Number owning farm animals	4,623	2,462	3,258	2,699	3,141
Percentage of owners/lessees in this category	87.3	90.1	88.6	84.6	82.0
Percentage of all animal owners in the county	34.1	28.3	28.9	27.1	32.7
Number owning horses	1,154	685	1,035	704	762
Percentage of owners/lessees in this category	21.8	25.1	28.1	22.1	19.9
Number of horses	1,523	879	1,353	850	929

Note: * The numbers given in these two rows are the totals for all in the "below two hectares" category.

	Borshchiv	Chortkiv	Husiatyn	Terebovlia	Zalishchyky
Percentage of all horses in the county	13.7	7.2	9.4	7.1	11.6
Number owning cattle	3,282	2,034	2,851	2,460	1,907
Percentage of owner/lessees in this category	62.0	74.5	77.5	77.1	49.8
Number of cattle	5,588	2,872	4,403	3,481	2,817
Percentage of all cattle in the county	22.0	17.2	18.8	17.5	19.3
Number owning sheep	1,404	220	95	37	1,086
Percentage of owners/lessees in this category	26.5	8.1	2.6	1.2	28.4
Number of sheep	6,653	942	449	164	5,178
Percentage of all sheep in the county	23.8	12.1	6.2	4.8	25.6
Number owning pigs	2,211	1,356	1,594	944	1,481
Percentage of owners/lessees in this category	41.7	49.6	43.3	29.6	38.7
Number of pigs	3,836	2,040	2,335	1,259	1,712
Percentage of all pigs in the county	25.8	21.5	21.8	20.4	23.0

(d) *Landholdings of 2-5 hectares of "productive area," 1902*

	Borshchiv	Chortkiv	Husiatyn	Terebovlia	Zalishchyky
Number of agricultural operations	5,079	3,621	4,396	4,051	3,673
Percentage of total agricultural operations	32.9	37.7	34.7	35.2	31.3
Number with grazing rights	2,091	1,257	389	1,772	1,427
Percentage of agricultural operations in this category	41.2	34.7	8.9	43.7	38.9
Number with woodland rights	131	1	0	245	216
Percentage of agricultural operations in this category	2.6	n/a	-	6.0	5.9
Number of owners/lessees working as agricultural labourers	2,251	1,637	1,566	1,322	1,500
Percentage of owners/lessees in this category	44.3	45.2	35.6	32.6	40.8
Number also working as craftsmen or in industry	10	32	11	49	1
Number engaging in unspecified wage labour	344	138	11	244	225

	Borshchiv	Chortkiv	Husiatyn	Terebovlia	Zalishchyky
Percentage of owners/lessees in this category	6.8	3.8	0.3	6.0	6.1
Number also engaging in domestic industry	146	40	59	89	44
Number also engaging in an "industrial" business	127	46	61	162	82
Number also engaging in another agricultural business	11	23	15	37	15
Number owning farm animals	4,878	3,500	4,250	3,869	3,470
Percentage of owners/lessees in this category	96.0	96.7	96.7	95.5	94.5
Percentage of all animal owners in the county	36.0	40.3	37.7	38.8	36.1
Number owning horses	2,564	2,466	3,208	2,913	1,834
Percentage of owners/lessees in this category	50.5	68.1	73.0	71.9	49.9
Number of horses	4,053	5,279	5,351	4,606	2,673
Percentage of all horses in the county	36.9	43.3	37.1	38.6	33.4

	Borshchiv	Chortkiv	Husiatyn	Terebovlia	Zalishchyky
Number owning cattle	4,035	3,145	3,951	3,617	2,635
Percentage of owner/lessees in this category	79.4	86.9	89.9	89.3	71.7
Number of cattle	8,737	5,627	7,443	6,149	4,664
Percentage of all cattle in the county	34.5	33.8	31.8	31.0	32.0
Number owning sheep	1,775	534	167	88	1,290
Percentage of owners/lessees in this category	34.9	14.7	3.8	2.2	35.1
Number of sheep	10,611	2,780	832	392	7,245
Percentage of all sheep in the county	37.9	35.8	11.6	11.4	35.9
Number owning pigs	2,718	2,180	2,373	1,560	1,829
Percentage of owners/lessees in this category	53.5	60.2	54.0	38.5	49.8
Number of pigs	5,812	3,750	3,895	2,194	2,837
Percentage of all pigs in the county	39.2	39.5	36.3	35.5	38.1

Appendix X

Deaths from Smallpox and Cholera and Total Deaths, Southern Podillia, 1880-1900

	1880	1881	1882	1883	1884	1885	1886	1887	1888	1889	1890
a) Smallpox											
Borshchiv	7	56	605	405	82	4	0	15	18	23	37
Chortkiv	18	9	65	4	41	0	1	12	54	65	7
Husiatyn	0	9	104	54	22	3	1	31	135	76	29
Terebovlia	2	10	35	35	22	5	0	85	350	24	0
Zalishchyky	11	363	244	143	49	18	5	6	27	244	42
b) Cholera											
Borshchiv	3	0	0	0	0	6	0	4	5	1	0
Chortkiv	12	16	13	3	10	6	8	0	0	0	0
Husiatyn	0	0	0	0	0	0	0	0	0	0	0
Terebovlia	0	0	0	0	10	1	0	0	0	0	0
Zalishchyky	3	1	0	0	1	3	0	0	1	0	0
c) Total deaths (excluding suicides and deaths due to injuries)											
Borshchiv	3,466	3,401	3,974	3,916	3,720	3,097	2,967	3,387	3,346	2,936	3,934
Chortkiv	2,243	1,951	2,229	2,325	2,683	2,204	2,059	2,422	2,237	2,251	2,295
Husiatyn	2,830	2,405	2,723	2,765	3,134	2,469	2,353	2,800	2,825	2,855	2,669
Terebovlia	2,056	2,229	2,190	2,649	2,733	2,124	2,377	2,525	2,407	2,282	2,363
Zalishchyky	3,024	3,109	3,218	2,941	2,982	3,006	2,794	2,624	2,695	2,742	2,474
Total	13,619	13,095	14,334	14,596	15,252	12,900	12,520	13,758	13,510	13,066	13,735

	1891	1892	1893	1894	1895	1896	1897	1898	1899	1900
a) Smallpox										
Borshchiv	1	7	1	1	n/a	36	15	136	155	21
Chortkiv	3	4	1	1		1	9	12	7	0
Husiatyn	4	2	5	5		0	46	61	40	10
Terebovlia	0	0	0	0		8	12	57	23	4
Zalishchyky	0	0	1	0		2	27	24	29	0
b) Cholera										
Borshchiv	0	9	40	700	n/a	0	0	0	0	0
Chortkiv	0	0	12	357		0	0	0	0	0
Husiatyn	0	22	2	377		0	0	0	0	0
Terebovlia	0	0	0	109		0	0	0	0	0
Zalishchyky	0	0	1	749		0	0	0	0	0
c) Total deaths (excluding suicides and deaths due to injuries)										
Borshchiv	2,904	3,956	3,146	3,943	3,512	3,208	2,975	3,507	3,167	2,859
Chortkiv	1,972	2,474	1,892	2,109	2,311	1,934	1,771	2,200	2,018	1,901
Husiatyn	2,574	3,122	2,216	2,604	3,035	2,383	2,284	2,196	3,115	2,503
Terebovlia	2,392	2,686	2,023	2,181	2,528	2,077	1,804	1,808	2,230	2,294
Zalishchyky	2,485	2,544	2,466	3,034	3,193	2,168	2,272	2,608	2,491	2,052
Total	12,327	14,782	11,743	13,871	14,579	11,770	11,105	12,319	13,021	11,609

Sources: *Oesterreichische Statistik*, vols. III(1), V(2), VIII(3), XII(4), XIII(3), XVIII(4), XXI(4), XXII(3), XXVIII(2), XXXI(4), XXXVII(2), XXXVIII(2), XL(2), XLIV(3), XLVIII(3), LII(2), LIV(1), LV(3), LXVII(1).

BIBLIOGRAPHY

Primary Sources

Archival Sources

AUSTRIA

The files cited here were transferred to Poland by Austria after World War I and are now in Archiwum Główne Akt Dawnych, Warsaw (AGAD).

Handels-Ministerium

HG 1 "Einschränkungen des Vieh- und Fleisch-Transport, 1888-1896"

Ministerium des Innern

B 9 "Bau der Strassen u. Chausseen 1888-89"

B 10 "Karpaten Routen 1890-92"

B 11 "Bau der Strassen u. Chausseen 1893-5"

B 50 "Brückenbau 1888-93"

V 6 "Viehtransport 1889"

Government Publications

1. AUSTRIA

Reichsgesetzblatt

Ackerbau-Ministerium

Bericht über das oesterreichische Veterinarwesen für das Jahr 1902. Vienna, 1908.

Statistisches Jahrbuch des k.k. Ackerbau-Ministeriums. Vienna, 1875ff.

Eisenbahn-Ministerium

Statistik der in den im Reichsrat vertretenen Königreiche und Länder im Betriebe gestandenen Lokomotiveisenbahnen, vol. V. Vienna, 1902.

Verordnungsblatt für Eisenbahnen und Schiffahrt. Vienna, 1896ff.

Finanz-Ministerium

Mittheilungen des k.k. Finanz-Ministeriums. Vienna, 1895ff.

Statistisches Jahrbuch über die direkten Steuern im Jahre 1887.

Handels-Ministerium

Verordnungsblatt des k.k. Handels-Ministerium für Eisenbahnen und Schiffahrt. Vienna, 1878-96.

Militär-geografisches Institut

Galizien (map 1:228,000). Vienna, 1872.

Statistische Central-Commission

Gemeindelexicon der im Reichsrate vertretenen Königreiche und Länder, vol. XII: *Galizien*. Vienna, 1906 (for 1900).

Oesterreichische Statistik. Vienna, 1880ff.

Oesterreichisches statistisches Handbuch. Vienna, 1882ff.

Orts-Repertorium des Königreiches Galizien und Lodomerien mit dem Grossherzogthume Krakau. Vienna, 1874 (for 1869).

Schematismus der allgemeinen Volksschulen und Bürgerschulen in den im Reichsrathe vertretenen Königreichen und Ländern. Vienna, 1891 (for 1890). Vienna, 1902 (for 1900).

Special-Orts-Repertorien der im oesterreichischen Reichsrathe vertretenen Königreiche und Länder, vol. XII: *Galizien*. Vienna, 1886 (for 1880). Vienna, 1893 (for 1890).

Statistisches Jahrbuch der autonomen Landesverwaltung. Vienna, 1900 ff.

2. CANADA

Department of the Interior

"Report of Inspector of Agencies in Europe." *Sessional Papers*, nos. 13 (1900), 25 (1901), 26 (1902).

3. GALICIA

Krajowe Biuro Statystyczne

Podręcznik statystyki Galicyi. Lviv, 1900-13.

Rocznik statystyki Galicyi. Lviv, 1887-98.

Wiadomości statystyczne o stosunkach krajowych. Lviv, 1873-1917.

Sejm

Stenograficzne sprawozdanie sejmu krajowego Królewstwa Galicyi i Lodomeryi z Wielkiem Księstwem Krakowskiem. Lviv, 1861-1914.

4. GREAT BRITAIN

Board of Education, *Report on Technical and Commercial Education in East Prussia, Poland, Galicia, Silesia and Bohemia*, Cd. 419. London, 1900.

Report of the Royal Commission on Alien Immigration, Cd. 1741. London, 1903.

Royal Commission on Labour. *Foreign Reports.* Vol. XI: *Austria-Hungary and the Balkan States*. London, 1893 (by G. Drage).

5. UNITED STATES OF AMERICA

52nd Congress, 1st Session. *Special Consular Reports on Streets and Highways in Foreign Countries. House Misc. Docs.*, No. 20. Washington, 1892.

Department of the Interior. Bureau of Education. Bulletin 54, "The Schools of Austria-Hungary." Washington, 1919.

Contemporary Newspapers and Periodicals (with publication dates)

Ukrainian

Batkivshchyna. Lviv, 1879-96.

Chytalnia. Lviv, 1893-96.

Dilo. Lviv, 1880-1918, 1922-39.

Halychanyn. Lviv, 1893-1913.

Hospodar. Peremyshl, 1898-1913.

Hospodar i promyshlennyk. Stanyslaviv, Lviv, 1879-87.

Hromadskyi holos. Lviv, 1892-1914, 1922-39.

Kalendar Misionara. Zhovkva, 1913.

Khliborob. Lviv, Kolomyia, 1891-4.

Lastivka. Lviv, 1869-81.

Literaturno-naukovyi vistnyk. Lviv, Kiev, 1898-1914, 1917-9, 1922-32.

Narod. Lviv, Kolomyia, 1890-5.

Nauka. Kolomyia, Lviv, Vienna, Chernivtsi, 1871-99, 1902-14, 1924-39.

Novost. Lviv, 1881-3.

Pravda. Lviv, 1867-80, 1884, 1888-96.

Priiatel ditei. Lviv, 1881-2.

Prolom. Lviv, 1880-2.

Prosveshchenie. Vienna, 1893-1902.

Russkaia rada. Kolomyia, 1871-1912.

Svoboda. Lviv, 1896-1919.

Uchytel. Lviv, 1889-1914.

Viche. Lviv, 1880-2.

Zapysky Naukovoho tovarystva imeny Shevchenka. Lviv, 1892-1937.

German and Polish

Parlamentar. Vienna, 1880ff.

Przegląd polski. Cracow, 1884-1936.

Ruthenische Revue. Vienna, 1903-5.

Statistische Monatschrift. Vienna, 1875ff.

Ukrainische Rundschau. Vienna, 1906-17.

Books and Articles

Anczyc, S. *O przemyśle tkackim w Galicyi*. Cracow, 1903.

Atkinson, D. "Society and the Sexes in the Russian Past." In *Women in Russia*, edited by D. Atkinson, A. Dallin, and G.A. Lapidus. Stanford, 1977.

Bachinger, K. "Das Verkehrswesen." In *Die Habsburgermonarchie*, edited by Wandruszka and Urbanitsch. Vol. I.

Badeni, S.H. "Schulpflicht und Schulbesuch in Oesterreich." *Statistische Monatschrift* XXVI.

Baranowski, M. *Pogląd na rozwój szkolnictwa ludowego w Galicyi od 1772 do 1895 roku*. Cracow, 1897.

Bartel, W. "Zur Geschichte des Galizischen Landesschulrates, 1867-1918." *Anzeiger der phil.-hist. Klasse der Oesterreichischer Akademie der Wissenschaften* 114. Vienna, 1977.

Batowski, H. "Die Polen." In *Die Habsburgermonarchie*, edited by Wandruszka and Urbanitsch, vol. III: 1.

Batschynskyj, W. "Das ukrainische Schulwesen in Galizien." *Ukrainische Rundschau*, no. 2 (1909).

Benedikt, H. *Die wirtschaftliche Entwicklung in der Franz-Jozefzeit*. Vienna, 1958.

Berend, I.T. and G. Ranki. *Economic Development in East-Central Europe in the 19th and 20th Centuries*. New York, 1974.

"Bericht über die Tätigkeit des statistischen Seminares und der anschliessenden statistischen Übungen an der Universität Wien im Wintersemester 1899-1900." *Statistische Monatschrift* XXVI.

Biegeleisen, L.W. *Rozwój gospodarczy nowoczesnej wsi Polskiej*. Cracow, 1916.

Bihl, W. "Die Ruthenen." In *Die Habsburgermonarchie*, edited by Wandruszka and Urbanitsch, Vol. III: 1.

Bilash, R. "Ukrainian Material Culture Change in East Central Alberta until 1930." Paper presented at the Canadian Association of Slavists, Guelph, Ontario, 5 June 1984.

Bilinski, L. von. "Das Verkehrswesen." In *Oesterreichisch-ungarische Monarchie in Wort und Bild*, 19.

Bilous, M. *Russkoe vesilie pislia zvychaiv i obychaiv narodnykh nad Prutom i na Podoliu*. Kolomyia, 1909.

Birnboim, A. *From My Father's House* (in Yiddish). Jerusalem, 1960.

Blanning, T.C.W. *Joseph II and Enlightened Despotism*. New York, 1970.

Bobińska, C. and A. Pilch. "Employment-Seeking Emigrations of the Poles World-Wide XIX and XX C." *Zeszyty naukowe*, Uniwersytetu Jagiellońskiego, Prace Polonijne, Zeszyt I. 1975.

Bogardus, E.S. "Measuring Social Distance." *Journal of Applied Sociology* 9 (1925).

Borovsky, M. *Materiialy do bibliohrafii hospodarskoi literatury vydanoi v Halychyni, na Volyni, Zakarpatti i Bukovyni*. Winnipeg, 1968.

Bratassević, E. "Die Bewegung im Stande der Sanitätspersonen in den letzten 40 Jahren." *Statistische Monatschrift* XXIX.

_____. "Die Infektionskrankheiten in Oesterreich während des letzten Decenniums 1890-1899." *Statistische Monatschrift* XXVIIII.

_____. "Die Sterblichkeit in den grösseren Städten Oesterreichs im Jahre 1893." *Statistische Monatschrift* XX.

_____. "Die Sterblichkeit in den im Reichsrat vertretenen Ländern im Jahre 1894." *Statistische Monatschrift* XXI.

_____. "Vergleichende Statistik der wichtigsten Todesursachen während der Jahre 1873-1890 in den im Reichsrat vertretenen Ländern." *Statistische Monatschrift* XIX.

Brix, E. *Die Umgangssprachen in Altösterreich zwischen Agitation und Assimilation.* Vienna, 1982.

Brock, P. "Ivan Vahylevych (1811-1866) and the Ukrainian National Identity."In *Nationbuilding*, edited by Markovits and Sysyn.

Brownlow, M.E. *Herbs and the Fragrant Garden.* 2d ed. London, 1963.

Bryk, I., and M. Kotsiuba, eds. *Pershyi Ukrainskyi prosvitno-ekonomichnyi konhres v 40-littia T-va "Prosvity."* Lviv, 1910.

Budzynovsky, V. *Khlopska posilist.* Lviv, 1901.

Bujak, F. "Budżet chłopa." *Ekonomista*, no. 2 (1902).

_____. *Galicya,* 2 vols. Lviv, 1908-10.

_____. "Rozwój gospodarczy Galicji (1772-1914)." In *Studja historyczne i społeczne.* Lviv, 1924.

_____. "Wieś zachodnio-Galicyjska u schyłku XIX wieku." In *Wybór pism*, vol. II (1976).

Buszko, J. "Zum Wandel der Gesellschaftstruktur in Galizien und in der Bukowina." In Oesterreichische Akademie der Wissenschaften, philosophisch-historische Klasse, *Sitzungsberichte*, 343. Vienna, 1978.

Bużek, J. "Das Auswanderungsproblem und die Regelung des Auswanderungswesen in Oesterreich." In *Zeitschrift für Volkswirtschaft, Sozialpolitik und Verwaltung* 10 (1901).

_____. "Der Einfluss der Ernten, respective der Getreidepreise auf die Bevölkerungsbewegung in Galizien in den Jahren 1878-1898." *Statistische Monatschrift* XXVII.

_____. *Studya z zakresu administracyi i wychowania publicznego*: I, *Szkolnictwo ludowe.* Lviv, 1904.

_____. "Własność tabularna w Galicyi według stanu z końcem roku 1902." In *Wiadomości statystyczne o stosunkach krajowych* XX: iii.

Caro, L. *Auswanderung und Auswanderungspolitik in Oesterreich.* Leipzig, 1909.

_____. "Lichwa na wsi w Galicyi w latach 1875-1891." In *Studya społeczne*, edited by L. Caro, 2d ed. Cracow, 1908.

Chmelar, H. "The Austrian Emigration, 1900-1914." *Perspectives in American History* 7 (1973).

Chyzhov, M.P. *Ukrainskyi lisostep*. Kiev, 1961.

Cooper, J. "Ukrainian Cookery," unpublished manuscript, Dauphin, 1982.

Crankshaw, E. *The Fall of the House of Habsburg*. London, 1970.

Cras, N.S.B. *A History of Agriculture in Europe and America*. New York, 1925.

Cwiklinski, L., ed. *Wirtschaftliche Zustände Galiziens in der Gegenwart*. Vienna and Leipzig, 1913.

Cybulski, N. *Próba badań nad żywieniem się ludu wiejskiego w Galicyi*. Cracow, 1894.

Czołowski, B. "Urzędnicy galicyjskich wydziałów powiatowych w 1894." *Wiadomości statystyczne o stosunkach krajowych* XV: 1.

Czumer, W. *Recollections About the Life of the First Ukrainian Settlers in Canada*. Edmonton, 1981.

Daszyńska-Golińska, Z. "Neuere Literatur über galizisches Agrarwesen." *Archiv für Sozialwissenschaft und Sozialpolitik* 20 (1904).

_____. *Własność rolna w Galicyi*. Warsaw, 1900.

Dawidowa, J. *Kółka rolnicze w Galicyi*. Warsaw, 1890.

Dinklage, K. "Die landwirtschaftliche Entwicklung." In *Die Habsburgermonarchie*, edited by Wandruszka and Urbanitsch, I.

Doroshenko, D. *A Survey of Ukrainian History*. Edited by O. Gerus. Revised ed. Winnipeg, 1975.

Drazniowsky, R. "Galizien unter oesterreichischer und polnischer Herrschaft: kulturpolitische und wirtschaftliche Entwicklung der Ukrainer," Ph.D. dissertation, University of Innsbruck, 1957.

Dubrav, K. von. "Die Organisation des Sanitätsdienstes in Oesterreich." In *Sociale Verwaltung in Oesterreich am Ende des 19. Jahrhunderts*, edited by P.E. von Phillipsberg. vol. II. Vienna, 1900.

Dudykevych, V. *Iak prokhodyly vybory v zakhidnii Ukraini za chasiv Avstrii ta panskoi Polshchi*. 1946.

Dulczewski, Z. *Walka o szkole na wsi Galicyjskiej.* Warsaw, 1953.

Dumont, René. "Agriculture as Man's Transformation of the Rural Environment." In *Peasants and Peasant Societies: Selected Readings*, edited by T. Shanin. Harmondsworth, 1975.

Dunin-Wąsowicz, K. *Czasopiśmiennictwo ludowe w Galicji.* Wrocław, 1952.

Ehrenberger, H. "Oesterreichs Sparkassen im Jahre 1897." *Statistische Monatschrift* XXV.

Eisenbahn-Schematismus für Oesterreich-Ungarn. Vienna, 1874ff.

Englisch, K. von. "Die oesterreichische Auswanderungsstatistik." *Statistische Monatschrift* XXXIX.

Entsiklopedicheskii slovar. Edited by F. A. Brokhaus and I. A. Efron. Vol. XIV A. St. Petersburg, 1895.

Estreicher, S. "Galicia in the Period of Autonomy and Self-Government." In *The Cambridge History of Poland*, vol. II, edited by W.F. Reddaway et al.

Ewanchuk, M. *Spruce, Swamp and Stone: A History of the Pioneer Ukrainian Settlements in the Gimli Area.* Steinbach, 1977.

Falski, N. ed. *S. Sempołowska: Pisma pedagogiczne i oświatowe.* Warsaw, 1960.

Feldman, W. *Stronnictwa i programy polityczne w Galicyi, 1846-1906*, vol. 2. Cracow, 1907.

Franklin, S.H. *The European Peasantry.* London, 1969.

Franko, Ivan. "Emihratsiini ahenty v Halychyni." In *Tvory: filosofski, ekonomichni ta istorychni statti* 19. Kiev, 1956.

_____. "Emihratsiia halytskykh selian." In *Tvory: filosofski, ekonomichni ta istorychni statti* 19. Kiev, 1956.

_____. "Zemelna vlastnist u Halychyni," in *Tvory: filosofski, ekonomichni ta istorychni statti* 19. Kiev, 1956.

Geograficheskii atlas dlia uchitelei srednei shkoly. Moscow, 1967.

Geschichte der Österreichischen Land- und Forstwirtschaft und ihrer Industrien, 1848-1898. Vienna, 1899.

Głuchowski, K. *Wśród pionerów polskich na Antypodach: materiały do problemy osadnictwa polskiego w Brazylii.* Warsaw, 1927.

Gorski, A. von. "Das Marktwesen." In *Geschichte der Österreichischen Land- und Forstwirtschaft* I.

Greene, V.M. "Soap leads march toward longer life, scientist says." *Winnipeg Free Press*, 21 Feb. 1984.

Groniowski, K. "Emihratsiia z Halychyny." *Ukrainske slovianoznavstvo*, no. 4 (1971).

_____. *Polska emigracya zarobkowa w Brazylii 1871-1914.* Warsaw, 1972.

Gruiński, S. *Materiały do kwestyi żydowskiej w Galicyi.* Lviv, 1910.

Grzybowski, K. *Galicja 1848-1914: historia ustroju politycznego na tle historii ustroju Austrii.* Cracow, 1959.

Gurnicz, A. *Kółka rolnicze w Galicji.* Warsaw, 1967.

Habakkuk, H.J., and M. Postan, eds. *The Cambridge Economic History of Europe.* Vol. II. Cambridge, 1965.

Havrysh, V. *Moia Kanada i ia: spohady i rozpovidi pro ukrainskykh pioneriv u Kanadi.* Edmonton, 1974.

Hellbling, E.C. "Die Landesverwaltung in Cisleithanien." In *Die Habsburgermonarchie*, edited by Wandruszka and Urbanitsch. Vol. II.

Herasymenko, M.P. *Ahrarni vidnosyny v periodi kryzy panshchynnoho hospodarstva.* Kiev, 1959.

Hempel, K. "Ekonomiczne stosunki Galicyi: stosunki większej własności ziemskiej w Galicyi." *Wiadomości statystyczne o stosunkach krajowych* VII: ii.

Himka, J.-P. "The Background to Emigration: Ukrainians of Galicia and Bukovyna, 1848-1914." In *A Heritage in Transition: Essays in the History of Ukrainians in Canada*, edited by M.R. Lupul. Toronto, 1982.

_____. "The Greek Catholic Church and Nationbuilding in Galicia." *Harvard Ukrainian Studies* VIII, nos. 3/4.

_____. "Hope in the Tsar: Displaced Naive Monarchism Among the Ukrainian Peasants of the Habsburg Empire." *Russian History* 7: 1-2.

_____. "Polish and Ukrainian Socialism: Austria, 1867-1890." Ph.D dissertation, University of Michigan, 1977.

_____. "Priests and Peasants: The Greek Catholic Pastor and the Ukrainian National Movement in Austria, 1867-1900." *Canadian Slavonic Papers* XXI, no. 1.

_____. *Socialism in Galicia: The Emergence of Polish Social Democracy and Ukrainian Radicalism (1860-1890).* Cambridge, Mass., 1983.

Hoffman, W., ed. *Taschenbuch für den oesterreich. Eisenbahn-Betriebs-Beamten für das Jahr 1896.* Vienna, 1895.

Hohenbruck, A. von. "Die Verteilung der Gesammtflache Oesterreichs zwischen Gross- und Kleingrundbezitz." *Statistische Monatschrift* XXVI.

Horn, P. *The Rural World 1750-1850: Social Change in the English Countryside.* London, 1980.

Hoszowski, S. *Ceny we Lwowie w latach 1701-1914.* Warsaw, 1934.

Hrushevsky, M. *A History of Ukraine.* Edited by O. Fredrickson. New York, 1970.

Hryniuk, S.M. "Peasant Agriculture in East Galicia in the Late Nineteenth Century." *Slavonic and East European Review* 63, no. 2 (April 1985).

_____. "The Peasant and Alcohol in Eastern Galicia in the Late Nineteenth Century: A Note." *Journal of Ukrainian Studies* 20.

_____. "A Peasant Society in Transition: Ukrainian Peasants in Five East Galician Counties 1880-1900." Ph.D. dissertation, University of Manitoba, 1985.

_____, and Yereniuk, R. "The Ukrainian Experience." In *Visions of the New Jerusalem: Religious Settlement on the Prairies,* edited by B. Smillie. Edmonton, 1983.

Humeniuk, P. *Hardships and Progress of Ukrainian Pioneers: Memoirs From Stuartburn Colony and Other Points.* Steinbach, 1974.

Iasinchuk, L. *50 lit Ridnoi Shkoly, 1881-1931.* Lviv, 1931.

Ihnatiienko, V. *Bibliohrafiia ukrainskoi presy 1816-1916.* Kharkiv, 1930. Reprinted, W. Luciw, ed., at State College, Pa., 1968.

Ilarion, Metropolitan. *Ukrainska tserkva za chas ruiny (1657-1687).* Winnipeg, 1956.

Iliustrovanyi kaliendar tovarystva "Prosvita" 1886. Lviv, 1886.

Inama-Sternegg, K.R. von. "Die landwirtschaftlichen Arbeiter und deren Löhne in den im Reichsrathe vertretenen Ländern." *Statistische Monatschrift* XXI.

Inglot, S. et al., eds. *Historia chłopów Polskich.* Vol. II: *Okres zaborów.* Warsaw, 1972.

Istoriia selianstva Ukrainskoi RSR. Kiev, 1967.

Istorychno-memuarnyi zbirnyk Chortkivskoi okruhy. Ukrainskyi arkhiv, XXVI. New York, 1974.

Iudenych, P. *Po richkakh Ukrainy.* Kiev, 1968.

Jasiński, K. "Obszary uprawione pod poszczególne płody rolnicze na własności tabularnej w 1896-7." *Wiadomości statystyczne o stosunkach krajowych* XVI: iii.

Jasny, N. *Competition Among Grains.* Stanford, 1940.

_____. *The Socialized Agriculture of the USSR.* Stanford, 1949.

Kann, R. A. *The Multinational Empire*, 2 vols., New York, 1970.

V. J. Kaye. *Early Ukrainian Settlements in Canada, 1895-1900: Dr. Josef Oleskow's Role in the Settlement of the Canadian Northwest.* Toronto, 1964.

_____. (V. J. Kaye-Kysilevsky). "The Descendants of the Boyars of Halych on the Prairies of the Canadian West," in A. Baran et al., eds., *The Jubilee Collection of the Ukrainian Free Academy of Sciences.* Winnipeg, 1976.

Kellner, L., P. Arnold and A. L. Delisle. *Austria of the Austrians and Hungary of the Hungarians.* London, 1914.

Kent-Jones, D. W. and A. J. Amos, *Modern Cereal Chemistry.* London, 1967.

Kerblay, B. "Chayanov and the Theory of Peasantry as a Specific Type of Economy." In *Peasants and Peasant Societies: Selected Readings*, edited by T. Shanin. Harmondsworth, 1975.

_____. *Modern Soviet Society.* New York, 1983.

Keywan, Z., and M. Coles. *Greater than Kings: Ukrainian Pioneer Settlements in Canada.* Quebec, 1977.

Kieniewicz, S. *Adam Sapieha 1823-1903.* Lviv, 1939.

_____. *The Emancipation of the Polish Peasantry.* Chicago, 1969.

_____. *Galicja w dobie autonomicznej 1850-1914, wybór tekstów*. Wrocław, 1952.

Killiches, A. *Statistik des Sanitätswesens nach den für das Jahr 1873 vorgelegten Berichten*. Vienna, 1877.

Kiniorski, M. "Większa i mniejsza własność ziemska wobec parcelacyi." *Ekonomista*, no. 1, 1903.

Kiriak, I. *Sons of the Soil*. Winnipeg, 1983.

Klabouch, J. "Die Lokalverwaltung in Cisleithanien." In *Die Habsburgermonarchie*, edited by Wandruszka and Urbanitsch, vol. II.

Kleczyński, J. "Ekonomiczne stosunki Galicyi: stosunki włościańskie w Galicyi." In *Wiadomości statystyczne o stosunkach krajowych*, Lviv, VII, pt. i.

_____. "Życie gminne w Galicyi." In *Wiadomości statystyczne o stosunkach krajowych* IV.

Kobrynska, N. "Ruske zhinotstvo v Halychyni v nashykh chasakh." In *Pershyi vinok*. Lviv, 1884.

Koenig, S. "The Ukrainians of East Galicia," Ph.D. dissertation, Yale University, 1935.

Kolberg, O. "Ruś Czerwona." In *Dzieła wszystkie*, vol. 56. Wrocław, 1956.

Kolossa, T. "The Social Structure of the Peasant Class in Austria-Hungary: Statistical Sources and Methods of Research." *East European Quarterly*, vol. III, no. 4.

Konta, I. "Geschichte der Eisenbahnen Oesterreichs." In *Geschichte der Eisenbahnen der Oesterreichisch-ungarischen Monarchie*, edited by I. Konta, vol. I, pt. ii. Vienna, 1898.

_____. *Eisenbahn-Jahrbuch der oesterreichisch-ungarischen Monarchie* XXI, Vienna, 1892.

Kowalczyk, S., et al., eds. *Zarys historii polskiego ruchu ludowego*, vol. I, *1864-1918*. Warsaw, 1963.

Kozik, J. *The Ukrainian National Movement in Galicia 1815-1849*. Edmonton, 1986.

Kravets, O. *Simeinyi pobut i zvychai ukrainskoho narodu*. Kiev, 1966.

Kristensen, T. *Development in Rich and Poor Countries*. New York, 1982.

Kubiiovych, V., ed. *Entsyklopediia ukrainoznavsta*. Munich/New York/Paris, 1949-1980.

_____. (V. Kubijowycz). *Ukrainskyj statystycznyj ricznyk.* Warsaw, 1938.

_____. (V. Kubijovyč), ed. *Ukraine: A Concise Encyclopaedia*, 2 vols. Toronto, 1963 and 1973.

Kula, W. *Historia gospodarcza Polski w dobie popowstaniowej 1864-1918*. Warsaw, 1947.

Kupka, P. "Das Localbahnenwesen." In *Geschichte der Eisenbahnen*, ed. Konta, vol. I, pt. ii.

Labrousse, E. "The Evolution of Peasant Society in France from the Eighteenth Century to the Present." In *French Society and Culture since the Old Regime*, ed. by E. M. Acomb and M. L. Brown. New York, 1966.

Lehr, J. "The Pattern and Process of Ukrainian Rural Settlement in Western Canada, 1891-1914," Ph.D. dissertation, University of Manitoba, 1978.

_____. "Ukrainian Houses in Alberta." *Alberta Historical Review* 21 (1973).

Levytsky, K. *Istoriia politychnoi dumky halytskykh ukraintsiv 1848-1914*. Lviv, 1926.

Lipp, Adolf. *Verkehrs- und Handelsverhältnisse Galiziens.* Prague, 1870.

Lototsky, L. "Na robotu." *Dlia vsikh.* Lviv, 1908.

Lowell, A. *Government and Parties in Continental Europe.* London, 1896.

Lozynsky, M. *Sorok lit diialnosty 'Prosvity.'* Lviv, 1908.

Ludkiewicz, Z. *Kwestia rolna w Galicji.* Lviv, 1910.

Łukasiewicz, J. *Kryzys agrarny na ziemiach polskich w końcu XIX wieku.* Warsaw, 1968.

Lydolph, P. *Geography of the U.S.S.R.* New York, 1977.

Macartney, C.A. *Maria Theresa and the House of Austria.* London, 1969.

Magocsi, P.R. *Galicia: A Historical Survey and Bibliographic Guide.* Toronto, 1983.

_____. "The Language Question as a Factor in the National Movement in East Galicia." In *Nationbuilding*, edited by Markovits and Sysyn.

_____. "Old Ruthenianism and Russophilism: A New Conceptual Framework for Analyzing National Ideologies in Late 19th Century Eastern Galicia." *American*

Contributions to the Ninth International Congress of Slavists, II, edited by P. Debreczeny. Columbus, Ohio, 1983.

Makovei, O. *Zalisia*. 1897.

Marasse, M. "O wolności parcelowania gruntów ze względu na stosunki galicyjskie." *Przegląd Polski* III (1868).

Markovits, A.S., and F. E. Sysyn, eds. *Nationbuilding and the Politics of Nationalism: Essays on Austrian Galicia*. Cambridge, Mass., 1982.

Marlsburg, K. von der. "Die Rindviehzucht in Galizien." *Geschichte der österreichischen Land- und Forstwirtschaft* II.

Martin, J., and W. Leonard. *Principles of Field Crop Production*. 2d ed. New York, 1967.

Martynowych, O.T. *The Ukrainian Bloc Settlement of East-Central Alberta, 1890-1930: A History*. Edmonton, 1985.

_____. "Village Radicals and Peasant Immigrants: The Social Roots of Factionalism Among Ukrainian Immigrants in Canada." M.A. thesis, University of Manitoba, 1978.

Marunchak, M. *The Ukrainian Canadians: A History*. 2d edition. Winnipeg, 1982.

März, E., and K. Socher. "Währung und Banken in Cisleithanien." In *Die Habsburgermonarchie*, edited by Wandruszka and Urbanitsch. Vol. I.

Materyały do klimatografii Galicyi. Cracow, 1890ff.

May, A.J. *The Hapsburg Empire, 1867-1914*. Cambridge, Mass., 1951.

McCallum, J. "15% of GNP goes underground." *Winnipeg Free Press* (3 Nov. 1982).

McPhee, P. "A Reconsideration of the 'Peasantry' of Nineteenth-Century France." *Peasant Studies* 9, no. 1.

Mechtler, P. "Striflichter auf des Nationalitätenproblem bei den österreichischen Eisenbahnen." *Mitteilungen des österreichischen Staatsarchiv* 15.

Meinzigen, von. "Die häusliche Nutzthiere in Oesterreich nach dem Stande von 31 December 1900." *Statistische Monatschrift* XXVII.

Melnyk, P. "Das ukrainische landwirtschaftliche Genossenschaftswesen in Galizien." Dissertation. Vienna, 1944.

Morawski, F. "Dzierżawy w obrębie własności tabularnej." *Wiadomości statystyczne o stosunkach krajowych* XV: ii.

Morton, W.L. *Manitoba - A History.* 2d ed. Toronto, 1967.

Muchin, H. "The Evolution of the Ukrainian Family and its Portrayal in Illya Kiriak's novel *Sons of the Soil.*" M.A. thesis, (in Ukrainian), University of Manitoba, 1978.

Murdzek, B.P. *Emigration in Polish Social-Political Thought 1870-1914.* New York, 1977.

Murzynowska, K. "Polska emigracja zarobkowa przed 1914 r." *Historia Polski* III, 2 (1974).

Myska, M. "Fossores Ex Galicia: udział emigrantów z Galicji w formowaniu się klasy robotniczej w górnictwie węglowym Morawskiej Ostrawy w drugiej połowie XIX wieku." *Małopolskie studia historyczne* IX, 3-4 (1966).

Najdus, W. *Szkice z historii Galicji.* Vol. I. Warsaw, 1958.

[Navrotsky, Volodymyr]. "Piianstvo i propinatsiia na Halychyni." *Hromada* (Geneva) 5 (1882).

Nelli, H.S. *From Immigrants to Ethnics: The Italian Americans.* New York, 1983.

Neubauer, F. *Die Gendarmerie in Österreich 1849-1924.* Vienna, 1924.

Niederhauser, E. "The Problems of Bourgeois Transformation in Eastern and South-Eastern Europe." *Nouvelles Études Historiques* 1 (1965).

"Observator." "Lysty z-nad Poltvy." *Literaturno-naukovyi vistnyk* V (1899).

Oesterreichisch-ungarische Monarchie in Wort und Bild. Vol. 19: *Galizien.* Vienna, 1898.

Ogris, W. "Die Rechtsentwicklung in Cisleithanien." In *Die Habsburgermonarchie*, edited by Wandruszka and Urbanitsch. Vol. II.

Oleskiv, O. *O emigratsii.* Lviv, 1895.

_____. *Pro vilni zemli.* Lviv, 1895. (Reprinted, with an introduction by M. Marunchak, Winnipeg, 1975).

Orłowicz, M. *Co zwiedzać w Galicji (Wskazówki dla turystów).* Lviv, 1913.

Osechynsky, V.K. *Halychyna pid hnitom Avstro-Uhorshchyny.* Lviv, 1954.

_____. "Kolonialne stanovyshche Halychyny v skladi Avstro-Uhorshchyny." *Naukovi zapysky Lvivskoho derzhavnoho universytetu im. I. Franka* XXXVI, *Seriia istorychna*, 4. Lviv, 1955.

Otchet russko-narodnoho instytuta "Narodnyi Dim" vo Lvovi za 1881 hod. Lviv, 1881.

Pacher, G. von. *Die Arbeiterwanderungen zwischen Oesterreich-Ungarn und Nord-Amerika.* Vienna, 1897.

Palmer, F.H.E. *Austro-Hungarian Life in Town and Country.* New York, 1903.

Pavlyk, M. "Pro rusko-ukrainski chytalni." In *Tvory.* Kiev, 1959.

Paximadis, M. *Look Who's Coming: The Wachna Story.* Oshawa, 1976.

Persky, S. *Populiarna istoriia tovarystva "Prosvity" v Lvovi.* Lviv, 1932.

Philippsberg, P.E. von, ed. *Sociale Verwaltung in Oesterreich am Ende des 19. Jahrhunderts.* Vienna, 1900.

Pilat, T. "Die Auswanderung aus den podolischen Bezirken nach Russland." *Statistiche Monatschrift* XIX.

_____. "Grunta podlegające wspólnemu używaniu w Galicyi." *Wiadomości statystyczne o stosunkach krajowych* XV: ii.

_____. "Der landtäflicher Grundbesitz in Galizien." *Statistische Monatschrift* XVIII.

_____. "Landwirtschaft und Viehzucht." *Oesterreichisch-ungarische Monarchie in Wort und Bild.* Vol. 19.

_____. *Skorowidz dóbr tabularnych w Galicji z wielkim ks. Krakowskiem.* Lviv, 1897.

Pipes, R. *Russia under the Old Regime.* Harmondsworth, 1977.

Popowich, Sister C.H. *To Serve is to Love.* Toronto, 1971.

Presl, F.C. "Die öffentliche Gesundheitspflege in Oesterreich seit dem Jahre 1848." *Statistische Monatschrift* XXIV.

_____. "Produktion, Ausschank alkoholhältiger Getränke und die Trunkenheitsgesetzgebung." *Statistische Monatschrift* XXII.

Preston, W.T.R. "Report of Inspector of Agencies in Europe." Canada, *Sessional Papers*, vol. 10 (1900).

Prinzing, F. "Die Todesursachen in den Europäischen Staaten 1891-1900." *Statistische Monatschrift* XXIX.

Probst, F. "Die überseeische österreichische Auswanderung insbesondere 1889 und 1890." *Statistische Monatschrift* XVIII.

_____. "Die überseeische österreichische Auswanderung im Jahre 1891." *Statistische Monatschrift* XIX.

_____. "Die überseeische österreichische Auswanderung in den Jahren 1892 bis 1895." *Statistische Monatschrift* XXIII.

_____. "Die überseeische österreichische Auswanderung in den Jahren 1896 bis 1898." *Statistische Monatschrift* XXVI.

_____. "Die überseeische österreichische Auswanderung in den Jahren 1899-1901." *Statistische Monatschrift* XXIX.

"Pro zasnovannia NTSh." *Zapysky Naukovoho tovarystva im. Shevchenka.*

Pruski, W. *Hodowla zwierząt gospodarskich w Galicji w latach 1772-1918*. Wrocław, 1975.

Raczynski, J. von. "Die galizische Landwirtschaft der Gegenwart." In *Wirtschaftliche Zustände Galiziens in der Gegenwart*, edited by L. Cwiklinski. Vienna and Leipzig, 1913.

Radianska entsyklopediia istorii Ukrainy. Vol. 4. Kiev, 1972.

Rauchberg, H. "Der Bildungsgrad der Bevölkerung Oesterreichs nach Altersstufen." *Statistische Monatschrift* XIX.

Reddaway, W.F., et al., eds. *The Cambridge History of Poland*, 2 vols. Cambridge, 1941, 1951.

Reinicke, P. "Die Gold Funde von Michalkow und Fokoru." *Zeitschrift für Ethnologie* 31 (1899).

Remez, O. *Cherez kordon (z dnevnyka emihranta)*. Scranton, 1906.

Rosenfeld, S. "Die internationale Nomenklatur der Todesursachen." *Statistische Monatschrift* XXVI.

_____. "Die Totgeburten in Österreich während der Jahre 1886-1898." *Statistische Monatschrift* XXIX.

Rothenberg, G.E. *The Army of Francis Joseph.* West Lafayette, Indiana, 1976.

Rozdolski, R. *Wspólnota gminna w b. Galicji wschodniej i jej zanik.* Lviv, 1936.

Rudnitsky, S. *Ukraine: The Land and Its People.* New York, 1910.

Rudnytsky, I.L. "The Ukrainians in Galicia under Austrian Rule." In *Nationbuilding*, edited by Markovits and Sysyn.

[N. V.] *Ruska sprava v rokakh 1891-1894.* Lviv, 1895.

Rutkowski, J. *Historia gospodarcza Polski: Czasy porozbiorowe.* Poznań, 1950.

Salamon, R. *The History and Social Influence of the Potato.* Cambridge, 1949.

Schiff, W. "Bericht über die Tätigkeit der statistisches Seminares im Jahre 1896/7." *Statistische Monatschrift* XXIII.

Schmid, F. "Die Gemeinde- und Bezirksdarlehnskassen in Galizien." *Geschichte der österreichischen Land- und Forstwirtschaft* I: 2.

Schullern-Schrattenhoffen, H. von. "Die Bewegung der Getreidepreise in Oesterreich." *Statistische Monatschrift* XXI.

Sefer Borszczow (in Hebrew). Tel Aviv, 1960.

Segall, A. "Prof finds folk cures alive, well." *Winnipeg Free Press* (11 May 1984).

Serczyk, W. "The Participation of Ethnic Minorities in Emigration from Poland, with Particular Attention to the Ukrainians." Paper presented to Conference on Polish Immigration to the United States, Wayne State University, May 1979.

Shanin, T., ed. *Peasants and Peasant Societies: Selected Readings.* Harmondsworth, 1975.

Shcherbatiuk, I.E. "Sotsialno-ekonomicheskie prichiny emigratsii trudiashchikhsia mass iz Galitsii, ee formy i posledstviia." Avtoreferat dissertatsii. Kiev, 1965.

Shcherbina, F.A. *Krestianskie biudzety.* Voronezh, 1900.

Shlepakov, A.M. *The Emigration of Ukrainians to Canada: Reasons and Circumstances.* Toronto, 1981.

_____. *Ukrainska trudova emihratsiia v SSha i Kanadi (kinets XIX-pochatok XX st.).* Kiev, 1960.

Sirka, A. *The Nationality Question in Austrian Education: The Case of the Ukrainians in Galicia 1867-1914*. Frankfurt, 1980.

Sojka-Zielińska, K. *Prawne problemy podziału gruntów chłopskich w Galicji na tle austriackiego ustawodawstwa agrarnego*. Warsaw, 1966.

Sommerlad, E.L. *The Press in Developing Countries*. Sydney, 1966.

Stearns, P. *European Society in Upheaval: Social History since 1750*. New York, 1975.

Stefanyk, V. *The Stone Cross*. Translated by J. Wiznuk. Toronto, 1971.

Strigl, A. von. *Die österreichischen Staatsbahnen, 1896-1908*. Vienna, 1910.

Stys, W. *Rozdrąbnienie gruntów chłopskich w byłym zaborze austrjackim od roku 1787 do 1931*. Lviv, 1934.

Suligowski, A. "Pierwszy zjazd prawników i ekonomistów polskich." *Ateneum* 48 (1887).

Svystun, F.I. *Shcho to est-ukrainofilstvo? Eho istoriia i tepereshniaia kharakterystyka*. Lviv, 1912.

Swidomyj, V. "Das galizische Volksschulwesen in Ziffern." *Ruthenische Revue*, no. 21 (1904).

Sykes, J.B., ed. *The Pocket Dictionary of Current English*. 6th ed. Oxford, 1978.

Szczepanowski, S. *Nędza Galicyi w cyfrach i program energicznego rozwoju gospodarstwa krajowego*. Lviv, 1888.

Tittel, I. *Schematismus und Statistik des Grossgrundbesitzes*. Prague, 1913.

Treadgold, D. *The Great Siberian Migration*. Princeton, 1957.

Trusevych, S.M. *Suspilno-politychnyi rukh u skhidnii Halychyni v 50-70kh rokakh XIX st*. Kiev, 1978.

Tyktor, I., ed. *Velyka istoriia Ukrainy*. Winnipeg, 1948.

Ukrainsko-Polska sprava v Avstriiskim parliamenti. Lviv, 1908.

Umlauft, F. *Die Österreichisch-ungarische Monarchie*. Vienna, 1897.

Volak, J., and J. Stodola. *Plantes Médicinales*. Paris, 1983.

Vovk, F. *Studii z ukrainskoi etnohrafii ta antropolohii.* Prague, 1916.

Vozniak, M. "Korotkyi pohliad na doteperishniu dialnist 'Prosvity'." *Prosvita do ukrainskoho narodu.* Lviv, 1921.

Vynnytsky, I., ed. *Terebovelska zemlia: Istorychno-memuarnyi zbirnyk.* Ukrainskyi arkhiv XX. New York, 1968.

Vytanovych, I. *Istoriia ukrainskoho kooperatyvnoho rukhu.* New York, 1964.

_____. [E. Wytanowicz]. "Polityka agrarna Sejmu Galicyjskiego w cyfrach budżetów krajowych." *Studja z historyi społecznej i gospodarczej poświęcone Franciszkowi Bujakowi.* Lviv, 1931.

_____. "Sotsiialno-ekonomichni ideii v zmahanniakh halytskykh ukraintsiv na perelomi XIX-XX v." *Naukovi zapysky, Ukrainskyi tekhnichno-hospodarskyi instytut,* no. XXI. Munich, 1970.

Wandruszka, A., and P. Urbanitsch, eds. *Die Habsburgermonarchie 1848-1918.* Vienna, I: 1973, II: 1974, III: 1980.

Wandycz, P. "The Poles in the Habsburg Monarchy." In *Nationbuilding,* edited by Markovits and Sysyn.

Warner, C. *Agrarian Conditions in Modern European History.* New York, 1966.

Warriner, D., ed. *Contrasts in Emerging Societies: Readings in the Social and Economic History of South-Eastern Europe in the Nineteenth Century.* London, 1965.

Weber, Eugen. *Peasants into Frenchmen: The Modernization of Rural France, 1870-1914.* Stanford, 1976.

Wiedersperg, G.R. von. "Die Entwicklung des Veterinärwesens in Oesterreich." *Geschichte der österreichischen Land- und Forstwirtschaft* 1.

Wojciechowski, K. *Oświata ludowa 1863-1905.* Warsaw, 1954.

Wygoda, B. *Ustrój gospodarstw włościańskich w Galicyi.* Lviv, 1916.

Wynar, L. "Iuliian Bachynsky, vydatnyi doslidnyk ukrainskoi emihratsii." *Ukrainske istorychne tovarystvo, Seriia: Istorychni studii,* no. 8. New York, 1971.

Wysocki, J. "Die österreichische Finanzpolitik." In *Die Habsburgermonarchie,* edited by Wandruszka and Urbanitsch, I.

Zakharchyshyn, P., ed. *Iosyfinska i Frantsyskanska Metryky, pershi pozemelni kadastry Halychyny, pokazhchyk naselenykh punktiv.* Kiev, 1965.

Zhyvotko, A. "Istoriia ukrainskoi presy." Regensburg, 1946, mimeographed.

"Zur Statistik der Umlagen der Selbstverwaltungskörper." *Mitteilungen des k.k. Finanz-Ministeriums*, I, no. 3.

Interviews

Mrs. K. Chubaty, Stuartburn, 9 July 1979.

Mr. J. Horobec, Stuartburn, 20 June 1979.

Mr. E. Michaels, Portage la Prairie, 6 Oct. 1983 and 25 July 1984, and Winnipeg, 30 Dec. 1983.

Mr. W. Michalchyshyn, Winnipeg, 23 May 1981, 13 July, 6 Oct., 29 and 30 Dec. 1983, and 25 July 1984.

Mr. J. Patrick, Winnipeg, 6 July 1980.

Mrs. M. Rekunyk, Stuartburn, 12 July 1979.

Mrs. L. Salamandyk, Vita, 19 June 1979.

Mrs. A. Sokolyk, Dominion City, 19 July 1979.

Mr. M. Sokolyk, Dominion City, 19 July 1979.

Mr. J. Storoschuk, Vita, 20 June 1979.

INDEX

This index is divided into two parts. The first is a general alphabetical name and subject index. Because of the frequency of reference to them, it does not include Southern Podillia or its five countries, or some other possible entries such as Galicia, Land Executive and Poles. The second part of the index consists of the names of the towns and villages of Southern Podillia.

PART I

PART II
Villages and Towns of Southern Podillia

CIUS Press Publications in Ukrainian Studies

John Basarab	*Pereiaslav 1654: A Historiographical Study*
Martha Bohachevsky-Chomiak	*Feminists Despite Themselves: Women in Ukrainian Community Life, 1884-1939*
Jurij Borys	*The Sovietization of Ukraine 1917-1923: The Communist Doctrine and Practice of National Self-Determination*
Yury Boshyk, ed.	*Ukraine during World War II: History and Its Aftermath*
E.N. Burstynsky and R. Lindheim, ed.	*In Working Order: Essays Presented to G.S.N. Luckyj*
S.S. Dukelsky	*CHEKA na Ukraine*
Volodymyr Gzhytsky	*Night and Day*
John-Paul Himka	*Galician Villagers and the Ukrainian National Movement in the Nineteenth Century*
Assya Humesky	*Modern Ukrainian*
Mykola Khvylovy	*The Cultural Renaissance in Ukraine: Polemical Pamphlets, 1925-1926*
Filiaret Kolessa	*Ukrainska usna slovesnist*
I.S. Koropeckyj	*Development in the Shadow: Studies in Ukrainian Economics*
I.S. Koropeckyj, ed.	*Soviet Regional Economics: Selected Works of Vsevolod Holubnychy*
I.S. Koropeckyj, ed.	*Ukrainian Economic History: Interpretive Essays*

Hryhorii Kostiuk	*Zustrichi i proshchannia. Spohady*
Jan Kozik	*The Ukrainian National Movement in Galicia, 1815-1849*
Bohdan Krawchenko	*Social Change and National Consciousness in Twentieth-Century Ukraine*
Bohdan Krawchenko, ed.	*Ukraine After Shelest*
Emile Kruba and Arcady Joukovsky, eds.	*La Renaissance nationale et culturelle en Ukraine de 1917 aux années 1930*
Volodymyr Kubijovyč, ed.	*Encyclopedia of Ukraine. Vol. 1 (A-F), Vol. 2 (G-K)*
Borys Lewytzkyj	*Politics and Society in Soviet Ukraine, 1953-1980*
George S.N. Luckyj, ed.	*Vaplitianskyi zbirnyk*
Paul R. Magocsi, ed.	*Morality and Reality: The Life and Times of Andrei Sheptyts'kyi*
Ivan Maistrenko	*Istoriia moho pokolinnia. Spohady uchasnyka revoliutsiinykh podii v Ukraini*
Irena R. Makaryk, ed.	*About the Harrowing of Hell: A Seventeenth-Century Ukrainian Play in its European Context*
Stéphane Mallarmé	*Poésies/Poezii*, trans. Oleh Zujewskyj
David R. Marples	*Chernobyl and Nuclear Power in the USSR*
Leonid Pliushch	*Ekzod Tarasa Shevchenka*
M.L. Podvez'ko and M.I. Balla	*English-Ukrainian Dictionary*
Peter J. Potichnyj, ed.	*Poland and Ukraine: Past and Present*

Peter J. Potichnyj and Yevhen Shtendera, eds.	*Political Thought of the Ukrainian Underground, 1943-1951*
Peter J. Potichnyj and Howard Aster, eds.	*Ukrainian-Jewish Relations in Historical Perspective*, 2nd ed.
Janusz Radziejowski	*The Communist Party of Western Ukraine, 1919-1929*
Ivan L. Rudnytsky	*Essays in Modern Ukrainian History*
Ivan L. Rudnytsky, ed.	*Rethinking Ukrainian History*
Ihor Rymaruk, ed.	*Visimdesiatnyky: Autolohiia novoi ukrainskoi poezii*
David Saunders	*The Ukrainian Impact on Russian Culture, 1750-1850*
Roman Serbyn and Bohdan Krawchenko, eds.	*Famine in Ukraine, 1932-1933*
Iurii Shcherbak	*Chernobyl: A Documentary Story*
George Y. Shevelov	*A Historical Phonology of the Ukrainian Language*
Danylo Shumuk	*Life Sentence: Memoirs of a Ukrainian Political Prisoner*
Vasyl Sokil	*Zdaleka do blyzkoho. Spohady, rozdumy*
Danylo Husar Struk	*Ukrainian for Undergraduates*
Danylo Husar Struk	*Ukrainian for Undergraduates: Lab Drills*
George Tarnawsky and Patricia Kilina, trans.	*Ukrainian Dumy*
Volodymyr Vynnychenko	*Shchodennyk. Tom pershyi, 1911-1920*

Volodymyr Vynnychenko	*Schodennyk. Tom druhyi, 1921-1925*
Mykola Zerov	*Lektsii z istorii ukrainskoi literatury (1798-1870)*
Orest Zilynsky, ed.	*Antolohiia ukrainskoi liryky. Chastyna persha--do 1919*

For a complete catalogue of CIUS Press publications, please write to:

Canadian Institute of Ukrainian Studies Press
352 Athabasca Hall
University of Alberta
Edmonton, Alberta, CANADA
T6G 2E8

Printed in Canada

Cartography by Department of Geography, University of Toronto
Original research by S. Hryniuk